European Union and its Neighbours in a Globalized World

Volume 24

The series publishes monographs and edited volumes in the field of European and international law and policy. A special focus is put on the European neighbourhood policy, current problems in European and international law and policy as well as the role of the European Union as a global actor. The series supports the publishing and distribution of research results of cross-border research consortia. Besides renowned scientists the series is also open for publication projects of young academics. The series emphasizes the interplay of the European Union and its neighbouring countries as well as the important role of the European Union as a key player in the international context of law, economics and politics.

Thomas Giegerich

The Human Right to Democracy in Multilevel Systems at a Time of Democratic Backsliding: Global, Regional and European Union Perspectives

Springer

Thomas Giegerich
Europa-Institut
Saarland University
Saarbrücken, Saarland, Germany

ISSN 2524-8928 ISSN 2524-8936 (electronic)
European Union and its Neighbours in a Globalized World
ISBN 978-3-032-01688-1 ISBN 978-3-032-01689-8 (eBook)
https://doi.org/10.1007/978-3-032-01689-8

This Springer imprint is published by the registered company Springer Nature Switzerland AG
The registered company address is: Gewerbestrasse 11, 6330 Cham, Switzerland

Preface

This book is based on an online presentation I gave at Bilkent University, Ankara, on 14 December 2023. I thank my colleague Professor Ece Göztepe Çelebi for having invited me.

The manuscript has grown much longer in these past fifteen months. My wife, Professor Dagmar Richter, has read and criticised an earlier, even less perfect version. My assistants, Annika Blaschke, Maurizio Mammo Zagarella and Mika Schieffer, have helped me with corrections, formatting and materials. Katrin Lück, the head of the library of the Europa-Institut not only got me relevant articles and books, but also the financial support for this online open access publication from the Publication and Research Support Department of the Saarland University and State Library. Many thanks to all of them. For the remaining imperfections, I of course bear the sole responsibility.

This book is intended to help defend and promote democracy when it is facing grave challenges. As the bearers of the human right to democracy, we are jointly responsible for that great project of rational government by the free and equal humans on all levels—national, supranational, regional and global.

Saarbrücken, Saarland, Germany — Thomas Giegerich

Competing Interests The author has no competing interests to declare that are relevant to the content of this manuscript.

Contents

Chapter 1
Introduction: Human Rights and Democracy in the Post-National Era of Limited Sovereignty and Human Dignity

1.1 Human Rights Revolution Gives Rise to Democratic Entitlements

While humans are still primarily organised in sovereign (nation) states and ruled by national governments, we have long reached the post-national era. That era is characterised by governmental systems beyond States, such as international and supranational organisations in which Member States pool their forces for tackling issues beyond their individual problem-solving capacity. In this context, they also increasingly submit to hard-law and soft-law parameters concerning their own governmental structure and the basic rights of all their inhabitants as well as corresponding supervision by international or supranational courts or court-like treaty bodies. Member States have jointly made the sovereign decision to accept limitations on their sovereignty in order to ensure good governance sustainably across the entire membership of the respective organisation. "Good governance" denotes government that serves the public at large and not narrow special interests and that is accordingly characterised by the "principles of transparency, responsibility, accountability, participation, and responsiveness to all members of the public."[1]

Such international and supranational parameters for governmental structure and basic rights have been greatly promoted by the human rights[2] revolution that went

[1] Statement by the UN High Commissioner for Human Rights on 4 September 2023 on "good governance in the promotion and protection of human rights". Available via https://www.ohchr.org/en/statements/2023/09/good-governance (13 February 2025).

[2] In this book, the terms "basic rights" and "human rights" are used interchangeably. Technically, one can distinguish the guarantees of the fundamental rights of humans as subject matter of international regulation ("human rights") and national (constitutional) regulation ("basic rights"). See in this sense, e.g., Article 1 (2) and (3) of the German Basic Law.

T. Giegerich, *The Human Right to Democracy in Multilevel Systems at a Time of Democratic Backsliding: Global, Regional and European Union Perspectives*,
European Union and its Neighbours in a Globalized World 24,
https://doi.org/10.1007/978-3-032-01689-8_1

along with the establishment of the United Nations Organization in 1945[3] and first crystallised in the Universal Declaration of Human Rights (UDHR) in 1948.[4] The human rights revolution has gone a long way in realising Hersch Lauterpacht's demand of turning the individual human being into the ultimate unit of all law, including international law, instead of the sovereign State.[5] In the UN era, a network of human rights treaty systems has been developed in the world's regions, primarily in Europe, the Americas and Africa, as well as on the global level. The basic rights guarantees of these treaty systems inevitably and intentionally also shape the governmental structures of the systems' Member States because human rights, democracy and the rule of law are inextricably interlinked.[6] The human rights revolution has thus transformed objective discourse on appropriate forms of government into subjective discourse on entitlements to a human rights-friendly democratic governmental structure in States. It has also begun to modify the many undemocratic features of classical international law beyond States.[7]

The human rights revolution constitutes an important aspect of the constitutionalisation of public international law observed by some authors.[8] This constitutionalisation is said to denote firstly the adoption by international law of regulatory topics typical of constitutions, such as basic rights protection from governmental interference as well as other structural parameters for governmental systems, including democracy and secondly the transformation of the international legal order into a paramount system of effective legal constraints on States' governments, with the resulting necessity of ensuring minimum standards of democratic legitimacy of those international rules and global governance as a whole. While the first phenomenon is undeniable, the second one has not yet been fully thought through.[9]

---

[3] Charter of the United Nations of 26 June 1945, 1 UNTS XVI. Available via https://www.un.org/en/about-us/un-charter (13 February 2025).

[4] Of 10 December 1948 (UN General Assembly Resolution 217 A (III)). Available via https://www.un.org/en/about-us/universal-declaration-of-human-rights (13 February 2025).

[5] Lauterpacht (1945, republished in 2013), p. 47. See also Sparks and Peters (2024) on the historical and theoretical foundations of the post-1945 "individualisation" of international law. According to Tomuschat (1999), p. 162, today there is a tendency to assume that "States are no more than instruments whose inherent function it is to serve the interests of their citizens as legally expressed in human rights".

[6] See the UN sources cited below in Sect. 2.1.

[7] As to those features, see Crawford (1993), p. 116 ff.

[8] de Wet (2012), p. 1209 ff.; Peters (2017, 2022).

[9] But see Peters (2009), p. 263 ff.

What exactly "democracy" means, has been a controversial question for over 2500 years.[10] Today, there is a consensus on the following basics: The foundations of democracy are human liberty and equality in the sense that in a democratic system, the whole of free and equal citizens rule themselves and co-determine their common fate.[11] "Democracy is the form of government of the free and equal. It is based on the concept of the free self-determination of all citizens."[12] But liberty and equality are also the foundations of any human rights system, as evidenced by classical human rights catalogues,[13] and they are the essential consequences deriving from the dignity of all humans. Humans' equal dignity translates into their equal liberty and equal claim to democratic co-determination. Periodic, genuine, free, equal and fair elections that transfer governmental power for a limited period of time are a necessary, but not sufficient condition for democracy.[14]

1.2 Human Dignity as Source of Human Rights and Democracy

The democratic consequence of the human rights revolution is unsurprising if one takes into account that both human rights and democracy share human dignity as their source. After having been introduced by the preamble of the UN Charter[15] and placed in the first article of the UDHR,[16] the concept of human dignity has most clearly been identified as human rights source in the identical 2nd recital of both the preamble of the International Covenant on Civil and Political Rights (ICCPR)[17] and the International Covenant on Economic, Social and Cultural Rights (ICESCR)[18] and repeated in the 2nd recital of the preamble of the Convention against Torture

[10] See Frankenberg (2012), p. 250 ff. See also the quotation from Thukydides used by the European Convention as a motto for their 2003 draft Treaty establishing a Constitution for Europe: "Our Constitution … is called a democracy because power is in the hands not of a minority but of the greatest number." (OJ 2003 C 169, p. 1)

[11] Kelsen, who considered normative order (= rule) as indispensable for the possibility of society and State, identified freedom and equality as "negative" ideas opposed to heteronomous rule and contrariwise as positive foundations of autonomous rule (= democracy), *i.e.*, the rule of the equally free citizens over themselves (Kelsen (1929, trans.: 2013), p. 27 ff. Kelsen cites Cicero's De re publica as a reference.

[12] German FCC, judgment of 17 January 2017 (2 BvB 1/13), BVerfGE 144, 20, para. 542; judgment of 23 January 2024 (2 BvB 1/19), para. 211 (my translation).

[13] Déclaration des droits de l'homme et du citoyen of 26 August 1789, Article premier: "Les hommes naissent et demeurent libres et égaux en droits. …"; Article 1 sentence 1 UDHR: "All human beings are born free and equal in dignity and rights."

[14] See Pildes (2012), p. 529.

[15] 2nd recital. See Petersen (2020), paras. 8 ff., 24 ff.

[16] See also the 1st and 5th recital of the UDHR's preamble and Articles 22, 23.

[17] Of 16 December 1966, UNTS vol. 999, p. 171.

[18] Of 16 December 1966, UNTS vol. 993, p. 3.

and Other Cruel, Inhuman or Degrading Treatment or Punishment.[19] Human dignity is also part and parcel of the more recent Agenda for Sustainable Development because without sustainable development there is no life in dignity for large segments of the world's population.[20] Last not least, respect for human dignity and human freedom has been recognised by the ECtHR as the very essence of the ECHR[21] and enshrined as a fundamental right in Art. 1 of the Charter of Fundamental Rights of the EU (CFR).[22] The official explanation on Art. 1 CFR refers to the UDHR and underlines that "the dignity of the human person is not only a fundamental right in itself but constitutes the real basis of fundamental rights."[23]

The derivational link between human dignity and democracy has been less clearly elaborated by international legal texts. The 3rd recital of the preamble of the Constitution of the United Nations Educational, Scientific and Cultural Organization (UNESCO) qualifies the "principles of the dignity, equality and mutual respect of men" as "democratic principles".[24] The UN Secretary-General made clear that democratisation was based on and promoted human dignity.[25] The German Federal Constitutional Court has expressly identified human dignity as the source also of democracy: "The citizens' right to determine freely and equally, by means of elections and other votes, the personal and substantive aspects of public authority, is the fundamental element of the principle of democracy. The right to free and equal participation in public authority is enshrined in human dignity (Art. 1 (1) of the

[19] Of 10 December 1984, UNTS vol. 1465, p. 85. See also 2nd recital of preamble of the UN Charter; 1st and 5th recital of preamble and Article 1 of the UDHR; 1st recital of preamble of Protocol No. 13 to the ECHR; Article 1 CFR; Article 1 (1) and (2) of the German Basic Law. The settled case law of the German Federal Constitutional Court (FCC) has identified human dignity as the source and root of all other basic rights (Häberle 2004, § 22 para. 6 with references). See FCC, judgment of 17 January 2017 (2 BvB 1/13), BVerfGE 144, 20, paras. 538 ff.

[20] UN General Assembly Resolution 70/1 of 25 September 2015: Transforming our world: the 2030 Agenda for Sustainable Development (A/RES/70/1): preamble (under "people") and paras. 4, 8 and 14 of the Declaration.

[21] ECtHR (GC), judgment of 11 June 2002, Goodwin v. UK (Appl. No. 28957/95), para. 90. See Heselhaus and Hemsley (2019), p. 1 ff. See also Fikfak and Izvorova (2022).

[22] Before the CFR became part of primary law with the entry into force of the Treaty of Lisbon on 1 December 2009, the ECJ had confirmed that the fundamental right to human dignity was an unwritten general principle of Community law (judgment of 9 October 2001 [C-377/98], ECLI:EU:C:2001:523, paras. 70 ff.).

[23] OJ 2007 C 303, p. 17. According to Art. 52 (7) CFR, the explanations "shall be given due regard by the courts of the Union and of the Member States" when interpreting the CFR.

[24] Of 16 November 1945. Available via https://www.unesco.org/en/legal-affairs/constitution (22 January 2025).

[25] UN Doc. A/51/761 of 20 December 1996, para. 66: "... just like democratization within States, democratization at the international level is based on and aims to promote the dignity and worth of the individual human being and the fundamental equality of all persons and all peoples." See also para. 3 of the Universal Declaration on Democracy of the Inter-Parliamentary Union of 16 September 1997 (see below Sect. 3.2. note 50).

Basic Law)."[26] In a democratic system, individuals are not merely objects, but equal co-bearers of public authority, as befits their equal human dignity. This at least suggests an individual right to live under a democratic government. The very recent Council of Europe Framework Convention on Artificial Intelligence and Human Rights, Democracy and the Rule of Law[27] indicates that democracy is also based on human dignity.[28]

The source character of human dignity for both human rights and democracy is confirmed in substance by European Union law. Art. 2 TEU determines the foundational values of the Union in this sequence: "respect for human dignity, freedom, democracy, equality, the rule of law and respect for human rights" which suggests that human dignity underlies both democracy and human rights. Accordingly, Title I of the Charter of Fundamental Rights of the EU (CFR) is devoted to human dignity and its Art. 1 enshrines human dignity as the first and foremost human right. The official Explanation on Art. 1 confirms that "[t]he dignity of the human person is not only a fundamental right itself but constitutes the real basis of fundamental rights … It results that none of the rights laid down in this Charter may be used to harm the dignity of another person, and that the dignity of the human person is part of the substance of the rights laid down in this Charter. It must therefore be respected, even where a right is restricted."[29] The dignity of all humans translates into the equal participation of all Union citizens in the government of the EU, in accordance with the democratic principles enshrined in Art. 9–12 TEU.

1.3 Consolidation of Multilevel Systems: Human Rights and Governmental Structure Parameters in Today's Organised World

Most sovereign States have since 1945 become integrated in multilevel systems of government on the regional and the global level. This institutionalisation process has been further accelerated by globalisation.[30] These systems typically establish

[26] FCC, judgment of 30 June 2009 (2 BvE 2/08 etc.), para. 211 (the English translation that is available via https://www.bundesverfassungsgericht.de/SharedDocs/Entscheidungen/EN/2009/06/es20090630_2bve000208en.html [22 January 2025]) has been used but adapted by the author). Reconfirmed, *e.g.*, by FCC, judgment of 23 January 2024 (1 BvB 1/19), para. 229. On the derivational link between human dignity and democracy see Häberle (2004), paras. 61 ff.; but see also Herdegen, in: Herzog et al. (2009), vol. 1, Artikel 1, para. 27. See further Bedford et al. (2022).

[27] Of 5 September 2024, CETS No. 225 (not yet in force).

[28] See 5th recital of preamble and Article 7. See the Explanatory Report, para. 10 ("human dignity and individual autonomy as foundational values and principles … are essential for the full realisation of human rights, democracy and the rule of law") and para. 54 ("all Parties recognise the inherent dignity of the human person as an underlying basis of human rights, democratic participation and the rule of law"). Available via https://rm.coe.int/1680afae67 (22 January 2025).

[29] OJ C 303 of 14 December 2007, p. 17. See Article 6 (1) (3) TEU, Article 52 (7) EUCFR.

[30] Mégret (2009).

and implement at least some human rights and governmental structure parameters for their Member States because pre-1945 experience shows that otherwise international peace and security cannot be safeguarded.[31] In Europe—the world region on which this book concentrates—there are actually two regional levels, the broader international one of the Council of Europe (CoE) and the narrower supranational one of the European Union (EU). This means that nearly all European States[32] have submitted to human rights and governmental structure parameters as well as pertinent supervision by courts or quasi-judicial expert bodies on at least two levels—a narrower regional (CoE) and a broader global one (UN). EU Member States are even subject to three levels of parameters and supervision—a narrow EU, an intermediate CoE and a broader UN one.

EU law parameters have a particular quality: in accordance with the settled case-law of the ECJ, they are supranational in the sense that many of them are directly applicable in EU and national courts and enjoy primacy over conflicting national legal rules, including constitutional rules, which they supersede but do not void.[33] While the primacy of Union law was never included in a provision of the EU Treaties as such, it was expressly confirmed in Declaration No. 17 annexed to the Final Act of the Intergovernmental Conference which adopted the Treaty of Lisbon.[34] This direct effect and primacy of Union law rules greatly enhances their effective implementation in comparison with the international parameters and brings the EU closer to a quasi-federal hierarchical system. In such federal systems, the federal level typically imposes human rights and governmental structure parameters on the constituent states.[35]

Apart from the EU, the concept of governmental levels does not necessarily indicate hierarchies between them. The parameters on the global level are broader than on the regional level in the sense that they are binding on a larger number of States; the same can be said of the CoE parameters in comparison with the EU ones. The higher-level parameters are also obligatory in the sense that the lower-level governments must respect them and adapt their own standards, if necessary. But they are not hierarchically superior in the sense that they automatically nullify or supersede incompatible standards on the lower level, including the national level.

---

[31] See the preambles of the UN Charter and the UDHR.

[32] Belarus and Russia are the exceptions.

[33] de Witte (2021), p. 187 ff.; Hartley (2014), p. 203 ff.; Lenaerts et al. (2021), paras. 23.008 ff. See the recent characterisations of EU law and the EU's constitutional framework by the ECJ, judgment of 2 September 2021 (C-741/19), CLI:EU:C:2021:655, paras. 43 ff.; judgment of 21 December 2021 (Joined Cases C-357/19, C-379/19, C-547/19, C-811/19 and C-840/19), ECLI:EU:C:2021:1034, paras. 245 ff.; judgment of 22 February 2022 (C-430/21), ECLI:EU:C:2022:99, paras. 47 ff.

[34] Of 13 December 2007 (OJ 2016 C 202, p. 344). See ECJ, judgment of 21 December 2021 (Joined Cases C-357/19, C-379/19, C-547/19, C-811/19 and C-840/19), ECLI:EU:C:2021:1034, para. 248.

[35] See, e.g., the parameters in the US (Article IV, Section 4 of the US Constitution of 1787, XIVth Amendment of 1868), in Germany (Article 1 (3), Article 28 Basic Law of 1949) and Switzerland (Article 35(2), 51 Federal Constitution of 1999).

The institutionalisation of world and regional governance has led to transfers of decision-making powers from democratic States to international and supranational organisations that go along with a decline in the overall level of democracy, unless decision-making processes within these organisations are also democratised. Otherwise, the public authority they exercise instead of the States lacks democratic legitimacy.[36] Currently, a democracy deficit seems to prevail there.[37] This is why any human right to democracy will only be fully effective if it also extends to decision-making at the international and supranational level in the sense of a right to international and supranational democracy. That establishing democracy beyond the State level is an extremely difficult challenge goes without saying.[38] But the core elements characterising national democracy—transparency, accountability, as well as temporal, procedural and material limitation of rule under law—can *mutatis mutandis* be transferred to the international and supranational levels.

1.4 Democracy's Ups and Downs: From the Fall of the Iron Curtain to Democratic Backsliding

1.4.1 Thomas Franck's Legacy

One of the great successes of the human rights revolution, in the guise of the human dimension of the CSCE process,[39] was the fall of the iron curtain in Europe and the end of the Cold War in 1989-90. Its transformative effects on the governmental structures of the former Communist dictatorships of Central, Eastern and South-eastern European countries, including Russia, were best paraphrased in the Charter of Paris for a New Europe.[40] This Charter heralded a "new era of democracy, peace and unity" in Europe where national governmental systems would only be based on human rights, democracy and the rule of law. These soft-law commitments were compounded by the access to the Council of Europe and the European Convention of Human Rights of all these European States (except for Belarus) that went along with hard-law commitments regarding human rights and democracy.

These and parallel events in other parts of the world prompted Thomas M. Franck in 1992 to analyse "The Emerging Right to Democratic Governance".[41] He came to

---

[36] Krajewski (2019), paras. 1 ff.

[37] See Wheatley (2010), pp. 2 ff., 22 ff.; Peters (2009), p. 291 ff.

[38] Wheatley (2011), p. 525 ff. (suggesting to apply Habermas' model of deliberative democracy to governance beyond the State). For a sceptical view on whether democracy beyond the State is possible at all, see Volkmann (2002), p. 575 ff.

[39] See below Sect. 4.2.1.3.

[40] Of 21 November 1990. Available via https://www.osce.org/files/f/documents/0/6/39516.pdf (22 January 2025).

[41] Franck (1992), p. 46 ff. See also Fox (1992).

the following conclusion: "Both textually and in practice, the international system is moving toward a clearly designated democratic entitlement, with national governance validated by international standards and systematic monitoring of compliance. The task is to perfect what has been so wondrously begun." Eight years later, Franck added this: "It thus appears that there is increasing support ... for the proposition that the democratic entitlement, abetted by links with other basic human rights and the accompanying international monitoring of compliance, has trumped the principle of non-interference."[42]

In the same time period as Thomas Franck, Francis Fukuyama ventured the thesis that with the victory of Western liberal democracy humanity had reached the end of history, "the end-point of mankind's ideological evolution and the universalization of Western liberal democracy as the final form of human government."[43] He was countered by Samuel P. Huntington's "clash of civilisations" paradigm.[44] There were also words of caution by international law experts regarding the sustainability of democratic achievements.[45]

In 2011, a critical stock-taking of Franck's thesis pointed, for instance, to the dismantling of democratic achievements by the war on terror after 9/11 as well as to the problematic relationship between democracy and neoliberalism that privileged the wealthy and marginalised the poor.[46] It also pointed to the rapid rise of non-democratic superpowers, first and foremost the People's Republic of China, the mounting critique of an allegedly imperialist and neo-colonialist Western agenda of democratic regime change as well as the pressures of economic crisis, terrorist and other security threats and environmental decline which made democratic conditionality regarding international cooperation and exchange unaffordable and promoted a return to more pragmatic and realist foreign policy agendas.[47] At the same time, another author found that it was "too early to sound swan songs on the future of democracy. The democratization of governance beyond the state can be coherently and plausibly conceived."[48]

The contributions to a symposium on the right to democracy organised in 2018—when the "war on terror" after 9/11 was continuing and the era of democratic backsliding had already begun[49]—were more pessimistic than Franck, while at the same time underlining the need to more clearly define the content of democracy.[50]

---

[42] Franck (2000), p. 46.

[43] Fukuyama (1992).

[44] Huntington (1996), which builds on an article published in 1993.

[45] Salmon (1993), p. 277; Marks (2000), p. 532 ff.; Koskenniemi (2003), p. 471 ff. For a process-based approach that frames democracy as a teleological principle of international law imposing objective obligations not necessarily translating into individual rights, see Petersen (2009).

[46] Marks (2011), p. 507 ff.

[47] d'Aspremont (2011), p. 549 ff.

[48] von Bogdandy (2012), p. 316.

[49] See Graber et al. (2018); Haggard and Kaufman (2021).

[50] AJIL Unbound (2018). See also the historical overview by Kurnosov (2021), p. 265 ff.

The results of a more recent symposium organised 30 years after the fall of the iron curtain under the title "International Law and Democracy Revisited"[51] have been paraphrased as follows: "... while the debate on the existence of a universal legal norm on democratic governance may seem dead or hibernating, scholarship on concepts that are considered aspects of democracy (accountability, participation, human rights) is thriving. The half fulls could emphasize that the ... articles epitomize a contemporary sensibility on international law and democracy that resonates with the particular concerns of our times. The half empties are likely to respond that the scholarship fails to get to the heart of 'the crisis of democracy', 'democratic backsliding' and deep democratic deficits."[52]

The introduction to the proceedings of another symposium held in 2020 asks the question whether democracy really is the fundamental building block of the international order and comes to a rather sobering assessment of the efforts at democracy-building and promotion by legal transplants and sometimes military interventions having taken place around the globe in the last decades. Yet, citing Hilary Charlesworth,[53] it ends with the call to turn away from a technocratic to an enlightened substantive concept of democracy tied to values and linked with human dignity, transforming it into an ideal with emancipatory force that would have a chance to be generally accepted as a global value.[54]

1.4.2 *Democracy's Current "Health Problems"*

Today, we are in the midst of an era of democratic backsliding. On its website, the Office of the United Nations High Commissioner for Human Rights states that the 2024 elections in more than sixty countries "are testing democracy's health". The current situation is characterised as follows: "According to a report by the V-Dem Institute, the quality of democracy enjoyed by the average global citizen in 2022 is back to the levels of 1986. V-Dem Institute, an independent research institute based at the University of Gothenburg in Sweden, assesses democracies' health on five principles: electoral, liberal, participatory, deliberative and egalitarian. Nearly three-fourths of the world's population now lives in autocracies, including "electoral autocracies," representing half of the world's countries, the report said. For its part, the Global State of Democracy Initiative, which analyses the state and quality of democracy in 173 countries across the world, found that in 2022 democracy continued to contract across every region for a sixth consecutive year."[55]

---

[51] EJIL (2021).

[52] Klabbers et al. (2021), p. 14 f.

[53] Charlesworth (2015), p. 43 ff.

[54] Oeter (2023), p. 30 f.

[55] Available via https://www.ohchr.org/en/stories/2024/03/2024-elections-are-testing-democracys--health (22 January 2025).

In its most recent edition, the conclusions of the BTI Transformation Index of the Bertelsmann Stiftung draw a mixed picture of "[a]uthoritarian regression and democratic resilience".[56] On the one hand, "democracies around the world faced much less pressure" twenty years ago, when the BTI project started. "Today, almost a third of the 137 countries surveyed by the BTI show the lowest level of political participation opportunities ever recorded by the BTI." On the other hand, this gradual erosion of democracy is counteracted in many countries by functioning "institutions and mechanism of oversight such as the judiciary, parliament and the media" and, most importantly, "the resilience of civil society." The conclusions "highlight the importance of uniting street-level activism with institutional checks on government power to effectively resist authoritarian trends. Strengthening and safeguarding these civic forces and institutions stand as paramount strategies for fortifying democracy." This is important to remember because the topic of this book, the "human right to democracy", constitutes a prime example of how civil society actors as plaintiffs and the courts as adjudicators can join forces to protect and promote democracy on the national, international and supranational levels.

Yet, today, we are not only faced with the gradual erosion of democracy in many parts of the world, but a war of aggression by an increasingly dictatorial Russia against the democratic self-determination of Ukraine in the heart of Europe.[57] This bellicose reaction to Ukraine's approximation to the European Union is the worst imaginable backlash: A State that has reneged on its own post-1990 hard-law and soft-law commitments to human rights, democracy and the rule of law is using military force to drag a neighbouring State with it into the authoritarian abyss. Taking that war of aggression already into account, the Freedom House Annual Report 2023 made the following five pretty mixed key findings: "Global freedom declined for the 17th consecutive year. … The struggle for democracy may be approaching a turning point. … While authoritarians remain extremely dangerous, they are not unbeatable. … Infringement on freedom of expression has long been a key driver of global democratic decline. … The fight for freedom persists across decades."[58] The Economist Intelligence Unit's Democracy Index 2023, entitled "Age of conflict", finds another drop in the global average index score that "marks a new low since the index began in 2006". While "almost half of the world's population live in a democracy of some sort (45.4%)", "[o]nly 7.8% reside in a 'full democracy'" and "[m]ore than one-third of the world's population live under authoritarian rule (39.4%), a share that has been creeping up in recent years."[59] It is also interesting to note that only 11 of the EU Member States are classified as "full democracies", and the other 16 as "flawed democracies".[60]

---

[56] Available via https://bti-project.org/en/reports/global-dashboard?&cb=00000 (22 January 2025). See Bertelsmann Stiftung (2024).

[57] Kyrychenko and Chyrkin (2024). ECtHR (GC), judgment of 9 July 2025, Ukraine and The Netherlands v. Russia - Merits (Appl. Nos. 8019/16, 43800/14, 28525/20 and 11055/22), para. 177.

[58] Freedom House (2023), p. 1.

[59] Economist Intelligence Unit (2023), p. 3.

[60] Id., p. 9 f.

While this paints a mixed picture of the current state of democracy around the globe, there are also bright colours, not least with regard to international democracy. Thus, a recent study found out that "[o]verwhelming majorities in various countries across the global South, North, East, and West support the creation of a democratic world government to tackle pressing global challenges like climate change."[61] Interestingly, the United States was the only exception—there, only a minority of 45% supported the concept of a world government.[62]

1.5 Conclusion: Research Questions and Outline

This book takes stock of the current situation of the human right to democracy in multilevel systems of government—at a time of renewed struggles with antidemocratic forces. In such an era, the defenders of democracy should not only join forces, but also re-evaluate the potential of democratic rights that may earlier have seemed to be too general, indeterminate or uncertain to be of much help in promoting democracy, but now may assist in protecting it against threats heretofore unknown. In an approach different to the one used by Franck and the contributors to the aforementioned symposia, the subsequent chapters will be devoted to answering three questions: (1) Is there a human right to democracy in contemporary global and regional international law as well as European Union law and what consequences does that have for the States' governmental structure (top-down perspective on national democracy)? (2) Does the human right to democracy also extend to decision-making at the international and supranational level (bottom-up perspective on international/supranational democracy)? (3) What is the relation between national democracy and international democracy and the corresponding human rights (interdependence perspective)?

The first part of an answer to these questions in Chap. 2 derives from the elements of democracy proclaimed by the United Nations as a universal value. The second part in Chap. 3 results from an investigation of the national and international democratic ingredients of the right of self-determination of peoples, whose recognition and codification is the mainstay of the human rights revolution.[63] The third part in Chap. 4 adds a survey and comparison of the various democratic rights included in the global and regional human rights treaties that constitute the subjective cornerstones of democracy. The fourth part in Chap. 5 is devoted to analysing the EU as an exemplary but imperfect multilevel democracy. In all these parts, the enforcement of democratic entitlements will also be discussed. In the fifth part in Chap. 6, general conclusions will be drawn.

---

[61] Ghassim and Pauli (2024a), New Oxford/Dublin research. See Ghassim and Pauli (2024b), International Studies Quarterly, sqae 105.

[62] Id.

[63] For self-determination as the historic root of the democratic entitlement, see Franck (1992), p. 52 ff.

References

AJIL Unbound (2018) Symposium on Thomas Franck's "Emerging Right to Democratic Governance" at 25. Am J Int Law Unbound 112:64–93. Available via https://www.cambridge.org/core/journals/american-journal-of-international-law/volume/AB65B796FC9CCB0D26A26F44B5EF163C. Accessed 21 Feb 2025

Bedford D, Dupré C, Halmai G et al (eds) (2022) Human dignity and democracy in Europe. Edward Elgar Publishing, Cheltenham

Bertelsmann Stiftung (ed) (2024) Transformation Index BTI 2024: governance in international comparison. Bertelsmann Stiftung, Gütersloh

Charlesworth H (2015) Democracy and international law. Hague Acad Int Law, Recueil des Cours 371:43–162

Crawford J (1993) Democracy and international law. Br Yearb Int Law 64:113–133

d'Aspremont J (2011) The rise and fall of democracy governance in international law: a reply to Susan Marks. Eur J Int Law 22:549–570

de Wet E (2012) The constitutionalization of public international law. In: Rosenfeld M, Sajó A (eds) The Oxford handbook of comparative constitutional law, 1st edn. Oxford University Press, Oxford, pp 1209–1230

de Witte B (2021) Direct effect, primacy, and the nature of the legal order. In: Craig P, de Búrca G (eds) The evolution of EU law, 1st edn. Oxford University Press, Oxford, pp 187–227

Economist Intelligence Unit (2023) Democracy Index 2023: age of conflict. Available via https://image.b.economist.com/lib/fe8d13727c61047f7c/m/1/6e3d4542-1764-4d7a-b4c6-212bbbaba756.pdf?utm_campaign=MA00000491&utm_medium=email-owned&utm_source=eiu-marketing-cloud&utm_term=20241231&utm_id=2011174&sfmc_id=00QWT00000DwFXQ2A3&utm_content=cta-button-1&id_mc=278107246. Accessed 22 Jan 2025

EJIL (2021) International law and democracy revisited. Eur J Int Law 32

Fikfak V, Izvorova L (2022) Language and persuasion: human dignity at the European Court of Human Rights. Hum Rights Law Rev 22:1–24

Fox GH (1992) The right to political participation in international law. Yale J Int Law 17:539–607

Franck TM (1992) The emerging right to democratic governance. Am J Int Law 86:46–91

Franck TM (2000) Legitimacy and the democratic entitlement. In: Fox GH, Roth BR (eds) Democratic governance and international law, 1st edn. Cambridge University Press, Cambridge, pp 25–47

Frankenberg G (2012) Democracy. In: Rosenfeld M, Sajó A (eds) The Oxford handbook of comparative constitutional law, 1st edn. Oxford University Press, Oxford, pp 250–268

Freedom House (2023) Freedom in the World 2023: marking 50 years in the struggle for democracy. https://freedomhouse.org/sites/default/files/2023-03/FIW_World_2023_DigtalPDF.pdf. Accessed 22 Jan 2025

Fukuyama F (1992) The end of history and the last man. Free Press, New York

Ghassim F, Pauli M (2024a) New Oxford/Dublin research: public majorities worldwide support a democratic world government focused on global issues. Available via EJIL Talk. https://www.ejiltalk.org/new-oxford-dublin-research-public-majorities-worldwide-support-a-democratic-world-government-focused-on-global-issues/. Accessed 22 Jan 2025

Ghassim F, Pauli M (2024b) Who on earth wants a world government, what kind, and why? An international survey experiment. Int Stud Q 68:1–16

Graber MA, Levinson S, Tushnet M (eds) (2018) Constitutional democracy in crisis? Oxford University Press, Oxford

Häberle P (2004) Die Menschenwürde als Grundlage der menschlichen Gemeinschaft. In: Isensee J, Kirchhof P (eds) Handbuch des Staatsrechts, 3rd edn. C.F.Müller, Heidelberg, pp 317–368

Haggard S, Kaufman R (2021) Backsliding – democratic regress in the contemporary world. Cambridge University Press, Cambridge

Hartley TC (2014) The foundations of European Union law: an introduction to the constitutional and administrative law of the European Union, 8th edn. Oxford University Press, Oxford
Herzog R, Scholz R, Herdegen M et al (eds) (2009) GG-Kommentar, vol 1. C.H.Beck, Munich (quoted by: Author)
Heselhaus S, Hemsley R (2019) Human dignity and the European Convention on Human Rights. In: Becchi P, Mathis K (eds) Handbook of human dignity in Europe, 1st edn. Springer, Heidelberg, pp 943–967
Huntington SP (1996) The clash of civilizations and the remaking of world order. Simon & Schuster, New York City
Kelsen H (1929) Vom Wesen und Wert der Demokratie. J.C.B. Mohr, Tübingen. English edition: Kelsen H (2013) The essence and value of democracy (trans: Graf B). Rowman & Littlefield Publishers, Lanham, Maryland
Klabbers J, Lustig D, Nollkaemper A et al (2021) International law and democracy revisited: introduction to the symposium. Eur J Int Law 32:9–15
Koskenniemi M (2003) Legal cosmopolitanism: Tom Franck's Messianic World. N Y Univ J Int Law Polit 35:471–486
Krajewski M (2019) International organizations or institutions, democratic legitimacy. Max Planck Encyclopedia of Public International Law (OUP online edition)
Kurnosov D (2021) Pragmatic adjudication of election cases in the European Court of Human Rights. Eur J Int Law 32:255–279
Kyrychenko J, Chyrkin A (2024) Our fighting democracy. A letter from Ukraine. Available via https://verfassungsblog.de/our-fighting-democracy/. Accessed 22 Jan 2025
Lauterpacht H (1945, republished in 2013 with an introduction by Philippe Sands) An international bill of the rights of man. Oxford University Press, Oxford
Lenaerts K, van Nuffel P, Corthaut T (2021) EU constitutional law. Oxford University Press, Oxford
Marks S (2000) International law, democracy and the end of history. In: Fox GH, Roth BR (eds) Democratic governance and international law, 1st edn. Cambridge University Press, Cambridge p, pp 532–566
Marks S (2011) What has become of the emerging right to democratic governance? Eur J Int Law 22:507–524
Mégret F (2009) Globalization. Max Planck Encyclopedia of Public International Law (OUP online edition)
Oeter S (2023) Democracy – fundamental building-block of the international order? In: Khan D-E, Lagrange E, Oeter S et al (eds) Democracy and sovereignty. Rethinking the legitimacy of public international law, 1st edn. Brill Nijhoff, Brill/Leiden, pp 1–32
Peters A (2009) Dual democracy. In: Klabbers J, Peters A, Ulfstein G (eds) The constitutionalization of international law, 1st edn. Oxford University Press, Oxford, pp 263–341
Peters A (2017) Constitutionalisation. Max Planck Institute for Comparative Public Law & International Law, Research Paper Series No. 2017-08. Available via https://papers.ssrn.com/sol3/papers.cfm?abstract_id=2941412. Accessed 22 Jan 2025
Peters A (2022) Against a deconstitutionalisation of international law in times of populism, pandemic, and war. Max Planck Institute for Comparative Public Law & International Law, Research Paper Series No. 2022-22. Available via https://papers.ssrn.com/sol3/papers.cfm?abstract_id=4259946. Accessed 22 Jan 2025
Petersen N (2009) Demokratie als teleologisches Prinzip: Zur Legitimität von Staatsgewalt im Völkerrecht, 1st edn. Springer, Berlin
Petersen N (2020) Human dignity, international protection. Max Planck Encyclopedia of Public International Law (OUP online edition)
Pildes RH (2012) Elections. In: Rosenfeld M, Sajó A (eds) The Oxford handbook of comparative constitutional law, 1st edn. Oxford University Press, Oxford, pp 529–546
Salmon J (1993) Internal aspects of the right to self-determination: towards a democratic legitimacy principle? In: Tomuschat C (ed) Modern law of self-determination, 1st edn. Nijhoff, Dordrecht, pp 253–282

Sparks T, Peters A (eds) (2024) The individual in international law. Oxford University Press, Oxford
Tomuschat C (1999) International law: ensuring the survival of mankind on the eve of a new century. Nijhoff, The Hague
Volkmann U (2002) Setzt Demokratie den Staat voraus? Archiv des öffentlichen Rechts 127:575–611
von Bogdandy A (2012) The European lesson for international democracy: the significance of Articles 9-12 EU Treaty for international organizations. Eur J Int Law 23:315–334
Wheatley S (2010) The democratic legitimacy of international law. Bloomsbury Publishing, Oxford
Wheatley S (2011) A democratic rule of international law. Eur J Int Law 22:525–548

Chapter 2
Democracy as a Universal Value: United Nations Sources

There is no better introduction to this chapter than the following statement by the Office of the UN High Commissioner of Human Rights: "The majority of States in the world today describe themselves as democratic. However, democracy is a dynamic social and political system which is neither linear nor irreversible, and all countries can benefit from continued improvement of their democratic processes. In the twenty-first century, we face the triple challenge of building democracies, preserving democracies, and improving the quality of democracies."[1]

This statement suggests that more States pretend to be democratic than truly are; that democracy requires promotion and consolidation[2] as well as adaptation and improvement; and that it is never irreversibly established and safe, but that constant vigilance is essential for its preservation. There is no better conceivable method to promote such vigilance than individual ownership in the sense of a judicially enforceable human right to democracy. The following subchapters will therefore not only identify UN commitments to democracy, but also look for references to a human right to democracy.

2.1 World Summit Outcome and Other Recent UN General Assembly Resolutions

In the World Summit Outcome, the Heads of State and Government of the UN Member States in 2005 reaffirmed "that democracy is a universal value based on the freely expressed will of people to determine their own political, economic, social

---

[1] Available via https://www.ohchr.org/en/democracy (22 January 2025).

[2] See UN General Assembly Resolution 55/96 "Promoting and consolidating democracy" of 4 December 2000.

T. Giegerich, *The Human Right to Democracy in Multilevel Systems at a Time of Democratic Backsliding: Global, Regional and European Union Perspectives*, European Union and its Neighbours in a Globalized World 24,
https://doi.org/10.1007/978-3-032-01689-8_2

and cultural systems and their full participation in all aspects of their lives. We also reaffirm that while democracies share common features, there is no single model of democracy, that it does not belong to any country or region, and reaffirm the necessity of due respect for sovereignty and the right of self-determination. We stress that democracy, development and respect for all human rights and fundamental freedoms are interdependent and mutually reinforcing."[3]

This statement identifies the "freely expressed will of people" as the sole legitimate basis of decisions regarding that people's political, economic, social and cultural system, marking popular sovereignty as the indispensable foundation of government.[4] It also requires the full participation of the people in all aspects of their lives. But it remains indeterminate because it fails to specify the "common features" shared by democracies, *i.e.* the characteristics a governmental system must have in order to ensure the implementation of the "freely expressed will of the people" and their effective participation. This is surprising because only nine months earlier, the UN General Assembly expressly declared "that the essential elements of democracy include respect for human rights and fundamental freedoms, inter alia, freedom of association and peaceful assembly and of expression and opinion, and the right to take part in the conduct of public affairs, directly or through freely chosen representatives, to vote and to be elected at genuine periodic free elections by universal and equal suffrage and by secret ballot guaranteeing the free expression of the will of the people, as well as a pluralistic system of political parties and organizations, respect for the rule of law, the separation of powers, the independence of the judiciary, transparency and accountability in public administration, and free, independent and pluralistic media".[5] It seems that the Heads of State and Government wanted to avoid the clear commitment which their UN ambassadors had readily made nine months before, but their silence cannot be interpreted as a clear distancing either from the self-evident core conditions of true democracy.

The World Summit Outcome stresses the interdependence and mutual reinforcement of democracy, development and respect for all human rights and fundamental freedoms, including the economic, social and cultural rights. This means that underdevelopment or disrespect for any category of human rights weakens democracy, while undemocratic systems constitute obstacles to development and the realisation of human rights.[6] Finally, the statement affirms that in conformity with their right of self-determination, peoples must retain a sufficient margin in designing their

[3] UN General Assembly Resolution 60/1 of 16 September 2005, para. 135. See already World Conference on Human Rights, Vienna Declaration and Programme of Action of 25 June 1993, para. 8. Available via https://www.ohchr.org/sites/default/files/vienna.pdf (22 January 2025).

[4] See in this sense already para. 8 of the Vienna Declaration and Programme of Action of 25 June 1993. Available via https://www.ohchr.org/en/instruments-mechanisms/instruments/vienna-declaration-and-programme-action (22 January 2025).

[5] UN General Assembly Resolution 59/201 of 20 December 2004, para. 1 (adopted by a vote of 172:0, with 15 abstentions).

[6] See also UN General Assembly Resolution 70/1 (Chap. 1, note 20): "democracy, good governance and the rule of law … are essential for sustainable development" (para. 9).

political, economic and cultural system, including that system's concrete democratic features. However, this margin is not unlimited because democracies do have certain inalienable "common features". Thus, States will not simply get away with arbitrarily redefining their dictatorial system as "democracy". On the other hand, a people can always accept limitations of their designing margin by voluntarily assuming pertinent treaty obligations, such as those arising from human rights treaties that include democratic human rights with concrete content.[7]

More recent statements at UN level have specified the concept of democracy as a universal value somewhat further. The UN General Assembly added "that democracy includes respect for all human rights and fundamental freedoms for all" and in this context re-emphasised "the need for universal adherence to and implementation of the rule of law at both the national and international levels …"[8] The UN General Assembly also reaffirmed "that human rights, the rule of law and democracy are interlinked and mutually reinforcing and that they belong to the universal and indivisible core values and principles of the United Nations".[9]

The UN General Assembly rightly points out the interlinkage and complementarity of democracy on the one hand and human rights and the rule of law on the other hand. As we shall see, democracy depends on the effective guarantee of specific democratic human rights such as the right to vote and stand as a candidate as well as the freedoms of expression, assembly and association. Such effective guarantee in turn presupposes legal bindingness and availability of judicial enforcement mechanisms which brings in the rule of law. Conversely, "the full exercise of fundamental freedoms and human rights … can only take place within democratic systems".[10] While democracy can be defined as the rule of the political majority of a people or their representatives, that rule cannot be unrestrained, lest it be turned against democracy itself. Democracy does not give the political majority existing at a certain point in time the right to perpetuate their rule and thereby abolish democracy. It does not carry the seeds of its own destruction. Rather, democratic majority rule always is limited rule—inherently limited not least by democratic and other human rights and the rule of law that protect the democratic *acquis* from backsliding into autocratic or totalitarian government.[11]

The recognition by the UN General Assembly that democracy belongs to the core values and principles of the United Nations,[12] whose primary objective is "to

---

[7] See in this sense ICJ, Military and Paramilitary Activities in and against Nicaragua (Nicaragua v. U.S.), Merits, judgment of 27 June 1986, ICJ Reports 1986, p. 14 (paras. 258 ff.).

[8] Resolution 77/215 of 15 December 2022, para. 5.

[9] Resolution 77/110 of 7 December 2022, 3rd recital of preamble; Resolution 79/126 of 4 December 2024, 3rd recital of preamble.

[10] Commission on Human Rights, Resolution 2002/46 "Further measures" to promote and consolidate democracy" (E/CN.4/RES/2002/46) of 23 April 2002 (adopted by 43 votes to none, with 9 abstentions), para. 2.

[11] See Crawford (1993), p. 114 f.; Bošnjak (2025), p. 7.

[12] Resolution 60/1 (note 3), para. 119.

save succeeding generations from the scourge of war",[13] seems to support the democratic peace thesis, according to which democracies are less likely to resort to war, at least against other democracies.[14] There are more specific statements by the UN General Assembly in this regard.[15] In our context, however, it is important to note that the UN General Assembly has not propagated any general *right* to democracy whose substance would indeed be unclear, in view of the uncertain definition of democracy and its indeterminate "common features".[16] This stands in contrast to the general right to peace which the UN General Assembly has indeed solemnly proclaimed for both peoples in 1984 and individuals in 2016.[17] Art. 1 of the Declaration of 2016 sets forth that "[e]veryone has the right to enjoy peace such that all human rights are promoted and protected and development is fully realized." Art. 2 of that Declaration clearly indicates that the General Assembly aims for liberal peace within and between societies, based on "equality and non-discrimination, justice and the rule of law, and … freedom from fear and want." Although not mentioned expressly in Art. 2, liberal peace is usually also based on democratic governance.[18] On that basis, the right to peace also includes a right to democracy.

In a follow-up to the World Summit Outcome, the UN Secretary-General published a "Guidance Note of the Secretary-General on Democracy".[19] Invoking the UDHR, he there reaffirmed the Outcome's stance that while there was no single model of democracy, there were universal norms and standards essential to democracy: "Democracy needs strong, accountable and transparent institutions of governance, based on the rule of law, and including an accountable executive, an effective legislature and an independent and impartial judiciary, efficient and inclusive public administration, as well as an informed, empowered and politically active civil

[13] 1st recital of the preamble of the UN Charter.

[14] See in this sense Boutros-Ghali, para. 82: "Democracy at all levels is essential to attain peace for a new era of prosperity and justice." See Fox (2008), para. 34; Franck (2018, Chap. 1), p. 87 ff.; Peters (2009), p. 280 ff. This concept can be traced back to Immanuel Kant's essay "Perpetual Peace" of 1795 (Wheatley 2010, p. 51 ff.). See also Vidal (2023), according to which the relationship between democracy and peace is complex and democracy alone does not ensure peace: "In essence, while democracies may demonstrate a reduced proclivity to initiate wars with other democracies, peace is not an automatic by-product of democracy.", p. 2; Economist Intelligence Unit (2023), p. 23: "there are many flaws in the democratic peace thesis".

[15] Resolution 59/201 of 20 December 2004, para. 6: "*Acknowledges* that democracy contributes substantially to preventing violent conflict, to accelerating reconciliation and reconstruction in post-conflict peacebuilding …".

[16] See Fox (2008), paras. 7 ff.

[17] See the Declaration on the Right of Peoples to Peace (UN General Assembly Resolution 39/11 of 12 November 1984, annex); Declaration on the Right to Peace (UN General Assembly Resolution 71/189 of 19 December 2016, annex). See also Article 23 of the African Charter on Human and Peoples' Rights and para. 38 of the ASEAN Human Rights Declaration.

[18] Turan (2023), p. 12.

[19] Of 27 August 2009. Available via https://www.ohchr.org/en/documents/tools-and-resources/guidance-note-secretary-general-democracy (22 January 2025).

society and population." But the Secretary-General mentions no general *right* to democracy either.

One final UN effort at promoting democracy is worth mentioning: In Resolution 59/201 on "Enhancing the role of regional, subregional and other organizations and arrangements in promoting and consolidating democracy", the UN General Assembly invited "States members of intergovernmental regional organizations and arrangements to include or reinforce the provisions of the constitutive acts of the organizations and arrangements that are aimed at promoting democratic values and principles and protecting and consolidating democracy in their respective societies".[20] The HRC repeated this invitation in its Resolution 19/36 on "Human rights, democracy and the rule of law".[21] This parallels the utilisation of regional arrangements by the UN Security Council for purposes of maintaining international peace and security according to Art. 52 ff. UNCh.

There is of course no doubt that the political systems of too many small and large UN Member States do not come up to the democracy standard solemnly proclaimed in so many UN documents. They nevertheless support or at least do not contest these proclamations because they hope to gain legitimacy and improve their international standing by portraying themselves as democratic.[22] Their behaviour regarding democracy corresponds to that in respect of human rights—States that are among the worst human rights violators routinely confirm their commitment to the UDHR and do not hesitate to accede to global human rights treaties. We should not let the offenders undermine the hard-won international hard law and soft law standards of democracy and human rights, but rather take them at their word, constantly reminding them of their commitments and using all available political, legal and judicial means to make promises and practice match.[23]

2.2 UN Summit of the Future 2024: More National and International Democracy?

In the Declaration on the commemoration of the seventy-fifth anniversary of the United Nations, the UN General Assembly, gathering at the level of the Heads of State and Government of the Member States "representing the peoples of the world", noted the following: "There is no other global organization with the legitimacy, convening power and normative impact of the United Nations."[24] The UN

[20] UN General Assembly Resolution 59/201 of 20 December 2004, para. 9.

[21] A/HRC/RES/19/36 of 19 April 2012, para. 20.

[22] See d'Aspremont (2011), p. 556.

[23] See ICJ, judgment of 27 June 1986, Case Concerning Military and Paramilitary Activities in and against Nicaragua (Nicaragua v. USA), Merits, ICJ Reports 1986, p. 14, para. 186 (regarding customary international law).

[24] UN General Assembly Resolution 75/1 of 21 September 2020 (A/RES/75/1), para. 1.

Charter was identified as "the cornerstone of international law".[25] Our interconnected present and future challenges could only be addressed through reinvigorated multilateralism which was not an option but a necessity.[26] Multilateralism institutionalised in the United Nations is certainly more compatible with the requirements of international democracy than unilateralism outside. For the future, the Heads of State and Government promised to abide by international law, ensure justice and "continue to promote respect for democracy and human rights and to enhance democratic governance and the rule of law by strengthening transparent and accountable governance and independent judicial institutions."[27] This relates to national democracy. A further promise was made to upgrade the United Nations that needed to be reformed, strengthened and revitalised,[28] which may implicitly include an agenda for democratisation of the world organisation.[29]

Following up on this, the UN General Assembly recalled "our pledge to strengthen global governance for the sake of present and future generations" and decided to hold a "Summit of the Future: multilateral solutions for a better tomorrow" on 22 and 23 September 2024 that should "adopt a concise, action-oriented outcome document entitled "A Pact for the Future", agreed in advance by consensus through intergovernmental negotiations".[30] But it is unlikely that the Pact will transform the UN Charter into a truly democratic constitution of mankind.[31] Rather, the consensus requirement—which is democratic in itself—will ensure a compromise that represents the smallest common denominator.

Germany and Namibia, the co-facilitators of the Summit, presented a 20-page zero draft of the Pact for the Future in January 2024 that served as a basis for continuing negotiations.[32] The zero draft was rather general and abstract, offering the prospect of "a multilateral system that is fit for the future", "meaningful changes to global governance" and a "multilateral system, with the United Nations at its centre [that] is fit for purpose", primarily emphasising the need to increase effectiveness. While the zero draft referred to human rights and gender equality as well as the rule of law, democracy was nowhere expressly mentioned, neither its national nor its international variant.

---

[25] Id., para. 2.

[26] Id., para. 5.

[27] Id., para. 10.

[28] Id., para. 14. On previous reform efforts, see Giegerich (2005), p. 29 ff.

[29] See expressly in this sense Boutros-Ghali (1992), para. 82: "Democracy within the family of nations means the application of its principles within the world Organization itself. This requires the fullest consultation, participation and engagement of all States, large and small, in the work of the Organization."

[30] UN General Assembly Resolution 76/307 of 8 September 2022 (A/RES/76/307), 2nd recital of the preamble and paras. 2, 4.

[31] See Giegerich (2009), p. 31 ff.

[32] Zero draft of 26 January 2024. Available via https://www.un.org/en/summit-of-the-future (22 January 2025).

On 22 September 2024, the General Assembly, meeting at the level of Heads of State and Government, adopted without a vote The Pact for the Future and its annexes[33] which goes further. The chiefs "reaffirm that the three pillars of the United Nations – sustainable development, peace and security, and human rights – are equally important, interlinked and mutually reinforcing."[34] They promise to uphold "the principles of political independence and self-determination".[35] They also "reaffirm the Universal Declaration of Human Rights and the fundamental freedoms enshrined therein. The implementation of the Pact will enhance the full enjoyment of human rights and dignity for all, which is a key goal. We will respect, protect, promote and fulfil all human rights, recognizing their universality, indivisibility, interdependence and interrelatedness …" This implicitly includes reaffirmation of the supplementary democratic human rights. National democracy is not expressly mentioned, but alluded to when the chiefs decide to "develop good governance at all levels and transparent, inclusive, effective and accountable institutions at all levels".[36] However, there is no reference to any individual or collective human right to national democracy.

In contrast to national democracy, the Pact for the Future deals with international democracy explicitly and quite extensively—that was already alluded to in the passage on good governance just cited, because it refers to governance and institutions "at all levels". The Heads of State and Government already in the introduction "recognize that the multilateral system and its institutions, with the United Nations and its Charter at the centre, must be … just, democratic, equitable and representative of today's world".[37] Chapter V of the Pact is then entirely devoted to "[t]ransforming global governance". Trust in global institutions must be renewed "by making them more representative of … today's world".[38] Accordingly, the chiefs "resolve to make the multilateral system, with the United Nations at its centre, more … (c) Just, democratic, equitable and representative of today's world to ensure that all Member States, especially developing countries, can meaningfully participate in global decision-making in multilateral institutions and better integrating the voice of developing countries in global decision-making; (d) Inclusive, to allow for the meaningful participation of relevant stakeholders in appropriate formats, while reaffirming the intergovernmental character of the United Nations and the unique and central role of States in meeting global challenges …".[39]

Lit. c obviously aims at enhancing the UN's democratic legitimacy by promoting the influence of the less powerful Member States. By cautiously opening the door to civil society input in the work of the UN, lit. d would further increase the

[33] UN General Assembly Resolution 79/1 (A/RES/79/1).

[34] Para. 9.

[35] Para. 12.

[36] Para. 26 lit. a.

[37] Para. 6.

[38] Para. 65.

[39] Para. 66.

organisation's democratic legitimacy. The chiefs, however, do not mention the demands that have long been made by civil society actors that a UN parliamentary body should be established in order to enhance the organisation's input and social legitimacy and make it more democratic.[40] Lit. d, however, takes up another long-standing demand of increasing NGO involvement in international decision-making in order to democratise it at least to a certain extent.[41] One can also interpret it as opening up the UN system to a greater role for Member State subunits, such as cities, which are closer to the people, so that their participation could enhance the world organisation's democratic credentials.[42] Yet, this advance is devalued by the fact that the statement underlines the intergovernmental character of the UN.

Paras. 67 ff. of the Pact are devoted to the reform of the most powerful organ of the UN, the Security Council, whose decisions bind the UN Member States,[43] not only in the sense of making it more effective, but also regarding its democratic legitimacy. It is proposed to enlarge the Security Council to make it more representative of the current UN membership, and in particular to improve the representation of the underrepresented and unrepresented regions and groups, such as Africa, Asia-Pacific, Latin America and the Caribbean.[44] Moreover, "[t]he working methods should ensure the inclusive, transparent, efficient, effective, democratic and accountable functioning of an enlarged Council".[45] In this regard, the Heads of State and Government promise to continue "to improve and democratize the working methods of the Security Council" and more specifically, to "[i]mprove the participation in and access to the work of the Security Council and its subsidiary organs for all members of the General Assembly, to enhance the Council's accountability to the membership and increase the transparency of its work."[46]

The Heads of State and Government also announce that they will increase their effort to revitalise the work of the General Assembly,[47] which is the main representative organ of the peoples of the United Nations and thus the most democratic UN institution. They also "[s]tress the need for the selection and appointment process of the Secretary-General to be guided by the principles of merit, transparency and

[40] See, *e.g.*, the Campaign for a United Nations Parliamentary Assembly. Available via https://www.unpacampaign.org/ (22 January 2025). Peters (2009), p. 322 ff. On the futile attempt to establish a parliamentary assembly of the League of Nations, see von Bogdandy (2012), p. 320.

[41] Peters (2009), p. 315 ff.; Krajewski (2019), para. 19.

[42] See Šikorská (2025).

[43] Article 25 UNCh. According to the ECJ, the decisions of the UN Security Council "are binding on all the EU Member States and institutions" (judgment of 4 October 2024 [Joined Cases C-779/21 P and C-799/21 P], ECLI:EU:C:2024:835, para. 69). Why the EU institutions should also be bound, even though the EU is not a UN member, remains unexplained.

[44] Para. 67 lit. a, b.

[45] Para. 67 lit. f.

[46] Para. 69 chapeau and lit. d. These proposals to reform and democratise the UN Security Council were confirmed by a pledge included in para. 64 of the G20 Rio de Janeiro Leaders' Declaration of 18–19 November 2024. Available via https://www.consilium.europa.eu/media/l11hh2mb/g20-rio-de-janeiro-leaders-declaration-final.pdf (22 January 2025).

[47] Action 42.

inclusiveness and with due regard to gender balance and regional rotation."[48] These principles are actually hallmarks of a democratic selection process of (national and international) governmental functionaries. Finally, moving beyond the UN proper to the specialised agencies, the chiefs "underscore the need to enhance the representation and voice of developing countries in global economic decision-making, norm-setting and global economic governance at international economic and financial institutions, including the International Monetary Fund and the World Bank, to deliver more effective, credible, accountable and legitimate institutions."[49]

Regarding international democracy, the Heads of State and Government take a purely objective approach and do not consider any individual or collective human right to international democracy, not even in the rather abstract sense of Art. 28 UDHR.

Annex I to the Pact contains the Global Digital Compact. Regarding cyberspace, the Heads of State and Government promise to "work together to promote information integrity, tolerance and respect in the digital space, as well as to protect the integrity of democratic processes."[50] They apparently mean national democratic processes, including elections.[51] They also formulate the objective to "enhance international governance of artificial intelligence for the benefit of humanity".[52] More specifically, they present a democratic approach to Internet governance which "must continue to be global and multi-stakeholder in nature, with the full involvement of Governments, the private sector, civil society, international organizations, technical and academic communities and all other relevant stakeholders in accordance with their respective roles and responsibilities."[53] Moreover, the chiefs "commit to respect, protect and promote human rights in the digital space" and to "uphold international human rights law throughout the life cycle of digital and emerging technologies".[54] This of course includes democratic rights.

2.3 UN Commission on Human Rights Resolution of 2002: Concise List of Democratic Essential

The Commission on Human Rights, which functioned as a subsidiary organ of the UN Economic and Social Council from 1946 until 2006 (when it was replaced by the Human Rights Council), adopted Resolution 2002/46 on "Further measures to

[48] Para. 70 lit. c.

[49] Para. 76.

[50] Annex I, para. 34.

[51] On international legal limits to foreign election interference, in particular with the help of AI, see Rothkirch (2022); Shrivastava (2023).

[52] Annex I, para. 5.

[53] Annex I, para. 27. See also paras. 50 ff.

[54] Annex I, para. 22.

promote and consolidate democracy".[55] In para. 1, it declared "that the essential elements of democracy include respect for human rights and fundamental freedoms, freedom of association, freedom of expression and opinion, access to power and its exercise in accordance with the rule of law, the holding of periodic free and fair elections by universal suffrage and by secret ballot as the expression of the will of the people, a pluralistic system of political parties and organizations, the separation of powers, the independence of the judiciary, transparency and accountability in public administration, and free, independent and pluralistic media".

This concise list of democratic essentials that are obviously geared to national democracy can serve as interpretive guidance to the "common features" shared by democracies mentioned, but not specified, three years later in the World Summit Outcome of 2005. This is all the more true as it overlaps for the most part with the list affirmed by the UN General Assembly in 2004.[56] The Commission on Human Rights emphasises the importance of human rights, the rule of law and political as well as media pluralism for democracy. It also identifies certain human rights that are specifically important for democracy, which one may call democratic rights. However, the resolution does not refer to any human right to democracy as such.

2.4 UN Human Rights Council Resolution of 2023: Extensive List of Democratic Essentials

On 3 April 2023, the HRC—a subsidiary organ established by the UN General Assembly under Art. 22 UNCh—adopted a resolution on "human rights, democracy and the rule of law" without a vote[57] whose preamble includes the most comprehensive global list of democratic essentials that builds on and enormously extends the concise list of 2002: "the full, equal and meaningful participation of women in decision-making is critical to democracy"; "human rights, democracy and the rule of law create an environment in which countries can promote sustainable development, protect individuals from discrimination and ensure equal access to justice for all"; "human rights, democracy and the rule of law are interdependent and mutually reinforcing"; there is a "link between human rights, democracy, the rule of law and good governance"; "the independence and impartiality of the judiciary, the integrity of the judicial system and an independent legal profession are essential prerequisites for the protection of human rights, the rule of law, good governance and democracy"; "the right of every citizen to vote and to be elected at genuine periodic elections, which shall be by universal and equal suffrage and shall be held by secret ballot or by equivalent free-voting procedures, guaranteeing the free expression of the will of the electors" is an important element of democracy; "democracy is based

[55] E/CN.4/RES/2002/46 of 23 April 2002, adopted by 43 votes to none, with 9 abstentions.

[56] UN General Assembly Resolution 59/201 of 20 December 2004 (see above note 5).

[57] Resolution 52/22.

on the freely expressed will of people, including through free and fair elections that are transparent and inclusive, to determine their own political, economic, social and cultural systems and their full participation in all aspects of their lives"; there is the "need for all stakeholders to be a part of the responses to global crises, to have access to timely and accurate information online and offline and to be involved in decisions that affect them, and acknowledging the importance of an active, inclusive and safe engagement of civil society in policymaking, free from reprisals and acts of intimidation, and of facilitating the private sector's contributions to these responses"; "the important contribution of civil society, human rights defenders, journalists and media workers, to the promotion of human rights, democracy and the rule of law" needs to be acknowledged; States should "promote access to the Internet for all and … encourage digital platforms to secure access to free, independent, reliable and plural information"; "the fundamental importance of education and training for human rights in consolidating democracy" needs to be acknowledged and young people need to be given "real opportunities to enable their full, effective and meaningful participation in designing and implementing policies, programmes and initiatives"; "the exercise of human rights, including the rights to seek, receive and impart information, to participate in the conduct of government and public affairs" is vital; "while States have the primary responsibility for safeguarding and strengthening democracy and the rule of law, the United Nations has a critical role in providing assistance and coordinating international efforts to support States, at their request, in their democratization processes".

The HRC's extensive list of democratic essentials concentrates on parameters for States' democratic governmental structure from a top-down perspective; this becomes evident from the last sentence quoted. This sentence also carefully delineates the supportive function of the UN, leaving the primary responsibility at State level, in accordance with the right of self-determination. The HRC underlines the link between democracy, good governance and sustainable development. Taking also into consideration the statements by the UN General Assembly, the emphasis on the interdependence and complementarity of democracy, human rights and the rule of law is of paramount importance in our context. The rule of law connection confirms that democracy as a universal value constitutes a legal—not only a political—concept dependent on the protection of and effective enforcement by the law and the (independent and impartial) courts. The human rights connection indicates not only the aforementioned relation between democracy and the collective third-generation human right of self-determination, but also the importance of individual first-generation (civil and political) human rights to flesh out the concept, and at the same time, make it legally enforceable by myriads of humans in national and international courts as well as human rights treaty bodies.

The following human rights-based democratic principles in the HRC's list are particularly important: the right to vote and to be elected in genuine (*i.e.*, competitive[58]) periodic, free, secret, equal, inclusive, transparent and fair elections; access to timely, accurate, reliable and plural information online and offline; the active, inclusive and safe engagement of civil society in policymaking; the right to seek, receive and impart information; the right to effective and meaningful participation in the conduct of government and public affairs, including by young people, without discrimination; the importance of education and training for consolidating democracy;[59] the contribution of human rights defenders, journalists and media workers to democracy; transparency and accountability of decision-making processes; the significance of an independent and impartial judiciary and legal profession with equal access to justice for all also for the protection of democracy.

As already stated, the HRC resolution concentrates on parameters for States' democratic governmental structure from a top-down perspective. There is just one element that indicates the bottom-up perspective: "that responsible, sustainable and ambitious global responses to planetary challenges require … democratic mechanisms, decision-making processes that are inclusive of women, girls and groups in vulnerable situations, innovative participatory practices, accountable processes and fully transparent approaches based on the respect for human rights, the rule of law and democratic principles". This seems to demand democratic, participatory and inclusive decision-making processes also on the global level for developing responses to planetary challenges.

All in all, the HRC has not formulated any general right to national or international democracy either. But it has underlined both the human rights foundation and the various human rights components of democracy at the national and to a certain extent also at the international level.

2.5 Election Monitoring by the UN to Protect Citizens' Right to Participate in Elections

The UN has also undertaken practical efforts to establish, strengthen and promote democratic systems within States. One important aspect of these practical efforts is election monitoring, since free, fair and orderly elections are the key element of democratic government. The UN, together with many other international organisations, such as the African Union, the Council of Europe, the European Union, the Organization of American States and the Organization of Security and Cooperation in Europe, has been actively engaged in election monitoring for decades. It began in the decolonisation period and continues until today as part of the UN's post-conflict

[58] See Inter-Parliamentary Union, Universal Declaration on Democracy of 16 September 1997, para. 12. Available via https://www.ipu.org/impact/democracy-and-strong-parliaments/ipu-standards/universal-declaration-democracy (22 January 2025) (Chap. 3, note 50).

[59] See also UN General Assembly Resolution 75/199 "Education for democracy" of 21 December 2020.

peacebuilding efforts.[60] Election monitoring by the UN has always been based on the "[r]espect for the principles of national sovereignty and diversity of democratic systems in electoral processes" and the recognition of "the right of peoples to determine methods and to establish institutions regarding electoral processes", there being no single obligatory model (like with regard to democracy as such).[61]

On a regular biannual basis, the UN General Assembly adopts a resolution entitled "Strengthening the role of the United Nations in the promotion of democratization and enhancing periodic and genuine elections".[62] In these resolutions it reaffirms "that United Nations electoral assistance and support for the promotion of democratization are provided only at the specific request of the Member State concerned" and "that the electoral assistance provided by the United Nations should continue to be carried out in an objective, impartial, neutral and in dependent manner".[63] This hints at the prohibition of intervention in matters which are essentially within Member States' domestic jurisdiction in Art. 2 (7) UN Charter.[64] In the last pertinent Resolution 78/208 of 19 December 2023, the General Assembly reaffirmed "the obligation of all States to take all appropriate measures to ensure that every citizen has the effective right and opportunity to participate in elections on an equal basis, and calls upon States to take measures to eliminate laws, regulations and practices that discriminate, directly or indirectly, against citizens in their right to participate in public affairs, including based on race, colour, ethnicity, national or social origin, sex, sexual orientation and gender identity, language, religion, political views or on the basis of disability".[65]

UN and other international election observation is conducted in accordance with the Declaration of Principles for International Election Observation and the Code of Conduct for International Election Observers of 27 October 2005 that have been endorsed, *e.g.*, by the African Union, the Council of Europe—Parliamentary Assembly, the European Commission, the Inter-Parliamentary Union, the Organization of American States, the Organization for Security and Cooperation in Europe—Office of Democratic Institutions and Human Rights and the United Nations Secretariat.[66] By a joint declaration of 27 October 2022, the UN Special Rapporteur on the rights to freedom of peaceful assembly and association and the UN Special Rapporteur on the situation of human rights defenders stressed "that election observers are human rights defenders and civil society actors. States should therefore enable independent and impartial election observation by all monitors,

[60] For an overview, see Binder and Pippan (2018), paras. 8 ff.; Binder (2023), p. 212 ff.

[61] UN General Assembly Resolution 60/164 of 16 December 2005 (A/RES/60/164).

[62] See the most recent Resolution 78/208 of 19 December 2023 (A/RES/78/208), adopted with a vote of 155-0-25.

[63] Id., preamble and paras. 2, 3.

[64] On the relevance of Article 2 (7) UN Charter for UNGA election monitoring, see Nolte, in: Simma et al. (2024), vol. I, Article 2 (7), paras. 66 ff.

[65] Id., para. 7.

[66] Available via https://www.osce.org/files/f/documents/e/c/215556.pdf (22 January 2025).

including from abroad."[67] The joint declaration was made at a time when "[a]cross the globe, the conditions in which democratic elections are held have become increasingly difficult."[68] It cites the former UN Commission on Human Rights Resolution 2000/61 of 26 April 2000 on Human Rights Defenders.[69]

2.6 Conclusion: Common Features of National Democracies and Promotion of International Democracy

The UN General Assembly reaffirmed democracy as a universal value, but also each people's right of self-determination, concluding that there was no single model of democracy. It recognised that democracies shared common features, but refrained from defining them. By contrast, the HRC adopted an extensive list of democratic essentials, underlining both the human rights foundation and the various human rights components of democracy at the national and to a limited extent also at the international level. While neglecting national democracy, the 2024 UN Pact for the Future promised to improve international democracy, including by making the UN itself more democratic. In practice, the UN has longed helped to sustain and promote national democracy through election monitoring in order to ensure that every citizen has the effective right to participate in elections on an equal basis. But UN documents do not refer to any individual or collective human right to national or international democracy.

References

Binder C (2023) Election observation and assistance. In: Khan D-E, Lagrange E, Oeter S et al (eds) Democracy and sovereignty. Rethinking the legitimacy of public international law, 1st edn. Brill Nijhoff, Brill/Leiden, pp 212–234

Binder C, Pippan C (2018) Election Monitoring, International. Max Planck Encyclopedia of Public International Law (OUP online edition)

Bošnjak M (2025) The role of courts in tackling democratic backsliding. Speech at Harvard University, 10 March 2025. Available via https://www.echr.coe.int/documents/d/echr/speech-20250310-bosnjak-harvard-eng. Accessed 14 Mar 2025

Boutros-Ghali B (1992) UN Secretary-General, an agenda for peace. Available via https://digitallibrary.un.org/record/145749?v=pdf. Accessed 22 Jan 2025

[67] Available via https://srdefenders.org/information/the-situation-of-election-observers-as-human-rights-defenders%EF%BF%BC/ (22 January 2025).

[68] Id.

[69] Available via https://ap.ohchr.org/documents/E/CHR/resolutions/E-CN_4-RES-2000-61.doc (22 January 2025). This resolution referred to UN General Assembly Resolution 53/144 of 9 December 1998 by which the Assembly adopted by consensus the Declaration on the Right and Responsibility of Individuals, Groups and Organs of Society to Promote and Protect Universally Recognized Human Rights and Fundamental Freedoms.

Crawford J (1993) Democracy and international law. Br Yearb Int Law 64:113–133
d'Aspremont J (2011) The rise and fall of democracy governance in international law: a reply to Susan Marks. Eur J Int Law 22:549–570
Economist Intelligence Unit (2023) Democracy Index 2023: age of conflict. Available via https://image.b.economist.com/lib/fe8d13727c61047f7c/m/1/6e3d4542-1764-4d7a-b4c6-212bbbaba756.pdf?utm_campaign=MA00000491&utm_medium=email-owned&utm_source=eiu-marketing-cloud&utm_term=20241231&utm_id=2011174&sfmc_id=00QWT00000DwFXQ2A3&utm_content=cta-button-1&id_mc=278107246. Accessed 22 Jan 2022
Fox GH (2008) Democracy, Right to, International Protection. Max Planck Encyclopedia of Public International Law (OUP online edition)
Franck T (2018) "Emerging Right to Democratic Governance" at 25. Am J Int Law 112:64–93
Giegerich T (2005) "A Fork in the Road" – constitutional challenges, chances and *Lacunae* of UN Reform. German Yearb Int Law 48:29–76
Giegerich T (2009) The *Is* and the *Ought* of international constitutionalism: how far have we come on Habermas's Road to a "well-considered constitutionalization of international law"? German Law J 10:31–62
Krajewski M (2019) International organizations or institutions, democratic legitimacy. Max Planck Encyclopedia of Public International Law (OUP online edition)
Peters A (2009) Dual democracy. In: Klabbers J, Peters A, Ulfstein G (eds) The constitutionalization of international law, 1st edn. Oxford University Press, Oxford, pp 263–341
Rothkirch P (2022) Foreign election interference: a violation of the right to self-determination. Available via Völkerrechtsblog. https://voelkerrechtsblog.org/de/foreign-election-interference/. Accessed 22 Jan 2025
Shrivastava A (2023) Tackling foreign election interference through self-determination: a response to Philipp Rothkirch. Available via Völkerrechtsblog. https://voelkerrechtsblog.org/de/tackling-foreign-election-interference-through-self-determination/. Accessed 22 Jan 2025
Šikorská J (2025) Forum of Mayors: a hook for cities in multilateral processes? Available via Völkerrechtsblog. https://voelkerrechtsblog.org/de/forum-of-mayors/. Accessed 22 Jan 2025
Simma B, Khan D-E, Nolte G et al (eds) (2024) The Charter of the United Nations – a commentary, vol I, 4th edn. Oxford University Press, Oxford (quoted by: Author)
Turan T (2023) The 2016 UN General Assembly Declaration on the Right to Peace: a step towards sustainable positive peace within societies? Hum Rights Law Rev 23:1–24
Vidal XR (2023) 11th World Forum for Democracy: Democracy = Peace?, Final Report. Available via https://rm.coe.int/world-forum-for-demoicracy-2023-final-report/1680ae2e2c. Accessed 22 Jan 2025
von Bogdandy A (2012) The European lesson for international democracy: the significance of Articles 9-12 EU Treaty for international organizations. Eur J Int Law 23:315–334
Wheatley S (2010) The democratic legitimacy of international law. Oxford University Press, Oxford

Chapter 3
Democratic Ingredients of the Right of Self-Determination

The United Nations democratic engagement can be explained by the close connection between democracy and the self-determination of peoples that has for many decades been one of the main concerns of the world organisation. When the UN was founded in 1945, many countries around the globe were colonies of founding Member States. But Art. 1 (2), 55 UNCh pronounced the "principle of equal rights and self-determination of peoples". Regarding non-self-governing territories, the colonial powers in Art. 73 lit. b UNCh promise "to develop self-government, to take due account of the political aspirations of the peoples, and to assist them in the progressive development of their free political institutions". Regarding territories under trusteeship, Art. 76 lit. b UNCh formulates the basic objective of promoting "progressive development towards self-government or independence". These provisions helped in triggering the decolonisation process which was heralded by the UN General Assembly's Declaration on the Granting of Independence to Colonial Countries and Peoples.[1] The Declaration determined in para. 1 that "[t]he subjection of peoples to alien subjugation, domination and exploitation constitutes a denial of fundamental human rights" and "is contrary to the Charter of the United Nations". In para. 2, it for the first time formulated that "(a)ll peoples have the right to self-determination; by virtue of that right, they freely determine their political status and freely pursue their economic, social and cultural development." Accordingly, in para. 5 it demanded that immediate steps be taken in all territories "which have not yet attained independence, to transfer all powers to the peoples of those territories … in accordance with their freely expressed will and desire … in order to enable them to enjoy complete independence and freedom."

[1] Resolution 1514 (XV) of 14 December 1960. See Khan (2011). See also the separate entries on the decolonization of Belgian Territories, British Territories, Dutch Territories, French India, other French Territories, Portuguese Territories and Spanish Territories in the MPEPIL.

T. Giegerich, *The Human Right to Democracy in Multilevel Systems at a Time of Democratic Backsliding: Global, Regional and European Union Perspectives*,
European Union and its Neighbours in a Globalized World 24,
https://doi.org/10.1007/978-3-032-01689-8_3

The right of self-determination, which today's international law guarantees to all peoples,[2] has two complementary democratic ingredients: From a top-down perspective, the right contains a general parameter for all States to have a democratic governmental structure.[3] From a bottom-up perspective, it entitles all peoples to a democratic international order enabling their self-determination, whose construction is the responsibility of States. The effective realisation of the right of self-determination by a people, including its democratic ingredients, is an essential condition for the effective exercise of all other human rights by the members of that people.[4] This is what makes that right so important for a human rights-based international order, and this is why the ICCPR and the ICESCR guarantee it in common Art. 1. In its para. 3, this provision obliges States Parties to both Covenants not only to respect the right of self-determination of all peoples, but also to promote its realisation, including the realisation of its democratic ingredients.[5]

On the other hand, the right of self-determination of all peoples constitutes the human rights underpinning of the prohibition of intervention in the domestic affairs of all States, their governmental structure being the archetypical domestic affair (*domaine réservé*). Under customary international law, no State may coercively interfere in another State's choice of its political, economic and social institutions.[6] Rather, "[e]very State has an inalienable right to choose its political, economic, social and cultural systems, without interference in any form by another State."[7] There thus is a tension between the democracy parameter and the non-intervention principle that are both embedded in the right of self-determination. That tension can be resolved by limiting the regulatory density of the parameter so that each people and State retains a sufficiently broad margin of discretion in determining the specific democratic structure of their own system. Only the outer limits of this discretion are drawn by international law and are thus not part of the *domaine réservé*. But even the obligatory minimum standards of democracy may not be enforced at will by other States. They may not use military force at all for that purpose,[8] and other

---

[2] See Thürer and Burri (2008), paras. 13 ff.

[3] Wheatley (2010), p. 213 ff.: "democratic self-determination".

[4] See Human Rights Committee (CCPR), General Comment No. 12 (1984), para. 1.

[5] See in this sense also the Declaration on Principles of International Law concerning Friendly Relations and Co-operation among States in accordance with the Charter of the United Nations, UN General Assembly Resolution 2625 (XXV) of 24 October 1970.

[6] See UN General Assembly Resolution 2131 (XX) of 21 December 1965: Declaration on the Inadmissibility of Intervention in the Domestic Affairs of States and the Protection of Their independence and Sovereignty. See already Article 3 of the Draft Declaration on Rights and Duties of States 1949 (Annex of UNGA Res. 375 [IV]). Kriener (2023).

[7] UNGA Res. 2131 (XX), para. 5; Declaration on Principles of International Law concerning Friendly Relations and Co-operation among States in accordance with the Charter of the United Nations, UN General Assembly Resolution 2625 (XXV) of 24 October 1970, third principle (non-intervention). International Court of Justice, judgment of 27 June 1986 (Case Concerning Military and Paramilitary Activities in and against Nicaragua – Merits), ICJ Reports 1986, 14, para. 205.

[8] Article 2 (4) UN Charter. See below Sect. 3.1 on the inadmissibility of pro-democratic military interventions.

means of coercion only within the narrow limits drawn by the rules of international law on State responsibility.[9]

3.1 Top-Down Perspective: Parameter for States' Democratic Structure

Peoples' right of self-determination is related with popular sovereignty, the main ingredient of democratic government. Several key documents for the historical development of the concept of self-determination make this obvious by advocating the doctrine of popular sovereignty.[10] This applies to the US Declaration of Independence of 4 July 1776,[11] that stands in a revolutionary and decolonisation context, and the Déclaration des droits de l'homme et du citoyen of 26 August 1789 that only stands in a revolutionary context.[12] The immediate predecessor of the UN-era self-determination concept, the third principle of the Atlantic Charter,[13] makes the connection between self-determination and democracy even clearer: "[T]hey [the US President and the UK Prime Minister] respect the right of all peoples to choose the form of government under which they will live; and they wish to see sovereign rights and self government restored to those who have been forcibly deprived of them [by Nazi Germany and its allies] …". Some months later, the Atlantic Charter was confirmed by more than forty other States in the Declaration by the United Nations.[14] It also influenced the UN Charter.

The UN Charter refers to the "*principle* of equal rights and self-determination of peoples" in Art. 1 (2), 55,[15] thereby triggering the decolonisation process in which the "right to self-determination" of all peoples was first formulated.[16] As part of the human rights revolution, the *right* of self-determination of all peoples as a collective third-generation human right was later codified in the identical Art. 1 ICCPR and

[9] See Articles 42 ff. of the Articles on Responsibility of States for Internationally Wrongful Acts, Annex to UN General Assembly Resolution 56/83 of 12 December 2001 which define admissible reactions by other States to an internationally wrongful act, such as a violation of legally binding minimum standards of democracy by a State.

[10] Thürer and Burri refer to the US Declaration of Independence of 1776 and the Déclaration des droits de l'homme et du citoyen of 1789 (note 2, para. 1).

[11] Available via https://www.archives.gov/founding-docs/declaration-transcript (22 January 2025).

[12] Available via https://www.conseil-constitutionnel.fr/le-bloc-de-constitutionnalite/declaration-des-droits-de-l-homme-et-du-citoyen-de-1789 (22 January 2025).

[13] Atlantic Charter (Joint Declaration of the US President and the UK Prime Minister) of August 14, 1941. Available via https://avalon.law.yale.edu/wwii/atlantic.asp (22 January 2025).

[14] Of 1 January 1942. Available via https://avalon.law.yale.edu/20th_century/decade03.asp (22 January 2025).

[15] Emphasis added.

[16] See the Declaration on the Granting of Independence to Colonial Countries and Peoples, UN General Assembly Resolution 1514 (XV) of 14 December 1960.

Art. 1 ICESCR. It became part of customary international law in the 1960s[17] and respect for it is an obligation *erga omnes.*[18] The right of self-determination has meanwhile been recognised by the international community of States as a whole as a peremptory norm of general international law *(jus cogens)* from which no derogation is permitted.[19] It has thus become one of the foundations of the contemporary international legal order. The International Court of Justice has called the evolution of the right of self-determination "one of the major developments of international law during the second half of the twentieth century".[20]

The most authoritative summary of that right's substance can be found in Principle 5 of the Declaration on Principles of International Law concerning Friendly Relations and Co-operation among States in accordance with the Charter of the United Nations.[21] The UN General Assembly claimed that the principles stated in this Declaration were, and today they are generally considered as, "basic principles of international law" that elaborate the rights and duties of UN Member States and the rights of peoples under the Charter.[22]

Principle 5 on equal rights and self-determination of peoples makes clear that the right of self-determination extends to political as well as economic, social and cultural matters. With regard to the political aspect ("political status"), Principle 5 also indicates a distinction between external and internal self-determination in the sense that political self-determination may be realised external to or within an existing sovereign State.[23] The external dimension of political self-determination was particularly relevant in the decolonisation context. It comprises the right of a people to the "establishment of a sovereign and independent State, the free association or integration with an independent State or the emergence into any other political

[17] ICJ, Legal Consequences of the Separation of the Chagos Archipelago from Mauritius in 1965, Advisory Opinion of 25 February 2019, para. 148 ff.

[18] Id., para. 180. ECJ, judgment of 21 December 2016 (C-104/16 P), ECLI:EU:C:2016:973, paras. 88 f.

[19] See International Law Commission, Draft Conclusions on Identification and legal consequences of peremptory norms of general international law (jus cogens), Conclusion 23 and Annex, A/77/10, 2022. Available via https://legal.un.org/ilc/texts/instruments/english/commentaries/1_14_2022.pdf (22 January 2025). ICJ, Legal Consequences Arising from the Policies and Practices of Israel in the Occupied Palestinian Territory, Including East Jerusalem, Advisory Opinion of 19 July 2024, para. 233 (regarding cases of foreign occupation). See also Article 53 sentence 2 of the Vienna Convention on the Law of Treaties of 23 May 1969 (UNTS vol. 1155, p. 331).

[20] ICJ, Advisory Opinion of 22 July 2010 – Accordance with International Law of the Unilateral Declaration of Independence in Respect of Kosovo, para. 82.

[21] UN General Assembly Resolution 2625 (XXV) of 24 October 1970.

[22] See paras. 2 and 3 in the General Part of the Declaration. On the legal significance of the Declaration, see also Keller (2021), paras. 29 ff.

[23] "The establishment of a sovereign and independent State, the free association or integration with an independent State or the emergence into any other political status freely determined by a people constitute modes of implementing the right of self-determination by that people." See Thürer and Burri (2008), para. 23.

status freely determined by a people". Obviously, the alien subjugation or domination—colonial or other—of a people is *per se* undemocratic.

The internal dimension of political self-determination is even more closely related with democracy. It comprises the right of a people "freely to determine, without external interference, their political status and to pursue their economic, social and cultural development".[24] It is further stated that a sovereign and independent State conducts itself in compliance with the principle of equal rights and self-determination of peoples only, if it is "possessed of a government representing the whole people belonging to the territory without distinction as to race, creed or colour". The context of this statement reveals that it primarily aims at restricting ethnic minorities in multi-ethnic States to exercising their self-determination in the form of regional autonomy or federalisation, in order to counteract secessionist tendencies disrupting the territorial integrity of States.[25] Nevertheless, the statement clearly indicates that the internal self-determination of a people overlaps with the democratic legitimacy of their State's government.[26] This is the "democratic substance" of self-determination, requiring the effective exercise of the democratic human rights that are enshrined in the ICCPR.[27]

All in all, current international law contains a democracy parameter with *jus cogens* character and *erga omnes* effects, as an ingredient of the right of self-determination of peoples. It requires States to have a democratically legitimate government. One can thus discern a collective peoples' right to national democracy. A reminder of caution is in order, however: According to Principle 5 of the Friendly Relations Declaration, the right of political self-determination protects a people's free choice of its form of government against external interference.[28] This means that no specific requirements on the concrete design of governmental systems can be derived from the right of self-determination, beyond the general obligation to ensure effective democratic legitimacy based on popular sovereignty.[29] The concrete democratic design belongs to the *domaine réservé* of each State and is thus protected by the prohibition of intervention. This is in accordance with the fact that many varieties of democracy compete with each other.[30] However, some designs

---

[24] The right to internal self-determination also sets limits to the extraterritorial legislation of other States (Criddle 2024, p. 607 ff.).

[25] See Kimminich (1993), p. 98 ff.

[26] See also CCPR, General Comment No. 25 (57), CCPR/C/21/Rev.1/Add.7 of 27 August 1996, paras. 1 f.; Schabas (2019), Article 1 CCPR, para. 36.

[27] Thornberry (1993), p. 134 ff. (citing Article 19, 21, 22 and 25 ICCPR). See also Rosas (1993), p. 232 ff.

[28] See already para. 5 of the Declaration on the Inadmissibility of Intervention in the Domestic Affairs of States and the Protection of Their Independence and Sovereignty, UN General Assembly Resolution 2131 (XX) of 21 December 1965: "Every State has an inalienable right to choose its political, economic, social and cultural systems, without interference in any form by another State."

[29] See in this sense also Cassese (1995), p. 332.

[30] See the overview by Frankenberg (2012), p. 250 ff.

such as dictatorial one-party systems are so obviously undemocratic[31] that they are incompatible with internal self-determination.[32]

If the right of internal self-determination includes a democracy parameter, then the democratic legitimacy of the government should be the main criterion for answering the question whether a new entity established by a people in exercising its right of self-determination is recognised as a new sovereign State by the other States. While this criterion indeed plays an increasingly important role, it is not the only aspect considered by the other States in such a situation.[33] Rather, promoting the effective exercise of the right to external self-determination may suggest recognition regardless of that criterion. Also, the pressures of *realpolitik* in international relations may trump democracy concerns. Democratic legitimacy has greater significance when it comes to recognising the new rulers of a State as this State's government because that is a decision which can be withheld more easily.[34] However, the need to deal with the undemocratic, but effective rulers of a State compels other States sooner or later to ignore their lack of democratic legitimacy.[35]

Thinking further about the parameter of democracy, the question arises as to whether the right of self-determination includes a people's right to revolution against undemocratic government or, conversely, a right to resist the violent overthrow of democratic government (such as by a military coup). An affirmative answer would be in line with the role models in the US (1776)[36] and France (1789),[37] but in international law, this is unchartered territory.[38] International law is rather averse to both revolutions and coups because they tend to create instability, cause bloodshed and may well endanger the maintenance of international peace and security. The

[31] Since 1993, the Human Rights Committee has constantly considered one-party elections as incompatible with Article 25 ICCPR (see Fox 2000), p. 57 ff.

[32] See Oeter, in: Simma et al. (2024), vol. I., Self-Determination, para. 41. The prohibition of destructive abuse of rights (Art. 30) is a general principle of law that also limits the right of self-determination (see common Art. 5 (1) of the ICCPR and the ICESCR).

[33] See, e.g., the European Community's Declaration on the 'Guidelines on the Recognition of New States in Eastern Europe and in the Soviet Union', adopted by an Extraordinary EPC Ministerial Meeting on 16 December 1991 (ILM 31 [1992], 1486 f.): "The Community and its Member States confirm their attachment to the principles of the Helsinki Final Act and the Charter of Paris, in particular the principle of self-determination. They affirm their readiness to recognize, subject to the normal standards of international practice and the political realities in each case, those new States which, following the historic changes in the region, have constituted themselves on a democratic basis, have accepted the appropriate international obligations and have committed themselves in good faith to a peaceful process and to negotiations."

[34] See Murphy (2000), p. 123 ff.

[35] The most recent example is the Taliban rulers of Afghanistan who returned back to power in August 2021 (see Hasar 2024).

[36] See the Declaration of Independence of 4 July 1776. On the "right of revolution" asserted therein see Maier (1997), p. 135.

[37] See Article 2 of the Déclaration des droits de l'homme et du citoyen of 26 August 1789: "résistance à l'oppression".

[38] But see the 3rd recital of the preamble of the Universal Declaration of Human Rights which mentions "rebellion against tyranny and oppression" as a last resort where human rights are not properly protected by the rule of law.

UN Security Council has several times imposed sanctions on the basis of Chapter VII of the UN Charter in order to ensure the return to power of a democratic regime that was ousted by a military or other coup.[39] But that practice is not coherent in the sense that the Council will always side with democratic governments. Accordingly, at the present stage of development of international law, the right of self-determination does not appear to include a right to democratic revolution or resistance, except as a means to shake of the yoke of alien subjugation.[40] Even less can there be a right to outside military intervention to overthrow an illegitimate regime.[41]

3.2 Bottom-up Perspective: Right to Democratic International Order

From the complementary bottom-up perspective, peoples' right of self-determination entitles them also to a democratic international order.[42] The international community must not be organised in a way that subjects peoples to what effectively amounts to alien domination or subjugation, contrary to their right of self-determination. This means that all peoples must be able to exercise their right of self-determination effectively, and if they have accordingly established their own sovereign States, these States are equal members of the international community and participate equally in international law-making, law enforcement and adjudication. In other words, the right to a democratic international order represents a further development of the right to external self-determination: This right firstly entitles peoples to establish their own sovereign and independent State. It secondly entitles them to an international order based on the sovereign equality of all States thus established and their equal participation in all instances of international government.

An individualised indication of this perspective can be found in Art. 28 UDHR, according to which "[e]veryone is entitled to a social and international order in which the rights and freedoms set forth in this Declaration can be fully realized." This can be taken as an earl blueprint of an individual right to international democracy. Correspondingly, the principle of sovereign equality of States[43]—established by peoples in the exercise of their right of self-determination—ensures that States are only bound by those rules of international law to which they have at least implicitly consented. While the equally sovereign States are the masters of the international

[39] Haiti: Resolution 841 (1993) of 16 June 1993; Resolution 875 (1993) of 16 October 1993. Sierra Leone: Resolution 1132 (1997) of 8 October 1997; Resolution 1156 (1998) of 16 March 1998. Côte d'Ivoire: Resolutions 1975, 1980, 1981, 1992 (2011).

[40] See Salmon (1993), p. 263 f.; Chemillier-Gendreau (2007), paras. 13 ff.

[41] Salmon (1993), p. 277 f. On the admissibility of pro-democratic military interventions, see Byers and Chesterman (2000), p. 259 ff.; Wippman (2000), p. 293 ff. See also Oeter (2023), p. 18 ff.; Pippan (2023), p. 35 ff.

[42] For a theoretical perspective on globalising democracy in a human rights framework, see Gould (2004), part III (p. 157 ff.).

[43] Article 2 (1) UN Charter.

legal order that regulates the international community, they can exercise their master position only collectively and consensually, which is an important element of the democratic international order.[44] The international community as such is too loosely integrated to allow majority decisions binding all members.

For many years, the UN General Assembly (UNGA) and the Human Rights Council (HRC), as its subsidiary organ pursuant to Art. 22 UNCh, have promoted a "democratic and equitable international order", which indicates that only a democratic international order will be equitable. The HRC has since 2011 mandated an Independent Expert on the promotion of a democratic and equitable international order.[45] In the view of the UNGA and the HRC, such an order requires, inter alia, the realisation of the following aspects (of which I selected those primarily pertaining to democracy while skipping those primarily pertaining to equity, although that distinction cannot always easily be made):

> (a) The right of all peoples to self-determination …;
>
> (e) The right to an international economic order based on equal participation in the decision-making process, interdependence, mutual interest, solidarity and cooperation among all States; …
>
> (g) The promotion and consolidation of transparent, democratic, just and accountable international institutions in all areas of cooperation, in particular through the implementation of the principle of full and equal participation in their respective decision-making mechanisms;
>
> (h) The right to equitable participation of all, without any discrimination, in domestic and global decision-making;
>
> (i) The principle of equitable regional and gender-balanced representation in the composition of the staff of the United Nations system;
>
> (j) The promotion of a free, just, effective and balanced international information and communications order based on international cooperation for the establishment of a new equilibrium and greater reciprocity in the international flow of information, in particular correcting the inequalities in the flow of information to and from developing countries; …
>
> (o) The shared responsibility of the nations of the world for managing worldwide economic and social development, including addressing pandemics and other health-related global challenges, as well as threats to international peace and security, which should be exercised multilaterally.[46]

It should be noted that the resolutions of both bodies pertaining to a "democratic and equitable international order" have always been controversial,[47] not least

[44] But see Neumann (2023), p. 110 ff., for a critique of the democratic character of the making of customary international law from a sovereigntist perspective. For a more internationalist approach, see Wheatley (2010), p. 123 ff.

[45] See, e.g., HRC Resolution 54/4 of 11 October 2023 (adopted by a vote of 31:13:3). The latest report of that expert of 31 July 2023 (A/78/262) is available via https://documents-dds-ny.un.org/doc/UNDOC/GEN/N23/225/85/PDF/N2322585.pdf?OpenElement (22 January 2025).

[46] See, e.g., UN General Assembly Resolution 77/215 of 15 December 2022, para. 6; UN General Assembly Resolution 78/196 of 19 December 2023, para. 6. See also HRC Resolution 18/6 of 29 September 2011, para. 6.

[47] The UN General Assembly Resolution 77/215 of 15 December 2022 was adopted by a vote of 122:54:10, i.e., 122 States voted yes, 54 (mostly Western) States voted no, and 10 abstained. The voting result for UNGA Resolution 78/196 was 125:54:6.

because they are related with the concept of a New International Economic Order.[48] It is a legitimate question, however, if true self-determination for peoples of the global South can be achieved without a profound reform of the world economic order.[49] In its Universal Declaration on Democracy, the Inter-Parliamentary Union thus stated the following regarding the international dimension of democracy as an objective principle: "Democracy must also be recognised as an international principle, applicable to international organisations and to States in their international relations. The principle of international democracy does not only mean equal or fair representation of States; it also extends to the economic rights and duties of States."[50] This takes up the promises made in the preamble of the UN Charter: "to promote social progress and better standards of life in larger freedom" and "to employ international machinery for the promotion of the economic and social advancement of all peoples".[51]

It is no coincidence that the UN Charter reaffirms the UN peoples' "faith … in the equal rights … of nations large and small"[52] and introduces "the principle of equal rights and self-determination of peoples"[53] which is reaffirmed by the Friendly Relations Declaration.[54] There is no effective self-determination without equal rights. If a people, in exercising its right of self-determination, establishes an independent State, that State will enjoy sovereign equality with all others.[55] Equal rights of peoples and sovereign equality of their States require their equal participation in international decision-making and thus respect for democratic principles in the international order. Sovereign equality of States is an instrument to protect and empower small peoples and their individual members.[56] Moreover, international and supranational organisations as instances of the growing institutionalisation of the international community must have transparent, democratic, just and accountable decision-making processes that enable the full and equal participation of the peoples of all Member States. This all translates into a collective peoples' right to international democracy in a very general sense as a component of their right of self-determination.

---

[48] See Giegerich (2022), p. 214.

[49] See Schabas (2019), Article 1 CCPR, para. 4.

[50] Inter-Parliamentary Union, Universal Declaration on Democracy of 16 September 1997, para. 24. Available via https://www.ipu.org/impact/democracy-and-strong-parliaments/ipu-standards/universal-declaration-democracy (22 January 2025). The IPU is the global organisation of 180 national parliaments, while 15 international and supranational parliaments are associate members.

[51] 4th and 7th recital of the preamble.

[52] 2nd recital of the preamble.

[53] Article 1 (2) UN Charter. Article 1 ICCPR and Article 1 ICESCR only codify the right of self-determination of peoples without also expressly mentioning their equal rights. But equality is implicitly included in the formulation "[a]ll peoples".

[54] See above note 5.

[55] Article 2 (1) UN Charter.

[56] Giegerich (2020), p. 53 f.

There of course is a mismatch between *de jure* equality of all sovereign States as the cornerstone of international democracy and the *de facto* inequality of the many small and poor States, especially in the global South.[57] But this discrepancy between legal theory and practical reality corresponds to the one between the legal equality of individual citizens as the cornerstone of national democracies and their factual inequality. Here and there, the permanent task is to offset the consequences of that discrepancy as far as possible in order to enhance the credibility of the democratic claim both within States and between States.

International democracy (and the right to it) is primarily people-centred, not individual-centred, in the sense that the exercise of international governmental powers—law-making, enforcement and adjudication—must be based on the sovereignty of the world's peoples that have established sovereign States as equal bearers of the right of external self-determination: It therefore actually is an international "demoicracy" in the sense of the first sentence of the preamble of the UN Charter: "We the peoples of the United Nations …" However, each of these peoples is entitled to their own national democracy as a consequence of their right of internal self-determination comprising a right to a government based on popular sovereignty,[58] and that collective right has individual rights offshoots.[59] Thus, even those who think that democracy in the true sense can only be realised within the confines of a nation State with a *demos* should be able to support demands for international democracy firmly rooted in national democracy: There is no international "demoicracy" without national democracies. Conversely, however, national democracies will be undermined, if States are compelled to transpose international requirements in whose formulation they were not equally involved.

3.3 Interdependence of National Democracy and International Democracy: Adequate Overall Standard of Democracy as Goal

The relationship between democracy within States (national democracy) and democracy between States (international democracy) is not easy to determine. On the one hand, one can reasonably assume that international democracy should be based on national democracy: If a dictatorship prevents a people from effective participation in national political affairs, that people is also prevented from effectively participating in international political affairs. On the other hand, excluding dictatorial States from equal participation in international decision-making deprives those States' peoples completely of any influence on international decisions

[57] See Vanspranghe (2023), p. 119 ff.

[58] See the first sentence of the preamble of the Constitution of the United States of America of 17 September 1787: "We the People of the United States …".

[59] See below Chap. 4.

affecting them and worsens their democratic plight. Accordingly, Art. 4 (1) UN Charter, in difference to the Covenant of the League of Nations,[60] admits to membership in the UN as a true "world organisation" all "peace-loving" States without setting any standards concerning their democratic governmental structure.[61]

While this leniency on parameters for membership may be appropriate for the UN as a relatively loosely integrated model of multilevel government, it is unsuitable for more closely integrated organisations like the Council of Europe and the supranational European Union. Similar to federal States, which according to experience require consensus on certain fundamental constitutional values in order to function properly and survive in the long run,[62] these more closely integrated models of multilevel government usually set minimum constitutional standards for the Member States. These also include minimum standards of democracy that are all the stricter the higher the organisation's own demands on democracy are, as will be demonstrated below with regard to the Council of Europe and the EU. This is because the democratic character of the organisation and of each Member States also depends on the democratic character of all the Member States.[63] There is a *prima facie* assumption: the more democratic Member States are, the more democratic their organisation will be; and *vice versa*, the more democratic the organisation, the more democratic its Member States. This means that a State's membership in closely integrated international and supranational organisations can help protect and even promote democracy in that State. National democracy and international/supranational democracy are obviously interdependent.

On the other hand, the international and supranational integration of States can also have a detrimental effect on democracy: The transfer of decision-making powers from the State to the international or supranational level can weaken the democratic legitimacy of decisions affecting individual peoples because their influence is diluted. Such deterioration of overall democratic standards will be exacerbated if international decision-making is dominated by executives and its procedure non-transparent. Conversely, the more democratic (*i.e.*, participatory, transparent and parliamentarised) international decision-making is, the less will democratic standards at national level be impaired. This obvious interdependence between national and international democracy was already explained in detail by the UN Secretary-General in a supplement to his reports on democratisation almost thirty years ago.[64]

---

[60] Article 1 (2) of the Covenant of the League of Nations of 28 June 1919 opened up membership to "[a]ny fully self-governing State, Dominion or Colony". Available via https://libraryresources.unog.ch/ld.php?content_id=32971179 (22 January 2025). See Schücking and Wehberg (1931), commentary on Article 1, p. 273 ff.

[61] Fastenrath and Riznik, in: Simma et al. (2024), vol. I, Article 4, paras. 5–6, 16 and 21.

[62] See Giegerich (2019), p. 186 (referring to Abraham Lincoln's "house divided" speech of 1858 and the subsequent Civil War in the U.S.).

[63] On structural interdependencies in democratic federations, see Möllers and Schneider (2018), p. 18 ff. Available via https://www.boell.de/sites/default/files/endf_boell_demokratiesicherung-i-d-europ-union_v03_kommentierbar.pdf (22 January 2025).

[64] UN Doc. A/51/761 of 20 December 1996, paras. 61 ff.

The right to international democracy requires that international decision-making processes are democratised (i.e., made participatory, transparent and parliamentarised) as much as possible.[65] However, adaptations in the national decision-making processes may still be necessary to uphold democratic standards on the Member State level, in particular the adequate power balance between the national parliament and the executive branch of the government which represents the Member State on the international and supranational level. To the extent that the right of self-determination sets minimum standards for national democracies, it also obliges States to mitigate by compensatory mechanisms the effects which power transfers to international and supranational levels have on their domestic democratic standards of government. In order to attain an adequate overall standard of democracy in multilevel systems of government, an appropriate mixture of international democratisation and national compensatory adaptation is necessary.

Arguably, the right of self-determination of peoples favours decision-making close to each individual people, leaving as much as possible for them to decide autonomously within their sovereign national democratic systems.[66] In this sense, sovereign statehood protects a people's democratic self-determination.[67] But self-determination is not opposed to the voluntarily agreed transfer of decision-making powers from States to international or supranational institutions with regard to those regional or global problems that cannot be solved effectively at State level. In these cases, the joint or collective self-determination of a group of peoples is the only way to prevent two much more detrimental options—either leaving those problems unresolved or putting up with solutions imposed by more powerful external actors.

Nor does the right of self-determination preclude majority decisions in international or supranational institutions binding outvoted States. It only requires adequate democratic legitimacy and accountability of international and supranational decision-making, coupled with appropriate safeguards against and compensatory measures for detrimental effects that the institutionalisation at regional and global levels can have on national democracies. This means, *e.g.*, that any upgrading of the executive branch which represents the State internationally at the expense of the directly elected legislative branch because of the international institutionalisation must be compensated appropriately in order to maintain a proper national balance of powers. Democratic standards at all levels are interdependent and complementary. The ultimate objective is to ensure an adequate overall standard of democracy in multilevel systems of government where international, supranational and national decision-making are intertwined and together affect peoples. This may also permit a limited balancing between the levels of democratic legitimacy in the national and the international or supranational system in the sense that a deficit here can to a certain extent be compensated by a surplus there (and *vice versa*).

---

[65] See Arndt (2013); Giegerich (2020), p. 56 ff.

[66] See below Sect. 5.3.2 on the corresponding principle of subsidiarity of EU law.

[67] Wheatley (2010), p. 33 ff.

Another aspect of the relationship between international and national democracy is worth remembering: If States transfer powers to an international or supranational organisation in order to enhance their problem-solving capacity, they must ensure that the organisation's decision-making is both democratic and effective. Majority decisions constitute the best possible synthesis between democratic legitimacy and effectiveness, while veto powers by individual Member States not only decrease the organisation's effectiveness (*i.e.*, output legitimacy) but are also inherently undemocratic, because they give a small minority excessive influence and thereby distort the organisation's input legitimacy.[68] Since veto powers therefore decrease the level of international democracy, they can only be justified by a complementary/compensatory increase in the level of national democracy so that the overall standard of democracy remains adequate. Such an increase in the level of national democracy can only be assumed, if the veto power protects the core area of national self-determination.[69]

3.4 Enforcement Procedures for the Right of Self-Determination

Enforcement procedures only exist for the right's codified variants in Art. 1 ICCPR and ICESCR and their democratic ingredients. Focussing on Art. 1 ICCPR, because there is clear practice with respect to this provision, all States Parties are required by Art. 1 (3) ICCPR to promote the realisation of that right and respect it, in conformity with the UN Charter. They are all subject to the reporting procedure (Art. 40 ICCPR).[70] Those of them that have made the necessary declaration are also subject to the inter-State communication procedure (Art. 41 ICCPR) that has never been used.[71]

The individual communication procedure provided for in the Optional Protocol to the ICCPR (OP-ICCPR)[72] can only be initiated by individuals against States Parties of the Covenant that have also acceded to the OP-ICCPR. The Human Rights Committee (CCPR) has made clear that individuals cannot bring claims of violation of Art. 1 ICCPR which enshrines a right of peoples.[73] In contrast to the OP-ICCPR, the newer Optional Protocol to the ICESCR[74] permits communications also by or on behalf of "groups of individuals, under the jurisdiction of a State Party, claiming to be victims of a violation of any of the economic, social and cultural rights set forth

68 Peters (2009), p. 289 f.

69 See below Sect. 5.6 on the parallel problem in the EU.

70 Schabas (2019), Article 1 CCPR, para. 22.

71 Id., para. 23.

72 Of 16 December 1966, UNTS vol. 999, p. 171.

73 Schabas (2019), Article 1 CCPR, paras. 23 ff.

74 Of 10 December 2008 (UN General Assembly Resolution 63/117 [A/RES/63/117]).

in the Covenant by that State Party". It remains to be seen if the competent Committee on Economic, Social and Cultural Rights will qualify peoples as groups of individuals and the right of self-determination codified in Art. 1 ICESCR as an economic, social and cultural right. This seems unlikely but not impossible.

3.5 Conclusion: Peoples' Right to National and International Democratic Self-Determination

All in all, peoples' right of self-determination comprises a collective general right to democratically legitimate government in States, but with no specific requirements beyond certain minimum standards that ensure democratic legitimacy based on popular sovereignty. The concrete governmental design is left to each people and belongs to the *domaine réservé* of each State that is protected by the prohibition of intervention. The equal rights of peoples and ensuing sovereign equality of their States require their equal participation in international decision-making and thus respect for democratic principles in the international order, including international and supranational organisations. Accordingly, the UN General Assembly has for many years advocated a "democratic and equitable international order" in resolutions that have remained controversial. These democratic ingredients share the *jus cogens* character and *erga omnes* effects of the general right of self-determination.

Taking the two aspects together, that are obviously interdependent, one can speak of a collective right of peoples to national and international democratic self-determination which also includes an entitlement to democratic decision-making in international and supranational organisations as well as to adequate safeguards against detrimental effects that regional and global institutionalisation can have on national democracies. The goal is to ensure an adequate overall standard of democracy in multilevel systems of government. Since that collective right is rather vague, however, violations can only be established in clear-cut cases of dictatorships (national component), manifestly illegitimate denials of equal participation in international decision-making (international component) and obviously inadequate safeguards against disruptions in national democracies as a consequence of the international institutionalisation process (interdependence component). But even these rather elementary democratic standards deriving from the right of self-determination of peoples are difficult to enforce, as has been demonstrated in the preceding sub-chapter. This draws the attention to individual human rights that may help better to implement democratic standards at national and international/supranational levels, as will be demonstrated in the next chapter.

References

Arndt F (2013) Parliamentary Assemblies, International. Max Planck Encyclopedia of Public International Law (OUP online edition)

Byers M, Chesterman S (2000) 'You, the People': pro-democratic intervention in international law. In: Fox GH, Roth BR (eds) Democratic governance and international law, 1st edn. Cambridge University Press, Cambridge, pp 259–292

Cassese A (1995) Self-determination of peoples: a legal reappraisal. Cambridge University Press, Cambridge

Chemillier-Gendreau M (2007) Resistance, right to, international protection. Max Planck Encyclopedia of Public International Law (OUP online edition)

Criddle EJ (2024) Extraterritoriality's empire: how self-determination limits extraterritorial law-making. Am J Int Law 118:607–658

Fox GH (2000) The right to political participation in international law. In: Fox GH, Roth BR (eds) Democratic governance and international law, 1st edn. Cambridge University Press, Cambridge, pp 48–90

Frankenberg G (2012) Democracy. In: Rosenfeld M, Sajó A (eds) The Oxford handbook of comparative constitutional law, 1st edn. Oxford University Press, Oxford, pp 250–268

Giegerich T (2019) Federalist and antifederalist forces in the multilevel system of human rights protection in Europe. In: Denizeau-Lahaye C (ed) L'idée fédérale européenne à la lumière du droit comparé, 1st edn. Éditions Panthéon-Assas, Paris, pp 185–209

Giegerich T (2020) The political dimension of equality in the European Union: equality of citizens and equality of Member States in a supranational representative democracy. In: Giegerich T (ed) The European Union as protector and promoter of equality, 1st edn. Springer, Cham, pp 45–95

Giegerich T (2022) Supply chains responsibilities in the "Democratic and Equitable international Order" – the tasks for the European Union and its Member States. Zeitschrift für Europarechtliche Studien 25:213–220

Gould CC (2004) Globalizing democracy and human rights. Cambridge University Press, Cambridge

Hasar S (2024) Representation of Afghanistan before the International Court of Justice. Available via EJIL Talk. https://www.ejiltalk.org/representation-of-afghanistan-before-the-international-court-of-justice/. Accessed 22 Jan 2025

Keller H (2021) Friendly relations declaration. Max Planck Encyclopedia of Public International Law (OUP online edition)

Khan R (2011) Decolonization. Max Planck Encyclopedia of Public International Law (OUP online edition)

Kimminich O (1993) A "federal" right of self-determination? In: Tomuschat C (ed) Modern law of self-determination, 1st edn. Nijhoff, Dordrecht, pp 83–100

Kriener F (2023) Intervention, Prohibition of. Max Planck Encyclopedia of Public International Law (OUP online edition)

Maier P (1997) American Scripture. Knopf Doubleday Publishing Group, New York

Möllers C, Schneider L (2018) Demokratiesicherung in der Europäischen Union. Available via https://www.boell.de/sites/default/files/endf_boell_demokratiesicherung-i-d-europ-union_v03_kommentierbar.pdf. Accessed 22 Jan 2025

Murphy SD (2000) Democratic legitimacy and the recognition of States and governments. In: Fox GH, Roth BR (eds) Democratic governance and international law, 1st edn. Cambridge University Press, pp 123–154

Neumann V (2023) Demokratie und Völkerrecht. Mohr Siebeck, Tübingen

Oeter S (2023) Democracy – fundamental building-block of the international order? In: Khan D-E, Lagrange E, Oeter S et al (eds) Democracy and sovereignty. Rethinking the legitimacy of public international law, 1st edn. Brill Nijhoff, Brill/Leiden, pp 1–32

Peters A (2009) Dual democracy. In: Klabbers J, Peters A, Ulfstein G (eds) The constitutionalization of international law, 1st edn. Oxford University Press, Oxford, pp 263–341

Pippan C (2023) Pro-democratic interventionism revisited. In: Khan D-E, Lagrange E, Oeter S et al (eds) Democracy and sovereignty. Rethinking the legitimacy of public international law, 1st edn. Brill Nijhoff, Brill/Leiden, pp 35–59

Rosas A (1993) Internal self-determination. In: Tomuschat C (ed) Modern law of self-determination, 1st edn. Nijhoff, Dordrecht, pp 225–252

Salmon J (1993) Internal aspects of the right to self-determination: towards a democratic legitimacy principle? In: Tomuschat C (ed) Modern law of self-determination, 1st edn. Nijhoff, Dordrecht, pp 253–282

Schabas WA (2019) Nowak's CCPR Commentary, 3rd edn. N.P. Engel, Kehl

Schücking W, Wehberg H (1931) Die Satzung des Völkerbundes, Erster Band, 3rd edn. Franz Vhalen, Berlin

Simma B, Khan D-E, Nolte G et al (eds) (2024) The Charter of the United Nations – a commentary, vol I, 4th edn. Oxford University Press, Oxford (quoted by: Author)

Thornberry P (1993) The democratic or internal aspect of self-determination with some remarks on federalism. In: Tomuschat C (ed) Modern law of self-determination, 1st edn. Nijhoff, Dordrecht, pp 101–138

Thürer D, Burri T (2008) Self-determination. Max Planck Encyclopedia of Public International Law (OUP online edition)

Vanspranghe E (2023) La relation contariée entre souveraineté et démocratie au prisme des approches critiques du droit international. In: Khan D-E, Lagrange E, Oeter S et al (eds) Democracy and sovereignty. Rethinking the legitimacy of public international law, 1st edn. Brill Nijhoff, Brill/Leiden, pp 119–142

Wheatley S (2010) The democratic legitimacy of international law. Oxford University Press, Oxford

Wippman D (2000) Pro-democratic intervention by invitation. In: Fox GH, Roth BR (eds) Democratic governance and international law, 1st edn. Cambridge University Press, Cambridge, pp 293–327

Chapter 4
Human Rights as Cornerstones of Democracy

4.1 Global Democratic Rights Standards

4.1.1 Soft Law: Universal Declaration of Human Rights

While constituting the first international human rights catalogue in comprehensive form, including civil, political, economic, social and cultural rights, the UDHR has the character of a UN General Assembly resolution that is not legally binding as such.[1] It is only a soft-law document proclaiming human rights without codifying them as legal rights. Yet the UDHR informs the interpretation of the human rights obligations deriving from the UN Charter,[2] has meanwhile at least partly developed into customary international law and can also be qualified as reflecting general principles of law.[3] The UDHR is accordingly used by the UN Human Rights Council as one of the bases for the universal periodic review of the fulfilment by each UN Member State of its human rights obligations and commitments.[4] On the occasion of the 75th anniversary of the UDHR, the UN General Assembly stressed the Declaration's importance with regard to the promotion and protection of human rights and fundamental freedoms and urged States "to redouble their efforts in fulfilling their *duty* … to implement the provisions enshrined in the Universal Declaration of Human Rights …"[5]

---

[1] See Articles 10, 13 UNCh.

[2] See Article 1 (3), 55 lit. c, 56 UNCh.

[3] See Charlesworth (2008), paras. 14 ff.

[4] UN General Assembly Resolution 60/251 of 15 March 2006, para. 5 (e); HRC Resolution 5/1 of 18 June 2007, para. I.A.1 (b).

[5] UN General Assembly Resolution 78/194 of 19 December 2023 (A/RES/78/194), paras. 1 and 3 (emphasis added).

T. Giegerich, *The Human Right to Democracy in Multilevel Systems at a Time of Democratic Backsliding: Global, Regional and European Union Perspectives*, European Union and its Neighbours in a Globalized World 24,
https://doi.org/10.1007/978-3-032-01689-8_4

There is no "right to democracy" as such in the UDHR. However, it contains several guarantees of civil and political rights that protect essential prerequisites of a democratic system. The most important provision is Art. 21 UDHR, setting forth three such essentials: the right to participate in the government directly or indirectly through freely chosen representatives (para. 1); the right of equal access to public service (para. 2); and the right to vote and be elected in periodic, genuine, universal, free, equal and secret elections as the basis of popular sovereignty (para. 3).[6] As the formulation "his country" indicates, however, only citizens of the respective State, who are part of the people sustaining this State in exercising their right of self-determination, are entitled to participation in government.

Supplementary democratic guarantees are enshrined in Art. 15 UDHR (right to nationality that may not be arbitrarily withdrawn)[7] and—irrespective of citizenship—in the following provisions: Art. 2, 7 UDHR (non-discrimination and equality); Art. 18 UDHR (freedom of opinion and expression, of information and the media, regardless of frontiers); Art. 20 UDHR (freedom of peaceful assembly and association); Art. 26 UDHR (right to and freedom of education aimed at promoting democratic values); and Art. 8 UDHR (right to an effective remedy by competent national tribunals for violations of rights). Democracy is referred to only once, in Art. 29 (2) UDHR that regulates limitations on human rights. There it serves as a counterbalance—such limitations are only permitted to the extent that they are necessary for meeting just requirements "in a democratic society". Art. 30 UDHR is the last piece in the democratic mosaic of the UDHR: It protects the human rights bases of democracy by prohibiting States, groups and individuals from abusing any position under the UDHR for the purpose of destroying any right and freedom set forth in that Declaration. Since democracy cannot be destroyed without first dismantling its human rights bases, Art. 30 UDHR indirectly protects democratic governmental systems from antidemocratic exercises of rights set forth in the UDHR.

The UDHR was proclaimed by the UN General Assembly "as a common standard of achievement for all peoples and all nations"[8] and primarily has democratic and other human rights within States in mind. But according to Art. 28 UDHR, the Declaration also strives for an "international order in which the rights and freedoms set forth in this Declaration [including the democratic rights] can be fully realized". This indicates that the human rights proclaimed therein are also intended to promote international democracy, without which democratic self-determination remains

---

[6] Glazewski, in: Cantú Rivera (2004), Article 21 – Political Rights, p. 487 ff. According to the Venice Commission of the Council of Europe (see below note 60), Article 21 UDHR "may be considered to reflect customary international law" (Opinion No. 695/2012 of 18 June 2013, para. 9. Available via https://www.venice.coe.int/webforms/documents/?pdf=CDL-AD(2013)018-e (22 January 2025).

[7] The prohibition of arbitrary withdrawal of citizenship in Article 15 (2) UDHR reproduces a general principle of international law (ECJ, judgment of 2 March 2010 [C-135/08], ECLI:EU:C:2010:104, para. 53).

[8] Preamble.

precarious, and Art. 28 UDHR is formulated as an individual entitlement to such an international order.[9]

One final democratic aspect is enshrined in the last paragraph the UDHR's preamble. According to it, the UDHR was proclaimed by the UN General Assembly "to the end that every individual and every organ of society, keeping this Declaration constantly in mind, shall strive … to promote respect for these rights and freedoms and … to secure their universal and effective recognition and observance …". The implementation of human rights, including the democratic rights, thus is a concern of civil society and its individual members, in other words a democratic concern. The protection and promotion of human rights is a democratic endeavour because only their firm anchoring as inalienable and imprescriptible rights in the consciousness of all humans can ultimately secure them.[10] It is therefore important constantly to remind every human on earth that human rights are the rights of us all, *i.e.*, of the individual and collective ownership of each and all member(s) of the human family over human rights.

The question whether—based on the UDHR—there is a "human right to democracy" in present-day customary international law is difficult to answer.[11] This is because the democratic ingredients of the UDHR have meanwhile been adopted by numerous human rights treaties on the global and regional level which dominate the international discourse.[12] It is therefore hard to distinguish between treaty-based and extra-treaty State practice and *opinio juris* in the sense of Art. 38 (1) lit. b of the ICJ Statute, only the latter being capable of supporting customary international law relevant in our context.[13]

4.1.2 Hard Law: Human Rights Treaties at UN Level

4.1.2.1 Right to National Democracy

Most of the civil and political rights proclaimed in the UDHR were later codified in treaty form in the ICCPR. The Covenant does not include a "right to democracy" as such either, but reflects Art. 21 UDHR in Art. 25 ICCPR which guarantees three democratic essentials: the right and opportunity of every citizen, without

[9] See Decaux, in: Cantú Rivera (2004), Article 28 – The Right to a Social and International Order, p. 733 ff.

[10] See Judge Hand (1944). Available via https://www.btboces.org/Downloads/1_The%20Spirit%20of%20Liberty%20by%20Learned%20Hand.pdf (22 January 2025).

[11] The question is answered in the negative by Alfadhel (2017), p. 13 ff.

[12] See below Sect. 4.1.2 ff.

[13] See International Law Commission, Draft conclusions on identification of customary international law (2018), Conclusion 11 with Commentary (7). Available via https://legal.un.org/ilc/texts/instruments/english/commentaries/1_13_2018.pdf (22 January 2025). See UN General Assembly Resolution 73/203 of 20 December 2018 (A/RES/73/203) which takes note of these conclusions.

discrimination contrary to Art. 2 ICCPR and unreasonable restrictions, to take part in the conduct of public affairs, directly or indirectly through freely chosen representatives (lit. a); to vote and be elected at genuine, periodic, universal, free, equal and secret elections, guaranteeing the free expression of the will of the electors (lit. b); to have equal access to public service in their country (lit. c).[14] The right to vote and be elected covers all elections organised in the respective State, not only the elections to the legislature.[15]

Supplementary democratic guarantees that apply irrespective of citizenship are enshrined in Art. 2 (1), 26 ICCPR (non-discrimination and equality); Art. 19 ICCPR (freedom of opinion and expression, of information and the media, regardless of frontiers);[16] Art. 21 ICCPR (right of peaceful assembly);[17] Art. 22 ICCPR (right to freedom of association); and Art. 2 (3) ICCPR (right to an effective remedy by competent national authority for violations of rights). The ICCPR does not guarantee any right to nationality in the sense of Art. 15 UDHR.[18] The right to and freedom of education aimed at promoting democratic values in the sense of Art. 26 UDHR is enshrined in Art. 13 ICESCR.[19] In parallel with Art. 29 (2) UDHR, democracy is referred to three times in the ICCPR,[20] always in connection with limitations on human rights. There it serves as a counterbalance in the sense that such limitations must be necessary to protect certain public interests "in a democratic society".[21] The Covenant also includes a parallel provision to Art. 30 UDHR in Art. 5 (1) ICCPR[22] which prohibits States, groups and individuals from abusing any position under the Covenant for the purpose of destroying any right and freedom set forth in it, thereby indirectly protecting democratic governmental systems. Finally, Art. 4 ICCPR restricts governmental powers even in states of emergency in order to prevent a pretextual slide into autocracy.

---

[14] See CCPR, General Comment No. 25 (57), para. 1: "Article 25 lies at the core of democratic government based on the consent of the people and in conformity with the principles of the Covenant." For an overview of the HRC's case law pertaining to Article 25 ICCPR, see Alfadhel (2017), p. 36 ff.

[15] This is in contrast to the narrower Article 3 of the Additional Protocol to the ECHR (see below Sect. 4.2.1.2.1.1). See Schabas (2019), Article 25 CCPR, para. 22.

[16] See CCPR, General Comment No. 34 on Article 19 (Freedom of opinion and expression) of 29 July 2011 (CCPR/C/GC/34), para. 2: "Freedom of opinion and freedom of expression … constitute the foundation stone for every free and democratic society."

[17] See CCPR, General Comment No. 37 (2020) on the right of peaceful assembly of 17 September 2020 (CCPR/C/GC/37), para. 1: "The right of peaceful assembly … [t]ogether with other related rights, … also constitutes the very foundation of a system of participatory governance based on democracy, human rights, the rule of law and pluralism."

[18] Schabas (2019), Article 25 CCPR, para. 11 (p. 704). But see Article 24 (3) CCPR.

[19] As the Committee on Economic, Social and Cultural Rights stated in its General Comment No. 13 (E/C.12/1999/10 of 8 December 1999), "[e]ducation has a vital role in … promoting human rights and democracy" (para. 1).

[20] Articles 14 (1), 21 (1), 22 (2) ICCPR.

[21] See the parallel provision in Article 4 ICESCR.

[22] See in the same sense Article 5 (1) ICESCR.

Civic equality being a cornerstone of any democratic system, its guarantee in Art. 25 ICCPR is of primary importance. It is complemented by the general provisions on equal rights and non-discrimination in Art. 2 (1), 26 ICCPR. Unsurprisingly, the two global human rights instruments dedicated to combating discrimination, the International Convention on the Elimination of All Forms of Racial Discrimination (CERD)[23] and the Convention on the Elimination of All Forms of Discrimination against Women (CEDAW),[24] also specifically protect civic equality. In Art. 5 CERD, "States Parties undertake to eliminate racial discrimination ... and to guarantee the right of everyone, without distinction as to race, colour, or national or ethnic origin, to equality before the law, notably in the enjoyment of ... (c) [p]olitical rights, in particular the right to participate in elections – to vote and to stand for election – on the basis of universal and equal suffrage, to take part in the Government as well as in the conduct of public affairs at any level and to have equal access to public service".[25] Art. 7 CEDAW contains a parallel guarantee in favour of women, adding the obligation of States Parties to "ensure to women, on equal terms with men, the right ... (c) [t]o participate in non-governmental organizations and associations concerned with the public and political life of the country."

The Convention on the Rights of the Child (CRC),[26] which aims to protect people under the age of 18, does not specifically include voting and other political rights. But it does guarantee all the rights necessary to enable children to participate in public affairs, in accordance with their age and maturity: Art. 13 CRC (freedom of opinion and expression, of information and the media, regardless of frontiers); Art. 15 CRC (rights to freedom of association and peaceful assembly). Art. 28, 29 CRC on education enshrine a right of children to democratic education.

The Convention on the Rights of Persons with Disabilities (CRPD)[27] aims at ensuring the full, effective and equal participation and inclusion of persons with disabilities in society (Art. 1, 3 lit. b, c CRPD)—an obviously democratic goal. It is reflected in numerous provisions, primarily Art. 29 CRPD on participation in political and public life.

All these democracy-related human rights parameters are relatively concrete and have been further specified by international practice—the general comments or recommendations[28] and the case-law of the competent treaty bodies of independent experts which each of the aforementioned treaties establishes in order to monitor

[23] Of 21 December 1965, UNTS vol. 660, p. 195.

[24] Of 18 December 1979, UNTS vol. 1249, p. 13.

[25] See also HRC, Resolution 53/21 of 13 July 2023 on the incompatibility between democracy and racism (A/HRC/RES/53/21).

[26] Of 20 November 1989, UNTS vol. 1577, p. 3.

[27] Of 13 December 2006, UNTS vol. 2515, p. 3.

[28] See, e.g., CCPR, General Comment No. 25 on Article 25 of 27 August 1996 (CCPR/C/21/Rev.1/Add.7); General Comment No. 34 on Article 19 (Freedom of opinion and expression) of 29 July 2011 (CCPR/C/GC/34); General Comment No. 37 on Article 21 (Right of peaceful assembly) of 17 September 2020 (CCPR/C/GC/37); Committee on the Elimination of Discrimination against Women, General Recommendation No. 23: Political and Public Life of 1997.

implementation of treaty obligations. They have been concretised additionally by the HRC.[29] Thus, the global treaty bodies as well as their regional counterparts, including the human rights courts in Africa, the Americas and Europe, have consistently opined that political and public interest speech, as well as the press, enjoy heightened protection because of their central role in democratic societies.[30] On the other hand, penalising the spreading of false information in order to maintain the integrity of electoral processes has been accepted as legitimate, provided that it is proportionate.[31]

Reading the cited treaty provisions together, a rather clearly contoured individual human right to the essential ingredients of democratic national governments—an unwritten general right to national democracy—emerges as a synthesis of the special democratic rights. This still leaves States Parties sufficient margins in designing their governmental systems, in accordance with their peoples' right of self-determination. Thus, Art. 25 lit. a ICCPR gives States Parties discretion concerning the mixture of direct and representative elements in their democratic system, and lit. b concerning its parliamentary or presidential character. But the general human right to national democracy sets minimum standards that must not be disregarded and it imposes the obligation on States to justify each limitation, also in the light of the basic requirements of a "democratic society" that is prescribed as the general limitation benchmark in all relevant human rights treaties. The general right to democracy promotes the pro-democratic interpretation of the specific democratic rights, increases the demands for pro-democratic justification of limitations and may even help generating further supplementary unwritten democratic rights.

One further added value of the general right to democracy in an era of democratic backsliding is that it urges consideration of an overall negative trend regarding democracy in a certain State, instead of limiting the perspective to individual tiles of the entire gloomy mosaic. Thus broadening the horizon will help understand the seriousness of individual interferences with specific democratic rights which are part and parcel of a general attack on democracy as such. If victims of such individual interferences can show that their general right to democracy is also affected because of the systemic threat involved, the scales will more likely tip in their favour and a human rights violation be found. Finally, taking the general right to democracy into account may help in crossing the admissibility threshold of the complaint procedure before the Human Rights Council that was established "to address consistent patterns of gross and reliably attested violations" of human rights and fundamental freedoms.[32] Thus, the general right to democracy may play an important role in countering democratic backsliding. This has not yet received sufficient attention.

---

[29] See, e.g., Resolution 39/11 on equal participation in political and public affairs of 28 September 2018 (A/HRC/RES/39/11), read together with the detailed Draft guidelines for States on the effective implementation of the right to participate in public affairs prepared by the Office of the UN High Commissioner for Human Rights (A/HRC/39/28 of 20 July 2018).

[30] Clooney (2024), p. 50 ff.; Murray (2019), p. 276 ff. (on Article 9 AfrChHPR).

[31] Milanovic and Webb (2024), p. 242. See also UN Human Rights Council Resolution 49/21 of 1 April 2021 on the role of States in countering the negative impact of disinformation on the enjoyment and realization of human rights; ECtHR, judgment of 22 July 2025, Bradshaw and Others v. UK (Appl. No. 15653/22) - not yet final.

[32] UN Human Rights Council Resolution 5/1 of 18 June 2007, paras. 85 ff.

4.1.2.2 Right to International Democracy

The human rights in those various treaties seem exclusively to represent the top-down approach of international parameters for democratic government on the State level. There is no provision similar to Art. 28 UDHR that clearly takes the bottom-up perspective, formulating parameters for democratic government on the international level. However, it must be ensured that any form of government beyond the State which is established by States also complies with human rights, including democratic human rights, that bind those States. After all, States Parties to human rights treaties have committed themselves not only to respect, but also to ensure to all humans within their jurisdiction the rights enshrined in those treaties.[33] This includes an obligation to protect everyone under their jurisdiction from negative impacts on their human rights, and also their citizens from negative impacts on their democratic rights, in particular if these impacts are caused by the States. States cannot be permitted to establish and empower international or supranational organisations without paying attention to their democratic legitimacy as well as potential threats to democratic human rights within States arising from the exercise of their powers. It is therefore necessary to interpret the various human rights provisions, including the democratic rights, in a way that also protects humans from potential threats to liberty, equality and democracy emanating from international and supranational organisations in which their States participate.

Thus, the right of citizens to take part in the conduct of public affairs according to Art. 25 lit. a ICCPR extends to the formulation and implementation of policy also at the international level,[34] all the more since lit. a, in contrast to lit. c of Art. 25 ICCPR, does not limit the scope of the right to the citizens' own country. The freedom of information and expression in Art. 19 ICCPR explicitly crosses frontiers and also covers the policies of international and supranational organisations. The rights of peaceful assembly and association pursuant to Art. 21, 22 ICCPR also protects assemblies and associations critical of government beyond the State. The Office of the UN High Commissioner for Human Rights in 2018 drafted guidelines for States on the effective implementation of the right to participate in public affairs[35] that were endorsed by the HRC.[36] Paras. 95–114 of these guidelines explain in detail the "[r]ight to participate in public affairs at the supranational level, including in international organizations".

Since international and supranational organisations have so far not acceded to any global or regional human rights treaty enshrining democratic rights,[37] they are

---

[33] See Article 2 (1) ICCPR.

[34] CCPR, General Comment No. 25 (57), para. 5. See also Peters (2009), p. 300 ff.

[35] A/HRC/39/28 of 20 July 2018.

[36] Resolution 39/11 of 28 September 2018 (A/HRC/RES/39/11).

[37] Most of these treaties are only open for accession by States (see, e.g., Article 48 ICCPR).

not directly bound by any of their provisions.[38] This is why it is not possible to invoke any treaty-based democratic right directly against these organisations. Arguably, international and supranational organisations are bound by human rights that are part of customary international law, but this will include only the most elementary rights, such as the minimum standards of democratic participation prescribed by the right of self-determination.[39] However, the organisations' Member States that are parties to the relevant human rights treaties are obliged to ensure that their citizens can effectively exercise their democratic rights enshrined therein also *vis-à-vis* those organisations. This is a consequence of the States' obligation not only to respect, but also to ensure the rights enshrined in human rights treaties.[40] The States can fulfil this obligation by including democratic human rights provisions in the statutes of the organisations and by prompting them to accede to human rights treaties (if possible) and thereby submitting to external control of their compliance with (democratic) human rights.

These considerations based on customary international law and treaty law permit us to recognise a general individual human right to international democracy that is primarily addressed to States. They are obliged to ensure respect for democratic principles in regional or global decision-making, in particular when they establish international and supranational institutions. But evidence of such a right is scarcer and its contours are less clear than those of the general right to national democracy.

4.1.2.3 Right to Adequate Overall Standard of Democracy in Multilevel Systems

Taking the general human rights to national democracy and international democracy together and combining them with the States' obligation to protect their citizens' democratic rights in multilevel systems of government, one can also construct a citizens' entitlement to adequate safeguards against potentially negative impacts of international institutionalisation on national democratic standards. Forming a synthesis of the rights to national and international democracy as well as that entitlement, one obtains a general individual human right to an adequate overall standard of democracy in systems of multiple and interdependent democratic levels of government.

As already explained in the context of the right of self-determination, the right to an adequate overall standard of democracy requires adequate democratic legitimacy

[38] The EU, however, acceded to the CRPD in 2010 (Council Decision of 26 November 2009, OJ 2010 L 23, p. 35). It is also currently preparing to accede to the ECHR and Protocol No. 1, based on Article 6 (2) TEU and Article 59 (2) ECHR. See the Draft revised Agreement on the Accession of the European Union to the Convention for the Protection of Human Rights and Fundamental Freedoms, CDDH(2023)R_EXTRA ADDENDUM, 4 April 2023. Available via https://rm.coe.int/steering-committee-for-human-rights-cddh-interim-report-to-the-committ/1680aace4e (22 January 2025).

[39] See above Chap. 3.

[40] See Art. 2 (1) ICCPR.

and accountability of international and supranational decision-making, coupled with appropriate safeguards against and compensatory measures for detrimental effects that the institutionalisation at regional and global levels may have on national democracies. The right may also permit a limited balancing between the levels of democratic legitimacy in the national and the international or supranational system in the sense that a deficit here can to a certain extent be compensated by a surplus there (and *vice versa*). Otherwise, the contours of that right are also rather vague.

4.1.2.4 Enforcement Procedures

The human rights treaties at UN level establish treaty bodies of independent experts that are tasked with supervising the implementation of the treaty obligations by the States parties. The three available standard procedures that could also be employed to enforce the rights to national and international democracy are: State reports, State complaints and individual complaints.[41] Using the example of the ICCPR, the State reporting procedure is obligatory for all States parties but it results only in concluding observations by the CCPR that identify implementation problems and make recommendations how to solve them.[42] Even though the Committee will take up such issues in the next reporting cycle, the compliance push of these concluding observations is not very strong.

The State complaint procedure pursuant to Art. 41 ICCPR is only available against States parties that have expressly recognised the competence of the CCPR to consider such complaints ("communications"). Its main aim is to reach a settlement between the disputing parties, in the absence of which the Committee can but write a report confined to a brief statement of the facts. It is not permitted to include any legal evaluation. No wonder that the procedure has never been used.[43]

The individual complaint procedure was moved to the Optional Protocol (OP)[44] so that it is available only against those States Parties to the ICCPR that are also parties to the OP. The procedure results in "views" which the CCPR forwards to the applicant and the respondent State.[45] If the Committee expresses the view that the State Party has violated rights of the applicant, this view will not legally bind that State and accordingly, there is no enforcement procedure. But the CCPR expressly requests States to be informed about measures taken to give effect to its views within 180 days and can also take up unresolved issues when considering the next States reports.

---

[41] Kälin and Künzli (2019), p. 203 ff.

[42] Article 40 ICCPR.

[43] The parallel procedure pursuant to Article 11 CERD has been used once, by Palestine against Israel, with little effect (see Keane 2024).

[44] Of 16 December 1966 (UNTS vol. 999, p. 171).

[45] Article 5 (4) OP.

Recently, obviously based on the pertinent Waite and Kennedy case of the ECtHR,[46] the CCPR addressed threats to civil and political rights emanating from international organisations and thereby indirectly took up the interdependence problem of national and international democracies and the respective democratic rights. It did so in a labour dispute involving the Asian Development Bank, an intergovernmental organisation headquartered in the Philippines. Quoting the Waite and Kennedy judgment almost verbatim, the Committee opined that "where States establish international organizations in order to pursue or strengthen their cooperation in certain fields of activity, and where they transfer to those organizations certain competencies and accord them immunities, there may be implications as to the protection of fundamental rights. It would therefore be incompatible with the object and purpose of the Covenant if States parties were thereby absolved of their obligations under the Covenant in relation to the field of activity covered by such transfer. The Committee recalls that the Covenant is intended to guarantee not theoretical or illusory rights, but rights that are practical and effective."[47] The Committee somewhat vaguely drew the conclusion that as the respondent State, the Philippines, had granted immunity to the Asian Development Bank from the jurisdiction of its courts, it was required to ensure that the Bank provided for reasonable alternative means of dispute resolution in order to fulfil its obligations pursuant to Art. 14 (1) ICCPR. It ultimately opined that the Philippines had not violated this standard.[48] This obligation to establish compensatory mechanisms for upholding the Covenant standards also applies in substance with respect to the democratic rights enshrined therein.

All in all, however, the effective enforcement of the democratic rights included in global human rights treaties is not sufficiently guaranteed. But there are at least some starting points at the global level for protecting democratic entitlements. One should also not underestimate the positive impact which the Universal Periodic Review Procedure in the UN Human Rights Council[49] may have on the preservation or restoration of democracy in UN Member States. In most serious cases, the complaint procedure before the Human Rights Council may also be available.[50]

---

[46] See below Sect. 4.2.1.2.3.

[47] Human Rights Committee, views adopted on 18 July 2024 concerning communication No. 3581/2019 (M.L.D. v. Philippines), CCPR/C/141/D/3581/2019, para. 9.6 (quoting para. 67 of the ECtHR's judgment in Waite and Kennedy v. Germany).

[48] For a critique, see Burchardt (2024).

[49] See above Sect. 4.1.1.

[50] See above Sect. 4.1.2.1.

4.2 Regional Human Rights Standards

4.2.1 Europe: Common Heritage of Democratic Ideals and Values

In Europe, there are democracy-related international standards at the Council of Europe level and further reaching supranational standards of the European Union. They place democracy on a more solid and effective legal basis than at UN level, not least because of a common European heritage of democratic ideals and values.[51] This is in accordance with the general rule of human rights protection in multilevel systems that the higher level provides minimum standards which the lower levels may exceed.[52] However, where the global level guarantees democratic rights that are either missing or less developed on the regional level, they remain binding and help close gaps in the regional human rights protection.[53]

4.2.1.1 Council of Europe: Organisation of Genuine Democracies

4.2.1.1.1 Democracy as Condition for Membership

The Council of Europe (CoE) is a regional organisation devoted to the protection and promotion of democracy, human rights and the rule of law. In its Statute,[54] the 46 Member States reaffirm their devotion to "individual freedom, political liberty and the rule of law, principles which form the basis of all genuine democracy",[55] and aim at achieving greater unity for the purpose of realising their common ideals and principles (Art. 1 Statute). This is the earliest version of the triad democracy, human rights and the rule of law, whose interdependence and complementarity has since been reaffirmed many times on the global level.[56] According to Art. 3 Statute, Member States of the CoE must accept the principles of the rule of law and the protection of human rights. European States qualify for membership only, if they are able and willing to fulfil Art. 3; if they seriously violate that commitment, they can be excluded (Art. 8 Statute).

While democracy is not expressly mentioned in Art. 3 Statute, it is also protected, since, according to the preamble, it forms the superstructure above a rule of law and human rights base. Russia is the only State that has so far been excluded

---

[51] See 2nd recital of the preamble and Article 1 lit. a of the Statute of the Council of Europe of 5 May 1949, ETS No. 1.

[52] See Article 5 (2) ICCPR; Article 53 ECHR.

[53] See, e.g., Art. 25 ICCPR that goes further than the democratic guarantees in the ECHR and Prot. No. 1.

[54] See above note 48.

[55] 2nd recital of the preamble.

[56] See above Sects. 2.1 and 2.3.

from the CoE, based on Art. 8 read together with Art. 3 Statute. But this was done because of its military aggression against Ukraine, another CoE Member State, and not because of the systematic violation of democratic principles in Russia.[57] However, the Heads of State and Government of the CoE Member States later qualified Russia's offence as follows: "Russia's war of aggression against Ukraine is not just a violation of international law, but an attack on our democracies."[58] This attack, together with democratic backsliding and new challenges arising from digitalisation and artificial intelligence, has placed "democratic security" in Europe firmly on the agenda of the CoE.[59] "Democratic security" actually is synonymous with the effective exercise of the right of peoples to internal and external self-determination.[60]

The primary objective of the CoE has always been human rights protection. It uses soft-law instruments (recommendations made by the Committee of Ministers and/or the Parliamentary Assembly), also regarding the protection and promotion of democracy,[61] and hard-law instruments, *i.e.* treaties which are drafted under its auspices. While the Member States remain free to decide which of those treaties they ratify or accede to, their membership in the CoE as such already includes a firm commitment to democracy, human rights and the rule of law. Moreover, it can be argued that today CoE membership requires States to be also party to the European Convention on Human Rights to lend credibility to their human rights commitment under Art. 3 of the CoE Statute.[62]

4.2.1.1.2 European Commission for Democracy Through Law (Venice Commission)

Immediately after the end of the Cold War, the "European Commission for Democracy through Law (Venice Commission)" was established by 18 CoE Member States as an independent consultative body on constitutional matters in

---

[57] Giegerich (2022), p. 519 ff.

[58] Reykjavík Declaration of 16/17 May 2023. Available via https://rm.coe.int/4th-summit-of-heads-of-state-and-government-of-the-council-of-europe/1680ab40c1 (22 January 2025).

[59] Giegerich (2023), p. 558 ff., calling the CoE "Europe's Specialised Agency for 'Democratic Security'". See also "Towards a New Democratic Pact for Europe: Report of the Secretary General of the Council of Europe 2025" has recently emphasised the fundamental importance of democratic security as "one built on free and fair elections, independent courts, free media, anti-corruption frameworks, gender equality, diversity, social justice, inclusive civic space and active participation in public life." (p. 5, 45). Available via https://rm.coe.int/2025-report-of-the-secretary-general-of-the-council-of-europe-en-final/1680b5ad96 (26 August 2025).

[60] Id., p. 565.

[61] See, e.g., Recommendation CM/Rec(2023)5 of the Committee of Ministers to member States on the principles of good democratic governance of 6 September 2023. Available via https://search.coe.int/cm/pages/result_details.aspx?objectid=0900001680abeb87 (22 January 2025); Recommendation CM/Rec(2023)6 of the Committee of Ministers to member States on deliberative democracy of 6 September 2023. Available via https://search.coe.int/cm/pages/result_details.aspx?objectid=0900001680ac627a (22 January 2025).

[62] Contrariwise, according to Article 58 (3) ECHR, cessation of membership of the CoE automatically terminates membership in the ECHR.

order to promote the rule of law and democracy.[63] It now has 61 Member States and several observers, extending far beyond Europe into Africa, the Americas and Asia. Its function is to provide legal advice and assist Member States "wishing to bring their legal and institutional structures into line with European standards and international experience in the fields of democracy, human rights and the rule of law".[64]

According to Art. 1 (1) sentence 2 of the Commission's Revised Statute, "[i]ts own specific field of action shall be the guarantees offered by law in the service of democracy." On the definition of democracy, the Venice Commission said this: "While there is no generally accepted concept of what constitutes a democracy and while there is a large variety of political systems and practices across states that are considered democracies, there is a European consensus on the core components of what a democracy is."[65] On this basis, it determined that the characteristic of Monaco's "*sui generis system* of limited monarchy ... raise an obvious issue of democracy" and urged improvements.[66]

In pursuit of its mandate, the Venice Commission has, for instance, adopted "Parameters on the Relationship between the Parliamentary Majority and the Opposition in a Democracy: A Checklist", which was endorsed by the Committee of Ministers.[67] While the institutional relations between the parliamentary opposition, the majority and other State institutions is of fundamental importance for a functioning democracy, enforceable "human rights standards are of little help" in this sphere which is primarily governed by international soft law precepts.[68]

Two recent opinions, both issued at the request of the Parliamentary Assembly, demonstrate the Venice Commission's relevance regarding the protection of democracy in the CoE and the EU as its subset. Regarding Hungary, the Venice Commission published a critical opinion on the Act LXXXVIII of 2023 on the Protection of National Sovereignty which prohibits foreign funding in electoral campaigns and establishes a new Sovereignty Protection Office.[69] While in principle acknowledging the legitimacy of certain restrictions on foreign funding of political parties and election campaigns, it criticised the overbreadth of the act: "Such wide regulations may have a chilling effect on the free and democratic debate in Hungary and on citizens' engagement in elections."[70] The European Commission has meanwhile initi-

[63] See the Commission's revised Statute adopted by the Committee of Ministers in Res (2002) 3 of 21 February 2002. Available via https://www.venice.coe.int/WebForms/documents/default.aspx?pdffile=CDL(2002)027-e (22 January 2025). For an overview of the Commission's evolution, see Nußberger and Miklasová (2023), p. 269 ff.

[64] Id. See, *e.g.*, the Venice Commission's Code of Good Practice in Electoral Matters, CDL-AD(2002)023rev2-cor, 25 October 2018. Available via https://www.venice.coe.int/webforms/documents/default.aspx?pdffile=CDL-AD(2002)023rev2-cor-e (22 January 2025).

[65] Opinion No. 695/2012 of 18 June 2013. Available via https://www.venice.coe.int/webforms/documents/?pdf=CDL-AD(2013)018-e (22 January 2025), para. 8.

[66] Id., paras. 98 ff.

[67] Opinion No. 845/2016 of 24 June 2019. Available via https://www.venice.coe.int/webforms/documents/?pdf=CDL-AD(2019)015-e (22 January 2025), endorsed by the Committee of Ministers on 5 February 2020.

[68] Id., para. 11.

[69] CDL-AD(2024)001 of 18 March 2024. Available via https://www.venice.coe.int/webforms/documents/default.aspx?pdffile=CDL-AD(2024)001-e (22 January 2025).

[70] Id., para. 82.

ated an infringement procedure pursuant to Art. 258 TFEU against Hungary regarding the same Act.[71]

Concerning Georgia, the Venice Commission issued a much more critical urgent opinion on the Law on Transparency of Foreign Influence, the controversial "foreign-agents law".[72] It regretted that the Georgian Parliament did not wait for the Venice Commission's assessment and that it adopted the law "in a procedure which left no space for genuine discussion and meaningful consultation, in open disregard for the concerns of large parts of the Georgian people."[73] Substantively, "it concludes that the restrictions set by the Law to the rights to freedom of expression, freedom of association and privacy are incompatible with the strict test set out in Articles 8(2), 10(2), and 11(2) of the ECHR and Article 17(2), 19(2) and 22(2) of the ICCPR as they do not meet the requirements of legality, legitimacy, necessity in a democratic society and proportionality, as well as with the principle of non-discrimination set out in Article 14 of the ECHR."[74]

Since Georgia is a candidate for EU accession, the European Council also reacted by reiterating "its serious concern regarding the course of action taken by the Georgian government, which runs counter to the values and principles upon which the European Union is founded. … The European Council recalls that such a course of action jeopardises Georgia's European path, and de facto halts the accession process. It calls on Georgia to adopt democratic, comprehensive and sustainable reforms, in line with the core principles of European integration."[75] Meanwhile, the Georgian government decided not to pursue the opening of accession negotiations and rejecting EU financial support until 2028. This has been regretted by the EU that also reiterated "its serious concerns about the continuous democratic backsliding of the country, including the irregularities which took place in the run up and during the recent Parliamentary elections."[76]

---

[71] European Commission, Press Release IP/24/4865 of 3 October 2024. Available via https://ec.europa.eu/commission/presscorner/api/files/document/print/en/ip_24_4865/IP_24_4865_EN.pdf (22 January 2025). The case is pending under file number C-829/24. See also Martínez and Menéndez (2024).

[72] CDL-PI(2024)013 of 21 May 2024. Available via https://venice.coe.int/webforms/documents/?pdf=CDL-PI(2024)013-e (22 January 2025).

[73] Id., para. 95.

[74] Id., para. 96. For a parallel assessment of the similar Russian foreign agents law, see ECtHR, judgment of 22 October 2024, Kobaliya and Others v. Russia (Appl. No. 39446/16 and 106 others): "The legislation examined in this case … bears the hallmarks of a totalitarian regime." (para. 86). See Krupskiy (2025).

[75] European Council Conclusion of 17 October 2024, paras. 45 f. Available via https://www.consilium.europa.eu/media/2pebccz2/20241017-euco-conclusions-en.pdf (22 January 2025).

[76] Statement by the High Representative/Vice-President of the Commission Kaja Kallas and Commissioner for Enlargement Marta Kos on Georgia of 1 December 2024. Available via https://enlargement.ec.europa.eu/news/statement-high-representative-vice-president-commission-kaja-kallas-and-commissioner-enlargement-2024-12-01_en (22 January 2025).

4.2.1.1.3 Parliamentary Assembly of the Council of Europe

The democratic credibility of the CoE itself is enhanced by the fact that it was the first intergovernmental organisation with a parliamentary component in its institutional set-up—the Parliamentary Assembly (PACE), consisting of representatives elected or appointed by the national parliaments of the Member States from among their members.[77] This is an attempt by Member States to democratise international decision-making at CoE level. Although PACE has few hard powers and primarily fulfils an advisory function to the Committee of Ministers, it increases the legitimacy of the CoE, not least by establishing a direct link between that organisation and the parliaments of its Member States,[78] which demonstrates that the CoE is not a purely intergovernmental, but also an interparliamentary institution, bringing it somewhat closer to the peoples/the electorates of the Member States. PACE has also operated as a 'school of democracy' in which parliamentarians from new democracies can learn from their more experienced peers.[79]

It is also important to note that PACE has become a watchdog of human rights and democracy in the CoE Member States,[80] engages in election observation, often in cooperation with other organisations,[81] has since 1993 monitored compliance by Member States with their membership conditions[82] and has in particular voiced its concern about democratic backsliding in recent years.[83]

One instrument PACE has used to counter democratic backsliding is the review of credentials of delegated national parliamentarians whose ratification is denied if there are doubts regarding the conduct of free and fair elections in their Member State (or, for that matter, other serious violations of Art. 3 CoE Statute). This leads to the suspension of the respective delegation's participatory rights in PACE. Since Art. 8 of the CoE Statute appears to reserve the power of suspending Member States' rights of representation in reaction to violations of Art. 3 of the Statute to the Committee of Ministers, the legality of PACE's measures are indeed not beyond doubt.[84] In 2024, PACE resolved not to ratify the credentials of the delegation of

[77] Articles 22 ff. CoE Statute. Leach (2017), p. 166 ff.

[78] Leach (2017), para. 7.88.

[79] Id.

[80] See, e.g., Resolution 1547 (2007) of 18 April 2007 "State of democracy and human rights in Europe". Available via https://assembly.coe.int/nw/xml/XRef/Xref-XML2HTML-en.asp?fileid=17531&lang=en (22 January 2025).

[81] See Leach (2017), paras. 7.80 ff.

[82] Leach (2017), paras. 7.49 ff. See also Ailincai (2021).

[83] Resolution 2437 (2022) and Recommendation 2232 of 28 April 2022 "Safeguarding and promoting genuine democracy in Europe". Available via https://pace.coe.int/en/files/30029/html (22 January 2025).

[84] See Polakiewicz and Kirchmayr (2021), p. 362. In footnote 4, the authors cite an unpublished Opinion by the CoE's Directorate of Legal Advice and Public International Law (Role and responsibilities of the Council of Europe's statutory organs with special emphasis on the limitation of membership rights, DLAPIL 18/2018) of 25 September 2018. On the dispute regarding the ratifi-

Azerbaijan for a number or reasons, including "serious concerns … as to [Azerbaijan's] ability to conduct free and fair elections, the separation of powers, the weakness of its legislature vis-à-vis the executive, the independence of the judiciary and respect for human rights, as illustrated by numerous judgments of the European Court of Human Rights and opinions of the European Commission for Democracy through Law (Venice Commission)".[85] More recently, PACE provisionally ratified the Georgian delegation's credentials, while at the same time suspending certain rights of its members, in reaction to rapid and serious democratic backsliding, as documented by concerns regarding the correctness and fairness of the parliamentary elections of 26 October 2024, and human rights abuses in Georgia.[86] In reaction, the Georgian delegation has withdrawn from PACE.[87]

In 2020, a new "Complementary joint procedure between the Committee of Ministers and the Parliamentary Assembly in response to a serious violation by a member State of its statutory obligations" was agreed which can be initiated by either of the two organs as well as the Secretary General.[88] The primary aim of this procedure "is to bring a member State, through constructive dialogue and co-operation, into compliance with the obligations and principles of the Organisation, and avoid imposing sanctions".[89]

4.2.1.1.4 Reykjavík Principles for Democracy

The commitment of the CoE in particular to democracy, complementary to human rights and the rule of law, was reconfirmed by the Reykjavík Summit of 16/17 May 2023. In the Reykjavík Declaration,[90] the Heads of State and Government of the CoE Member States underlined their "common responsibility to fight autocratic tendencies and growing threats to human rights, democracy and the rule of law. Those core values are the bedrock of our continued freedom, peace, prosperity and security for Europe. … We are committed to securing and strengthening democracy and good governance at all levels throughout Europe. We will work together to protect and promote the three fundamental, interdependent and inalienable principles of democracy, rule of law and human rights, as enshrined in the Statute of the

cation of the credentials of Russian parlamentarians between 2014 and 2019, see Giegerich (2022), p. 528 ff.

[85] PACE Resolution 2527 (2024) of 24 January 2024. On its legality, see Ailincai (2024b) The Parliamentary Assembly of the Council of Europe is at it again.

[86] Resolution 2585 (2025) of 29 January 2025.

[87] https://pace.coe.int/en/news/9762/pace-president-regrets-decision-of-georgian-delegation-to-withdraw-from-the-assembly (31 January 2025).

[88] PACE Resolution 2319 (2020) of 29 January 2020; CM Decision CM/Del/Dec(2020)1366/1.7-app of 5 February 2020; PACE Resolution 2360 (2021) of 26 January 2021.

[89] PACE Resolution 2319 (2020) of 29 January 2020, para. 4.1.

[90] Available via https://rm.coe.int/4th-summit-of-heads-of-state-and-government-of-the-council--of-europe/1680ab40c1 (22 January 2025).

Council of Europe and in the European Convention on Human Rights. However, democratic backsliding, external threats and new challenges lead us to strengthen our resolve and to adopt the Reykjavík Principles for Democracy, set forth in Appendix III."

In the preamble of Appendix III, the Heads of State and Government explain that they "consider democracy as the only means to ensure that everyone can live in a peaceful, prosperous and free society. We will meet our obligations under international law. We will prevent and resist democratic backsliding in our continent, including in situations of emergency, crisis and armed conflict and will stand firm against authoritarian tendencies by enhancing our shared commitments as member States of the Council of Europe." The following ten Reykjavík Principles for Democracy are formulated as objective principles and commitments by governments rather than as individual rights. But they of course constitute the interpretative background for the individual democratic rights guaranteed by the European Convention on Human Rights and the Additional Protocol.[91] The principles cover the following ten areas: (1) democratic participation; (2) elections and referenda; (3) independent and effective parliaments and other democratic institutions; (4) separation of powers against excessive concentration of power; (5) independent, impartial and effective judiciaries; (6) fight against corruption; (7) expressive, academic and artistic freedoms; (8) democratic future; (9) civil society; (10) full, equal and meaningful participation in public life for all, including women and girls, without violence, harassment or discrimination.

Regarding principle (2), the chiefs promise to "take all appropriate measures against any interference in electoral systems and processes" and ensure that elections are "grounded in respect for relevant human rights standards", such as the freedom to create political parties. Repelling illicit foreign interference in elections has become an urgent task.[92] Regarding principle (7), it is stated that "[f]ree, independent, plural and diverse media constitutes one of the cornerstones of democratic society and journalists and other media workers should be afforded full protection under the law.[93] Disinformation and misinformation posing a threat to democracy and peace will be countered, in a manner compatible with international law, including the right to freedom of expression and freedom of opinion". Regarding principle (8), the importance of "education about human rights and core democratic values, such as pluralism, inclusion, non-discrimination, transparency and accountability" is underlined. Finally, in principle (9) the chiefs reaffirm that civil society

---

[91] See below Sect. 4.2.1.2.

[92] On the decision of the Romanian Constitutional Court to annul the first round of the 2024 presidential elections because of alleged interference in the electoral process by Russia using AI mechanisms, see Selejan-Gutan (2024); Maftean (2024); Kuti (2024); Carrozzini (2024); Shattock (2025). See below Sects. 4.2.1.2.1.4.2 and 5.4.2.2.

[93] On the importance of pluralism in the audio-visual sector, see ECtHR, judgment of 17 September 2009, Manole and Others v. Moldova (Appl. No. 13936/02), paras. 95 ff.; (GC), judgment of 7 June 2012, Centro Europa 7 S.R.L. and Di Stefano v. Italy (Appl. No. 38433/09), paras. 129 ff. (Footnote not in the original).

"is a prerequisite for a functioning democracy and commit to supporting and maintaining a safe and enabling environment in which civil society, as well as human rights defenders, can operate free from hindrance, insecurity and violence".

While the Reykjavík Principles are clearly focussed on national democracy, the reference to "better global governance" in their last paragraph indicates that international democracy is also on the agenda of the CoE Heads of State and Government. They hope to join forces with non-European democratic powers in this regard.

Very briefly, the Reykjavík Declaration mentions an important point that has already briefly been touched upon above when discussing the relation between human rights and democracy on the global level[94]—the complementarity between social security and democratic security. The CoE Heads of State and Government confirmed that social justice was crucial for democratic stability and security and therefore reaffirmed their full commitment to the protection and implementation of social rights as guaranteed by the European Social Charter system.[95] They accordingly promised to "consider the organisation of a high-level conference on the European Social Charter, as a step to take further commitments under the Charter where possible."[96] This conference took place on 3 and 4 July 2024 and produced the Vilnius Declaration which reconfirmed "that social justice and the Council of Europe's action on social rights play a crucial role for democratic stability and security."[97] The Vilnius Declaration invokes the 1993 Vienna Declaration and Programme of Action, in which all human rights, including social rights, had been qualified as "universal, indivisible, interdependent and interrelated", as well as the Sustainable Development Goals as defined by the United Nations 2030 Agenda for Sustainable Development.[98]

In a follow-up to the Reykjavík Declaration and the Reykjavík Principles, the Committee of Ministers established a new Steering Committee on Democracy (CDDEM) that started work in May 2024.[99] The CDDEM is tasked with promoting and facilitating "thematic exchanges and peer reviews of experience and good practices among Council of Europe member States to develop common policy responses and standards, as well as tools, to strengthen democracy, its institutions and processes and good governance at all levels—national, regional and local; and to enhance the meaningful participation in democratic life of all members of society, notably of young persons and civil society."[100] One of its most important tasks is to

---

[94] See above Sect. 2.1.

[95] European Social Charter (revised) of 3 May 1996 (ETS No. 163).

[96] See above note 90.

[97] Available via https://rm.coe.int/en-vilnius-declaration/1680b0dcf3 (22 January 2025), paras. 2 and 5; Glas (2024).

[98] Id., para. 3.

[99] Available via https://www.coe.int/en/web/steering-committee-on-democracy/about-us (22 January 2025). It replaced the European Committee for Democracy and Governance as of 1 January 2024.

[100] CDDEM Terms of Reference. Available via https://rm.coe.int/terms-of-reference-of-the--steering-committee-on-democracy-cddem-/1680af951a (22 January 2025).

counter democratic backsliding.[101] As the CDDEM's terms of reference clearly indicate, democracy at the international and supranational level is beyond the scope of the CDDEM's work.

4.2.1.1.5 CoE Framework Convention on Artificial Intelligence and Human Rights, Democracy and the Rule of Law

This Convention (CoE-FrCAI)[102] is open for signature by the CoE Member States, the non-Member States which have participated in its elaboration[103] and the EU. Other non-Member States can be invited to accede.[104] It does not attempt to fully regulate AI and its impacts, but is only intended to address the risks for human rights, democracy and the rule of law deriving from AI systems, while also recognising the opportunities they offer in this regard.[105] The Convention is based on the "fact that human rights, democracy and the rule of law are inherently interwoven".[106] According to Art. 1 (1) CoE-FrCAI, "[t]he provisions of this Convention aim to ensure that activities within the lifecycle of artificial intelligence systems are fully consistent with human rights, democracy and the rule of law."

Art. 5 (1) CoE-FrCAI specifically requires the Parties "to seek to ensure that artificial intelligence systems are not used to undermine the integrity, independence and effectiveness of democratic institutions and processes, including the principle of the separation of powers, respect for judicial independence and access to justice." Democratic processes of course also comprise free and fair elections.[107] Art. 5 (2) CoE-FrCAI requires measures to protect "individuals' fair access to and participation in public debate, as well as their ability to freely form opinions." As the Explanatory Report explains, AI technologies "possess significant potential to enhance democratic values, institutions, and processes", but on the other hand also raise concerns regarding threats to democracy and human rights, such as the dissemination of disinformation and AI-enabled manipulation of authentic content.[108]

As already indicated by its designation as a framework convention, the provisions of the CoE-FrCAI impose legal obligations on the Parties, to be given effect by appropriate legislative, administrative or other measures,[109] but do not enshrine

---

[101] CM/Del/Dec(2024)133/2b of 17 May 2024, para. 6. Available via https://search.coe.int/cm#{%22CoEIdentifier%22:[%220900001680afa9e7%22],%22sort%22:[%22CoEValidationDate%20Descending%22]} (22 January 2025).

[102] Of 5 September 2024, CETS No. 225 – not yet in force.

[103] Argentina, Australia, Canada, Costa Rica, the Holy See, Israel, Japan, Mexico, Peru, the United States and Uruguay (see the pertinent Explanatory Report, para. 156).

[104] Article 30 (1), Article 31 (1) CoE-FrCAI.

[105] See 4th and 5th recitals of the preamble of the CoE-FrCAI.

[106] 8th recital of the preamble of the CoE-FrCAI.

[107] See the pertinent Explanatory Report, para. 46 lit. e.

[108] Paras. 42 f.

[109] Article 1 (2) CoE-FrCAI.

enforceable individual rights. The Convention is not even intended "to create new human rights or human rights obligations or undermine the scope and content of the existing applicable protections, but rather, by setting out various legally binding obligations contained in its Chapters II to VI, to facilitate the effective implementation of the applicable human rights obligations of each Party in the context of the new challenges raised by artificial intelligence."[110] This invites us to consider those other "applicable human rights obligations" regarding democracy within the CoE system.

4.2.1.2 European Convention on Human Rights and Additional Protocol

The CoE's most significant achievement is the European Convention on Human Rights (ECHR)[111] and complementary Protocols that constitute the most effective system of international human rights protection worldwide. The Convention system has rightly been characterised as "a mechanism to promote peace and stability in Europe and the Council of Europe's core values of human rights, democracy and the rule of law."[112] Human rights embodying democratic guarantees, similar to the ones at global level, are contained in the ECHR and the Protocol No. 1 to the ECHR (Prot. No. 1).[113] While the ECHR binds all 46 Member States of the CoE, the Protocol binds 44—only Monaco and Switzerland have not accepted it.

4.2.1.2.1 Right to National Democracy

In the 4th recital of its preamble, the ECHR subscribes to the interdependence and complementarity of human rights and democracy, a concept also advocated by the UN General Assembly and HRC: Fundamental freedoms "are best maintained by an effective political democracy". According to the settled case law of the ECtHR, "[d]emocracy … appears to be the only political model contemplated by the Convention and, accordingly, the only one compatible with it"[114] and "[d]emocracy constitutes a fundamental element of the 'European public order' …".[115] While neither the ECHR nor the Prot. No. 1 includes a right to democracy as such, they pro-

---

[110] Explanatory Report, para. 13.

[111] Convention for the Protection of Human Rights and Fundamental Freedoms of 4 November 1950 (ETS No. 5), as amended.

[112] Reykjavík Declaration (note 90), Appendix IV.

[113] Protocol to the Convention for the Protection of Human Rights and Fundamental Freedoms of 20 March 1952 (ETS No. 9).

[114] See ECtHR (GC), judgment of 13 February 2003, Refah Partisi (The Welfare Party) and Other v. Turkey (Appl. No. 41340/98 etc.), para. 86; GC judgment 16 March 2006, Ždanoka v. Latvia (Appl. No. 58278/00), para. 98.

[115] ECtHR, decision of 21 November 2017, Cumhuriyet Halk Partisi v. Turkey (Appl. No. 48818/17), para. 36; judgment of 16 April 2024, Guđmundur Gunnarson and Magnús Davíđ Norđdahl v. Iceland (Appl. Nos. 24159/22 and 25751/22), para. 57.

tect a number of human rights constituting the indispensable basis of democratic government. Since the ECtHR has emphasised both the "Convention's role as a 'constitutional instrument of European public order' in the field of human rights"[116] and the importance of democracy as the foundation of that European public order, one can draw the conclusion that the protection of democracy through the democratic rights at its basis is a particularly essential task of the Convention system and its Court.

4.2.1.2.1.1 Voting Rights: Art. 3 of Protocol No. 1

According to the ECtHR, "[t]he rights guaranteed under Article 3 of Protocol No. 1 are crucial to establishing and maintaining the foundations of an effective and meaningful democracy governed by the rule of law and are accordingly of prime importance in the Convention system".[117] The Court has also emphasised that "the Convention establishes a close nexus between an effective political democracy and the effective operation of Parliament [elected in accordance with Art. 3 Prot. No. 1]. Accordingly, there can be no doubt that the effective functioning of Parliament is a value of key importance for a democratic society ..."[118] This includes protection of parliamentary autonomy in the making and enforcement of rules regarding its internal operation, but limited by "the concepts of 'effective political democracy' and 'the rule of law' to which the Preamble to the Convention refers".[119]

Art. 3 Prot. No. 1, despite being formulated as an objective obligation of Convention States, in particular enshrines the democratically essential subjective right to vote and stand as a candidate in free, periodic, universal and secret elections.[120] But in contrast to Art. 25 lit. b ICCPR, that right covers only elections to "the legislature". The definition of this term depends on the constitutional structure of the respective Convention State. National parliaments and the European Parliament[121] are definitely included, regional assemblies only when they are

[116] ECtHR (GC), judgment of 30 June 2005, Bosphorus v. Ireland (No. 45036/98), para. 156.

[117] Judgment of 16 April 2024, Guðmundur Gunnarson and Magnús Davíð Norðdahl v. Iceland (Appl. Nos. 24159/22 and 25751/22), para. 57. See also judgment of 21 May 2019, G.K. v. Belgium (Appl. No. 58302/10), para. 49.

[118] (GC), judgment of 17 May 2016, Karácsony and Others v. Hungary (Appl. Nos. 42461/13 and 44357/13), para. 141.

[119] ECtHR, judgment of 16 April 2024, Guðmundur Gunnarson and Magnús Davíð Norðdahl v. Iceland (Appl. Nos. 24159/22 and 25751/22), para. 63.

[120] ECtHR (GC), judgment of 6 October 2005, Hirst v. UK (No. 2) (Appl. No. 74025/01), paras. 56 ff.; judgment of 24 October 2023, Myslihaka and Others v. Albania (No. 68958/17 etc.), para. 54. For an overview of the development of the Strasbourg case law, see Richter, in: Dörr et al. (2022), Kapitel 25 para. 33 ff., 147 ff.

[121] See below Sect. 4.2.1.2.2.

granted genuine legislative powers,[122] while local councils are excluded.[123] Presidential elections may be covered, if the president has the power to control the enactment of legislation,[124] whereas referenda fall under Art. 3 Prot. No. 1 only in exceptional cases.[125]

According to the case law of the ECtHR, Art. 3 Prot. No. 1 enshrines not only the right to elect and be elected, but also the right to sit and work effectively in the legislature once elected to it.[126] Elected parliamentarians' right to exercise political participation under Art. 3 Prot. No. 1 includes elements of Art. 10 and Art. 11 ECHR.[127] Read together with Art. 14 ECHR, that provision protects also from discrimination within its scope of application.[128] On this basis, the ECtHR decided "that the system that had been put in place to ensure the political representation of national minorities in Hungary had ended up limiting their political effectiveness and threatened to reduce, rather than enhance, diversity and the participation of minorities in political decision-making" and therefore violated Art. 3 Prot. No. 1 in conjunction with Art. 14 ECHR.[129] Moreover, Art. 3 Prot. No. 1 "entails a procedural positive obligation to put in place a domestic system for the effective examination of individual complaints and appeals in matters concerning electoral rights, and this system must be secured with procedural safeguards".[130]

While Art. 3 Prot. No. 1 does not limit active and passive electoral rights to citizens, States parties are free to thus limit them and have mostly done so.[131] In general, the ECtHR grants Convention States a broad margin of appreciation in

---

[122] See ECtHR, judgment of 28 April 2016, Partei Die Friesen v. Germany (Appl. No. 65480/10), para. 32, with regard to the German State legislatures.

[123] But see in this regard the Additional Protocol to the European Charter of Local Self-Government on the right to participate in the affairs of a local authority of 16 November 2009 (CETS No. 207) that binds 22 CoE Member States.

[124] For a counter-example, see ECtHR, decision of 6 March 2025, Georgescu v. Romania (Appl. No. 37327/24).

[125] For the relevant case law, see ECtHR, Press Unit, Factsheet – Right to Vote (September 2023). Available via https://www.echr.coe.int/documents/d/echr/FS_Vote_ENG (22 January 2025); ECtHR (Registry), Guide on Article 3 of Protocol No. 1 to the ECHR (Updated to 29 February 2024). Available via https://ks.echr.coe.int/documents/d/echr-ks/guide_art_3_protocol_1_eng (22 January 2025).

[126] ECtHR, judgment of 11 June 2002, Sadak and Others v. Turkey (No. 2) (Appl. No. 25144/94 etc.), para. 33 ff.

[127] ECtHR, decision of 11 February 2025, Costa i Rosselló v. Spain etc. (Appl. No. 29780/20 etc.), para. 122.

[128] ECtHR, judgment of 28 April 2016, Partei Die Friesen v. Germany (Appl. No. 65480/10), paras. 30 ff.

[129] ECtHR, judgment of 10 November 2022, Bakirdzi and E.C. v. Hungary (Appl. Nos. 49636/14 and 65648/14). The quote is from the Court's Press Release ECHR 354 (2022).

[130] ECtHR, judgment of 16 April 2024, Guđmundur Gunnarson and Magnús Davíđ Norđdahl v. Iceland (Appl. Nos. 24159/22 and 25751/22), paras. 42, 58 f.

[131] See Grabenwarter (2014), Protocol No. 1, Article 3, para. 2. See also Article 16 ECHR (below Sect. 4.2.1.2.1.3).

regulating elections and limiting electoral rights.[132] This is because "[t]here are numerous ways of organising and running electoral systems and a wealth of differences, inter alia, in historical development, cultural diversity and political thought within Europe which it is for each Contracting State to mould into their own democratic vision."[133] The Court has also underlined that the standards for establishing compliance with Art. 3 Prot. No. 1 are less stringent than those applied under Art. 8–11 ECHR.[134] The reason probably is that election cases are so close to the heart of national democratic systems that the ECtHR's own democratic legitimacy for overriding the Convention State parliaments will only be solid enough in clear-cut cases.[135] The Court has indeed generally explained the fundamentally subsidiary role of the Convention and of itself that translates into the Convention States' margin of appreciation[136] by reference to the national authorities' better democratic legitimation.[137]

On the other hand, the ECtHR has emphasised that despite the States' wide margin of appreciation, which depended on the special historico-political context of each State,[138] "it is for the Court to determine in the last resort whether the requirements of Article 3 of Protocol No. 1 have been complied with. In particular, it has to satisfy itself that the conditions do not curtail the rights in question to such an extent as to impair their very essence and deprive them of their effectiveness; that they are imposed in pursuit of a legitimate aim; and that the means employed are not disproportionate … Such conditions must not thwart the free expression of the people in the choice of the legislature – in other words, they must reflect, or not run counter to, the concern to maintain the integrity and effectiveness of an electoral procedure aimed at identifying the will of the people through universal suffrage".[139] The Court has also repudiated interferences with the active or passive right to vote based on arbitrary grounds.[140] But it has accepted a prohibition on standing for election after removal from office in impeachment proceedings for violations of the constitution that was imposed in order to protect "the proper functioning of the institution of

---

132 ECtHR (Registry), Guide on Article 3 (note 125), paras. 12 ff.

133 ECtHR (GC), judgment of 6 October 2005, Hirst v. UK (No. 2) (Appl. No. 74025/01), para. 61; judgment of 24 May 2016, Paunović and Milivojević v. Serbia (Appl. No. 41683/06), para. 59.

134 ECtHR (GC), judgment 16 March 2006, Ždanoka v. Latvia (Appl. No. 58278/00), para. 115.

135 See Bellamy (2015), p. 1019 ff.

136 See now the 6th recital of the preamble of the ECHR, as amended by Protocol No. 15 (CETS No. 213).

137 ECtHR (GC), judgment of 8 July 2003, Hatton and Others v. UK (Appl. No. 36022/97), para. 97.

138 ECtHR, judgment of 25 July 2024, Ždanoka v. Latvia (No. 2) (Appl. No. 42221/18), para. 56. Murauskas (2024).

139 ECtHR, judgment of 11 June 2015, Tahirov v. Azerbaijan (Appl. No. 31953/11), para. 54.

140 See, e.g., ECtHR, judgment of 3 September 2024, Shlosberg v. Russia (Appl. No. 32648/22): Disqualification of a candidate from standing for Parliament for having exercised his right pursuant to Article 11 ECHR. For a counter-example, see ECtHR, judgment of 11 June 2024, Kokëdhima v. Albania (Appl. No. 55159/16): Removal from office as a Member of Parliament because of a conflict of interests not arbitrary or insufficiently foreseeable.

which that person seeks to become a member, and indeed of the constitutional system and democracy as a whole in the State concerned", provided that the length of the ban was proportionate.[141]

On balance, it has been argued that regarding electoral rights, the Court's "pragmatic adjudication" seems to be influenced by external considerations, sometimes paying excessive deference to political sensitivities in the Convention States.[142]

In an era of democratic backsliding, the Court's deference to national political majorities in this respect is problematic and should be reconsidered. After all, the Court has meanwhile started to take rule of law backsliding seriously[143] and should do the same with regard to democratic backsliding. It has indeed always underlined its own function as the ultimate arbiter as to whether the requirements of Art. 3 Prot. No. 1 and their democratic underpinnings have been complied with.[144] But it should start to fulfil this obligation more thoroughly. One useful instrument for the ECtHR in this context would be to adopt the non-retrogression rule developed by the Court of Justice of the EU (ECJ) for instances of rule of law backsliding (erosion of judicial independence): Member States must not adopt laws which "bring about a reduction in the protection of the value of the rule of law".[145] The same rule should apply *mutatis mutandis* in regard of the value of democracy, also within the ECHR system. However, in order to preserve the Convention States' regulatory discretion, there should be no automatism that would, *e.g.*, exclude even a moderate extension of election periods. However, any retrogression regarding democratic standards should be treated with suspicion and thus be subject to particularly strict judicial scrutiny by the ECtHR, in the sense that a particularly strong reason is required to justify such retrogression.

4.2.1.2.1.2 Supplementary Democratic Rights

There are no equivalents in the ECHR to the other democratically essential rights of citizens which are included in the UDHR and the ICCPR: the right to take part in the conduct of public affairs, directly or indirectly through freely chosen representatives, and the right to have equal access to public service.[146] The pertinent global guarantees enshrined in Art. 25 ICCPR therefore remain important also in Europe,

---

[141] ECtHR (GC), advisory opinion of 8 April 2022 (Request No. P16-2020-002).

[142] Kurnosov (2021, Chap. 1).

[143] See, e.g., ECtHR (GC), judgment of 23 June 2016, Baka v. Hungary (Appl. No. 20261/12); judgment of 7 May 2021, Xero Flor w Polsce sp. z o.o. v. Poland (Appl. No. 4907/18); Judgment of 3 February 2022, Advance Pharma sp. z o.o v. Poland (Appl. Bo. 1469/20); GC judgment of 15 March 2022, Grzęda v. Poland (Appl. No. 43572/18); judgment of 6 July 2023, Tuleya v. Poland (Appl. Nos. 21181/19 and 51751/20). See also Bošnjak (2025), p. 8 ff.

[144] ECtHR (GC), judgment of 6 October 2005, Hirst v. UK (No. 2) (Appl. No. 74025/01), para. 62.

[145] ECJ, judgment of 20 April 2021 (C-896/19), ECLI:EU:C:2021:311, para. 63 f.; judgment of 15 July 2021 (C-791/19), ECLI:EU:C:2021:596, para. 51.

[146] See Article 21 UDHR, Article 25 lit. a, c ICCPR.

where they may for instance serve as an interpretative background for adapting national or regional fundamental rights guarantees.

Supplementary democratic guarantees, irrespective of citizenship, are enshrined in Art. 10 ECHR (right to freedom of opinion and expression, of information and the media, regardless of frontiers);[147] Art. 11 ECHR (right to freedom of peaceful assembly and association);[148] Art. 13 ECHR (right to an effective remedy before a national authority for violations of rights). Art 6 (1) ECHR even sets forth an entitlement to a fair and public hearing within a reasonable time by an independent and impartial tribunal established by law, if civil rights and obligations are at stake. While the ECtHR has interpreted these terms broadly, they do not include political rights in connection with electoral disputes or disputes regarding political parties.[149] In these cases, only Art. 13 ECHR applies which is less strict regarding remedies.

The ECHR does not guarantee any right to nationality as such, but Art. 8 ECHR (private life), as interpreted by the European Court of Human Rights, protects against arbitrary expatriation[150] which would automatically cancel all political rights linked to citizenship. While the right to education is guaranteed in Art. 2 Prot. No. 1, it does not include specific requirements regarding the promotion of democratic values through education. The ECtHR has, however, emphasised the fundamental role that the right to education played in a democratic society, which was indispensable to the furtherance of human rights, so that Art. 2 Prot. No. 1 must not be interpreted restrictively.[151] It has also underlined that safeguarding pluralism in education was essential for the preservation of the "democratic society" as conceived by the Convention.[152]

The ECtHR has emphasised the importance for democracy of the freedom of expression, guaranteed by Art. 10 ECHR. According to settled case law, "there is little scope under Article 10 § 2 of the Convention for restrictions on political speech or debate. … [I]n a democratic society based on the rule of law, political ideas

[147] The ECtHR has derived from Art. 10 ECHR a right of journalists to have access to information held by a public authority, if that contributes to transparency in public life and in particular regarding public spending (judgment of 4 April 2024, Zöldi v. Hungary [Appl. No. 49049/189, paras. 32 ff.).

[148] ECtHR, judgment of 16 January 2025, Bodson et autres c. Belgique (Requête No. 35834/22 etc.): Militant activism in the form of trade union's blockade of highway in the course of a general strike against austerity measures that lead to criminal prosecutions is not protected. See the critique by Dejean de la Bâtie (2025).

[149] ECtHR (Registry) (2024), para. 97.

[150] For the relevant case law, see ECtHR, Press Unit, Factsheet – Deprivation of Citizenship (July 2023). Available via https://www.echr.coe.int/documents/d/echr/FS_Citizenship_Deprivation_ENG (22 January 2025). See also Articles 7–9 of the European Convention on Nationality of 6 November 1997 (ETS No. 166). In reaction to the denaturalisations during the Nazi period that were based on racial and political discrimination, Article 16 (1) sentence 1 of the German Basic Law categorically prohibits deprivation of German citizenship.

[151] ECtHR (GC), judgment of 10 November 2005, Leila Şahin v. Turkey (Appl. No. 44774/98), para. 137.

[152] ECtHR, decision of 11 September 2006, Konrad v. Germany (Appl. No. 35504/03), para. 1.

which challenge the existing order and whose realisation is advocated by peaceful means must be afforded a proper opportunity of expression … [I]t is the essence of democracy to allow diverse political programmes to be proposed and debated, even those that call into question the way a State is currently organised, provided that they do not harm democracy itself …"[153] On the other hand, the national constitution may impose limitations on parliamentary debates regarding the secession of provinces: "democratic legitimacy and constitutional legality cannot be set against each other to the detriment of the latter".[154]

Art. 10 ECHR "constitutes one of the essential foundations of a democratic society and one of the basic conditions for its progress", culminating in the freedom of the news media and in particular the audio-visual media which form the most sensitive sector under present-day conditions.[155] Regarding the latter, Art. 10 ECHR does not only impose a "negative duty of non-interference" on Convention States, but also "a positive obligation to put in place an appropriate legislative and administrative framework to guarantee effective pluralism". Convention States must prevent a public broadcaster, but also powerful economic or political groups in society "to obtain a position of dominance over the audio-visual media and thereby exercise pressure on broadcasters and eventually curtail their editorial freedom". Otherwise, the fundamental role of freedom of expression in a democratic society is undermined and the public's entitlement to receive information and ideas of general interest curtailed.[156] This case-law constitutes the basis of the protection as well as regulation of the media also within the EU.[157]

The ECtHR has also repeatedly emphasised the primordial role of political parties in democratic systems and drawn the following pro-democratic conclusions in its case law:[158] Firstly, a political party is protected by Art. 11 ECHR even if it promotes "a change in the law or the legal and constitutional structures of the State on two conditions: firstly, the means used to that end must be legal and democratic; secondly, the change proposed must itself be compatible with fundamental democratic principles. It necessarily follows that a political party whose leaders incite to violence or put forward a policy which fails to respect democracy or which is aimed at the destruction of democracy and the flouting of the rights and freedoms recognised in a democracy cannot lay claim to the Convention's protection against

[153] ECtHR, decision of 11 February 2025, Costa i Rosselló v. Spain etc. (Appl. No. 29780/20 etc.), paras. 134 f.

[154] Id., paras. 139 f.

[155] ECtHR (GC), judgment of 7 June 2012, Centro Europa 7 S.R.L. and Di Stefano v. Italy (Appl. No. 38433/09), para. 131.

[156] Id., para. 133 f.

[157] Recital 15 in the preamble of the EU's European Media Freedom Act (see below Sect. 5.7.1) expressly invokes this case of the ECtHR. See also Art. 52 (3) CFR.

[158] See the overview in ECtHR (Press Unit), Factsheet "Political parties and associations" (May 2022). Available via https://www.echr.coe.int/documents/d/echr/FS_Political_parties_ENG (22 January 2025).

penalties imposed on those grounds …".[159] Secondly, the Court always strictly scrutinises limitations imposed on political parties, allowing Convention States just a limited margin of appreciation, and in particular in respect of prohibitions or dissolutions of parties that may be used only in the most serious cases.[160] The German FCC took these requirements thoroughly into account when deciding on, and ultimately dismissing, an application to prohibit a political party in Germany pursuant to Art. 21 (2) Basic Law.[161]

Civic equality is guaranteed by the accessory prohibition of discrimination in Art. 14 ECHR that prohibits discrimination regarding the exercise of any of the aforementioned democratic rights enshrined in the ECHR. The independent general prohibition of discrimination in Art. 1 of Protocol No. 12 (P-12)[162] binds only 20 CoE Member States. The ECtHR applied it to the elections to the Presidency of Bosnia and Herzegovina, irrespective of whether these elections fell within the scope of Art. 3 Prot. No. 1, and determined that the applicants' ineligibility to stand as candidates violated Art. 1 P-12.[163]

Convention rights that are not specifically democracy-related can also play an important role in the maintenance of democracy. Thus, the right to liberty and security of person enshrined in Art. 5 ECHR also protects opposition parliamentarians and government critics from being deprived of their liberty to silence them, in conjunction with Art. 18 ECHR, where applicable.[164] In one case, the ECtHR applied Art. 18 ECHR in conjunction with Art. 5 ECHR after finding "that it has been established beyond reasonable doubt that the applicant's detention, especially during two crucial campaigns relating to the referendum and the presidential election, pursued the ulterior purpose of stifling pluralism and limiting freedom of political debate, which is at the very core of the concept of a democratic society."[165]

Art. 10 ECHR provides an elevated level of protection for the freedom of expression of members of national and regional parliaments. Speech in Parliament is "political speech par excellence", since "Parliament is a unique forum for debate in

---

[159] ECtHR, judgment of 9 April 2002, Yazar and Others v. Turkey (Appl. No. 22723/93 etc.), para. 49.

[160] ECtHR (GC), judgment of 13 February 2003, Refah Partisi (The Welfare Party) and Others v. Turkey (Appl. No. 41340/98 etc.), para. 100.

[161] FCC, judgment of 17 January 2017 (2 BvB 1/13), paras. 607 ff. English translation available via https://www.bundesverfassungsgericht.de/SharedDocs/Entscheidungen/EN/2017/01/bs20170117_2bvb000113en.html (22 January 2025).

[162] Of 4 November 2000 (ETS No. 177).

[163] ECtHR (GC), judgment of 22 December 2009, Sejdić and Finci v. Bosnia and Herzegovina (Appl. Nos. 27996/06 and 34836/06), paras. 52 ff.; Chamber judgment of 29 August 2023, Kovačević v. Bosnia and Herzegovina, Appl. No. 43651/22), paras. 69 ff. (referred to the Grand Chamber which upheld the Government's objection to the admissibility of the application—see Press Release ECHR 157 (2025) of 25 June 2025).

[164] See, *e.g.*, ECtHR, judgment of 10 December 2019 and GC judgment of 11 July 2022 in proceedings under Article 46 (4) ECHR in the case Kavala v. Turkey (Appl. No. 28749/18).

[165] ECtHR (GC), judgment of 22 December 2020, Selahattin Demirtaş v. Turkey (No. 2) (Appl. No. 14305/17), para. 437; confirmed in judgment of 8 July 2025, Selahattin Demirtaş v. Turkey (No.4) (Appl. No. 13609/20), paras. 307 ff.

a democratic society, which is of fundamental importance."[166] However, although "the freedom of parliamentary debate is of fundamental importance in a democratic society, it is not absolute in nature."[167] Interpreting Art. 10 ECHR in the light of Art. 3 Prot. No. 1, the ECtHR also determined that Convention States' margin of appreciation regarding the necessity of restricting the freedom of speech was particularly narrow in the context of election campaigns, because there, freedom of expression was an essential condition of ensuring "the free expression of the opinion of the people in the choice of the legislature".[168] It had thus been incompatible with Art. 10 ECHR to impose an administrative fine on the leader of a political party, which was traditionally supported by voters belonging to the Turkish minority in Bulgaria, for using the Turkish language in a campaign speech. In this context, the ECtHR considered it appropriate to underline "l'importance du pluralisme, de la tolérance et de la protection des minorités dans une société démocratique, et d'affirmer que le respect des minorités, loin d'affaiblir les démocraties, ne peut que les renforcer."[169]

The importance of Art. 10 ECHR for national democracy can be illustrated by a recent case of the ECtHR concerning Hungary, a country which the Orbán government has turned into the leading example of democratic backsliding in Europe.[170] The applicants are Members of the Hungarian Parliament belonging to an opposition parliamentary group. They unsuccessfully requested permission from the Speaker to use posters during a parliamentary session in order to demonstrate the extent of deforestation. When they used the posters anyway, they were fined by the Speaker who belonged to the governing majority. They claimed a violation of their rights under Art. 10 ECHR, emphasising the importance of the posters in Parliament for attracting media attention, since they otherwise had limited access to the media that were mostly controlled by the government. The Chamber unanimously dismissed their application. It emphasised the national parliaments' autonomy to regulate their procedure, including the use of expressive means, and granted them a wide margin of appreciation in this respect. Unfortunately, the Chamber disregarded the weakened state of democracy in Hungary which the political majority there has been eager to transform into an "illiberal democracy".[171] The hope that the Grand Chamber would intervene in the case and take democratic backsliding in Hungary more seriously was dashed when the panel rejected the referral request (Art. 43 ECHR).[172]

---

[166] ECtHR (GC), judgment of 17 May 2016, Karácsony and Others v. Hungary (Appl. Nos. 42461/13 and 44357/13), paras. 137 f.

[167] Id., para. 139.

[168] ECtHR, judgment of 2 May 2023, Mestan v. Bulgaria (Appl. No. 24108/15), para. 54.

[169] Id., para. 62.

[170] ECtHR, judgment of 5 October 2023, Ikotity and Others v. Hungary (Appl. No. 50012/17).

[171] See Nugraha (2023). On the features of an "illiberal democracy", see Nußberger and Miklasová (2023), p. 272 f.

[172] Press release ECHR 040 (2024) of 20 February 2024. See Karsai and Kazai (2024). See also ECtHR, judgment of 11 February 2025, Novaya Gazeta and Others v. Russia (Appl. Nos. 11884/22 etc.)—concurring opinion of Judge Pavli on the necessity to take "the general democratic credentials of a particular political system, at a particular moment in time" into account when assessing individual cases.

4.2.1.2.1.3 Democratic Society Counterbalance to Human Rights Limitations Prescribed by Law

In parallel with the UDHR and the ICCPR, democracy is referred to several times in the ECHR connection with limitations on human rights.[173] There it also serves as a counterbalance in the sense that such limitations must always be necessary to protect certain public interests "in a democratic society" whose acknowledged hallmarks in the Convention system are pluralism, tolerance and broadmindedness.[174] Moreover, as a general rule, limitations of rights enshrined in the ECHR and Protocols must be in accordance with or prescribed by "law".[175]

According to the settled case law of the ECtHR, limitation rules qualify as "law" in that sense only if they meet the following two standards: Firstly, the legal rule (which can be a statutory or common law rule) must be adequately accessible in the sense that citizens have an indication which legal rules apply in their cases. Secondly, these rules must be "formulated with sufficient precision to enable the citizen to regulate his conduct: he must be able – if need be with appropriate advice – to foresee, to a degree that is reasonable in the circumstances, the consequences which a given action may entail."[176] These two standards derive from the rule of law principle and are intended to prevent arbitrariness regarding human rights limitations.

Contrary to the Inter-American Court of Human Rights,[177] the ECtHR has not yet been confronted with the question whether the term "law" also implies fulfilment of democratic minimum standards. In that case, limitations could not be justified if they were based on statutes enacted by a legislature not established by democratic elections in accordance with Art. 3 Prot. No. 1 (such as a military junta). It seems safe to assume that the ECtHR would not qualify such undemocratic rules as "law", not least because of the "democratic society" counterbalance that is directly linked to the "law" and must therefore inform the interpretation of this term. In this context, it is interesting to note that the ECtHR has accepted rules of EU law as "law" for purposes of Convention rights limitations without questioning their democratic credentials.[178] This confirms that the Court considers secondary EU law as sufficiently democratic, despite the allegation of a democratic deficit in the EU.

If the ECtHR finds that the limitation of a Convention right in the concrete case is prescribed by law in the aforementioned sense, it further examines its necessity in

---

[173] Articles 6 (1), 8 (2), 9 (2), 10 (2) and 11 (2) ECHR.

[174] ECtHR, judgment of 7 December 1976, Handyside v. UK (Appl. No. 5493/72), para. 49; (GC) judgment of 6 October 2005, Hirst v. UK (No. 2) (Appl. No. 74025/01), para. 70. For a survey of the case law, see Logemann (2004), p. 207 ff.

[175] Articles 5 (1), 7, 8 (2), 9 (2), 10 (2), 11 (2) ECHR. Article 1 Prot. No. 1; Articles 2 (3), (4) Prot. No. 4; Article 1, 2 Prot. No. 7.

[176] ECtHR, judgment of 26 April 1979, Sunday Times v. UK (Appl. No.6538/74), para. 49. See also the (GC) judgment of 16 June 2015, Delfi AS v. Estonia (Appl. No. 64569/09), paras. 120 ff.

[177] See below Sect. 4.2.2.1.3.

[178] ECtHR (GC), judgment of 30 June 2005, Bosphorus v. Ireland (No. 45036/98), paras. 143 ff. In the concrete case, the legal basis for the interference in the right to property was a Council sanctions regulation enacted unanimously without the participation of the European Parliament.

a democratic society. In this context, it has in recent years increasingly emphasised "the fundamentally subsidiary role of the Convention. The national authorities have direct democratic legitimation and are, as the Court has held on many occasions, in principle better placed than an international court to evaluate local needs and conditions".[179] On this basis, it has granted the Convention States a "margin of appreciation" whose breadth, however, depends on the circumstances, including "the quality of the parliamentary and judicial review of the necessity of a particular measure" on the national level.[180] The ECtHR therefore explicitly makes the granting of the margin of appreciation conditional on the legislature's democratic legitimacy.

In another parallel with the global level, Art. 17 ECHR prohibits States, groups and individuals from abusing any position under the Convention for the purpose of destroying any right and freedom set forth in it, thereby indirectly protecting democratic governmental systems against societal efforts to undermine them.[181] Art. 18 ECHR also prohibits the abuse of powers to restrict Convention rights for ulterior purposes, trying to prevent anti-democratic coups by the government.[182] Finally, Art. 15 ECHR restricts governmental powers even in states of emergency, in order to prevent a slide into autocracy under a pretext. Derogations permitted under Art. 15 ECHR must also always remain within the boundaries of that Convention State's other obligations under international law, including those regarding democracy. According to the ECtHR, "the existence of a 'public emergency threatening the life of the nation' must not serve as a pretext for limiting freedom of political debate, which is at the very core of the concept of a democratic society. … even in a state of emergency … the Contracting States must bear in mind that any measures taken should seek to protect the democratic order from the threats to it, and every effort must be made to safeguard the values of a democratic society, such as pluralism, tolerance and broadmindedness."[183]

Art. 16 ECHR that seems to give Convention States *carte blanche* to restrict political activities of aliens is a peculiar provision that expresses the *zeitgeist* of the 1950s and has no parallel on the global level. The ECtHR has interpreted it narrowly in the sense that it is "only capable of authorising restrictions on 'activities' that

---

[179] ECtHR (GC), judgment of 6 October 2005, Maurice v. France (Appl. No. 11810/03), para. 117. The principle of subsidiarity, according to which the Convention States have the primary responsibility for securing the Convention rights, has been inserted into the preamble of the ECHR by Protocol No. 15 (CETS No. 213).

[180] ECtHR (GC), judgment of 9 March 2023, L.B. v. Hungary (Appl. No. 36345/16), para. 125.

[181] See in this sense ECtHR, decision of 11 December 2006, Kalifatstaat c. Allemagne (Appl. No. 13828/04): "… compte tenu du lien très clair entre la Convention et la démocratie, nul ne doit être autorisé à se prévaloir des dispositions de la Convention pour affaiblir ou détruire les idéaux et valeurs d'une société démocratique".

[182] See ECtHR (GC), judgment of 25 June 2024, Ukraine v. Russia (*Re* Crimea) (Appl. Nos. 20958/14 and 38334/18), paras. 1334 ff.

[183] See ECtHR, judgment of 20 March 2018, Mehmet Hasan Altan v. Turkey (Appl. No. 13237/17), para. 210.

directly affect the political process."[184] This limits the effects of Art. 16 ECHR to those of the citizenship requirement of Art. 25 ICCPR. The general democratic participation rights, such as the ones enshrined in Art. 10, 11 ECHR, therefore also apply in favour of aliens. Since aliens are subject to the territorial jurisdiction of the country of residence or stay no less than citizens, the narrow interpretation of Art. 16 ECHR is appropriate from a democratic point of view.[185]

4.2.1.2.1.4 General Right to Democracy as Synthesis of Special Democratic Rights

Importance of General Right to National Democracy

The conclusion that can be drawn corresponds to and reinforces the one at the global level: From a synthesis of the cited specific ECHR provisions, a rather clearly contoured general Convention right to the essential ingredients of democratic national governments—a general right to democracy in Convention States—emerges that is implicitly guaranteed in the ECHR. In the CoE, as an organisation of genuine democracies, this general right has an even firmer basis. It still leaves States sufficient margins in designing their governmental systems, in accordance with the right of self-determination of their peoples. But the general Convention right to national democracy sets minimum standards that must not be disregarded and imposes the obligation on States to justify each limitation, also in the light of the basic requirements of a "democratic society" that is prescribed as the general limitation benchmark in the ECHR.

This general right to democracy promotes the pro-democratic interpretation in particular of the specific democratic Convention rights, increases the demands on justification of their limitations and can perhaps even generate further supplementary unwritten democratic rights, in order to close gaps in the ECHR. Remaining gaps will be filled by the supplementary guarantees in Art. 25 ICCPR that can also be used as orientation for the extensive interpretation of existing and the progressive development of further democratic Convention rights. Since all Convention States are also parties to the ICCPR, Art. 25 ICCPR constitutes the interpretative background of the ECHR in the sense of Art. 31 (3) lit. c of the Vienna Convention on the Law of Treaties (VCLT),[186] which codifies a rule of interpretation of customary international law. Like on the global level, a further added value of a general right to democracy in the ECHR in an era of democratic backsliding consists in broadening the horizon towards systemic threats that are included in individual interferences with specific democratic rights, making them more serious and facilitating the determination of a violation, where applicable, in conjunction with Art. 17 or Art. 18 ECHR.

Unfortunately, the ECtHR has not yet recognised such a general Convention right to national democracy. While it has indicated that violations of the passive right to vote of individual applicants guaranteed in Art. 3 Prot. No. 1 also "infringed

[184] ECtHR (GC), judgment of 15 October 2015 (No. 27510/08), Perinçek v. Switzerland, para. 122.

[185] On the even more limited role of Article 16 ECHR within the EU, see below Sect. 5.4.3.4.

[186] Of 23 May 1969 (UNTS vol. 1155, p. 331).

the sovereign power of the electorate" as a whole,[187] it has never derived a collective right of the electorate to democracy (which would correspond to the right of internal self-determination).[188] The Court should do so in these times of democratic backsliding. For after all, it has always emphasised that "the Convention is a living instrument which must be interpreted in the light of present-day conditions and of the ideas prevailing in democratic States today", that it "must have regard to the changing conditions in Contracting States", that it must take into account developments in international law beyond the ECHR[189] and that "[t]he Convention is intended to guarantee not rights that are theoretical or illusory but rights that are practical and effective".[190] If "present-day conditions" only in individual Convention States show threats to the democratic system, the ECtHR could and should counteract by making use of the potential lying dormant in the democratic rights enshrined in the ECHR and Prot. No. 1. If, however, democratic backsliding proliferates, the question arises whether this would lead to a general lowering of Convention standards or whether the ECtHR should instead adopt a general non-retrogression rule preserving standards of democracy previously established.[191] In this context, it is important to remember that the ECtHR has understood the "living instrument" concept as only supporting an upward trajectory of human rights standards which corresponds to a non-retrogression rule: "The Court reiterates that the Convention is a living instrument which must be interpreted in the light of present-day conditions and that the increasingly high standard being required in the area of the protection of human rights and fundamental liberties correspondingly and inevitably requires greater firmness in assessing breaches of the fundamental values of democratic societies ..."[192]

4.2.1.2.1.4.1 The ECtHR's Georgescu Case as Recent Example

The recent high-profile Georgescu case demonstrates how important it would be to develop a general right to national democracy as a synthesis of the various democratic rights guaranteed by the ECHR and Prot. No. 1:[193] The Romanian Constitutional Court had of its own motion annulled the first round of the 2024 presidential elections in Romania because of alleged interference in the electoral process by Russia using AI mechanisms. The candidate Georgescu, who had quite unexpectedly taken

[187] ECtHR, judgment of 11 June 2002, Sadak and Others v. Turkey (No. 2) (Appl. No. 25144/94 etc.), para. 40.

[188] See Richter, in: Dörr et al. (2022), Kapitel 25 para. 66.

[189] ECtHR (GC), judgment of 7 July 2011, Bayatyan v. Armenia (Appl. No. 23459/03), para. 102.

[190] See, *e.g.*, ECtHR, judgment of 9 October 1979, Airey v. Ireland (Appl. No. 6289/73), para. 24; GC judgment of 29 March 2006, Scordino v. Italy (No. 1) (Appl. No. 36813/97), para. 192; GC judgment of 25 June 2024, Ukraine v. Russia (*Re* Crimea) (Appl. Nos. 20958/14 and 38334/18), para. 1336.

[191] See above Sect. 4.2.1.2.1.1 (at the end).

[192] ECtHR (GC), judgment of 12 May 2005, Öcalan v. Turkey (Appl. No. 46221/99), para. 163.

[193] ECtHR, decision of 6 March 2025, Georgescu v. Romania (Appl. No. 37327/24).

the top spot after the first round of voting, lodged a complaint with the ECtHR, claiming violation of his rights under Art 6, 10, 11 and 13 ECHR and Art. 3 Prot. No. 1. He complained that his right to free elections under Art. 3 Prot. No. 1 had been interfered with on the basis of unsubstantiated allegations of external interference in the electoral process, that the Constitutional Court decision was the result of political interference by the ruling party in charge of the electoral process and that it undermined the freedom to participate in the democratic process. A three-judge Committee of the Court unanimously declared the application inadmissible. Regarding the complaint under Art. 3 Prot. No. 1, the Court reiterated that the provision was limited to "the choice of legislature" of which the Romanian President was not part. Regarding the complaints under Art. 6, 13 ECHR, the applicant's right to stand as a candidate in presidential elections was a political and not a civil right in the sense of Art. 6 (1) ECHR and he did not have an arguable claim under Art. 13 ECHR either. Regarding Art. 10, 11 ECHR, the Court found the claims to be unsubstantiated because the applicant had not raised any factual and legal arguments to support them.

Perhaps Georgescu's application to the ECtHR was poorly drafted. But the result is that the quite extraordinary judicial intervention in the Romanian presidential elections remains unreviewed by the ECtHR. If the applicant took the top spot after the first round of voting because of illicit external interference in the elections, the Constitutional Court intervention actually protected national democracy which proved to be a militant democracy. However, if there was no such interference or if it had no demonstrable impact on the result, the intervention massively distorted national democracy.[194] Either way, the case demonstrates that national democracy is inadequately protected by the ECHR and Prot. No. 1, as interpreted by the ECtHR. It is unacceptable that such a politically sensitive case going to the heart of Romanian national democracy has not been thoroughly reviewed at the European level.[195] According to media reports, the Romanian Central Electoral Bureau has meanwhile barred Georgescu from competing in the May 2025 rerun of the presidential elections and the Constitutional Court has upheld this decision.[196] Whether his exclusion is based on legitimate reasons in conformity with democracy should not remain without European judicial scrutiny.

This is why the recognition of a synthetical right to national democracy that could be used for thorough review in such a case would be so important. It would close the existing gap and bring the Convention standards in accordance with Art. 25 lit. b ICCPR. Since Romania is party to the ICCPR and the OP-ICCPR, Georgescu

---

[194] See Iancu (2025). See also Zysset A (2025) An Anxious-Avoidant Court: Adjudicating Democratic Infrastructure in Călin Georgescu v. Romania. Available via Strasbourg Observers. https://strasbourgobservers.com/2025/05/27/an-anxious-avoidant-court-adjudicating--democratic-infrastructure-in-calin-georgescu-v-romania/. Accessed 26 August 2025.

[195] On Georgescu's futile attempt to obtain judicial protection from the EU's GC, see below Sect. 5.4.2.2.

[196] https://www.politico.eu/article/romania-top-court-rejects-calin-georgescu-appeal/ (13 March 2025).

could consider lodging a communication against Romania alleging violation of his right under Art. 25 lit. b ICCPR. Pursuant to Art. 5 (2) lit. a OP-ICCPR, the Committee is not prevented from considering a communication whose subject matter has already been examined by the ECtHR. But Romania has entered a reservation against Art. 5 (2) lit. a OP-ICCPR to the effect that the Human Rights Committee "shall not have competence to consider communications from an individual if the matter … has already been examined under another procedure of international investigation or settlement."[197] Such reservations are routinely made by CoE Member States to prevent the Committee from reviewing the judgments of the ECtHR, and the Committee accepts them, provided that the ECtHR, in issuing an inadmissibility decision, sufficiently examined the merits of the case.[198] This arguably happened in the Georgescu case, so that the Human Rights Committee would not consider his communication because of the Romanian reservation.

But it would be embarassing for the European system of democracy protection, if in a comparable case, a European appealed to the Human Rights Committee, for lack of effective remedies in Europe, and obtained the Committee‘s determination that his rights under Art. 25 lit. b ICCPR had been violated. It is therefore essential that the ECtHR raises the Convention standards to the level of the ICCPR by recognising a right to national democracy.

4.2.1.2.2 Right to International Democracy

After this survey of the human rights parameters for national democracy in the ECHR and Prot. No. 1 (top-down perspective), the question arises whether the Convention system also includes the bottom-up perspective, setting minimum democratic standards for international or supranational organisations. Just as their counterparts on the global level, the democratic rights enshrined in Art. 10, 11 ECHR naturally also protect the search for information, the expression of opinions as well as peaceful assemblies and the establishment of associations that concern activities of such organisations. Moreover, in the famous *Matthews* case, the ECtHR extended the right to free elections in Art. 3 Prot. No. 1 to elections to the European Parliament (EP), keeping pace with the transfer of considerable legislative powers to the EP in the course of deepening European integration.[199]

In conclusion, from an overall view of the cited treaty provisions one can also discern a general Convention right to international democracy, but just as on the global level, its contours are much less clear than those of the Convention right to national democracy. The pertinent case law of the ECtHR is still in development.

---

[197] https://treaties.un.org/Pages/ViewDetails.aspx?src=TREATY&mtdsg_no=IV-5&chapter=4&clang=_en#EndDec (12 March 2025).

[198] Schabas (2019), Article 5 First OP, paras. 13 ff.

[199] ECtHR (GC), judgment of 18 February 1999, Matthews v. UK (Appl. No. 24833/94). See the criticism by Crawford (2000), p. 118 ff.

4.2.1.2.3 Right to Adequate Overall Standard of Democracy in Multilevel Systems

The ECtHR has also addressed threats to Convention rights emanating from international and supranational organisations and thereby indirectly taken up the interdependence problem of national and international/supranational democracies and the respective democratic rights. This became necessary because so far, no international or supranational organisation has acceded to the ECHR and thereby become directly subject to the Court's supervision. Accordingly, the acts of such organisations which interfere with Convention rights can only be challenged in Strasbourg indirectly, by lodging an application under Art. 34 ECHR against the Convention State implementing those acts, after having unsuccessfully exhausted the national remedies, or against all the Convention States which are members of the organisation, depending on the circumstances of the case.[200]

In the case Waite and Kennedy v. Germany,[201] the ECtHR determined that Convention States are free to establish international and supranational organisations "in order to pursue or strengthen their cooperation in certain fields of activities" and to "attribute these organisations certain competences and accord them immunities" for ensuring their proper functioning. But the possible human rights implications had to be kept under control, all the more since the organisations were not themselves parties to the ECHR: "It would be incompatible with the purpose and object of the Convention, … if the Contracting States were … absolved from their responsibility under the Convention in relation to the field of activity covered by such attribution. It should be recalled that the Convention is intended to guarantee not theoretical or illusory rights, but rights that are practical and effective."[202]

The ECtHR therefore held that in view of the right of access to a court guaranteed in Art. 6 (1) ECHR, a Convention State may grant an international organisation (in this case the European Space Agency) immunity from the jurisdiction of its courts only if the statute of that organisation offered plaintiffs "reasonable alternative means to protect effectively their rights under the Convention".[203] Convention States are, in other words, required by Art. 6 (1) ECHR to ensure that such alternative means are available when they conclude the treaty founding the organisation and grant it immunity.[204] This obligation to establish compensatory mechanisms for upholding the Convention standards also applies in substance with respect to the democratic rights enshrined in the ECHR. The Matthews case, where the ECtHR extended Art. 3 Prot. No. 1 to cover elections to the European Parliament, is one example. The Matthews judgment covers all cases in which the obligation for

---

[200] See Lawson and Shrugged (2024), p. 647 ff.

[201] ECtHR (GC), judgment of 18 February 1999, Waite and Kennedy v. Germany (Appl. No. 26083/94).

[202] Id., paras. 63, 67.

[203] Id., paras. 68 ff.

[204] The Austrian Constitutional Court in 2022 decided that Austria had failed the Waite and Kennedy standard when granting immunity to the Organization of Petrol Exporting Countries (OPEC) headquartered in Vienna (see Janig 2024, p. 331 ff.).

Convention States arises directly under the treaty establishing the international or supranational organisation. The content of this obligation is subject to the consent of every single Member State, so that each of them can be held individually responsible for provisions included in or missing from that treaty, in violation of the ECHR. This obligation to establish compensatory mechanisms for upholding the Convention standards also applies in substance with respect to the democratic rights enshrined in the ECHR.

With regard to the supranational European Union, the ECtHR has further developed and generalised the Waite and Kennedy approach in the Bosphorus case, although not specifically regarding democratic rights, but the right to property (Art. 1 of Prot. No. 1). The Bosphorus judgment covers cases in which the obligation for Convention States arises from secondary acts adopted by the organs of the international or supranational organisation. In Bosphorus, the Court struck a compromise between the interest in effective human rights protection and the interest in promoting European integration, of which the ECHR in fact is part and parcel. Convention States taking action in compliance with their commitments from other treaties establishing international or supranational organisations to abide by such secondary acts may interfere with Convention rights "as long as the relevant organisation is considered to protect fundamental rights, as regards both the substantive guarantees offered and the mechanisms controlling their observance, in a manner which can be considered at least equivalent to that for which the Convention provides. … If such equivalent protection is considered to be provided by the organisation, the presumption will be that a State has not departed from the requirements of the Convention when it does no more than implement legal obligations flowing from its membership of the organisation. However, any such presumption can be rebutted if, in the circumstances of a particular case, it is considered that the protection of Convention rights was manifestly deficient."[205] In case of rebuttal, the ECtHR will review Convention State action under ordinary Convention standards and in so doing disregard that State's other treaty commitments. The same applies if either no equivalent protection is provided in the first place[206] or if the State acts outside its strict international legal obligations arising from the membership in the organisation.[207] The Bosphorus approach also applies with regard to democratic Convention rights, but there have been no pertinent cases yet.

[205] ECtHR (GC), judgment of 30 June 2005, Bosphorus v. Ireland (Appl. No. 45036/98), paras. 155 f. See also judgment of 6 December 2012, Michaud v. France (Appl. No. 12323/11); GC judgment of 23 May 2016, Avotiņš v. Latvia (Appl. No. 17502/07); judgment of 25 March 2021, Bivolaru and Moldovan v. France (Appl. Nos. 40324/16 and 12623/17). For an overview, see Lenaerts et al. (2021), para. 25.014.

[206] This is, e.g., the case if the national courts fail to make a reference to the ECJ pursuant to Art. 267 (3) TFEU which would have been necessary to deploy the full potential of the EU's machinery for supervising fundamental rights (ECtHR, judgment of 6 December 2012, Michaud v. France [Appl. No. 12323/11], paras. 114 ff.).

[207] Bosphorus Case, para. 157. See Rizcallah (2023), p. 1062 ff.

In the latest case in point, Al-Dulimi, the ECtHR emphasized that the Convention States were required to ensure judicial review even of UN Security Council decisions imposing sanctions that they enforce (and that are practically not subject to judicial review at UN level) to the extent necessary for avoiding arbitrariness: "… [T]he Convention being a constitutional instrument of European public order …, the States Parties are required … to ensure a level of scrutiny of Convention compliance which, at the very least, preserves the foundations of that public order. One of the fundamental components of European public order is the principle of the rule of law, and arbitrariness constitutes the negation of that principle."[208] While interferences with democratic Convention rights by the UN Security Council will not occur often, they are not inconceivable, for instance in the context of post-conflict peacebuilding which may require restrictions on voting rights and the media. Art. 103 UN Charter which seems to give the UN Charter obligations precedence over Convention obligations, was brushed aside by the ECtHR in Al Dulimi with the remark that the UN Security Council had not explicitly prohibited judicial review of its decisions by regional courts.[209]

All in all, the case law of the ECtHR indicates that the Convention contains a right to an adequate overall standard of human rights, including democratic human rights, in multilevel systems of government. But that right is still developing and therefore not yet entirely clear. There is no Strasbourg case law yet requiring Convention States to ensure both the democratic legitimacy of governmental authority exercised by their international or supranational organisations and the protection of their domestic democracy against detrimental effects that their membership may have for instance on the national separation of powers.

The constitutional situation in Germany may provide an example in both regards: Art. 23 (1) of the Basic Law (BL) provides that "[w]ith a view to establishing a united Europe, the Federal Republic of Germany shall participate in the development of the European Union that is committed to democratic … principles … The establishment of the European Union, as well as changes in its treaty foundations … shall be subject to paragraphs (2) and (3) of Article 79."[210] Sentence 1 of this paragraph requires Germany to ensure democracy at EU level, while the last sentence refers to Art. 79 (3) BL. Read together with Art. 20 (2) BL, that provision requires adequate safeguards for the German democratic system *vis-à-vis* detrimental effects of European integration.[211] It remains to be seen if the ECtHR interprets the Convention standards accordingly, if pertinent cases come up.

---

[208] ECtHR (GC), judgment of 21 June 2016, Al-Dulimi and Montana Management Inc. v. Switzerland (Appl. No. 5809/08), para. 146.

[209] Id., paras. 135 ff.

[210] English translation available via https://www.gesetze-im-internet.de/englisch_gg/englisch_gg.html (22 January 2025).

[211] See, e.g., Federal Constitutional Court, judgment of 30 June 2009 (2 BvE 2/08 etc.). Available via https://www.bundesverfassungsgericht.de/SharedDocs/Entscheidungen/EN/2009/06/es20090630_2bve000208en.html (22 January 2025) (English translation). On the fundamental "right to democracy" in German constitutional law, as developed by the FCC, see below Sect. 5.5.2.

When the EU finally fulfils its obligation under Art. 6 (2) TEU to accede to the ECHR,[212] it will become directly subject to the supervision of the ECtHR, also with regard to violations of democratic rights.[213] Victims of interferences of Convention rights attributable to the EU will then be able to lodge a complaint directly against the EU, and the Matthews and Bosphorus judgments will become obsolete.

4.2.1.2.4 Enforcement Procedures

The democratic human rights of the ECHR and Prot. No. 1 are primarily enforceable in the national courts of the Convention States, in accordance with the principle of subsidiarity that has been added to the preamble of the ECHR by Art. 1 of Protocol No. 15.[214] After the exhaustion of (effective) domestic remedies,[215] the ECtHR can be involved. The Court has compulsory jurisdiction over individual applications by victims (Art. 34 ECHR) as well as inter-State applications by other Convention States (Art. 33 ECHR). There is no need first to exhaust domestic remedies in an inter-State case, if an administrative practice of the respondent State is challenged, *i.e.*, a repetition of acts incompatible with the Convention that are officially tolerated by that State.[216] This means that an antidemocratic restructuring in a Convention State can immediately be brought before the ECtHR by other Convention States. In practice, however, inter-State cases are infrequent, and if they are initiated at all, this is mostly done for egoistic purposes (the realisation of the applicant State's national interests, such as the protection of its citizens), and not for altruistic purposes (the enforcement of the common values of the CoE, such as democracy, in other States).

Pursuant to Art. 46 ECHR, the final judgments of the ECtHR have binding force. Their execution is supervised by the Committee of Ministers of the CoE that can call upon the ECtHR to determine whether a Convention State has violated its obligation to abide by a judgment. If the Court finds a violation of Art. 46 (1) ECHR, it is up to the Committee of Ministers to decide on measures to be taken (Art. 46 (5) ECHR). The nuclear option would be for the Committee to exclude that State from the CoE, according to Art. 8 CoE Statute: The persistent refusal to abide by a judgment of the ECtHR can be characterised as a serious violation of Art. 3 CoE Statute, *i.e.*, the obligation to observe the rule of law principle and respect human rights. But this has not yet happened.

---

[212] See the revised draft accession instruments of 2023 (that provide for the EU's accession to the ECHR as well as Prot. No. 1 and No. 6) in the appendix to CoE – Steering Committee for Human Rights, Interim to the Committee of Ministers, CDDH(2023)R_EXTRA ADDENDUM, 4 April 2023. Available via https://rm.coe.int/steering-committee-for-human-rights-cddh-interim-report-to-the-committ/1680aace4e (22 January 2025).

[213] On the current state of play in this respect, see Øby Johansen et al. (2024), p. 641 ff.

[214] Of 24 June 2013 (CETS No. 213).

[215] Article 35 (1) ECHR.

[216] ECtHR (GC), decision of 16 December 2020, Ukraine v. Russia (re Crimea), Appl. No. 20958/14, 38334/18, paras. 363 ff.

4.2.1.2.5 Conclusion: Incomplete Protection of Democratic Rights by the ECHR

The CoE is the most closely knit regional community of democratic States and its most significant achievement, the ECHR and Protocols, provide the most advanced system of human rights protection in the world under the reasonably effective supervision of the ECtHR. Yet, the specific democratic rights expressly contained in the ECHR and Prot. No. 1 are incomplete, if compared with Art. 25 ICCPR, while the supplementary democratic rights are largely congruent. The ECtHR has not yet recognised a general Convention right to national democracy which would help filling the gaps. On the contrary, the Court still leaves too much regulatory margin to Convention States regarding limitations of democratic rights. In an era of democratic backsliding, its excessive deference to national prerogatives is detrimental and should be reconsidered. Since the Court has started to take rule of law backsliding seriously, there is hope that in the future it will do the same with regard to democratic backsliding. For, even in the CoE, respect for democratic essentials can no longer be taken for granted.

While so far, instances of democratic backsliding have not yet caused any major set-back regarding democratic rights in Europe, the phenomenon should be taken more seriously. An important first step would be the recognition of a general right to democracy implicit in the ECHR. The CoE and the ECtHR have been steadfast supporters and defenders of the human rights that constitute the foundation of democratic government. The composition of the ECtHR has not changed in a way that could cast doubt on its role as the guardian of democratic rights.[217] But the question has rightly been posed whether the influence of NGOs on the selection process of the Strasbourg judges should be increased, using models of Africa and the Americas, in order to counter the 'democratic deconsolidation' of European States which control that process.[218]

On the positive side, the ECtHR's approaches to a right to international democracy are more advanced than on the global level, as demonstrated by the Matthews case, though not yet fully developed. The Court also seems to be sensitive to the interdependence problem, but it has not yet transferred the compensatory mechanisms from the Waite and Kennedy as well as Bosphorus cases to democratic rights, for a lack of pertinent cases.

[217] See Burgorgue-Larsen (2024), p. 215 f. See also Ailincai (2024a) The Long-Awaited Election.

[218] Id., p. 197.

4.2.1.3 The Human Dimension of the Organisation for Security and Co-operation in Europe (OSCE)

The OSCE began in 1973 during the Cold War as the cross-block Conference on Security and Co-operation in Europe (CSCE) that produced the politically binding Helsinki Final Act.[219] In this Act, the participating States—Western democracies and Eastern communist dictatorships—did not commit themselves to democratic government as such, but they embraced the promotion of fundamental rights, including political rights.[220] This was the "human dimension" of the CSCE's security concept.[221] Accordingly, Principle VII of the Declaration on Principles Guiding Relations between Participating States in the Helsinki Final Act pertained to respect for human rights and fundamental freedoms and—making reference to the Charter of the United Nations and the Universal Declaration of Human Rights—included the following paragraph: "They will promote and encourage the effective exercise of civil, political, economic, social, cultural and other rights and freedoms all of which derive from the inherent dignity of the human person and are essential for his free and full development."

After the fall of the Iron Curtain, the Heads of State or Government of the CSCE States adopted the Charter of Paris for a New Europe which heralded "a new era of democracy, peace and unity" in Europe.[222] In that political document, the chiefs undertook "to build, consolidate and strengthen democracy as the only system of government of our nations", underlining the following essentials: "Democratic government is based on the will of the people, expressed regularly through free and fair elections. Democracy has as its foundation respect for the human person and the rule of law. Democracy is the best safeguard of freedom of expression, tolerance of all groups of society, and equality of opportunity for each person. Democracy, with its representative and pluralist character, entails accountability to the electorate, the obligation of public authorities to comply with the law and justice administered impartially. No one will be above the law." They finally promised that "[o]ur States will co-operate and support each other with the aim of making democratic gains irreversible."

The Charter of Paris institutionalised the CSCE by establishing permanent institutions meeting on a regular basis such as the Council of Ministers (now Ministerial Council) and the Permanent Council that were shortly afterwards complemented by the CSCE Parliamentary Assembly consisting of delegates from the national parliaments, following the model of the CoE Parliamentary Assembly. Importantly, an Office for Free Elections was established in order to "foster the implementation of paragraphs 6, 7 and 8 of the Document of the Copenhagen Meeting of the Conference

---

[219] Of 1 August 1975. Available via https://www.osce.org/files/f/documents/5/c/39501.pdf (22 January 2025).

[220] Last recital of the preamble of the Helsinki Final Act.

[221] See Giegerich (2023), p. 580 ff.

[222] Of 21 November 1990. Available via https://www.osce.org/files/f/documents/0/6/39516.pdf (22 January 2025).

on the Human Dimension of the CSCE".[223] These paragraphs on free, fair, periodic and genuine elections and election observation were quoted in Annex 1. In 1995, the CSCE was transformed into the OSCE, without, however, changing the status of the project or the non-legal character of the 57 Participating States' commitments.[224]

In 1992, the Office for Free Election was transformed into the Office for Democratic Institutions and Human Rights (ODIHR) and its role enhanced towards overall responsibility for the implementation of the "human dimension".[225] It is based in Warsaw and mandated with assisting the OSCE Participating States to "ensure full respect for human rights and fundamental freedoms, to abide by the rule of law, to promote principles of democracy and … to build, strengthen and protect democratic institutions, as well as promote tolerance throughout society."[226] Election observation, including the observation of European Parliament elections,[227] is an important aspect of the ODIHR's work.

Because of its importance for the maintenance of democracy, the OSCE Representative on Freedom of the Media also deserves to be mentioned. The office, located in Vienna, was established by the Permanent Council Decision No. 193 of 5 November 1997[228] and constitutes "the world's only intergovernmental media watchdog".[229] Defending free media online and offline is an important prerequisite for effective democracy in the digital age.[230] At a time when media freedom is increasingly threatened also in Europe, the Office works to protect journalists, media pluralism and access to information and counteract fake news and hate speech.[231]

The CSCE and OSCE soft-law documents do not mention any general right to national or international democracy, but the Helsinki process has since its inception assisted in the protection and promotion of supplementary democratic human rights in Europe and in fact made a major contribution towards the democratisation of the formerly Communist States in Central, East and South East Europe, including Belarus, Russia and the other successor States of the former Soviet Union. It is

---

[223] Supplementary document to give effect to certain provisions contained in the Charter of Paris for a New Europe, chapter I.G.

[224] See Fastenrath and Fastenrath (2019), paras. 6 ff., 38 ff. For an extensive discussion of the OSCE's status and role, see Steinbrück Platise et al. (2019).

[225] See Fastenrath and Fastenrath (2019), para. 29.

[226] CSCE Helsinki Document 1992, VI (2). Available via https://www.osce.org/files/f/documents/7/c/39530.pdf (22 January 2025).

[227] OSCE ODHIR, Special Election Assessment Mission – European Parliament Elections, 6–9 June 2024, Statement of preliminary findings and conclusions. Available via https://www.osce.org/files/f/documents/1/8/570492_2.pdf (22 January 2025).

[228] Available via https://www.osce.org/files/f/documents/b/9/40131.pdf (22 January 2025). See Fastenrath and Fastenrath (2019), para. 33.

[229] The OSCE Representative on Freedom of the Media, p. 3. Available via https://www.osce.org/files/f/documents/9/9/186381.pdf (22 January 2025).

[230] Id., p. 2.

[231] Id., p. 4 ff.

cooperating in this regard with the UN as well as regional organisations, such as the CoE and the EU.[232] Its practical role has been paraphrased as follows: "The OSCE works to build and sustain stability, peace and democracy for more than one billion people, through political dialogue and projects on the ground."[233]

Since the end of the Cold War, the human dimension of the OSCE has comprised the political commitments of the Participating States regarding human rights and democracy. Also at that time, the Human Dimension Mechanism was established in order to monitor the implementation of these commitments under the auspices of the ODIHR. The Human Dimension Mechanism is based on the Vienna Concluding Document of 1989 (Vienna Mechanism) that was further elaborated at the Conference on the Human Dimension in Moscow in 1991 (Moscow Mechanism).[234] The Moscow Mechanism, which has so far been used fifteen times, permits the establishment of *ad hoc* missions of independent experts whose purpose is "to facilitate resolution of a particular question or problem relating to the human dimension".[235] Such a mission may be invited by a Participating State into its own territory, but it may also deal with "a particularly serious threat to the fulfilment of the provisions of the CSCE human dimension [which] has arisen in another participating State", if requested by at least ten Participating States.[236]

While the OSCE has survived the new division of Europe caused by Russia's aggression against Ukraine since 2014, there is no denying that it has been weakened considerably. Yet, as the only regional organisation still including Russia and Ukraine as well as the latter's allies on both sides of the Atlantic, it may have a role to play in the settlement of the conflict and the resurrection of democracy in Russia and Belarus.

4.2.2 *Right to Democracy Beyond Europe: Brief Look at Other World Regions*

This subchapter concentrates on the two longest and best established as well as most researched regional human rights systems in the Americas and in Africa. It is complemented by a brief review of the human rights systems of the League of Arab States and ASEAN.

---

[232] See Boisson de Chazournes and Gadkowski (2019), p. 199 ff.

[233] What is the OSCE, p. 2. Available via https://www.osce.org/files/f/documents/d/d/35775_10.pdf (22 January 2025).

[234] Human Dimension Mechanisms. Available via https://www.osce.org/odihr/human-dimension-mechanisms (22 January 2025).

[235] Moscow Mechanism (as amended), para. 5. Available via https://www.osce.org/files/f/documents/5/e/20066.pdf (22 January 2025).

[236] Id., paras. 4 ff., 13.

4.2.2.1 Western Hemisphere: The Americas

4.2.2.1.1 Representative Democracy as "Gold Standard" in the Organization of American States (OAS)[237]

The Charter of the Organization of American States[238] includes several references to democracy. The most important ones are these: The 3rd recital of the preamble identifies representative democracy as "an indispensable condition for the stability, peace and development of the region". The 4th recital projects "the consolidation on this continent, within the framework of democratic institutions, of a system of individual liberty and social justice based on respect for the essential rights of man" as a consequence of American solidarity and good neighbourliness. Art. 1 of the Charter identifies the OAS as a regional agency within the UN whose purpose is, among others, to promote the solidarity of the American States, but only with the powers expressly conferred by the Charter and without intervening in matters that are within the internal jurisdiction of the Member States. This addresses the tension between international obligations regarding a State's constitutional set-up and the prohibition of intervention protecting the self-determination of that State's people regarding their constitution.[239]

Two of the essential purposes of the OAS, proclaimed in Art. 2 of the Charter, are "[t]o promote and consolidate representative democracy, with due respect for the principle of non-intervention" (lit. b) and "[t]o eradicate extreme poverty, which constitutes an obstacle to the full democratic development of the peoples of the hemisphere" (lit. g). In Art. 3 of the Charter, the American States reaffirm a series of principles, three of which pertain to democracy: "d) The solidarity of the American States and the high aims which are sought through it require the political organization of those States on the basis of the effective exercise of representative democracy; e) Every State has the right to choose, without external interference, its political, economic, and social system and to organize itself in the way best suited to it, and has the duty to abstain from intervening in the affairs of another State …; f) The elimination of extreme poverty is an essential part of the promotion and consolidation of representative democracy and is the common and shared responsibility of the American States".

The most interesting provision, Art. 9 OAS Statute, was added by the Protocol of Washington.[240] It provides for the suspension of membership rights, if a democratic government is overthrown by force, as has happened quite frequently in Latin

---

[237] The protection of democracy by sub-regional organisation in the Americas (see the examples given by Nemitz and Ehm 2019, p. 375 f.) is omitted in this book.

[238] Of 30 April 1948, as amended. Available via https://www.oas.org/en/sla/dil/docs/inter_american_treaties_A-41_charter_OAS.pdf (22 January 2025). Not all the amendments are in force for all OAS Member States (see Articles 140, 142 OAS Charter).

[239] See above Chap. 3 and Sect. 3.1.

[240] Of 14 December 1992 (A-56). Available via http://www.oas.org/dil/treaties_A-56_Protocol_of_Washington.htm (22 January 2025).

America and the Caribbean. Art. 9 OAS Statute, which has been applied in practice several times to various *coups* in OAS Member States that had ratified the Protocol of Washington,[241] reads as follows:

> A Member of the Organization whose democratically constituted government has been overthrown by force may be suspended from the exercise of the right to participate in the sessions of the General Assembly, the Meeting of Consultation, the Councils of the Organization and the Specialized Conferences as well as in the commissions, working groups and any other bodies established.
>
> a) The power to suspend shall be exercised only when such diplomatic initiatives undertaken by the Organization for the purpose of promoting the restoration of representative democracy in the affected Member State have been unsuccessful;
> b) The decision to suspend shall be adopted at a special session of the General Assembly by an affirmative vote of two-thirds of the Member States;
> c) The suspension shall take effect immediately following its approval by the General Assembly;
> d) The suspension notwithstanding, the Organization shall endeavor to undertake additional diplomatic initiatives to contribute to the re-establishment of representative democracy in the affected Member State;
> e) The Member which has been subject to suspension shall continue to fulfill its obligations to the Organization;
> f) The General Assembly may lift the suspension by a decision adopted with the approval of two-thirds of the Member States;
> g) The powers referred to in this article shall be exercised in accordance with this Charter.

Nine of the 34 OAS Member States have not ratified the Protocol inserting Art. 9, most notably Mexico, and are therefore not bound by it.[242] Mexico explained its opposition in a declaration made at the time of the adoption of the Protocol of Washington by referring to the principles of non-intervention and self-determination:

> The Government of Mexico reiterates its bent for and commitment to democracy based on the strictest respect for and adherence to the principles of nonintervention and self-determination. Mexico has reacted swiftly and firmly to disruptions of the constitutional order on numerous occasions in the past but remains convinced, nonetheless, that democracy is a process which comes from the sovereign will of the people, and cannot be imposed from outside. Mexico is categorically opposed to any attempt to disrupt the constitutional order in any country and further expresses a deep commitment to democracy and the amelioration of our political systems. It insists, however, that it is unacceptable to give to regional organizations supra-national powers and instruments for intervening in the internal affairs of our states.
>
> The Government of Mexico maintains that the preservation and strengthening of democracy in our region cannot be enhanced through isolation, suspension or exclusion, and hence believes that the wording on suspension of member states as approved here today, has changed the original purpose of our Organization.
>
> Mexico is opposed to the punitive character ascribed to the OAS and reaffirms its conviction that cooperation and dialogue are the most effective means of resolving internal conflicts within states or conflicts between states.

---

241 Arrighi (2017), para. 57.

242 See Arrighi (2017), para. 23.

> Consequently, the Government of Mexico is placing on record its opposition to these amendments to the charter as approved at the XVI Special Session of the General Assembly.[243]

Art. 9 OAS Charter reconfirms that the OAS Member States are taking their reciprocal treaty commitment to representative democracy seriously and are ready to enforce it. Contrary to the Mexican declaration, this is fully compatible with the principle of non-intervention, as enshrined in Art. 1 (2), 19 OAS Charter, and the right to self-determination. The overthrow of a democratically constituted government of an OAS Member State by force is not a matter within that State's internal jurisdiction, in view of contrary OAS Charter commitments. The ratification of the Washington Protocol introducing the suspension power in Art. 9 OAS Charter constitutes an exercise of the right of self-determination. One can of course always question whether suspension of membership rights will be an effective means against coups. But each Member State is free to give its own answer to that question when casting its vote in the General Assembly pursuant to Art. 9 lit. b OAS Charter.

The OAS Charter is exclusively focussed on parameters for Member States' democratic governmental structure from a top-down perspective. It neglects the bottom-up perspective on international democracy and accordingly has no parliamentary body of its own, in contrast to the CoE. Decision-making at OAS level is completely dominated by the Member States' executives.[244]

4.2.2.1.2 American Declaration of the Rights and Duties of Man (ADRDM)

This Declaration,[245] the earlier regional equivalent of the UDHR, was adopted together with the OAS Charter by the Ninth International Conference of American States in 1948.[246] It emphasises the duties more than the UDHR.[247] While the ADRDM as such, just like the UDHR, does not create legal obligations, it has become an authoritative tool for interpreting the legally binding human rights obligations deriving from the OAS Charter. Accordingly, it has long been used by the Inter-American Commission on Human Rights (IACommHR), an OAS organ,[248] as an obligatory standard of review *vis-à-vis* those OAS Member States that have not ratified the American Convention on Human Rights (ACHR).[249] The ADRDM and the ACHR are implemented by the IACommHR as two distinct but complementary

---

[243] Available via http://www.oas.org/dil/treaties_A-56_Protocol_of_Washington_sign.htm (22 January 2025).

[244] See Articles 53 ff. OAS Charter.

[245] Available via https://www.oas.org/dil/access_to_information_human_right_American_Declaration_of_the_Rights_and_Duties_of_Man.pdf (22 January 2025).

[246] Grossman (2010), para. 2.

[247] But see Article 29 (1) UDHR.

[248] Article 106 OAS Charter.

[249] Grossman (2010), paras. 11 ff., 21 f.; Cançado Trindade and González-Salzberg (2024), p. 302 ff.

international legal instruments.[250] Thus, in contrast to the UDHR, the ADRDM as a whole has been transformed from an international soft-law to an international hard-law instrument.

Like the UDHR, the ADRDM identifies human dignity as the source of human rights (and duties).[251] And like its global equivalent, it knows no "right to democracy" as such, but contains several guarantees of civil and political rights that protect essential prerequisites of a democratic system. The most important provision is Art. XX, the equivalent of Art. 21 UDHR, which proclaims the entitlement of "[e]very person having legal capacity … to participate in the government of his [!] country, directly or through his representatives, and to take part in popular elections, which shall be by secret ballot, and shall be honest, periodic and free."[252] In difference to Art. 21 UDHR, Art. XX ADRDM does not guarantee the right of equal access to public service. On the other hand, Art. XXXIV ADRDM enshrines the duty to serve the community and the nation, including by holding "any public office to which he may be elected by popular vote in the state of which he is a national." Moreover, pursuant to Art. XXXII ADRDM, "[i]t is the duty of every person to vote in the popular elections of the country of which he is a national, when he is legally capable of doing so." Contrariwise, Art. XXXVIII imposes a duty on every person "to refrain from taking part in political activities that, according to law, are reserved exclusively to the citizens of the state in which he is an alien."[253]

Supplementary democratic guarantees are contained in the following provisions of the ADRDM: Art. XVII (right to recognition of juridical personality and civil rights), Art. II (right to equality before the law), Art. IV (right to freedom of investigation, opinion, expression and dissemination of ideas), Art. XXI (right of peaceable assembly), Art. XXII (right of association), Art. XXIV (right of petition), Art. XII (right to an education that prepares everyone to be a useful member of society) and Art. XVIII (right to an effective remedy in a court to ensure respect for legal and constitutional rights). Art. XIX (right to nationality) constitutes a further supplementary democratic guarantee that does not appear in the ECHR.[254] This is because the main democratic human right in Art. XX is limited to citizens. Art. XIX ensures that this right cannot be taken away by arbitrarily denaturalising persons.

Democracy as such is referred to only once in Art. XXVIII that regulates limitations on human rights and permits limitations to the rights of man specifically also regarding "the just demands of … the advancement of democracy." In difference to Art. 29 (2) UDHR, democracy in the ADRDM does not serve as a general counterbalance for all limitations but as a separate ground for limiting human rights.

---

[250] Grossman (2010), para. 18.

[251] 1st recital of the preambles of both the Conference document and the ADRDM as part of that document; 2nd recital of the ADRDM preamble.

[252] The exclamation mark was added to underline that this main democratic right is limited to the citizens of the respective country, using the generic masculine form common at the time.

[253] See Article 16 ECHR (above Sect. 4.2.1.2.1.3).

[254] But see above Sect. 4.2.1.2.1.2 on the ECtHR's use of Article 8 ECHR against arbitrary deprivations of citizenship.

4.2.2.1.3 American Convention on Human Rights (ACHR)

Just like the ADRDM, the American Convention on Human Rights (ACHR)[255] does not contain any "right to democracy" as such, but enshrines specific democratic rights, most importantly the right of citizens to participate in government (Art. 23 ACHR) that "reflects one of the basic principles and the democratic aim of the OAS."[256] Art. 23 (1) ACHR guarantees three democratic essentials closely modelled on Art. 25 ICCPR: the right to take part in the conduct of public affairs, directly or indirectly through freely chosen representatives (lit. a); to vote and be elected at genuine, periodic, universal, free, equal and secret elections, guaranteeing the free expression of the will of the electors (lit. b); to have equal access to public service in their country (lit. c). Art. 23 (2) ACHR permits limited regulation by law of the exercise of these rights.[257]

The other typical democratic rights are also included in the ACHR: Art. 8 (general right to a fair trial before an independent and impartial tribunal previously established by law),[258] Art. 13 (freedom of thought, expression and information, regardless of frontiers),[259] 15 (right of assembly), 16 (freedom of association, including for political purposes), 20 (right to a nationality that indirectly protects the right of citizens to participate in government [Art. 23 ACHR][260]), 24 (equality before the law and right to equal protection), 25 (right to judicial protection against acts that violate fundamental rights). The IACtHR "has recognized the relationship that exists between political rights, freedom of expression, the right of assembly and freedom of association, and that these rights, taken as a whole, make the democratic process possible."[261]

Interestingly, Art. 27 ACHR that permits derogation from human rights obligations in time of war, public danger or other emergency expressly excludes any suspension of the core democratic right in Art. 23 ACHR, of the right to nationality in Art. 20 ACHR and of the judicial guarantees essential for their protection. Art. 13 of the Additional Protocol to the ACHR in the Area of Economic, Social and Cultural

[255] Of 22 November 1969 (OAS Treaty Series No. 36). Available via https://www.oas.org/dil/treaties_b-32_american_convention_on_human_rights.pdf (22 January 2025).

[256] See Hennebel and Trigoudja (2022), p. 690.

[257] Id., p. 706 ff.

[258] See Hennebel and Trigoudja (2022), p. 336.

[259] On the freedom of expression as a major tool for the functioning of democracy, based on the core values of pluralism, transparency, and tolerance see id., p. 432 ff., 445 f. On positive obligations, such as the protection of journalists and the media, see id., p. 440 f. On the democratic importance of the right of access to information see id., p. 448 ff.

[260] See IACtHR, Proposed Amendments of the Naturalization Provisions of the Constitution of Costa Rica. Advisory Opinion OC-4/84 of January 19, 1984. Series A No. 4, paras. 34 f.

[261] IACtHR, judgment of 5 October 2015, Case of López Lone et al. v. Honduras (Preliminary objection, merits, reparations and cost), Series C No. 302, para. 160 (with further references).

Rights[262] on the right to education requires that education ought to enable everyone to participate effectively in a democratic and pluralistic society.

Art. 29 lit. c ACHR expressly states that "[n]o provision of the Convention shall be interpreted as … precluding other rights or guarantees that are … derived from representative democracy as a form of government". In parallel with the ECHR, the "democratic society" serves as a general counterbalance on restrictions of those rights.[263] Art. 30 ACHR further limits the scope of permissible restrictions that need to be "in accordance with laws enacted for reasons of general interest and in accordance with the purpose for which such restrictions have been established."[264] When asked to give an advisory opinion on the interpretation of the word "laws" in this provision,[265] the IACtHR unanimously determined that only those laws could restrict the rights embodied in the ACHR that were "passed by democratically elected legislative bodies established by the Constitution".[266]

Reading all these ACHR provisions together, one can derive an unwritten general individual right to national democracy, but that has not yet been recognised by the IACtHR. In any event, international democracy seems to be of no concern to the ACHR.

4.2.2.1.4 Inter-American Democratic Charter

The democratic guarantees of the OAS-Charter, the ADRDM and the ACHR are supplemented by an important soft-law document: the Inter-American Democratic Charter (IADC).[267] Technically, it is a resolution with 28 articles that was unanimously adopted at a special session of the OAS General Assembly and signed by the OAS Member States. Art. 1 (1) of the Charter states that "[t]he peoples of the Americas have a right to democracy and their governments have an obligation to promote and defend it." This clearly expresses a collective right to national democracy *vis-à-vis* governments, with several components—an implicit duty to respect and explicit duties to protect and to promote. Art. 2 IADC identifies the effective exercise of representative democracy as the basis of the constitutional regimes of the OAS Member States. The Charter thus also clearly concentrates on national democracy.

---

[262] Of 17 November 1988 (OAS Treaty Series No. 69. Available via https://www.oas.org/juridico/english/treaties/a-52.html (22 January 2025).

[263] Articles 15, 16 (2), 32 (2) ACHR. See also Article 5 of the Additional Protocol (note 229).

[264] See Article 18 ECHR.

[265] The advisory jurisdiction of the Court is regulated in Article 64 (1) ACHR.

[266] Advisory Opinion OC-6/86 of May 9, 1986. Available via https://www.corteidh.or.cr/docs/opiniones/seriea_06_ing.pdf (22 January 2025). See Pasqualucci (2013), p. 48 f.

[267] Of 11 September 2001. Available via https://www.oas.org/charter/docs/resolution1_en_p4.htm (22 January 2025). See also OAS, Tenth Anniversary of the Inter-American Democratic Charter. Available via https://www.oas.org/docs/publications/tenth%20anniversary%20of%20the%20inter-american%20democratic%20charter.pdf (22 January 2025).

Art. 3 IADC contains a non-exhaustive list of the essential elements of representative democracy: "… respect for human rights and fundamental freedoms, access to and the exercise of power in accordance with the rule of law, the holding of periodic, free, and fair elections based on secret balloting and universal suffrage as an expression of the sovereignty of the people, the pluralistic system of political parties and organizations, and the separation of powers and independence of the branches of government." Art. 4 IADC adds a list of essential components of the exercise of democracy, including transparency in government activities and freedom of the press. According to Art. 5 IADC, "[t]he strengthening of political parties and other political organizations is a priority for democracy." The IACtHR has not been ready to derive an autonomous and justiciable general "right to democracy" from the combination of Art. 3 IADC and Art. 29 lit. c and d ACHR.[268] On the other hand, the Court has used the OAS Charter and the IADC to confirm that national judges who protested against the 2009 *coup d'état* in Honduras exercised a right and fulfilled a duty to defend democracy.[269]

Art. 19 ff. IADC expand Art. 9 OAS Charter by setting forth that "an unconstitutional interruption of the democratic order or an unconstitutional alteration of the constitutional regime that seriously impairs the democratic order in a member state constitutes, while it persists, an insurmountable obstacle to its government's participation" in the OAS bodies.[270] Art. 23 ff. IADC provide for electoral observation missions by the OAS in Member States in order to help ensuring free and fair electoral processes, but only upon the request of the Member State concerned. The IACommHR on 30 April 2024 adopted Resolution 1/24, based on Art. 41 lit. b ACHR, in which it recognised national and international election observers as human rights defenders and reaffirmed the States' duties to respect and protect them in their important mission for the defence of the democratic systems and the rule of law.[271]

The IADC that is based on the consensus of all OAS Members can be taken into account in interpreting the democracy-related provisions of the OAS Charter, ADRDM and ACHR[272] or at least used as a supplementary means of interpreting those provisions.[273] Accordingly, the last recital of the preamble of the IADC refers to "the advisability of clarifying the provisions set forth in the OAS Charter and

---

[268] IACtHR, judgment of 5 August 2008, Case of Apitz Barbera et al. ("First Court of Administrative Disputes") v. Venezuela (Preliminary objection, merits, reparations and costs), Series C No. 182, paras. 216 ff. See Hennebel and Trigoudja (2022), p. 691.

[269] IACtHR, judgment of 5 October 2015, Case of López Lone et al. v. Honduras (Preliminary objection, merits, reparations and cost), Series C No. 302, paras. 152 ff. See Hennebel and Trigoudja (2022), p. 691.

[270] On the application of Articles 19 ff. in practice, see Tenth Anniversary of the Inter-American Democratic Charter (note 234), p. 26 ff.; Prezas (2023), p. 246 ff.

[271] Available via https://www.oas.org/es/cidh/decisiones/pdf/2024/Res-1-24-Personas-Observadoras.pdf (22 January 2025). See Tullio (2024).

[272] See Article 31 (3) lit. a VCLT.

[273] See Article 32 VCLT.

related basic instruments on the preservation and defense of democratic institutions, according to established practice". Some consider the IADC as a legally binding authoritative interpretation of the OAS Charter, in parallel with the ADRDM,[274] and the IACtHR refers to it in its case law.[275]

4.2.2.1.5 Enforcement Procedures

The IACommHR, an OAS organ that has also been included in the ACHR,[276] and the Inter-American Court of Human Rights, established by the ACHR,[277] are the two supervisory organs of the Inter-American human rights system.[278] The IACommHR supervises the human rights record of OAS Member States that have not acceded to the ACHR (in particular, the United States and Canada) by the ADRDM and also decides on individual petitions.[279] With regard to ACHR parties, the right of individual petition is enshrined in Art. 44 ff. ACHR. The Commission's jurisdiction over petitions concerning both the ADRDM and the ACHR is compulsory, and in contrast to Art. 1 OP-ICCPR and Art. 34 ECHR that permit individual applications only by victims of an alleged human right violation, Art. 44 ACHR is open for petitions by any person, group of persons or nongovernmental entity legally recognised in one or more OAS Member States that know of a human rights violation (*actio popularis*).[280] This possibility of autonomous NGO involvement may be particularly important to counteract general antidemocratic measures by States.

The IACommHR decides on whether the defendant State is responsible for the claimed human rights violation and can also make recommendations regarding redress, including legislative changes.[281] While such recommendations are not binding, the IACommHR may publish a report about unadjusted violations that subjects the uncooperative State to the forum of public opinion.[282] Instead, it can refer the case to the IACtHR, provided that the State is a party to the ACHR and has recognised the jurisdiction of the Court pursuant to Art. 62 ACHR. In contrast to the ECtHR, individuals have no access to the IACtHR.[283] If the IACommHR or the defendant State have submitted a case to the IACtHR, the Court will make a final

[274] See Benz (2024), p. 117, note 350 (with further references).
[275] See the references given by Hennebel and Trigoudja (2022), p. 690, note 7.
[276] Articles 34 ff.
[277] Articles 52 ff.
[278] Grossman (2021), para. 1.
[279] Id., para. 35.
[280] Id., para. 31.
[281] Id., para. 35. See Article 50 ACHR.
[282] Id., para. 36. See Article 51 ACHR.
[283] Article 61 ACHR.

decision by judgment that is legally binding.[284] Pursuant to Art. 63 (1) ACHR, the Court has broad reparation authority.[285]

According to Art. 64 ACHR, all OAS Member States, including those not party to the ACHR, as well as the OAS organs,[286] may request an advisory opinion from the IACtHR regarding the interpretation of the ACHR as well as other treaties concerning the protection of human rights in the American States (which, according to the Court's case law, include the ADRDM[287] and the IADC[288]). Every Member State may furthermore request an opinion regarding the compatibility of any of its domestic laws with the aforementioned human rights treaties. This procedure can also be used to protect and promote the democratic human rights enshrined in those treaties, and it has indeed been so used.[289] In December 2024, Guatemala requested a comprehensive advisory opinion "regarding democracy and political rights" which is still pending, giving the Court the opportunity to clarify the existence and scope of a human right to democracy in the Americas at a time of increasing challenges.[290] While the advisory opinions are not legally binding, they are highly authoritative and have a considerable impact, not least because the IACtHR cites them when rendering binding judgments in contentious cases, and so do national courts.[291]

4.2.2.2 Africa: African Union[292]

4.2.2.2.1 Constitutive Act of the African Union

The Constitutive Act of the African Union (AUCA)[293] does not put the same emphasis on democracy as the OAS Charter, but makes several references to it. One of the objectives of the AU is "to promote democratic principles and institutions, popular

[284] Articles 67, 68 ACHR. See Neuman (2007), para. 24.

[285] Id., para. 23.

[286] Those listed in Chapter VIII of the OAS Charter (as amended since the formulation of Article 64 ACHR); see Hennebel and Trigoudja (2022), p. 1356.

[287] Id., p. 1360.

[288] Benz (2024), p. 117 f. But see also id., p. 179 ff. on the rejection by the Court of a pertinent request by the IACommHR.

[289] See, e.g., Presidential reelection without term limits in the context of the Inter-American Human Rights System (Interpretation and scope of articles 1, 3, 24, and 32 of the American Convention on Human Rights, XX of the American Declaration of the Rights and Duties of Man, 3(d) of the Charter of the Organization of American States and of the Inter-American Democratic Charter), Advisory Opinion OC-28/21, Series A No. 28 (7 June 2021). See Benz (2024), p. 229 ff.

[290] Amor Vásquez (2025).

[291] Pasqualucci (2013), pp. 37, 77 ff.; Hennebel and Trigoudja (2022), p. 1365 ff.

[292] The protection of democracy by the eight African sub-regional economic communities such as ECOWAS (which counts "promotion and consolidation of a democratic system of governance in each Member State" among its fundamental principles. Available via https://ecowas.int/fundamental-principles-2/ [22 January 2025]) are omitted in this book. In this regard, see, *e.g.*, Viljoen (2012), pp. 469 ff., 502 ff. (who also mentions sub-regional parliaments); Buchan and Tsagourias (2023).

[293] Of 11 July 2000. Available via https://au.int/sites/default/files/treaties/7758-treaty-0021_-_CONSTITUTIVE_ACT_OF_THE_AFRICAN_UNION_E.pdf (22 January 2025).

participation and good governance".[294] The AU shall function in accordance with the principle of "respect for democratic principles, human rights, the rule of law and good governance".[295] The two cited provisions at least primarily refer to national democracy, but the second one also addresses democracy at AU level. Another of the functioning principles of the AU is also related to national democracy: the "condemnation and rejection of unconstitutional changes of governments".[296] Art. 30 AUCA provides for the automatic suspension of membership, if governments come to power through unconstitutional means. Art. 4 lit. h AUCA even sets forth "the right of the Union to intervene in a Member State pursuant to a decision of the Assembly in respect of grave circumstances, namely: war crimes, genocide and crimes against humanity" to which a more recent Protocol, that has not yet entered into force because no Member State has ratified it so far, adds "as well as a serious threat to legitimate order to restore peace and stability to the Member State of the Union upon the recommendation of the Peace and Security Council".[297] This amendment cannot be interpreted as permitting armed outside intervention to protect national democracy, because this would be contrary to Art. 53 (1) sentence 2 UNCh which requires authorisation by the UN Security Council for all enforcement action by regional arrangements.[298]

There are further clear references to international democracy in the AU Constitutive Act: Firstly, in another of the AU's functioning principles: "participation of the African peoples in the activities of the Union";[299] secondly, in the Pan-African Parliament (PAP) as an organ of the AU.[300] This PAP is established "[i]n order to ensure the full participation of the African peoples in the development and economic integration of the continent."[301] Its composition, powers, functioning and organisation is to be regulated in a separate protocol,[302] the Protocol to the Constitutive Act of the African Union Relating to the Pan-African Parliament (PAP Protocol).[303] According to Art. 4 and 5 of the Protocol, each State Party shall initially be repre-

---

[294] Article 3 lit. g AU Constitutive Act.

[295] Article 4 lit. m AU Constitutive Act.

[296] Article 4 lit. p AU Constitutive Act.

[297] Protocol on Amendments to the Constitutive Act of the African Union of 11 July 2003 – not yet in force. Available via https://au.int/sites/default/files/treaties/35423-treaty-0025_-_PROTOCOL_ON_THE_AMENDMENTS_TO_THE_CONSTITUTIVE_ACT_OF_THE_AFRICAN_UNION_E.pdf (22 January 2025).

[298] See Roth (2000), p. 328 ff.; Pippan (2023), p. 54 f. (who points out that armed interventions in Africa absent SC authorisation have in practice always additionally been based on the invitation by the *de jure* government of the target State).

[299] Article 4 lit. c AU Constitutive Act.

[300] Article 5 (1) lit. c AU Constitutive Act.

[301] Article 17 (1) AU Constitutive Act.

[302] Article 17 (2) AU Constitutive Act.

[303] Of 27 June 2014, not yet in force. Available via https://au.int/sites/default/files/treaties/7806-treaty-0047_-_protocol_to_the_constitutive_act_of_the_african_union_relating_to_the_pan-african_parliament_e.pdf (22 January 2025). But the Pan-African Parliament already exists as an organ of the African Economic Community (see Viljoen 2011, paras. 25 ff.).

sented by an equal number of five parliamentarians (two of them women), to be elected by the national parliaments in a way ensuring that the representation of each State Party reflects the diversity of opinion in the respective national parliament. Membership of a national parliament and the PAP are incompatible. The democracy and human rights-related objectives of the PAP are clearly provided in the PAP Protocol: it shall "promote the principles of human and peoples' rights and democracy in Africa; … encourage good governance, respect for the rule of law, transparency and accountability in Member States".[304] While the second part of the quotation concerns national democracy, the first part, referring to "democracy in Africa", also encompasses international democracy in the African world region.

4.2.2.2.2 African (Banjul) Charter on Human and Peoples' Rights

The African (Banjul) Charter on Human and Peoples' Rights (AfChHPR)[305] with 54 States Parties—all African States except Morocco—does not mention democracy as such, but enshrines both collective and individual democratic rights. Art. 20 (1) AfChHPR codifies the collective right of all peoples to self-determination with its democratic ingredients. Among the individual democratic rights, Art. 13 AfChHPR stands out. In para. 1, it guarantees the right of every citizen "to participate freely in the government of his country, either directly or through freely chosen representatives in accordance with the provisions of the law." Para. 2 enshrines every citizen's "right of equal access to the public service of his country", para. 3 the right of every individual of equal access to public property and services.[306] Surprisingly, the AfChHPR does not include a specific guarantee of the right to vote and be elected which is only implicitly assumed in Art. 13 (1) AfChHPR but has been enforced by the African Commission on Human and Peoples's Rights.[307] This gap is partly filled by a soft-law document issued by the OAU Heads of State and Government, the Declaration on the Principles Governing Democratic Elections in Africa of 2002.[308] On this basis, the AU (as the OAU's successor) engages in electoral observation and monitoring missions.[309] The other typical democratic rights are also included in the

[304] Article 3 lit. c, d. See also the 10th and 11th recital of the preamble. Viljoen (2012), p. 174 f.

[305] Of 27 June 1981. https://au.int/sites/default/files/treaties/36390-treaty-0011_-_african_charter_on_human_and_peoples_rights_e.pdf (22 January 2025).

[306] Article 13 (3) AfChHPR is an anti-apartheid provision.

[307] Murray (2019), pp. 344 ff., 353 ff.

[308] Available via https://archives.au.int/bitstream/handle/123456789/572/AHG%20Decl%201%20%28XXXVIII%29%20_E.pdf?sequence=1&isAllowed=y (22 January 2025).

[309] See the Guidelines for African Union Electoral Observation and Monitoring Missions – EX. CL/91 (V) Annex II. Available via https://archives.au.int/bitstream/handle/123456789/2060/Guidelines%20for%20Electoral%20Observation%20and%20Monitoring%20Missions_E.pdf (22 January 2025).

AfChHPR.[310] In contrast to the ACHR and the ECHR, however, there is no "democratic society" counterbalance on restrictions of those rights.

Art. 30 ff. AfChHPR establish the African Commission on Human and Peoples' Rights that is mandated with promoting these rights and ensuring their protection in Africa. The Commission assesses State reports submitted under Art. 62 AfCHHPR and adopts concluding observations.[311] It can also deal with communications from States parties[312] as well as "other" (*i.e.*, individual and NGO) communications.[313] The Commission has also been called upon to determine the content of the right to self-determination (Art. 20 (1) AfChHPR) in cases of secessionist movements.[314] It has also recognised that unconstitutional changes of government violate Art. 13 (1) and the democratic ingredients of the right to self-determination.[315] When dealing with alleged violations of the AfChHPR, the Commission is required to draw inspiration from (among others) the provisions of various African instruments on human and peoples' rights, which includes the treaties dealt with in the following sections.[316] The Commission renders decisions on the merits of inter-State and individual communications which are arguably binding on the State Party concerned.[317]

The African Court on Human and Peoples' Rights (AfCtHPR) was established by the Protocol to the AfChHPR (Prot.) of 10 June 1998 that is in force for 34 States Parties.[318] It still constitutes the basis for the Court's work because the Protocol on the African Court of Justice and Human Rights of 1 July 2008,[319] which is intended to replace it, has not yet entered into force.[320] According to Art. 3 (1) Prot., the AfCtHPR's comparatively broad contentious jurisdiction extends to "all cases and disputes submitted to it concerning the interpretation and application of the Charter, this Protocol and any other relevant Human Rights instrument ratified by the States concerned." The latter include African human rights instruments, but also global ones, such as the ICCPR.[321] The scope of the Court's jurisdiction is therefore much broader than that of the Commission, which is limited to violations of the AfChHPR.[322] The judgments of the Court are legally binding.[323] Access to the Court

---

310 2, 3, 9, 10 and 11 AfChHPR. On the special importance of political speech in the context of Article 9 AfCHHPR, see Murray (2019), p. 278 f.

311 Viljoen (2012), p. 349 ff.

312 Articles 47 ff. AfChHPR.

313 Articles 55 ff. AfChHPR. See Ouguergouz (2010), para. 35.

314 Viljoen (2012), p. 224 ff.

315 Murray (2019), pp. 357 f., 504.

316 See below Sects. 4.2.2.2.3 and 4.2.2.2.4.

317 Viljoen (2012), pp. 335 ff., 339.

318 Available via https://au.int/sites/default/files/treaties/36393-treaty-0019_-_protocol_to_the_african_charter_on_human_and_peoplesrights_on_the_establishment_of_an_african_court_on_human_and_peoples_rights_e.pdf (22 January 2025).

319 Available via https://au.int/sites/default/files/treaties/36396-treaty-0035_-_protocol_on_the_statute_of_the_african_court_of_justice_and_human_rights_e.pdf (22 January 2025).

320 On the so far unsuccessful efforts to develop the AfCtHPR further, see De Silva (2024).

321 Ouguergouz (2010), para. 42; Viljoen (2012), p. 435 ff. See also Article 7 Prot.

322 Id., para. 43.

323 Articles 27 ff. Prot.

is open only to the Commission, the State Party which has lodged a complaint to the Commission as well as the State Party against which such a complaint has been lodged, the State Party whose citizen is a victim of human rights violation and African Intergovernmental Organisations.[324] NGOs and individuals may only institute cases directly before the Court if the defendant State Party has made a declaration accepting the competence of the Court to examine such cases.[325] The Court may also deliver non-binding advisory opinions on the matters circumscribed in Art. 3 (1) Prot. at the request of an AU Member State, the AU, any of its organs, or any African organisation recognised by the AU, but only if the subject matter is not related to a matter being examined by the Commission.[326]

The comparatively weak anchoring of democracy in the AfChHPR is partly compensated by a number of other treaties in the AU system, starting with the Protocol to the African Charter of Human and Peoples' Rights on the Rights of Women in Africa.[327] In the 10th recital of its preamble, "democracy" is mentioned among the bases of African values. Art. IX of the Protocol enshrines women's right to participation in the political and decision-making process, requiring States Parties to take specific positive action to promote participative governance and to ensure that "[w]omen participate without any discrimination in all elections; … are represented equally at all levels with men in all electoral processes".

4.2.2.2.3 African Charter on Democracy, Elections and Governance

The most important supplementary democratic guarantees are embodied in the African Charter on Democracy, Elections and Governance (AfChDEG), an international treaty which 46 of 55 AU Member States have signed and 39 ratified.[328] Its 53 articles comprise detailed rules on the establishment, functioning, protection and improvement of democratic systems of national government, including provisions on democratic elections and election observation (Art. 17 ff.) and sanctions in cases of unconstitutional changes of government (Art. 23 ff.).[329]

---

[324] Article 5 (1) Prot. See Viljoen (2012), p. 426 ff.

[325] Article 5 (3), Article 34 (6) Prot. Currently, only eight States Parties have made such a declaration; four other States Parties had made, but later withdrawn their declaration. Available via https://au.int/sites/default/files/treaties/36393-sl-PROTOCOL_TO_THE_AFRICAN_CHARTER_ON_HUMAN_AND_PEOPLESRIGHTS_ON_THE_ESTABLISHMENT_OF_AN_AFRICAN_COURT_ON_HUMAN_AND_PEOPLES_RIGHTS_0.pdf (22 January 2025).

[326] Article 4 Prot. Viljoen (2012), p. 446 ff.

[327] Of 11 July 2003. Available via https://au.int/sites/default/files/treaties/37077-treaty-charter_on_rights_of_women_in_africa.pdf (22 January 2025).

[328] Of 30 January 2007. Available via https://au.int/sites/default/files/treaties/36384-treaty-african-charter-on-democracy-and-governance.pdf (22 January 2025).

[329] See de Wet (2021), p. 199 ff. On international criminal sanctions in such cases, see the Protocol on Amendments to the Protocol on the Statute of the African Court of Justice and Human Rights of 2014 (below in Sect. 4.2.2.2.4).

Among the objectives of the African Charter on Democracy, Elections and Governance listed in Art. 2 AfChDEG are these: to "[p]romote adherence … to the universal values and principles of democracy and respect for human rights" (no. 1); "[p]romote the holding of regular free and fair elections to institutionalize legitimate authority of representative government as well as democratic change of governments" (no. 3); "[p]rohibit, reject and condemn unconstitutional change of government in any Member State …" (no. 4); "[n]urture, support and consolidate good governance by promoting democratic culture and practice, building and strengthening governance institutions and inculcating political pluralism and tolerance" (no. 6). Art. 3 AfChDEG lists eleven principles that are to guide the implementation of the Charter, including representative government; regular, transparent, free and fair elections; separation of powers; gender equality; effective citizen participation; "[c]ondemnation and total rejection of unconstitutional changes of government; and "[s]trengthening political pluralism and recognising the role, rights and responsibilities of legally constituted political parties, including opposition political parties, which should be given a status under national law."

In Art. 23 AfChDEG, "the State Parties agree that the use of, inter alia, the following illegal means of accessing or maintaining power constitute an unconstitutional change of government and shall draw appropriate sanctions by the Union:

1. Any putsch or coup d'Etat against a democratically elected government.
2. Any intervention by mercenaries to replace a democratically elected government.
3. Any replacement of a democratically elected government by armed dissidents or rebels.
4. Any refusal by an incumbent government to relinquish power to the winning party or candidate after free, fair and regular elections; or
5. Any amendment or revision of the constitution or legal instruments, which is an infringement on the principles of democratic change of government."[330]

Art. 27 ff. AfChDEG extend democratic standards beyond the political to the economic and social governance. One approach is to "ensure and promote strong partnerships and dialogue between government, civil society and private sector" (Art. 28 AfChDEG), the inclusion of women (Art. 29 AfChDEG), citizen participation in the development process (Art. 30 AfChDEG) and participation of groups with special needs, such as young persons and persons with disabilities, in the governance process (Art. 31 AfChDEG). Art. 32 AfChDEG requires only efforts to institutionalise good political governance, while Art. 33 AfChDEG directly mandates the institutionalisation of good economic and social governance. According to Art. 34 AfChDEG, "State Parties shall decentralize power to democratically elected local authorities as provided in national laws."[331] Even more importantly, pursuant to Art. 36 AfChDEG "State Parties shall promote and deepen democratic governance by

[330] Article 30 AUCA and Article 25 AfChDEG provide the basis for sanctions in the cases listed in Article 23 AfChDEG. On the pertinent practice of the AU, see Prezas (2023), pp. 237 ff., 241, 245 f.

[331] On the democratic value of decentralisation, see below Sect. 4.2.2.2.4.

implementing the principles and core values of the NEPAD Declaration on Democracy, Political, Economic and Corporate Governance and, where applicable, the African Peer Review Mechanism (APRM)."[332]

All the provisions of the AfChDEG are formulated as State obligations and not as individual rights. However, since they constitute the interpretative background of the democratic human rights enshrined in the AfChHPR,[333] they can reinforce individual rights otherwise guaranteed. Put differently, these other individual rights can be used to enforce the Charter's objective democratic standards.

4.2.2.2.4 Other Treaties Relevant for the Protection and Promotion of Democracy

Further provisions to protect and promote aspects of democracy are added by the African Union Convention on Preventing and Combating Corruption[334] and the African Charter on Values and Principles of Public Service and Administration.[335] Corruption in the public and private sector indeed is the antithesis of democracy, the rule of law, human rights and good governance.[336]

The democratic value of decentralisation has already been addressed by Art. 34 AfChDEG[337] which imposes what seems to be a rather soft obligation on States Parties to decentralise powers to "democratically elected local authorities", but only if provided in national laws. It thus appears to be no more than a suggestion to consider passing such laws. It is true that the level of democracy in a State increases, if decision-making power is delegated to democratically accountable lower levels of government that are closer to the citizens which makes the connection between the voters and the elected functionaries stronger. One further democratic benefit of

---

[332] New Partnership for Africa's Development (NEPAD) Declaration on Democracy, Political, Economic and Corporate Governance. Available via https://archives.au.int/bitstream/handle/123456789/495/2002%20AHG%20235%20%28XXXVIII%29%20Annex%201%20_E.pdf?sequence=1&isAllowed=y (22 January 2025). The APRM is a Specialised Agency of the AU that was established in 2003 and organises a peer review process of a State's record in political, economic and corporate governance on a voluntary basis: "Member countries within the APRM undertake self-monitoring in all aspects of their governance and socio-economic development. African Union (AU) stakeholders participate in the self-assessment of all branches of government – executive, legislative and judicial – as well as the private sector, civil society and the media.". Available via https://au.int/en/organs/aprm (22 January 2025). See Frans Viljoen (2012), pp. 166 ff., 198 ff.

[333] See Article 60 AfChHPR, Article 3 (1) Prot. and Article 31 (3) lit. c of the Vienna Convention on the Law of Treaties of 23 May 1969 (UNTS vol. 1155, p. 331).

[334] Of 11 July 2003. Available via https://au.int/sites/default/files/treaties/36382-treaty-0028_-_african_union_convention_on_preventing_and_combating_corruption_e.pdf (22 January 2025).

[335] Of 31 January 2011. Available via https://au.int/sites/default/files/treaties/36386-treaty-charter_on_the_principles_of_public_service_and_administration.pdf (22 January 2025).

[336] See 1st recital of the preamble of UN Convention against Corruption of 31 October 2003 (UNTS vol. 2349, p. 41). See also Viljoen (2012), p. 272 ff.

[337] See above Sect. 4.2.2.2.3.

decentralisation is the increase in the opportunities for civil society to participate in governance, both at the local level and also at higher levels, if local authorities are empowered to provide input to national decision-making processes. Decentralisation therefore translates into democratisation in the sense of improving the overall democratic legitimacy of government.

This underlines the democratic importance of the African Charter on the Values and Principles of Decentralisation, Local Governance and Local Development.[338] According to Art. 5 (1) of this Charter, the States Parties "shall enact domestic laws/regulations, recognising different levels of government with the mandate to exercise their competencies through clearly defined regulatory mechanisms." This constitutes a hard-law obligation to decentralise. Art. 5 (2) of the Charter adds that the local governments and authorities shall manage their administration and finances in an accountable and transparent manner through democratically elected deliberative assemblies and executive organs. Under Art. 5 (4) of the Charter, local governments or authorities shall be consulted on higher-level projects that directly or indirectly affect them. Art. 6 of the Charter introduces the principle of subsidiarity. The Charter is based on the conviction that "local governments or local authorities are key cornerstones of any democratic governance system" and the collective will of the AU Member States "to deepen participatory democracy, citizens and community empowerment [and] to promote accountability and transparency of public institutions".[339] Accordingly, Art. 12 of the Charter regulates in detail participation, based on the general rule that "[d]emocracy shall be the foundation of local governance and shall take a participatory and representative form".[340] Finally, Art. 13 of the Charter on representation requires the central governments of States Parties to enact electoral laws "that promote regular, democratic, free, fair and transparent local government elections" and also "establish innovative measures and appropriate mechanisms to ensure the full participation of all eligible citizens, including specific measures for the representation of women and marginalised groups in local government elections". Local residents and communities are also to be encouraged "to provide feedback to their locally elected representatives, make their grievances heard, and seek redress".

In order to demonstrate how serious the protection of democracy is taken in the AU, international criminal sanctions for certain antidemocratic actions have meanwhile been introduced by the Protocol on Amendments to the Protocol on the Statute of the African Court of Justice and Human Rights.[341] This Protocol, which has not

[338] Of 27 June 2014 – not yet in force. Available via https://papsrepository.africa-union.org/bitstream/handle/123456789/543/african_charter_on_the_values_and_principles_of_decentralisation_local_governance_and_local_development_en.pdf?sequence=1&isAllowed=y (22 January 2025).

[339] 8th and 9th recital of the preamble. See also Article 2 lit. i, Article 4 lit. a, g of the Charter.

[340] Article 12 (2) of the Charter.

[341] Of 27 June 2014 - not yet in force (see above Sect. 4.2.2.2.1). Available via https://au.int/sites/default/files/treaties/36398-treaty-0045_-_protocol_on_amendments_to_the_protocol_on_the_statute_of_the_african_court_of_justice_and_human_rights_e-compressed.pdf (22 January 2025).

yet entered into force, intends to invest that Court also with international criminal jurisdiction, in an attempt to divert the attention of the International Criminal Court from Africa, in accordance with the principle of complementarity enshrined in Art. 1 sentence 1 of the Rome Statute of the International Criminal Court.[342] In the Protocol's preamble, the States Parties recall "their commitment to the right of the Union to intervene in a Member States pursuant to a decision of the Assembly in respect of grave circumstances, namely war crimes, genocide and crimes against humanity as well as a serious threat to legitimate order to restore peace and stability to the Member State of the Union upon the recommendation of the Peace and Security Council" and reiterate "their respect for democratic principles, human and people's [sic] rights, the rule of law and good governance".[343] In the annexed Statute of the African Court of Justice and Human and Peoples' Rights (as the Court is henceforth to be called under Art. 8 of the Protocol), the Court's international criminal jurisdiction is extended beyond genocide, crimes against humanity, war crimes and the crime of aggression to ten other crimes, including "[t]he crime of unconstitutional change of government" (Art. 28A (1) No. 4 of the Statute). Based on Art. 23 AfChDEG,[344] Art. 28E of the Statute defines that crime as follows:

1. For the purposes of this Statute, 'unconstitutional change of government' means committing or ordering to be committed the following acts, with the aim of illegally accessing or maintaining power:
   a) A putsch or coup d'état against a democratically elected government;
   b) An intervention by mercenaries to replace a democratically elected government;
   c) Any replacement of a democratically elected government by the use of armed dissidents or rebels or through political assassination;
   d) Any refusal by an incumbent government to relinquish power to the winning party or candidate after free, fair and regular elections;
   e) Any amendment or revision of the Constitution or legal instruments, which is an infringement on the principles of democratic change of government or is inconsistent with the Constitution;
   f) Any substantial modification to the electoral laws in the last six (6) months before the elections without the consent of the majority of the political actors.
2. For purposes of this Statute, "democratically elected government" has the same meaning as contained in AU instruments.

Finally, in the preamble of the Agreement Establishing the African Continental Free Trade Area,[345] the Member States of the African Union recognise "the importance

[342] Of 17 July 1998, UNTS, vol. 2187, No. 38544.

[343] 8th and 9th recital. The 8th recital cites Article 4 lit. h of the Constitutive Act of the AU, as amended by the Protocol on Amendments to the Constitutive Act of the African Union of 11 July 2003 – not yet in force (see above Sect. 4.2.2.2.1).

[344] See above Sect. 4.2.2.2.3.

[345] Of 21 March 2018, entered into force on 30 May 2019. Available via https://au-afcfta.org/wp-content/uploads/2022/06/AfCFTA-Agreement-Legally-scrubbed-signed-16-May-2018.pdf (22 January 2025).

of international security, democracy, human rights, gender equality and the rule of law, for the development of international trade and economic cooperation".[346]

4.2.2.3 The Human Rights Systems of the Arab World and ASEAN

4.2.2.3.1 Democratic Rights in the Arab World

The (revised) Arab Charter on Human Rights[347] is a treaty that was concluded under the auspices of the League of Arab States,[348]—whose founding treaty makes no reference to democracy.[349] The Arab Charter invokes the UN Charter, the UDHR, the ICCPR, the ICESCR and the Cairo Declaration on Human Rights in Islam. It enshrines the right of self-determination of all peoples, comprising the right to freely choose their political system,[350] and the usual supplementary democratic rights of everyone, such as the right to information, to freedom of opinion and expression as well as the right to seek, receive and impart information and ideas through any medium, regardless of geographical boundaries,[351] the protection against discrimination and the right to equality[352] as well as the right to an effective remedy against violations of human rights recognised in the Arab Charter.[353] One aim of the education to be provided by States Parties is "to strengthen respect for human rights and fundamental freedoms".[354]

The most important democratic rights of citizens are, however, contained in Art. 24 Arab Charter, namely the rights to "freely pursue a political activity"; to "take part in the conduct of public affairs, directly or through freely chosen representatives"; to "stand for elections or choose [their] representatives in free and impartial elections, in conditions of equality among all citizens that guarantee the free expression of [their] will";[355] to "the opportunity to gain access, on an equal footing with others, to public office in [their] country in accordance with the principle of equality of opportunity"; to "freely form and join associations with others"; and to "freedom

[346] 7th recital.

[347] Of 22 May 2004. Available via https://digitallibrary.un.org/record/551368?v=pdf (22 January 2025).

[348] Pact of the League of Arab States of 22 March 1945. Available via https://avalon.law.yale.edu/20th_century/arableag.asp (22 January 2025).

[349] Article 8 of the Pact (see preceding fn.) provides that "[e]very member State of the League shall respect the form of government obtaining in the other States of the League, and shall recognize the form of government obtaining as one of the rights of those States, and shall pledge itself not to take any action tending to change that form."

[350] Article 2 (1).

[351] Article 32.

[352] Articles 3, 11.

[353] Article 23.

[354] Article 41 (4). See also Article 41 (5).

[355] For gaps in this guarantee, see Rishmawi (2008), paras. 55, 57.

of association and peaceful assembly". According to Art. 24 (7), restrictions placed on the exercise of any of these rights need to be "prescribed by law and ... necessary in a democratic society" in order to safeguard certain overriding public interests.[356] This brings in the general democracy counterbalance for all limitations which we also find at the global level and in the ECHR, but not in the Americas and in Africa. Since the democratic rights in Art. 24 Arab Charter are limited to citizens, Art. 29 (1) Arab Charter introduces an important supplementary protection against the arbitrary or unlawful deprivation of nationality.

As regards enforcement, the Arab Charter establishes the Arab Human Rights Committee of independent experts that is charged with reviewing periodic reports to be submitted by the States Parties.[357] There is no individual or inter-State complaints procedure.[358] The effectiveness of the Arab regional human rights regime has been questioned, not least with regard to the right to democracy: "... it is safe to say that there is no concrete regional Arab custom affirming democracy (in its procedural sense) as a right."[359] The hope for democratisation in North Africa and the Middle East that were sparked by the Arab Spring uprising starting in 2011 has largely been disappointed.[360]

4.2.2.3.2 Democratic Rights in ASEAN

The Charter of the Association of Southeast Asian Nations (ASEAN)[361] makes several references to national as well as international democracy. In the 7th recital of the preamble, the peoples of the Member States proclaim their adherence "to the principles of democracy, the rule of law and good governance, respect for and protection of human rights and fundamental freedoms". Two of ASEAN's purposes in Art. 1 of the Charter relate to democracy: "[t]o ensure that the peoples and Member States of ASEAN live in peace with the world at large in a just, democratic and harmonious environment" (4.); and "[t]o strengthen democracy, enhance good governance and the rule of law, and to promote and protect human rights and fundamental freedoms, with due regard to the rights and responsibilities of the Member States

---

[356] Article 4 Arab Charter permits derogation from these rights in exceptional situations of emergency.

[357] Article 45–48 Arab Charter.

[358] The Statute of the Arab Court of Human Rights that was adopted in 2014 by the League of Arab States and would introduce an inter-State dispute settlement mechanism has not yet entered into force (Almutawa 2023).

[359] Alfadhel (2016b), The Right to Democracy in International Law & the Arabs State Practice, pp. 20, 27. The author also states that nearly all Arab States parties to the ICCPR did not fulfil the standards of Article 25 ICCPR in accordance with General Comment No. 25 (p. 25).

[360] Alfadhel (2016a), The Failure of the Arab Spring.

[361] Of 20 November 2007. Available via https://asean.org/book/the-asean-charter-30th-reprint/ (22 January 2025). On the traditional "ASEAN way" of non-interference into the domestic affairs and informal mechanisms of confidence-building and consensus, see Malanczuk (2017), paras. 12 ff.

of ASEAN" (7.). Purpose 4 seems to allude to international democracy, purpose 7 instead to national democracy. Among the principles in Art. 2 (2) of the Charter, two are democracy-related: "adherence to the rule of law, good governance, the principles of democracy and constitutional government" (lit. h); "respect for fundamental freedoms, the promotion and protection of human rights …" (lit. i). There is no parliamentary body among the organs of ASEAN, but an ASEAN human rights body in Art. 14 of the Charter. On this basis, the ASEAN Intergovernmental Commission on Human Rights (AICHR) was established in 2009 as a consultative body.[362]

The ASEAN Inter-Parliamentary Assembly (AIPA), which dates back to the 1970s, is not an official organ of ASEAN pursuant to the Charter, but a regional parliamentary organisation established by delegates of the national parliaments of the ASEAN Member States.[363] Its character is similar to the character of the Inter-Parliamentary Union at the global level.[364] According to Art. 3 of the AIPA Statutes on the aims and purposes, the following are most relevant in the current context: to promote cooperation and close relations among parliaments of ASEAN Member States, other parliaments and parliamentary organisations; "to offer parliamentary contributions to ASEAN integration"; "to promote the principles of human rights, democracy, peace, security and prosperity in ASEAN." According to the preamble, "more direct and active participation by the peoples of the ASEAN Member States is of great importance in further promoting the aims of the ASEAN", which indicates that AIPA is also intended to enhance the democratic legitimacy of ASEAN.

ASEAN has only produced a soft-law instrument for the protection of human rights, the ASEAN Human Rights Declaration, drafted by the AICHR and issued by the Heads of State/Government of the Member States.[365] In this Declaration, they reaffirmed their adherence to the principles of democracy, the rule of law and good governance as well as their commitment to the UDHR, the UN Charter, the Vienna Declaration and Programme of Action and other international human rights instruments to which their States are parties. The Declaration includes the usual supplementary democratic rights of everyone—the right to freedom of opinion, expression and information (para. 23); the right to freedom of peaceful assembly (para. 24); the protection from discrimination (para. 2); the right to an effective and enforceable remedy (para. 5). While a right to freedom of association, which is one of the democratic essentials,[366] is not specifically guaranteed, ASEAN Member States expressly "affirm all the civil and political rights in the Universal Declaration of Human Rights" (para. 10), so that the right to freedom of association in Art. 20 (1) UDHR

---

362 The Commission's Terms of Reference are available via https://aichr.org/wp-content/uploads/2020/02/TOR-of-AICHR.pdf (22 January 2025).

363 See The Statutes of the ASEAN Inter-Parliamentary Assembly, 8th ed. October 2024. Available via https://aipasecretariat.org/pages/statutes/ (22 January 2025).

364 On the IPU, see above Sect. 3.2. (fn. 50).

365 Of 18/19 November 2012. Available via https://asean.org/asean-human-rights-declaration/ (22 January 2025).

366 See Uerpmann-Wittzack (2023), p. 169 ff.

is implicitly also guaranteed in the ASEAN context. According to para. 31 (3), education is required to "strengthen the respect for human rights and fundamental freedoms in ASEAN Member States." Interestingly, para. 9 takes a democratic approach towards realising the rights and freedoms contained in the Declaration. This process "shall take into account peoples' participation, inclusivity and the need for accountability."

The main democratic rights are enshrined in para. 25 which provides: "(1) Every person who is a citizen of his or her country has the right to participate in the government of his or her country, either directly or indirectly through democratically elected representatives, in accordance with national law. (2) Every citizen has the right to vote in periodic and genuine elections, which should be by universal and equal suffrage and by secret ballot, guaranteeing the free expression of the will of the electors, in accordance with national law." According to para. 18, "[e]very person has the right to a nationality as prescribed by law. No person shall be arbitrarily deprived of such nationality …"

The general limitation clause in para. 8 provides that "the exercise of human rights and fundamental freedoms shall be subject only to such limitations as are determined by law solely for the purpose of" safeguarding specific overriding public interests "in a democratic society." This reflects the well-known general democracy counterbalance. Finally, para. 40 prohibits States, groups and individuals from abusing the Declaration as a pretext for undermining the purposes and principles of ASEAN or destroying" any of the rights and fundamental freedoms set forth in this Declaration and international human rights instruments to which ASEAN Member States are parties." This builds on models in the UDHR and the ECHR that indirectly protect democratic governmental systems.

Since the ASEAN Charter is a soft-law instrument, it lacks enforcement mechanisms. However, the AICHR uses the Charter to help it fulfil its mandate.[367] It serves as a basis for future ASEAN human rights conventions.

4.2.2.4 Conclusion: The Debits and Credits of Democratic Determination Outside Europe

Both the American and African regional organisations have had to cope with numerous coups against democratic governments as well as civil strife in their wake. This has led them to upgrade their defence of democracy through hard-law and soft-law instruments, compared to Europe. But all in all, the state of democracy has remained more precarious there than in Europe that possesses the most effective enforcement system for democratic human rights with the ECtHR and has only recently begun to experience instances of democratic backsliding.

[367] See in this sense the Five-Year Work Plan of the AICHR 2021-2025. Available via https://aichr.org/wp-content/uploads/2020/10/AICHR-FYWP-2021-2025-approved-at-53rd-AMM_for-web.pdf (22 January 2025).

Both the African and the American system have some distinct features concerning democracy protection. In the Americas, we find the following ones: On the positive side, the OAS Charter makes the promotion and consolidation of representative democracy in the Member States one of its essential purposes, a soft-law Inter-American Democratic Charter which includes a collective people's right to national democracy, the possibility of autonomous NGO involvement in the enforcement of democratic rights by *actio popularis* applications to the IACommHR and the IACtHR, the use of an advisory opinion procedure in the IACtHR for protecting and promoting democratic human rights; on the negative side, since important States (in particular the United States and Canada) have remained outside the ACHR, there are gaps in the enforcement of democratic human rights in the Americas; international democracy is neglected regarding both the regional and global levels.

The African system has the following special features: On the positive side, decentralisation as a specific democratic endeavour, a hard-law African Charter on Democracy as a special instrument to protect and improve national democracy; an international criminal law component of democracy protection against unconstitutional changes of government and the inclusion of international democracy; on the negative side, comparatively weak enforcement mechanisms.

Neither in the Americas, nor in Africa has a general right to national democracy, let alone international democracy, been recognised so far.

In the Arab world, democratic human rights are protected by hard-law provisions, but effective enforcement is largely lacking. ASEAN has so far mostly relied on soft-law in this regard. Neither region has devoted attention to a general right to national democracy or to international democracy.

4.3 General Conclusion: Human Rights Foundations of Democracy Around the World

At global level, essential democratic standards as well as supplementary democratic guarantees are enshrined in the soft-law UDHR, primarily regarding national democracy, but also international democracy. In hard-law form, these essentials and guarantees are primarily codified in the ICCPR. They are relatively concrete and have been further specified by treaty-body practice. From these provisions, a rather clearly contoured unwritten human right to national democracy can be synthesised which may play an important role in countering democratic backsliding, but has not yet been clearly established. Evidence of a general human right to international democracy is scarcer and its contours are less clear. From a synthesis of those general rights to national and international democracy one obtains a general human right to an adequate overall standard of democracy in multilevel systems of government whose contours are also rather vague.

At regional level, the ECHR and Prot. No. 1 provide more effective protection of supplementary democratic rights, while the specific democratic rights are less complete than those in the ICCPR. The ECtHR has not yet recognised a general right to national democracy and not yet begun to take democratic backsliding seriously enough. The Court's approach to a right to international democracy and the interdependence problem are more advanced than at the global level. American and African regional organisations have upgraded their defence of democracy through hard-law and soft-law instruments, but the state of democracy has remained more precarious there than in Europe. The same holds true regarding the Arab world and ASEAN. Neither of the latter four regions recognises any general right to national or international democracy.

References

Ailincai MA (2021) Who monitors compliance with fundamental values in EU Member States? Available via Verfassungsblog. https://verfassungsblog.de/who-monitors-compliance-with-fundamental-values-in-eu-member-states/. Accessed 22 Jan 2025

Ailincai MA (2024a) The long-awaited election of a judge to the ECtHR in respect of Poland. Available via EJIL Talk. https://www.ejiltalk.org/the-long-awaited-election-of-a-judge-to-the-ecthr-in-respect-of-poland/. Accessed 22 Jan 2025

Ailincai MA (2024b) The Parliamentary Assembly of the Council of Europe is at it again. On the non-ratification of the credentials of Azerbaijan's parliamentary delegation. Available via Strasbourg Observers. https://strasbourgobservers.com/2024/03/08/the-parliamentary-assembly-of-the-council-of-europe-is-at-it-again-on-the-non-ratification-of-the-credentials-of-azerbaijans-parliamentary-delegation/. Accessed 22 Jan 2025

Alfadhel KA (2016a) The failure of the Arab Spring. Cambridge Scholars Publishing, Newcastle upon Tyne

Alfadhel KA (2016b) The right to democracy in international law & the Arabs State practice. J Islam State Pract Int Law 12:20–30

Alfadhel KA (2017) The right to democracy in international law. Between procedure, substance and the philosophy of John Rawls. Taylor and Francis, Florence

Almutawa A (2023) Arab Court of Human Rights. Max Planck Encyclopedia of Public International Law (OUP online edition)

Amor Vásquez A (2025) In defense of a human right to democracy: Reflections on the pending Advisory Opinion before the Inter-American Court of Human Rights. Available via EJIL Talk. https://www.ejiltalk.org/in-defense-of-a-human-right-to-democracy-reflections-on-the-pending-advisory-opinion-before-the-inter-american-court-of-human-rights/. Accessed 29 Aug 2025

Arrighi J-M (2017) Organization of American States (OAS). Max Planck Encyclopedia of Public International Law (OUP online edition)

Bellamy R (2015) The democratic legitimacy of international human rights conventions: political constitutionalism and the European Convention on Human Rights. Eur J Int Law 25:1019–1042

Benz E (2024) The advisory function of the Inter-American Court of Human Rights. Nomos, Baden-Baden

Boisson de Chazournes L, Gadkowski A (2019) The external relations of the OSCE. In: Steinbrück Platise M, Moser C, Peters A (eds) The legal framework of the OSCE, 1st edn. Cambridge University Press, Cambridge, pp 199–214

Bošnjak M (2025) The role of courts in tackling democratic backsliding. Speech at Harvard University, 10 March 2025. Available via https://www.echr.coe.int/documents/d/echr/speech-20250310-bosnjak-harvard-eng. Accessed 14 Mar 2025

Buchan R, Tsagourias N (2023) The Niger Coup and the prospect of ECOWAS military intervention: an international law appraisal. Available via Articles of War. https://lieber.westpoint.edu/niger-coup-ecowas-military-intervention-international-law-appraisal/. Accessed 22 Jan 2025

Burchardt D (2024) Human Rights Committee Globalises Waite and Kennedy – but fails to protect judicial independence effectively. Available via EJIL Talk. https://www.ejiltalk.org/human-rights-committee-globalises-waite-and-kennedy-but-fails-to-protect-judicial-independence-effectively/. Accessed 22 Jan 2025

Burgorgue-Larsen L (2024) The 3 regional human rights courts in context. Oxford University Press, Oxford

Cançado Trindade AA, González-Salzberg DA (2024) International law of human rights. Oxford University Press, Oxford

Cantú Rivera H (ed) (2004) The Universal Declaration of Human Rights – a commentary. Brill Nijhoff, Brill/Leiden (quoted by: Author)

Carrozzini A (2024) Shooting democracy in the foot? Available via Verfassungsblog. https://verfassungsblog.de/shooting-democracy-in-the-foot/. Accessed 22 Jan 2025

Charlesworth H (2008) Universal Declaration of Human Rights (1948). Max Planck Encyclopedia of Public International Law (OUP online edition)

Clooney A (2024) Introduction. In: Clooney A, Neuberger D (eds) Freedom of speech in international law, 1st edn. Oxford University Press, Oxford, pp 1–70

Crawford J (2000) Democracy in international law – a reprise. In: Fox GH, Roth BR (eds) Democratic governance and international law, 1st edn. Cambridge University Press, Cambridge, pp 114–120

De Silva N (2024) The Malabo Protocol's 10th Anniversary Revives Advocacy for an African Criminal Court. Available via EJIL Talk. https://www.ejiltalk.org/the-malabo-protocols-10th-anniversary-revives-advocacy-for-an-african-criminal-court/. Accessed 22 Jan 2025

De Wet E (2021) The African Union's struggle against 'unconstitutional change of government': from a moral prescription to a requirement under international law? Eur J Int Law 32:199–226

Dejean de la Bâtie A (2025) Bodson et al. v. Belgium: a blow to organised activism. Available via Strasbourg Observers. https://strasbourgobservers.com/2025/03/14/bodson-et-al-v-belgium-a-blow-to-organised-activism/. Accessed 14 Mar 2025

Dörr O, Grote R, Marauhn T (eds) (2022) EMRK/GG. Konkordanzkommentar zum europäischen und deutschen Grundrechtsschutz, vol II, 3rd edn. 2022 Mohr Siebeck, Tübingen (quoted by: Author)

ECtHR (Registry) (2024) Guide on Article 3 of Protocol No. 1 to the ECHR (Updated to 29 February 2024). https://ks.echr.coe.int/documents/d/echr-ks/guide_art_3_protocol_1_eng. Accessed 22 Jan 2025

Fastenrath U, Fastenrath C (2019) Organisation for Security and Co-operation in Europe (OSCE). Max Planck Encyclopedia of Public International Law (OUP online edition)

Giegerich T (2022) Struggling for Europe's Soul: The Council of Europe and the European Convention on Human Rights Counter Russia's Aggression against Ukraine. Zeitschrift für Europarechtliche Studien 25:519–558

Giegerich T (2023) The expanding concepts of "peace and security" in international and European law: protecting sustainable peace and human life in dignity. Zeitschrift für Europarechtliche Studien 26:539–589

Glas LR (2024) The tide is turning for the European Social Charter: the Vilnius Declaration and the warm-up thereto. Available via Strasbourg Observers. https://strasbourgobservers.com/2024/07/19/the-tide-is-turning-for-the-european-social-charter-the-vilnius-declaration-and-the-warm-up-thereto/. Accessed 22 Jan 2025

Grabenwarter C (2014) European Convention on Human Rights – Commentary. C.H. Beck, Munich

Grossman CM (2010) American Declaration of the Rights and Duties of Man (1948). Max Planck Encyclopedia of Public International Law (OUP online edition)

Grossman CM (2021) Inter-American Commission on Human Rights (IACommHR). Max Planck Encyclopedia of Public International Law (OUP online edition)

Hand L (1944) The spirit of liberty. https://www.btboces.org/Downloads/1_The%20Spirit%20of%20Liberty%20by%20Learned%20Hand.pdf. Accessed 22 Jan 2025

Hennebel L, Trigoudja H (2022) The American Convention on Human Rights – a commentary. Oxford University Press, Oxford

Iancu B (2025) Romanian militant democracy and the time machine. Available via Verfassungsblog. https://verfassungsblog.de/romanian-militant-democracy-and-the-time-machine/. Accessed 16 Mar 2025

Janig P (2024) X v. OPEC. Am J Int Law 118:331–337

Kälin W, Künzli J (2019) The law of international human rights protection, 2nd edn. Oxford University Press, Oxford

Karsai D, Kazai V (2024) Decorum without democracy in the Hungarian Parliament: the Grand Chamber's potential intervention in Ikotity and Others v Hungary. Available via Strasbourg Observers. https://strasbourgobservers.com/2024/02/02/decorum-without-democracy-in-the-hungarian-parliament-the-grand-chambers-potential-intervention-in-ikotity-and-others-v-hungary/. Accessed 22 Jan 2025

Keane D (2024) A missed opportunity: the decision in Palestine v Israel. Available via EJIL Talk. https://www.ejiltalk.org/a-missed-opportunity-the-decision-in-palestine-v-israel/. Accessed 22 Jan 2025

Krupskiy M (2025) Kobaliya and others v. Russia: perverted transparency or when legislation on 'Foreign Agents' bears the hallmarks of a totalitarian regime? Available via Strasbourg Observers. https://strasbourgobservers.com/2025/01/17/kobaliya-and-others-v-russia-perverted-transparency-or-when-legislation-on-foreign-agents-bears-the-hallmarks-of-a-totalitarian-regime/. Accessed 22 Jan 2025

Kurnosov D (2021) Pragmatic adjudication of election cases in the European Court of Human Rights. Eur J Int Law 32:255–279

Kuti C (2024) On means and ends. Available via Verfassungsblog. https://verfassungsblog.de/on-means-and-ends/. Accessed 22 Jan 2025

Lawson R, Shrugged A (2024) An analysis of the ECtHR case law involving issues of EU law since *Opinion 2/13*. Eur Pap 9:647–671

Leach P (2017) The Parliamentary Assembly of the Council of Europe. In: Schmahl S, Breuer M (eds) The Council of Europe, 1st edn. Oxford University Press, Oxford, pp 166–211

Lenaerts K, van Nuffel P, Corthaut T (2021) EU constitutional law. Oxford University Press, Oxford

Logemann A (2004) Grenzen der Menschenrechte in demokratischen Gesellschaften. Nomos, Baden-Baden

Maftean MR (2024) A troubling triumph in Romania. Available via Verfassungsblog. https://verfassungsblog.de/triumph-in-romania/. Accessed 22 Jan 2025

Malanczuk P (2017) Association of Southeast Asian Nations (ASEAN). Max Planck Encyclopedia of Public International Law (OUP online edition)

Martínez E, Menéndez A (2024) Hungary's Sovereignty Protection Sham. Available via Verfassungsblog. https://verfassungsblog.de/sovereignty-protection-sham/. Accessed 22 Jan 2025

Milanovic M, Webb P (2024) False speech. In: Clooney A, Neuberger D (eds) Freedom of speech in international law, 1st edn. Oxford University Press, Oxford, pp 220–276

Murauskas D (2024) Manoeuvring between the constitutional order and the Convention rights – context dependent deliberation of Ždanoka v. Latvia (No. 2). Available via Strasbourg Observers. https://strasbourgobservers.com/2024/09/17/manoeuvring-between-the-constitutional-order-and-the-convention-rights-context-dependent-deliberation-of-zdanoka-v-latvia-no-2/. Accessed 22 Jan 2025

Murray R (2019) The African Charter on Human and Peoples' Rights: a commentary. Oxford University Press, Oxford

Nemitz P, Ehm F (2019) Strengthening democracy in Europe and its resilience against autocracy: daring more democracy and a European Democracy Charter. In: Garben S, Govaere I, Nemitz P (eds) Critical reflections on constitutional democracy in the European Union, 1st edn. Hart Publishing, Oxford, pp 345–384

Neuman GL (2007) Inter-American Court of Human Rights (IACtHR). Max Planck Encyclopedia of Public International Law (OUP online edition)
Nugraha IY (2023) Ikotity and Others v. Hungary: restricting the opposition's freedom of expression through a wide margin of appreciation in the context of democratic backsliding. Available via Strasbourg Observers. https://strasbourgobservers.com/2023/12/05/ikotity-and-others-v-hungary-restricting-the-oppositions-freedom-of-expression-through-a-wide-margin-of-appreciation-in-the-context-of-a-democratic-backsliding/. Accessed 22 Jan 2025
Nußberger A, Miklasová J (2023) Council of Europe as the guardian of democracy: the Venice Commission. In: Khan D-E, Lagrange E, Oeter S et al (eds) Democracy and sovereignty. Rethinking the legitimacy of public international law, 1st edn. Brill Nijhoff, Brill/Leiden, pp 269–288
Øby Johansen S, Ulfstein G, Follesdal A et al (2024) The revised draft agreement on the accession of the EU to the ECHR. Eur Pap 9:641–646
OSCE (2017) The OSCE representative on freedom of the media. https://www.osce.org/files/f/documents/9/9/186381.pdf. Accessed 22 Jan 2025
OSCE, What is the OSCE? https://www.osce.org/files/f/documents/d/d/35775_10.pdf. Accessed 22 Jan 2025
Ouguergouz F (2010) African Charter on Human and Peoples' Rights (1981). Max Planck Encyclopedia of Public International Law (OUP online edition)
Pasqualucci JM (2013) The practice and procedure of the Inter-American Court of Human Rights, 3rd edn. Cambridge University Press, Cambridge
Peters A (2009) Dual democracy. In: Klabbers J, Peters A, Ulfstein G (eds) The constitutionalization of international law, 1st edn. Oxford University Press, Oxford, pp 263–341
Pippan C (2023) Pro-democratic interventionism revisited. In: Khan D-E, Lagrange E, Oeter S et al (eds) Democracy and sovereignty. Rethinking the legitimacy of public international law, 1st edn. Brill Nijhoff, Brill/Leiden, pp 35–59
Polakiewicz J, Kirchmayr JK (2021) Sounding the alarm: the Council of Europe as the guardian of the rule of law in contemporary Europe. In: Von Bogdandy A, Bogdanowicz P, Canor I et al (eds) Defending checks and balances in EU Member States, 1st edn. Springer, Berlin, pp 361–382
Prezas I (2023) Democratic sanctions and international law. In: Khan D-E, Lagrange E, Oeter S et al (eds) Democracy and sovereignty. Rethinking the legitimacy of public international law, 1st edn. Brill Nijhoff, Brill/Leiden, pp 235–268
Rishmawi M (2008) Arab Charter on Human Rights (2004). Max Planck Encyclopedia of Public International Law (OUP online edition)
Rizcallah C (2023) The systemic equivalence test and the presumption of equivalent protection in European Human Rights Law – a critical appraisal. German Law J 24:1062–1077
Roth BR (2000) The illegality of 'pro-democratic' invasion pacts. In: Fox GH, Roth BR (eds) Democratic governance and international law, 1st edn. Cambridge University Press, Cambridge, pp 328–342
Schabas WA (2019) Nowak's CCPR commentary, 3rd edn. N.P. Engel, Kehl
Selejan-Gutan B (2024) The Second Round that Wasn't. Available via Verfassungsblog. https://verfassungsblog.de/the-second-round-that-wasnt/. Accessed 22 Jan 2025
Shattock E (2025) Electoral dysfunction: Romania's election annulment, disinformation, and ECHR positive obligations to combat election irregularities. Available via EJIL Talk. https://www.ejiltalk.org/electoral-dysfunction-romanias-election-annulment-disinformation-and-echr-positive-obligations-to-combat-election-irregularities/. Accessed 22 Jan 2025
Steinbrück Platise M, Moser C, Peters A (eds) (2019) The legal framework of the OSCE. Cambridge University Press, Cambridge
Tullio A (2024) Democracy's guardians: the Inter-American Commission recognizes electoral observers as human rights defenders. Available via Verfassungsblog. https://verfassungsblog.de/electoral-observers-human-rights-iachr/. Accessed 22 Jan 2025

Uerpmann-Wittzack R (2023) Freedom of association. The shrinking space of civil society. In: Khan D-E, Lagrange E, Oeter S et al (eds) Democracy and sovereignty. Rethinking the legitimacy of public international law, 1st edn. Brill Nijhoff, Brill/Leiden, pp 169–180

Viljoen F (2011) African Union (AU). Max Planck Encyclopedia of Public International Law (OUP online edition)

Viljoen F (2012) International human rights law in Africa, 2nd edn. Oxford University Press, Oxford

Chapter 5
The European Union as Exemplary But Imperfect Multilevel Democracy

5.1 Democracy as Inherent Element of the European Integration Process

The European Union is a liberal-democratic project at its core,[1] but a special case for a number of reasons: It is a quasi-federal non-State polity of still sovereign Member States[2] whose character oscillates between a confederation and a federal State and whose constitution remains unresolved.[3] So does its final destination: While Winston Churchill's demand of 1946 to build "a kind of United States of Europe"[4] provided the initial spark for the European integration project, and Robert Schuman's Declaration as one of its founding documents sketched out the vision of a "European federation" in 1950,[5] the language of the Treaties has never gone beyond the indeterminate goal of "an ever closer union among the peoples of Europe".[6]

But as this reference to "the peoples" proves, the European integration project has always had a democratic foundation and its future development—the deepening of the integration—is only conceivable in democratic forms, in accordance with the freely expressed will of the peoples of Europe. Accordingly, the ECJ has thus characterised the autonomy of the EU legal order and the framework it sets to further

---

[1] Lenaerts (2024), p. 380.

[2] Fassbender (2023), p. 1629 ff.

[3] Walker (2012), p. 1185 ff.; Nettesheim (2024), in: Grabitz/Hilf/Nettesheim, Artikel 9 EUV para. 4.

[4] Churchill (1946).

[5] Available via https://european-union.europa.eu/principles-countries-history/history-eu/1945-59/schuman-declaration-may-1950_en (22 January 2025).

[6] Article 1 (2) TEU. See also the 1st recital of the preamble of the TFEU, which is identical in wording with the 1st recital of the Treaty establishing the European Economic Community of 25 March 1957. See Oeter (2009), p. 55 ff.

T. Giegerich, *The Human Right to Democracy in Multilevel Systems at a Time of Democratic Backsliding: Global, Regional and European Union Perspectives*, European Union and its Neighbours in a Globalized World 24,
https://doi.org/10.1007/978-3-032-01689-8_5

integration progress: "… the Union possesses a constitutional framework that is unique to it. That framework encompasses the founding values set out in Article 2 TEU, which states that the Union 'is founded on the values of respect for human dignity, freedom, democracy, equality, the rule of law, and respect for human rights', the general principles of EU law, the provisions of the Charter, and the provisions of the EU and FEU Treaties, which include, inter alia, rules on the conferral and division of powers, rules governing how the EU institutions and its judicial system are to operate, and fundamental rules in specific areas, structured in such a way as to contribute to the implementation of the process of integration described in the second paragraph of Article 1 TEU …"[7] The enlargement of the EU in the form of accessions pursuant to Art. 49 TEU as well as its contraction in the form of withdrawals from the EU under Art. 50 TEU are also democratic processes.[8]

According to the settled case law of the ECJ, the EU legal order is characterised by its autonomy with respect both to the law of the Member States and to public international law. The autonomy is based on the Union's unique constitutional framework established by the Treaties which constitute the independent source of EU law.[9] This autonomy requires (1) that the EU institutions and their acts have a democratic legitimacy of their own which is not completely derived from the Member States; (2) that choices democratically made by the EU are not called in question by non-EU actors, including Member State, third State and international judicial and other actors.[10] In essence, this amounts to a claim of democratic European self-determination.

5.2 Top-Down, Bottom-Up and Horizontal Democratic Parameters of the EU

From the top-down perspective, the EU has set comparatively strict parameters regarding democracy in the Member States, both in the form of institutional standards and democratic human rights.[11] Because of their supranational character, these parameters have much greater effectiveness than their international counterparts. Thus, the direct effect and primacy of supranational rules on democracy and the rule of law can be important for the re-establishment of democracy and the rule

[7] ECJ, opinion 1/17 of 30 April 2019, ECLI:EU:C:2019:341, para. 110.

[8] Regarding withdrawal, see ECJ, judgment of 10 December 2018 (C-621/18), ECLI:EU:C:2018:999, paras. 66 f., 75.

[9] ECJ, opinion 2/13 of 14 December 2014, ECLI:EU:C:2014:2454, paras. 166, 170; opinion 1/17 of 30 April 2019, ECLI:EU:C:2019:341, paras. 109 f.; judgment of 18 March 2022 (C-156/21), ECLI:EU:C:2022:97, para. 125; judgment of 18 March 2022 (C-157/21), ECLI:EU:C:2022:98, para. 143.

[10] See Lenaerts (2024), p. 386 (referring to ECJ, opinion 1/17 of 30 April 2019, ECLI:EU:C:2019:341, paras. 160 f.).

[11] See below Sect. 5.4.

of law in Poland after the electoral defeat of the PiS party that is responsible for democratic and rule of law backsliding.[12] Primacy enables and obliges national executive and judicial decision-makers to disapply national legal and even constitutional provisions that are contrary to directly effective EU law precepts of democracy and the rule of law.[13]

From the bottom-up perspective, the EU is the most advanced model of a supranational democratic system,[14] with democratic rights firmly entrenched at Union level by the Member States as the contracting parties of the Treaties.[15] Moreover, mechanisms have been introduced by the EU and Member States to prevent negative repercussions on national democratic systems from the transfer of powers to the EU. The interdependence problem of national and supranational democracies and the respective democratic rights is clearly recognised and an adequate overall standard of democracy in the EU multilevel system is ensured.[16]

Beyond these two vertical components, democracy in the EU has a third, partly horizontal and partly vertical, component in the sense of an EU mission to "export" democratic standards to third States (horizontal) and the international community as a whole (vertical—bottom-up). This is all based on the conviction that democracy as one of the "universal values" derives from "the cultural, religious and humanist inheritance of Europe".[17] It is important to note, however, as the quotation indicates, that these democratic standards have long become universally accepted and enshrined in the UDHR, the ICCPR and regional human rights instruments around the globe.[18] Accordingly, the EU does not impose any foreign standards on third States but simply reconfirms the common ones and engages in joint efforts to realise them more effectively. This is why the term "export" is placed in inverted commas.

Because of their different contexts, the top-down, bottom-up and horizontal democratic parameters may differ, even if one takes into account that they can anyhow not go beyond basic requirements, respecting the constitutional identities of the Member States, pursuant to Art. 4 (2) TEU, the functionality of the supranational integration project and the right of internal self-determination of the peoples of third States: National democracy at Member State level functions differently than supranational democracy at EU level, the national democracies in non-European States and international democracy in global international organisations.[19]

---

[12] Von Bogdandy and Spieker (2023), p. 123 ff. On the problems involved in restoring the rule of law in Poland, see, e.g., Scheppele (2024), Schmidt (2024), Halmai (2025), Kristan (2025).

[13] Morijn (2024). See, e.g., ECJ, judgment of 13 July 2023 (Joined Cases C-615/20 and C-671/20), ECLI:EU:C:2023:562, regarding primacy of Article 19 (1) subpara. 2 TEU in the rule of law context.

[14] See Ruffert, in: Calliess and Ruffert (2022), Artikel 9 EUV, para. 2.

[15] See below Sect. 5.5.

[16] Ruffert, in: Calliess and Ruffert (2022), Artikel 10 EUV, para. 5.

[17] See 2nd recital of the preamble of the TEU.

[18] See above Chaps. 2–4.

[19] Chelini-Pont (2025), p. 7 f.

All this turns the EU into an exemplary (if imperfect) multilevel democracy, although there is no European *demos* yet.[20] What we have, however, are equal and self-determined citizens of the Union that in their combination function as the multinational subject of legitimation of the EU, reminding of the situation in a multiethnic federal State.[21] European democracy is therefore not an individualistic, but a holistic concept, even though there is no federal people, but only a community of Union citizens as a substitute.[22] The EU's remaining democracy deficit is a permanent construction site where improvements are constantly devised and gradually implemented.[23] It may well be true that the EU cannot be completely democratised without transforming it into a federal State in which the present problems of "disjunction between power and electoral accountability" and "executive dominance" would at least be mitigated, if not entirely resolved.[24] But that would constitute a quantum leap at the expense of the Member States' sovereignty and democratic autonomy that currently does not seem politically feasible (if it ever will).

Yet, without further approximation of the EU to a federal state, coupled with a reduction in the influence of Member States at EU level (and in particular their veto power), its further democratisation will be difficult.[25] As long as considerable political power is vested in the European Council (that defines the Union's general political directions and priorities [Art. 15 (1) sentence 1 TEU]) and the Council (that exercises legislative, budgetary, policy-making and coordinating functions), both of which are not democratically accountable as bodies at EU level, but only in their national components at the level of 27 Member States, the democratic legitimacy of EU measures will remain precarious: There is no "EU government" which could be voted out of office in the next elections to the European Parliament.[26]

---

[20] Von Bogdandy (2023), p. 23 ff. For a critique of the "no demos"thesis as an obstacle to the deepening of European integration, see Weiler (1995), p. 1655 ff. For a less ethno-centred version of the "no demos" thesis, see Grimm (1995), p. 292 ff. For recent attempts at deconstructing the "undemocratic" EU and returning it into a Europe of sovereign nation States ("great reset"), see Chelini-Pont (2025), p. 7 f.

[21] See Sydow (2024), p. 320. See also Oeter (2009), p. 67; Möllers (2025), p. 812 ff.

[22] But see von Bogdandy (2012), p. 321 f.

[23] See Nettesheim (2024), in: Grabitz/Hilf/Nettesheim, Artikel 10 EUV paras. 116 ff.

[24] On the features of the EU's democracy deficit, see Craig (2021b), Integration, p. 31 f.; Grimm (2017); id. (2022), p. 241 ff.; Haltern (2017), paras. 1188 ff.; Weiler (2011), p. 303 f.; Hailbronner (2018), p. 277 ff.; Weiler (2018), p. 629 ff.; Hatje (2019), p. 123 f.; Lenaerts (2013), p. 273 f., 279 f. See also Kelemen (2019), p. 47 ff.

[25] See below Sects. 5.5.4 and 5.6.2.

[26] See Weiler and Haltern (footnote 19).

5.3 Historical Overview of Democracy Parameters: From the Abortive European (Political) Community (1953) to the Treaty of Lisbon (2007) and Beyond

5.3.1 Draft Treaty Establishing the Statute of the European (Political) Community (1953)

Democratic requirements would have played an early role in the abortive draft of a Treaty establishing the Statute of the European (Political) Community.[27] Art. 1 defined the Community as an indissoluble union of peoples and States. One of the general objectives and tasks of the Community set forth in Art. 2 was to contribute to the protection of human rights and fundamental freedoms in Member States. Art. 3 made Section I of the ECHR with its democratic rights (but not Prot. No. 1 guaranteeing free elections which was not yet in force) an integral part of the Statute. The two-chamber Parliament, vested with legislative and budgetary powers, was to consist of a Peoples' Chamber of directly elected representatives and a Senate whose members were to be elected by the national parliaments (Art. 10 ff.). Art. 116 limited accession to Member States of the Council of Europe and other European States which guaranteed the rights referred to in Art. 3; Art. 104 would have permitted Member States to "request the European Executive Council for assistance in maintaining constitutional order and democratic institutions within their territory." The conditions under which the European Executive Council, with the unanimous concurrence of the Council of National Ministers, could intervene on its own initiative for that purpose were to be drafted and enacted in due course.

5.3.2 From the ECSC Treaty (1951) to the Single European Act (1986)

While democracy as a precept for the governmental structure of the Member States as well as the European Communities and European Union was expressly included in primary law only by the Treaty of Maastricht of 1992 and the Treaty of Amsterdam

[27] Adopted by the Common Assembly of the European Coal and Steel Community on 10 March 1953 (German text available via https://www.politische-union.de/epg1.htm [27 August 2025]), but not pursued further after the failure of the European Defence Community in 1954 with which it was closely affiliated. The Statute speaks only of "European Community"; the adjective "Political" was added in bracket to distinguish it from the later European Community, *i.e.* the renamed European Economic Community. For a detailed account of the negotiations on the European (Political) Community, see Griffiths (1994), p. 19 ff.; Griffiths (2000) (with an English version of the draft treaty on p. 189 ff.); Schorkopf (2023), p. 55 ff.

of 1997,[28] it had much earlier been officially recognised as a binding principle. The first instance is the Document on the European Identity, a political document that was adopted by the Foreign Ministers of the then nine Member States in Copenhagen in 1973: "The Nine … are determined to defend the principles of representative democracy, of the rule of law, of social justice … and of respect for human rights." They also stated that membership in their construction of a United Europe was open only to those "other European nations who share the same ideals and objectives."[29]

Enhancing supranational democracy beyond the fact that the representatives of democratic Member State governments in the Council held the decision-making power had been a goal from the very beginning of the European integration project. Art. 20–25 of the Treaty establishing the European Coal and Steel Community (ECSC)[30] already provided for an assembly of representatives of the peoples of the Member States (with rather limited supervisory powers), that could either be delegated by their national parliaments, according to the model of PACE, or directly elected, depending on the decision of each Member State. Art. 137–144 of the subsequent Treaty establishing the European Economic Community[31] also included such an assembly,[32] gave it advisory powers in addition to supervisory powers and charged it with drawing up "proposals for elections by direct universal suffrage in accordance with a uniform procedure in all Member States."[33] But since the entry into force of such a proposal was made contingent on the unanimous approval by the Council and the subsequent adoption by all the Member States, it took until 1976, before the Decision of the representatives of the Member States meeting in council relating to the Act concerning the election of the representatives of the Assembly by direct universal suffrage could be made.[34]

In view of the first direct election of the Members of the European Parliament in 1979, the European Council adopted a "Declaration on Democracy" in which the Heads of State or Government of the Member States qualified that election as "a vivid demonstration of the ideals of democracy shared by the peoples within" the

[28] See Erlbacher and Herrmann (2022), p. 32. On the attempts to democratise the European Communities since the early 1970, see Schorkopf (2023), p. 153 ff.

[29] Document on the European Identity of 14 December 1973, para. I.1. and 4. Available via https://www.cvce.eu/content/publication/1999/1/1/02798dc9-9c69-4b7d-b2c9-f03a8db7da32/publishable_en.pdf (22 January 2025).

[30] Of 18 April 1951 (original French version available via https://eur-lex.europa.eu/legal-content/FR/TXT/PDF/?uri=CELEX:11951K/TXT [22 January 2025]).

[31] Of 25 March 1957. Available via https://www.cvce.eu/en/obj/treaty_establishing_the_european_economic_community_rome_25_march_1957-en-cca6ba28-0bf3-4ce6-8a76-6b0b3252696e.html (22 January 2025).

[32] The accompanying Convention on certain institutions common to the European Communities of 25 March 1957 merged the ECSC and the EEC assemblies into a single Assembly. Available via https://www.cvce.eu/de/recherche/unit-content/-/unit/en/b9fe3d6d-e79c-495e-856d-9729144d2cbd/9f9228e1-9025-461f-b4fc-235670678e10#903872ca-002c-4ba4-b845-c25bbcb0f60f_en&overlay (22 January 2025).

[33] Article 138 (3) EEC Treaty.

[34] Of 20 September 1976 (OJ 1976 L 278), p. 1.

European Communities. They also "solemnly declare[d] that respect for and maintenance of representative democracy and human rights in each Member State are essential elements of membership of the European Communities."[35] In 1980, the Court of Justice made clear that democracy at the European level was more than a political commitment. Rather, it constituted a "fundamental democratic principle" of Community law "that the peoples should take part in the exercise of power through the intermediary of a representative assembly."[36]

In 1984, the first directly elected European Parliament adopted a draft Treaty on European Union by a large majority.[37] According to its preamble, this "Spinelli Draft", named after its main sponsor, Altiero Spinelli, was intended to continue and revive "the democratic unification of Europe" and make the European institutions "more democratic". It also reconfirmed the commitment of the Member States of the European Communities "to the principles of pluralist democracy, respect for human rights and the rule of law". Pursuant to para. 1 (2), only democratic European States could apply for membership. Para. 3 accorded all the citizens of the Member States an additional citizenship of the Union, entitling them to "take part in the political life of the Union in the forms laid down by this Treaty". Paras. 4.4. and 44 provided that "serious and persistent violation of democratic principles or fundamental rights by a Member State" could entail the imposition of penalties in the form of suspension of rights and participation in Union organs.

Based on the Stuttgart Solemn Declaration on European Union by the European Council[38] and also motivated by the Spinelli Draft, the Single European Act[39] was concluded by the then twelve Member States of the European Communities in the determination "to work together to promote democracy on the basis of the fundamental rights recognized in the constitutions and laws of the Member States, the Convention for the Protection of Human Rights and Fundamental Freedoms and the European Social Charter, notably freedom, equality, and social justice".[40] The fourth recital of the preamble referred to "the democratic peoples of Europe" and the fifth recital read in part as follows: "AWARE of the responsibility incumbent upon Europe ... in particular to display the principles of democracy and compliance with the law and with human rights to which they are attached, so that together they may

---

[35] European Council, Copenhagen, 7–8 April 1978, Conclusions of the Presidency, Annex D. Available via https://www.consilium.europa.eu/media/20773/copenhagen_april_1978__eng_.pdf (22 January 2025).

[36] ECJ, judgment of 29 October 1980 (C-138/79), ECR 1980, 3333, para. 33. Confirmed, *e.g.*, in the judgment of 11 June 1991 (C-300/89), ECR 1991, I-2867, para. 20 and in the judgment of 10 June 1997 (C-392/95), ECR 1997 I-03213, para. 14.

[37] Of 14 February 1984. Available via https://www.cvce.eu/content/publication/2002/5/6/0c1f92e8-db44-4408-b569-c464cc1e73c9/publishable_en.pdf (22 January 2025).

[38] Of 19 June 1983. Available via https://www.cvce.eu/en/obj/solemn_declaration_on_european_union_stuttgart_19_june_1983-en-a2e74239-a12b-4efc-b4ce-cd3dee9cf71d.html (22 January 2025).

[39] Of 17 February 1986 (OJ 1987 L 169, p. 1).

[40] 3rd recital of the preamble.

make their own contribution to the preservation of international peace and security in accordance with the undertaking entered into by them within the framework of the United Nations Charter". This alludes to the European responsibility to project the principles of democracy, the rule of law and human rights as well as to the concept of democratic peace.

5.3.3 Treaties of Maastricht (1992), Amsterdam (1997) and Nice (2001)

The Treaty of Maastricht founded the European Union. Art. F (1) of the new Treaty on European Union for the first time explicitly set forth that the Member States' "systems of government are founded on the principles of democracy" and that the Union should respect their (accordingly democratic) national identities.[41]

Together with the establishment of the European Union, the Treaty of Maastricht introduced the citizenship of the Union, now regulated in Art. 9 sentences 2 and 3 TEU and Art. 20 (1) TFEU, which complements without replacing national citizenship. It has remained inextricably linked with the citizenship in at least one Member State: It is automatically acquired with the acquisition of citizenship of a Member State and is automatically lost with the loss of that national citizenship, unless the person concerned has the nationality of another Member State.[42] According to the settled case law of the ECJ, Union citizenship "is destined to be the fundamental status of nationals of the Member States".[43] It has transformed the Member State nationals that had previously been only economic actors as Common Market citizens into political actors in the supranational European polity.[44]

When the Treaty of Maastricht came up for ratification in Germany, it was decided that the deepening of the integration brought about by it was so far-reaching that it required a firmer constitutional basis than the previously used Art. 24 (1) of the Basic Law. For this purpose, the new Art. 23 was added to the Basic Law.[45] Regarding democracy, Art. 23 (1) sentence 1 BL takes the bottom-up perspective in the sense that it makes German participation in the development of the new European Union conditional on the latter's commitment to democratic principles.[46] This

---

[41] OJ 1992 C 191, p. 1. See Schorkopf (2024), in: Grabitz/Hilf/Nettesheim, Artikel 2 EUV para. 1.

[42] ECJ, judgment of 9 June 2022 (C-673/20), ECLI:EU:C:2022:449, para. 48.

[43] Id., para. 49.

[44] See below Sect. 5.5.6.1.

[45] See above Sect. 4.2.1.2.3 (at the end).

[46] Art. 23 (1) sentence 1 BL reads as follows: "With a view to establishing a united Europe, the Federal Republic of Germany shall participate in the development of the European Union that is committed to democratic, social and federal principles, to the rule of law and to the principle of subsidiarity and that guarantees a level of protection of basic rights essentially comparable to that afforded by this Basic Law." (English translation available via https://www.gesetze-im-internet.de/englisch_gg/englisch_gg.html [7 March 2025]).

provision is complemented by the inward-looking sentence 2 of Art. 23 (1) BL which sets out that "[t]he establishment of the European Union, as well as changes in its treaty foundations … shall be subject to paragraphs (2) and (3) of Article 79." The reference to Art. 79 (3) BL brings in Art. 20 (2) BL on the sovereignty of the people, so that Art. 23 (1) sentence 2 BL in substance requires adequate safeguards for the German democratic system *vis-à-vis* detrimental effects of European integration.[47]

The Treaty of Amsterdam replaced Art. F (1) TEU by the following text: "The Union is founded on the principles of liberty, democracy, respect for human rights and fundamental freedoms, and the rule of law, principles which are common to the Member States."[48] It also renumbered the provision to become Art. 6 (1) TEU and transferred the Union's duty to respect Member States' national identities to Art. 6 (3) TEU. The Court of Justice reconfirmed that the principle of democracy that had already before formed part of European Community law was now expressly enshrined in Art. 6 (1) TEU as one of the foundations of the EU. As one of the principles common to the Member States, it had to be taken into consideration when interpreting acts of secondary law.[49] Finally, the Treaty of Amsterdam introduced the political procedure for enforcing the principles of Art. 6 (1) TEU (now Art. 2 TEU) *vis-à-vis* a Member State guilty of a "serious and persistent breach" in Art. 7 (1)–(5) TEU, which is now regulated in Art. 7 (2)–(5) TEU.

When it became apparent at the beginning of 2000 that in Austria a new government would be formed integrating the right-wing populist FPÖ party, whose position regarding the principles enshrined in Art. 6 (1) TEU (now Art. 2 TEU) seemed problematic, the EU could not react on the basis of Art. 7 TEU because Austria was obviously not in serious and persistent breach of those principles. Instead, the fourteen other Member State, on 31 January 2000, imposed sanctions on Austria in the form of unfriendly acts outside the EU framework, each of them on a bilateral basis.[50] These sanctions were lifted in September 2000 on the basis of a report by Martti Ahtisaari, Jochen Frowein and Marcelino Oreja.[51] This report recommended the "introduction of preventive and monitoring procedures into Article 7 of the EU Treaty [EUT] so that a situation similar to the current situation in Austria would be dealt with within the EU from the very start."[52]

---

[47] See, e.g., Federal Constitutional Court, judgment of 30 June 2009 (2 BvE 2/08 etc.). Available via https://www.bundesverfassungsgericht.de/SharedDocs/Entscheidungen/EN/2009/06/es20090630_2bve000208en.html (22 January 2025) (English translation). On the fundamental "right to democracy" in German constitutional law, as developed by the FCC, see below Sect. 5.6.2.

[48] OJ 1997 C 340, p. 1. See Schorkopf (2024), in: Grabitz/Hilf/Nettesheim, Artikel 2 EUV para. 2.

[49] ECJ, judgment of 9 March 2010 (C-518/07), ECLI:EU:C:2010:125, para. 41.

[50] For a detailed account and legal evaluation, see Schorkopf (2001); Cramér and Wrange (2001).

[51] Report on the Austrian Government's Commitment to the Common European Values, in Particular Concerning the Rights of Minorities, Refugees and Immigrants, and the Evolution of the Political Nature of the FPÖ (the Wise Men Report) of 8 September 2000 (International Legal Materials (2001) 40:102–123).

[52] Id., para. 120.

The Treaty of Nice followed this recommendation by adding a new paragraph 1 to Art. 7 TEU (today Art. 7 (1) TEU) which now permits the EU to determine "that there is a clear risk of a serious breach by a Member State of the values referred to in Article 2". It also provides for the possibility to make recommendations to the Member State in question. Meanwhile, this preventive early warning procedure has proved to be completely ineffective.[53]

5.3.4 *Treaty of Lisbon and Charter of Fundamental Rights (2007)*

The Treaty of Lisbon transformed the foundational "principles" of the Union, including democracy, that had already been recognised by the Treaty of Maastricht and further elaborated by the Treaty of Amsterdam, into foundational "values" in Art. 2 TEU.[54] Since then, democracy at Member State and Union level are firmly entrenched as a fundamental value of the EU in Art. 2, 9 and 10 TEU[55] and further elaborated by secondary legal acts.[56]

In a case concerning the rule-of-law value, the ECJ made the following statement with regard to all the values in Art. 2 TEU, including democracy: "The values contained in Article 2 TEU have been identified and are shared by the Member States. They define the very identity of the European Union as a common legal order. Thus, the European Union must be able to defend those values, within the limits of its powers as laid down by the Treaties."[57] In other words, the EU has its own constitutional identity which rests on the same values as the constitutional identities of the Member States, these values being common to all of them.[58] The whole legal structure of the EU "is based on the fundamental premise that each Member State shares with all the other Member States, and recognises that they share with it, a set of common values on which the EU is founded, as stated in Article 2 TEU."[59]

---

[53] See below Sect. 5.4.2.1.

[54] See Schorkopf (2024), in: Grabitz/Hilf/Nettesheim, Artikel 2 EUV paras. 3 ff.

[55] In Germany, the introduction of indeterminate values into constitutional discourse had long before been criticised by Schmitt (2020) as a destructive "tyranny of values". On this basis, the question has been raised whether the EU's fight against democratic backsliding in some Member States comes down to such a tyranny (on the resulting challenges see von Bogdandy [2019], p. 503 ff.). See also Assenbrunner (2023), p. 610 ff.

[56] See, e.g., Regulation (EU, EURATOM) 1141/2014 of 22 October 2014 on the statute and funding of European political parties and European political foundations, OJ 2014 L 317, 4 November 2014, p. 1 (based on Article 224 TFEU); Regulation (EU) 2024/900 of 13 March 2024 on the transparency and targeting of political advertising, OJ L, 2024/900, 20 March 2024 (based on Articles 16, 114 TFEU).

[57] ECJ, judgment of 16 February 2022 (C-156/21), ECLI:EU:C:2022:97, para. 145; judgment of 16 February 2022 (C-157/21), ECLI:EU:C:2022:98, para. 127.

[58] See Baquero Cruz and Keppenne (2022), p. 65.

[59] ECJ, opinion 2/13 of 14 December 2014, ECLI:EU:C:2014:2454, para. 168.

In a further case concerning the protection of fundamental rights against individualised sanctions imposed by the UN Security Council and implemented by the EU, which was decided when Art. 6 (1) TEU as amended by the Treaty of Amsterdam and left untouched by the Treaty of Nice was in force, the ECJ made another important statement: It emphasised that Art. 297 and Art. 307 of the EC Treaty[60] that permit Member States under certain conditions to derogate from their primary law obligations "cannot ... be understood to authorise any derogation from the principles of liberty, democracy and respect for human rights and fundamental freedoms enshrined in Article 6 (1) EU as a foundation of the Union. ... Article 307 EC may in no circumstances permit any challenge to the principles that form part of the very foundations of the Community legal order ..."[61] Applied to the current legal situation, this means that the foundational values enshrined in Art. 2 TEU, including democracy, have a special status and perhaps even a higher rank within primary law. Other provisions of primary law have to be interpreted in conformity with those values.[62]

Art. 9 sentence 1 TEU enshrines the principle of equality of Union citizens, in the sense of their democratic equality. The predecessor of this provision in Art. I-45 of the abortive Treaty establishing a Constitution for Europe (TCE)[63] was actually entitled "principle of democratic equality". The Treaty of Lisbon did, however, not adopt any of the article headlines of the TCE, so that the text of the current Art. 9 TEU does not explicitly refer to "democratic" equality.[64] But since it has been placed in "Title II Provisions on Democratic Principles", it obviously addresses no other than the specific "democratic" equality of citizens of the Member States in their capacity as Union citizens, all the more since the general right to equality is enshrined in Art. 20 of the Charter of Fundamental Rights (CFR),[65] which codifies a fundamental general principle of Union law.[66] In its immediate vicinity, Art. 10 (1) TEU expressly prescribes "representative democracy" as the foundation of the functioning of the Union. Art. 10 (2) TEU further defines the EU's dual-level/quasi-federal democracy by referring to the direct representation of Union citizens in the European Parliament and the representation of Member States in the European Council and the Council by organs (Heads of State or Government or governments)

[60] Now Art. 347 and Art. 351 TFEU.

[61] ECJ, judgment of 3 September 2008 (Joined Cases C-402/05 P and C-415/05 P), ECLI:EU:C:2008:461, paras. 303 f.

[62] See Potacs (2016), p. 172 ff.

[63] Of 29 October 2004 (OJ 2004 C 301, p. 1).

[64] The wording of Article 9 TEU is widely considered as botched—see, e.g., Ruffert, in: Calliess and Ruffert (2022), Artikel 9 EUV, paras. 26 f.; Schönberger, in: Grabitz et al. (2024), Artikel 9 EUV, paras. 4 ff.

[65] See Heselhaus, in: Pechstein et al. (2023a), vol. I, Artkel 9 EUV para. 14; Ruffert, in: Calliess and Ruffert (2022), Artikel 9 EUV, para. 30; Haag, in: von der Groeben et al. (2015), Artikel 9 EUV, para. 4 f.; Nettesheim (2024), in: Grabitz/Hilf/Nettesheim, Artikel 9 EUV paras. 6, 25.

[66] Recognised by the ECJ since the judgment of 19 October 1977 (Joined Cases 117/76 and 16/77), ECR 1977-01753, para. 7. See the explanation on Article 20 (OJ 2007 C 303, p. 17).

"that are themselves democratically accountable either to their national Parliaments, or to their citizens." The EU has therefore rightly been called a "composite democracy".[67] The two strands of the EU's democratic legitimacy—the supranational and the national one—complement and reinforce each other in the sense that the lower the supranational level of legitimation is, the higher the national level must be, and *vice versa*.[68]

Finally, the CFR, which Art. 6 (1) TEU (as amended by the Treaty of Lisbon) has turned into an essential component of primary law, states that "the Union is founded on the indivisible, universal values of human dignity, freedom, equality and solidarity; it is based on the principles of democracy and the rule of law."[69] This identifies the close relationship between human dignity and the human rights to freedom, equality and solidarity deriving from it on the one hand and the organisational principles of democracy and the rule of law on the other—they are "universal, indivisible, interrelated, interdependent and mutually reinforcing."[70] Accordingly, the CFR enshrines several fundamental rights that are democratically essential, such as the freedom of expression and information as well as the freedom and pluralism of the media (Art. 11), the freedom of assembly and association (Art. 12), the right to vote and stand as a candidate at elections to the EP and at municipal elections (Art. 39, 40) as well as a right to an effective judicial remedy in case of violation of any of these rights (Art. 47).

The ECJ considers that "like the ECHR, the Charter is a living instrument which must be interpreted in the light of present-day conditions and of the ideas prevailing in democratic States today, … with the result that regard must be had to changes in values and ideas, both in terms of society and legislation, in the Member States."[71] This "living instrument" approach by the ECtHR to the ECHR has led to an expansion of human rights protection in the CoE, and the parallel approach by the ECJ to the CFR is likely to have a similar effect regarding fundamental rights protection in the EU, also with regard to democratic rights. However, a word of caution seems appropriate, because the ECJ's explicit reference to "changes in values and ideas … in the Member States" can cut both ways: If the number of rule of law and democratic backsliding cases at Member State level increase, that may lead to a contraction of the CFR's protective scope. This is not unlikely, since the EU Agency for Fundamental Rights found that "[d]emocracy itself continued to be under threat in 2023."[72] However, the non-retrogression rule may prevent turning a trickle of democratic backsliding into an avalanche. This would correspond to the ECtHR's approach to the "living instrument" concept that only supports an upward trajectory

[67] Lenaerts (2013), p. 280 f.; Heselhaus, in: Pechstein et al. (2023a), vol. I, Artikel 9 EUV, paras. 3, 6: "Demokratieverbund".

[68] Huber, in: Streinz (2018), Artikel 10 EUV, paras. 34 ff.

[69] 2nd recital of the preamble.

[70] This borrows the formulation used by the UN General Assembly to designate the relationship between the different human rights generations (see, e.g., UNGA Resolution 60/251 of 15 March 2006, 3rd recital of the preamble).

[71] ECJ, judgment of 17 December 2020 (C-336/19), ECLI:EU:C:2020:1031, para. 77 (citing ECtHR [GC], judgment of 7 July 2011, Bayatyan v. Armenia [Appl. No. 23459/03], para. 102).

[72] European Union Agency for Fundamental Rights (2024), p. 3.

of human rights standards, all the more since the ECJ expressly referred to present-day conditions and ideas "prevailing in *democratic* States".[73]

5.3.5 Nobel Peace Prize 2012 for EU's Advancement of Democratic Peace

In 2012, the EU was awarded the Nobel Peace Prize, because "the union and its forerunners have for over six decades contributed to the advancement of peace and reconciliation, democracy and human rights in Europe."[74] This once again underlines the close relationship between peace, democracy and human rights which have in fact been realised together in post-War and post-Cold War Europe where democratic stability fostered international peace and stability, and vice versa: "The stabilizing part played by the EU has helped to transform most of Europe from a continent of war to a continent of peace."[75]

5.3.6 EU Measures for Enhancement and Defence of Democracy

The preamble of the TEU has ever since its beginnings in the Treaty of Maastricht of 1992 confirmed both the attachment of the European integration project to the principle of democracy and the necessity "to enhance further the democratic ... functioning of the institutions".[76] The European Commission has accordingly taken a number of steps to bolster democracy in the EU, such as the "European Democracy Action Plan"[77] and the more recent "Defence of Democracy" package[78] which includes a Recommendation on inclusive and resilient electoral processes in the Union and enhancing the European nature and efficient conduct of the elections to the European Parliament that covers elections at EU as well as Member State level.[79] This Recommendation invokes the Code of Good Practice in electoral matters of the Venice Commission of the CoE.[80] In the run-up to the European Parliament

[73] Emphasis added. See above Sect. 4.2.1.2.1.4.1.

[74] Press Release of the Norwegian Nobel Committee of 12 October 2012. Available via https://www.nobelprize.org/prizes/peace/2012/press-release/ (22 January 2025).

[75] Id. On democratic peace, see above Sect. 2.1.

[76] Recitals 4 and 7.

[77] Communication COM(2020) 790 final of 3 December 2020.

[78] Press Release IP/23/6453 of 12 December 2023.

[79] Commission Recommendation (EU) 2023/2829 of 12 December 2023, OJ 2023 L, 20 December 2023.

[80] See Chap. 4, footnote 64.

Elections 2024, the Council approved conclusions on democratic resilience: safeguarding electoral processes from foreign interference.[81]

Based on Art. 35 (3) in conjunction with Art. 34 (1) lit. c of the Digital Services Act,[82] the European Commission has recently published draft "Guidelines for Providers of Very Large Online Platforms and Very Large Online Search Engines on the Mitigation of Systemic Risks for Electoral Processes" for public consultation.[83] The "electoral processes" addressed by these documents comprise those "at local, regional, national, and European levels" that are all important elements of the representative democracy on which the Union is founded, according to Art. 10 (1) TEU.[84] In December 2024, in the context of the presidential election in Romania whose first round was annulled by the Romanian Constitutional Court because of foreign interference through AI mechanisms,[85] the Commission increased monitoring of Tik Tok under the Digital Services Act.[86]

The potentially negative influence of AI on democratic processes has also been addressed in the EU's recent Artificial Intelligence Act.[87] Based on Art. 16 and Art. 114 TFEU, the main purpose of the AI Act is "to improve the functioning of the internal market by laying down a uniform legal framework in particular for the development, the placing on the market, the putting into service and the use of artificial intelligence systems (AI systems) in the Union".[88] But at the same time, the AI Act also tries to ensure "a high level of protection of … fundamental rights as enshrined in the Charter of Fundamental Rights of the European Union …, including democracy, … to protect against the harmful effects of AI systems in the Union …"[89] and to prevent AI misuse contradicting EU values such as democracy.[90] This combination of purposes has also been incorporated in Art. 1 (1) AI Act. Accordingly, "AI systems intended to be used to influence the outcome of an election or referendum or the voting behaviour of natural persons in the exercise of

[81] Of 21 May 2024 (10119/24). Available via https://data.consilium.europa.eu/doc/document/ST-10119-2024-INIT/en/pdf (24 February 2025).

[82] Regulation (EU) 2022/2065 of 19 October 2022 on a Single Market For Digital Services (OJ L 277 of 27 October 2022 p. 1).

[83] Available via https://digital-strategy.ec.europa.eu/en/news/commission-gathering-views-draft-dsa-guidelines-election-integrity (22 January 2025). For a critique, see Peukert (2024).

[84] EC Vice-President Vestager, Press Release of 8 February 2024. Available via https://digital-strategy.ec.europa.eu/en/news/commission-gathering-views-draft-dsa-guidelines-election-integrity (22 January 2025).

[85] See above Sect. 4.2.1.2.1.4.2.

[86] European Commission, Press Release IP/24/6243 of 5 December 2024. Available via https://ec.europa.eu/commission/presscorner/detail/en/ip_24_6243 (22 January 2025).

[87] Regulation (EU) 2024/1689 of 13 June 2024 laying down harmonised rules on artificial intelligence etc. (OJ of 12 July 2024 L 2024/1689).

[88] Recital 1 of the Preamble.

[89] Id. See also recitals 2, 8 of the Preamble.

[90] Recital 28 of the Preamble.

their vote in elections or referenda should be classified as high-risk AI systems"[91] that are subject to particularly strict requirements. The necessity of enabling democratic control of AI systems by promoting AI literacy is also emphasised.[92] Providers of very large online platforms or very large online search engines are obliged "to identify and mitigate systemic risks that may arise from the dissemination of content that has been artificially generated or manipulated, in particular risk of the actual or foreseeable negative effects on democratic processes, civic discourse and electoral processes, including through disinformation."[93]

Moreover, the EU has established the necessary secondary acts in order to be able to impose targeted sanctions for protecting democracy at EU and Member State levels, but also in international organisations or third States against hybrid threats by foreign powers, currently first and foremost Russia. These consist of a Council Decision based on Art. 29 TEU and a Council Regulation based on Art. 215 TFEU, both concerning restrictive measures in view of Russia's destabilising activities.[94] These acts target "natural or legal persons, entities or bodies that are: (a) responsible for, implementing, supporting, or benefitting from actions or policies by the Government of the Russian Federation which undermine or threaten democracy, the rule of law, stability or security in the Union, or in one or more of its Member States, in an international organisation or in a third country, or which undermine or threaten the sovereignty or independence of one or several of its Member States, or of a third country", through any one of the listed specific actions which include, e.g., election interference, the destabilisation or overthrow of the constitutional order and information manipulation and interference.[95] On this basis, restrictive measures were recently imposed for the first time.[96] The European Council also strongly condemned "Russia's hybrid campaign, including sabotage, disruption of critical infrastructure, cyber-attacks, information manipulation and interference, and attempts to undermine democracy, including in the electoral process, against the European Union and its Member States."[97]

One specific sanctions case concerned the Russian-owned RT France, a company publishing specialised television channels. After the start of Russia's war of

---

[91] Recital 62 of the Preamble. See Art. 74 (8) AI Act and Annex III, para. 8 lit. b.

[92] Recital 20 of the Preamble.

[93] Recital 120 of the Preamble. See also recital 136 of the Preamble.

[94] Council Decision (CFSP) 2024/2643 of 8 October 2024 concerning restrictive measures in view of Russia's destabilising activities (OJ L 2024/2643 of 9 October 2024); Council Regulation (EU) 2024/2642 of 8 October 2024 concerning restrictive measures in view of Russia's destabilising activities (OJ L 2024/2642 of 9 October 2024).

[95] Article 2 (1) Council Decision (CFSP) 2024/2643; Article 2 (3) Council Regulation (EU) 2024/2642.

[96] Council of the EU, Press Release of 16 December 2024. Available via https://www.consilium.europa.eu/en/press/press-releases/2024/12/16/russian-hybrid-threats-eu-agrees-first-listings-in-response-to-destabilising-activities-against-the-eu-its-member-states-and-partners/ (22 January 2025).

[97] European Council Conclusions of 19 December 2024, para. 28. Available via https://www.consilium.europa.eu/media/jhlenhaj/euco-conclusions-19122024-en.pdf (22 January 2025).

aggression against Ukraine, RT France became subject of restrictive measures in the form of the temporary prohibition of broadcasting of content by any means in all EU countries. The General Court dismissed its action for annulment (Art. 263 TFEU) which RT France had based, *inter alia*, on an alleged infringement of its right of freedom of expression and information and the freedom of the media protected by Art. 11 CFR as well as Art. 10 ECHR. The Court emphasised in particular that the prohibition pursued a legitimate objective, namely to protect the EU and its Member States against "disinformation and destabilisation campaigns conducted by the media outlets under the control of the leadership of the Russian Federation which threatened the Union's public order and security, in a context marked by military aggression against Ukraine … Since the propaganda and disinformation campaigns are capable of undermining the foundations of democratic societies and are an integral part of the arsenal of modern warfare, the restrictive measures at issue also form part of the pursuit by the European Union of the objectives assigned to it in Article 3(1) and (5) TEU."[98] This shows that the protection of the democratic system as such can justify profound restrictions of important individual democratic rights.

In her statement to the European Parliament as a candidate for her second term in office, Commission President von der Leyen promised that the Commission would propose a comprehensive "European Democracy Shield" as a "dedicated structure for countering foreign information manipulation and interference" in order to defend European democracy.[99] The European Parliament has meanwhile established a special Committee on the European Democracy Shield.[100]

5.4 EU Law Parameters for Democracy in Member States and Pertinent Individual Rights

Pursuant to Art. 2 TEU, the Union is founded on values that are common to the Member States, in particular respect for democracy and human rights (including democratic rights).[101] According to the ECJ, Art. 2 TEU "contains values which … are an integral part of the very identity of the European Union as a common legal

[98] GC, judgment of 27 July 2022 (T-125/22), ECLI:EU:T:2022:483, margin notes 55 f., 162.

[99] Statement of 18 July 2024 (https://enlargement.ec.europa.eu/news/statement-european-parliament-plenary-president-ursula-von-der-leyen-candidate-second--mandate-2024-2024-07-18_en [7 February 2025]). See also Naja Bentzen (European Parliamentary Research Service), Information integrity online and the European democracy shield, PE 767.153 – December 2024 (https://www.europarl.europa.eu/RegData/etudes/BRIE/2024/767153/EPRS_BRI(2024)767153_EN.pdf [7 February 2025]).

[100] European Parliament, Press Release of 3 February 2025 (https://www.europarl.europa.eu/news/en/press-room/20250129IPR26563/european-democracy-shield-special-ep-committee-elects-chair-and-starts-work [7 February 2025]).

[101] Bouzoraa (2023), p. 809 ff.

order, values which are given concrete expression in principles containing legally binding obligations for the Member States."[102] While the democratic rights enshrined in the CFR are at least as concrete as those enshrined in the ECHR, there is no definition of "democracy" in the sense of Art. 2 TEU. That provision was originally formulated by the Convention which drafted the abortive Treaty establishing a Constitution for Europe of 2004. An explanatory note by the Praesidium of that Convention makes clear that what later became Art. 2 TEU should only contain "a hard core of values meeting two criteria at once: on the one hand, they must be so fundamental that they lie at the very heart of a peaceful society practising tolerance, justice and solidarity; on the other hand, they must have a clear non-controversial legal basis so that the Member States can discern the obligations resulting therefrom which are subject to sanction."[103] As Art. 2 sentence 2 TEU now shows, Art. 2 sentence 1 TEU obliges the Member States only to realise the "common core" of those values that is shared by all them, irrespective of the considerable differences in their concrete design and actual implementation from Member State to Member State.

5.4.1 *Democracy as Accession Criterion and Membership Obligation*

Art. 49 TEU makes respect for and the commitment to promote democracy (among others) a political criterion for EU membership, adopting the Copenhagen criteria that had been formulated in 1993, in view of the upcoming eastward enlargement after the fall of the 'iron curtain'.[104] On this basis, the European Parliament recently criticised the parliamentary and local elections in the accession candidate country Serbia on 17 December 2023 that were held in conditions contrary to Serbia's commitment to free and fair elections.[105] With regard to the accession candidate country Moldova, the EU has imposed financial and travel sanctions on "natural or legal persons, entities or bodies responsible for, supporting or implementing actions or policies which undermine or threaten the sovereignty and independence of the Republic of Moldova, or democracy, the rule of law, stability or security in the

[102] ECJ, judgment of 16 February 2022 (C-156/21), ECLI:EU:C:2022:97, para. 232; judgment of 16 February 2022 (C-157/1), ECLI:EU:C:2022:98, para. 264 (both concerning the rule of law); judgment of 19 November 2024 (C-808/21), ECLI:EU:C:2024:962, para. 160; judgment of 19 November 2024 (C-814/21), ECLI:EU:C:2024:963, para. 157 (both concerning the principles of democracy and equal treatment).

[103] Praesidium, Draft of Articles 1 to 16 of the Constitutional Treaty (CONV 528/03) of 6 February 2003, p. 11.

[104] Presidency Conclusions of the Copenhagen European Council – 21–22 June 1993. Available via https://www.europarl.europa.eu/enlargement/ec/pdf/cop_en.pdf (22 January 2025).

[105] See EP Press Release of 8 February 2024. Available via https://www.europarl.europa.eu/news/en/press-room/20240202IPR17327/serbia-did-not-fulfil-its-commitments-to-free-and-fair-elections-say-meps [22 January 2025).

Republic of Moldova through any of the following actions: (i) obstructing or undermining the democratic political process, including by obstructing or seriously undermining the holding of elections or attempting to destabilise or overthrow the constitutional order; (ii) planning, directing, engaging in, directly or indirectly, supporting or otherwise facilitating violent demonstrations or other acts of violence …".[106] But the ECJ has underlined that the values in Art. 2 TEU are not only important guideposts of the accession process, but remain valid for and legally binding on Member States after accession.[107]

Art. 10 (2) subpara. 2 TEU provides that one of the pillars supporting the democratic entablature of the EU is the domestic democratic accountability—direct or indirect—of the Member States' representatives in the European Council and the Council. Since the EU and Member States are closely intertwined legally and politically, the democratic character of the EU level depends also on the democratic character of each and every Member State, and *vice versa*.[108] This is why the EU and all Member States have a legitimate and even essential interest in the democratic credentials of each other.[109] If the member States cannot rely on each other to respect the values enshrined in Art. 2 TEU, the mutual trust as the corner stone of the integration project cannot be maintained.[110] On this background, EU institutions have occasionally assumed an informal role as intermediaries in constitutional disputes within Member States, with the consent of the competent national authorities, in order to foster the effective functioning of national democracies.[111]

However, the democracy parameters for Member States deriving from Art. 2 TEU are not limited to requiring the adequate democratic accountability of just the national representatives in the Council and the European Council pursuant to Art. 10 (2) subpara. 2 TEU, while disregarding the rest of the national constitutional structure. This is because a Member State cannot be partly democratic and partly autocratic, just as a Member State cannot partly (*i.e.*, in the fields covered by EU law) abide by the rule of law and partly (*i.e.*, in the other areas) indulge in the arbitrary reign of power.[112] Art. 2 TEU therefore obliges every Member State to be

[106] Article 2 (1) lit. a of Council Decision (CFSP) 2023/891 of 28 April 2023 concerning restrictive measures in view of actions destabilising the Republic of Moldova (OJ L 114 of 2 May 2023 p. 15) and Article 2 (3) lit. a of Council Regulation (EU) 2023/888 of 28 April 2023 concerning restrictive measures in view of actions destabilising the Republic of Moldova (OJ L 114 of 2 May 2023 p. 1). See General Court, judgment of 18 December 2024 (T-489/23), ECLI:EU:T:912; judgment of 18 December 2024 (T-493/23), ECLI:EU:T:913.

[107] ECJ, judgment of 16 February 2022 (C-156/21), ECLI:EU:C:2022:97, paras. 124 ff.; judgment of 16 February 2022 (C-157/21), ECLI:EU:C:2022:98, paras. 142 ff.

[108] Spieker (2023), p. 165 ff.; Möllers (2025), p. 840 f.

[109] See in this sense ECJ, judgment of 16 February 2022 (C-156/21), ECLI:EU:C:2022:97, para. 125 (regarding all the values of Article 2 TEU).

[110] ECJ, judgment of 20 April 2021 (C-896/19), ECLI:EU:C:2021:311, para. 62.

[111] See with regard to a rule of law issue Díez Sarasola (2024). See also Mangas (2024), p. 63 ff.

[112] See in this sense already Abraham Lincoln, speech at Springfield, Illinois, on 16 June 1858: "'A house divided against itself cannot stand.' I believe this government cannot endure, permanently half *slave* and half *free*." (Lincoln [1992], p. 131 [emphasis in the original]).

completely democratic and subject to the rule of law.[113] The values enshrined in Art. 2 TEU bind the Member States also outside the area of EU competences[114] and probably even outside the scope of application of Union law.

There is a discrepancy between democracy (and the other values of Art. 2 TEU) as an initial accession criterion and as a continuing membership obligation. While Art. 49 sentence 1 TEU requires from candidate countries both the respect of and the commitment to promote democracy, Art. 2 TEU requires Member States only to respect (*i.e.*, refrain from dismantling) it, but no more commitment to promote (*i.e.*, actively engage in improving and expanding) it. The reason for this difference may be the presumption that candidate countries have some catching up to do regarding the realisation of the values of Art. 2 TEU in order to reach the average Member State level.

As the democratic character of the EU also depends on the effective implementation of democratic standards in all Member States, the question arises if primary EU law imposes a duty on the Union to guarantee the democratic character of the latter. The Treaties do not contain any express provision to this effect.[115] The formulation of Art. 7 TEU establishing a political procedure to enforce the EU values vis-à-vis the Member States indicates that the EU organs have broad discretionary powers[116] whose exercise is not subject to any judicial review.[117] Regarding the initiation of infringement proceedings against a Member State pursuant to Art. 258 TFEU, the Commission also enjoys discretion.[118] Since the Member States are not subject to any continuing commitment to promote democracy after their accession, they are not legally required either to institute infringement proceedings pursuant to Art. 259 TFEU in order to enforce democracy parameters vis-à-vis other Member States. In the absence of any strict obligation under EU law to implement democratic standards in the Member States, there can accordingly not be any corresponding individual claims against the EU in this regard.

[113] See in this sense Sonnevend (2023), p. 580 f.

[114] Schorkopf (2024), in: Grabitz/Hilf/Nettesheim, Artikel 2 EUV para. 18.

[115] See, by contrast, Art. 28 (3) of the German Basic Law according to which the Federation shall guarantee that the constitutional order of the Länder conforms to basic democratic standards.

[116] Art. 7 (1) TEU: "... the Council ... may determine"; Art. 7 (2) TEU: "The European Council ... may determine".

[117] Art. 269 TFEU. See below Sect. 5.4.2.1.

[118] See below Sect. 5.4.2.2.

5.4.2 *Pro-Democracy Enforcement Procedures: Political, Judicial and Financial Sanctions*

5.4.2.1 Art. 7 (1) TEU Procedures Against Poland and Hungary

Art. 7 TEU, Art. 354 TFEU provide a political procedure to enforce the EU values against backsliding which is completely controlled by the discretion of the political organs of the EU—the Commission, the Council, the European Council and the European Parliament.[119] It thus leaves no room for any individual rights. That political procedure has proved to be utterly ineffective,[120] and it may also be normatively incoherent to the extent that the imposed sanction consists of the suspension of the Member State's voting rights in the Council while leaving its obligations unaffected, which impairs the democratic structure of the EU's decision-making process under Art. 10 (2) sentence 2 TEU.[121]

The two initiatives so far taken on the basis of Art. 7 (1) TEU (the preventive early warning procedure)[122]—one by the Commission against Poland,[123] the other by the European Parliament against Hungary[124]—have lingered in the Council for years and not produced any decision.[125] It is still interesting to note that the Commission's reasoned proposal for a Council decision "on the determination of a clear risk of a serious breach by the Republic of Poland of the rule of law" is entirely focussed on the rule of law value,[126] whereas the EP's reasoned proposal concerning Hungary is much broader.[127] The EP has also voiced several concerns pertaining to the value of democracy, such as "the functioning of the constitutional and electoral system", "freedom of expression" and "freedom of association". This pending procedure raised the question whether Hungary could be entrusted with the Council Presidency

[119] Both Article 7 (1) and (2) TEU give a right of proposal also to one third of the Member States, but the decision-making is monopolised by the political organs of the EU.

[120] Bouzoraa (2023), p. 835 f.

[121] See in this sense Theuns (2024), p. 65 ff.

[122] No initiative was ever taken on the basis of Article 7 (2) TEU (the repressive sanctions procedure).

[123] COM(2017) 835 final of 20 December 2020. Available via https://eur-lex.europa.eu/legal-content/EN/TXT/PDF/?uri=CELEX:52017PC0835 (22 January 2025).

[124] P8 TA(2018) 0340 of 12 September 2018. Available via https://www.europarl.europa.eu/doceo/document/TA-8-2018-0340_EN.html (15 November 2024).

[125] For an account, see Theuns (2024), p. 35 ff.

[126] COM(2017) 835 final of 20 December 2017. Available via https://eur-lex.europa.eu/legal-content/EN/TXT/PDF/?uri=CELEX:52017PC0835 (22 January 2025).

[127] European Parliament resolution of 12 September 2018 on a proposal calling on the Council to determine, pursuant to Article 7(1) of the Treaty on European Union, the existence of a clear risk of a serious breach by Hungary of the values on which the Union is founded. Available via https://www.europarl.europa.eu/doceo/document/TA-8-2018-0340_EN.html (22 January 2025).

on 1 July 2024.[128] In fact, Hungary held the presidency until 31 December 2024. The Art. 7 (1) procedure against Poland has meanwhile been closed, in view of the sincere efforts of the new Tusk government since December 2023 to reverse the encroachments on the judiciary by the previous government and restore the rule of law.[129]

There have also been suggestions that Member State representatives whose democratic credentials are dubious could be excluded from the Council and the European Council because they do not fulfil the requirements of Art. 10 (2) subpara. 2 TEU.[130] It is, however, more than questionable whether that provision is sufficiently concrete to be applied directly by EU institutions, all the more since this would have a similar effect as the suspension of voting rights under Art. 7 (2), (3) TEU which is permitted only in the Council and only by virtue of a unanimous European Council decision after obtaining the consent of the European Parliament.[131]

Art. 269 TFEU strictly limits the role of the ECJ in the Art. 7 TEU procedure: It can only be seised by the Member State concerned by a determination of the European Council or the Council that there is a clear risk of a serious breach or that there already is a serious and persistent breach of the values of Art. 2 TEU, and in respect solely of the procedural stipulations. This means that the Art. 7 TEU procedure does not involve any judicially enforceable individual rights.

5.4.2.2 Infringement Procedure (Art. 258 TFEU) and Reference Procedure (Art. 267 TFEU)

The ECJ has made it clear that the political procedure pursuant to Art. 7 TEU does not constitute the only avenue for enforcing the values of Art. 2 TEU.[132] It is yet uncertain, however, to what extent the infringement procedure under Art. 258 TFEU allows judicial enforcement of EU law parameters for Member State democracy. Undoubtedly, it empowers the Commission to pursue violations by Member States of specific democratic fundamental rights, such as the right to vote and the freedom of expression and association.[133] But the question is whether the value of democracy in Art. 2 TEU as such can be enforced. While the ECJ has confirmed that the rule of law parameters of Art. 2 TEU can be enforced under Art. 258 TFEU, in view of their

[128] Safradin et al. (2023), Bárd (2023), Kaźmierska (2024). See Article 16 (9) TEU and Council Decision (EU) 2016/1316 of 26 July 2016 (OJ L 208 of 2 August 2016 p. 42), on the exercise of the Presidency of the Council.

[129] European Commission, Press Release P/24/2461 of 6 May 2024. Available via https://ec.europa.eu/commission/presscorner/detail/en/ip_24_2461 (22 January 2025).

[130] Cotter (2020); id. (2022).

[131] Bradley (2020), Bouzoraa (2023), p. 826 ff.

[132] ECJ, judgment of 16 February 2022 (C-156/21), ECLI:EU:C:2021:97, para. 159; judgment of 16 February 2022 (C-157/21), ECLI:EU:C:2021:98, para. 195.

[133] On the protection of these rights by EU law *vis-à-vis* Member States, taking into account Article 51 (1) CFR, see below Sect. 5.4.3.4.

concretisation in Art. 19 (1) (2) TEU,[134] it is uncertain if Art. 10 (2) subpara. 2 TEU qualifies as an equivalent concretisation regarding democracy parameters.[135] Recently, in cases concerning the right of EU foreign nationals to become members of political parties in their Member State of residence pursuant to Art. 22 TFEU, the ECJ at least indicated that this may be the case.[136]

Whether and to what extent violations of Art. 2 TEU standing alone can be invoked in the infringement procedure is currently being tested by the Commission: In a case against Hungary, which is pending before the ECJ, the Commission claims that the human rights and equality aspects of Art. 2 TEU were violated by a Hungarian law directed against homosexual and transgender persons.[137] In the hearing before the full Court, in which the Commission was supported by the European Parliament and sixteen Member States, the most important issue was the justiciability of Art. 2 TEU as a self-standing provision, given the indeterminacy of the values enshrined therein.[138] In her opinion of 5 June 2025, the Advocate has meanwhile affirmed that the ECJ can find a violation of Art. 2 TEU as such in a case that is within the scope of EU law and where other provisions of primary and secondary Union law have also been violated.[139] In a more recent case against Poland, which still is in the preliminary procedure stage, the Commission claims that the democracy aspect of Art. 2 and Art. 10 TEU was violated by the Polish so-called "Lex Tusk" because of its undue interference with the national elections.[140]

On 7 February 2024, the Commission initiated a further infringement procedure against Hungary regarding its "Defence of Sovereignty Act" of 2023 that aims at preventing the use of foreign funding by candidates, political parties and associations in the context of elections.[141] The Commission claims that the Act violates the principle of democracy as well as several democratic fundamental rights, among

---

[134] See, *e.g.*, judgment of 15 July 2021 (C-791/19), ECLI:EU:C:2021:596; judgment of 5 June 2023 (C-204/21), ECLI:EU:C:2023:442. The ECJ has also issued several pertinent preliminary rulings pursuant to Article 267 TFEU—see, *e.g.*, judgment of 13 July 2023 (Joined Cases C-615/20 and C-671/20), ECLI:EU:C:2023:562.

[135] See Schuler (2023b), National Elections.

[136] ECJ, judgment of 19 November 2024 (C-808/21), ECLI:EU:C:2024:962, paras. 114 ff.; judgment of 19 November 2024 (C-814/21), ECLI:EU:C:2024:963, paras. 112 ff. See Schuler (2024a), Enforcement of Democracy.

[137] Case C-769/22. Okunrobo (2023); Bonelli and Claes (2023), p. 3 ff. The Hungarian law is also clearly incompatible with the ECHR—see ECtHR (GC), judgment of 23 January 2023, Macatė v. Lithuania (Appl. No. 61435/19).

[138] See Kaiser et al. (2024), Riedl (2024), de Cecco (2024).

[139] ECLI:EU:C:2025:408.

[140] European Commission, Press Release IP/23/3134 of 8 June 2023. Schuler (2023a), Taking democracy seriously; Vissers (2023); Feisel (2023). See also Sadurski (2023). On 26 July 2023, the Venice Commission issued a critical urgent opinion on that law, recommending its repeal (CDL-PI(2023)021). Available via https://www.venice.coe.int/webforms/documents/default.aspx?pdffile=CDL-PI(2023)021-e (22 January 2025).

[141] See above Sect. 4.2.1.1.2 on the pertinent opinion by the Venice Commission.

others.[142] In an earlier infringement procedure against Hungary concerning obligations of registration, declaration and publication by civil society organisations directly or indirectly receiving support from abroad the Commission had limited its claims to violations of Art. 63 TFEU read together with Art. 7, 8 and 12 CFR, only the latter guaranteeing the democratic freedom of association.[143] The EU is thus obviously beginning to counteract democratic backsliding in Member States more determinedly, as it has already taken resolute action against rule-of-law backsliding.[144]

In the legal literature it is suggested that the ECJ and other EU and national actors should make more determined use of Art. 2 TEU in combination with the primacy of EU law in order to stop and reverse democratic backsliding in Member States.[145] But such application of the indeterminate Art. 2 TEU by the ECJ in a "top down" manner has also been criticised as an over-constitutionalisation that excessively limits the political margins of democratically legitimated Member State parliaments.[146] This criticism of undemocratic judicial interference ignores the fact that the ECJ has only enforced most elementary common rule of law standards which definitely limit Member States' political discretion, not least because they correspond to the standards enshrined in Art. 6 (1) ECHR, as the ECtHR has made clear.[147] On this background, it is unlikely that the ECJ would not respect Art. 4 (2) TEU, if it were requested in the future to enforce the elementary common democratic standards of Art. 2 TEU. While judicial enforcement of the Art. 2 TEU values creates the risks of a "tyranny of values" incompatible with the rule of law, judicial overreach culminating in a non-democratic *gouvernement des juges* and, in the supranational context of the EU, a disruption of the (quasi-) federal balance, these risks are manageable.[148] As the ECtHR has underlined, "democracy cannot be reduced to the will of the majority of the electorate and elected representatives, in disregard of the requirements of the rule of law. … The remit of domestic courts and the Court is … complementary to … democratic processes. The task of the judiciary is to ensure the necessary oversight of compliance with legal requirements."[149] On

[142] See the Commission's press corner on "February infringement package: key decisions" of 7 February 2024 under "4. Justice". Available via https://ec.europa.eu/commission/presscorner/detail/EN/inf_24_301 (22 January 2025). Schuler (2024a), Regime Defence. The case is meanwhile pending before the ECJ under file number C-829/24.

[143] ECJ, judgment of 18 June 2020 (C-78/18), ECLI:EU:C:2020:476.

[144] Giegerich (2021b), The Rule of Law in the European Union, p. 9 ff.; Blanke and Sander (2023), p. 239 ff.

[145] Von Bogdandy and Spieker (2022).

[146] Schorkopf (2020), p. 477 ff.; Nettesheim (2024), p. 269 ff. But see Assenbrunner (2023), p. 609 ff.

[147] ECtHR, judgment of 7 May 2021, Xero Flor w Polsce sp. z o.o v. Poland (Appl. No. 4907/18); judgment of 3 February 2022, Advance Pharma sp. z o.o (Appl. No. 1469/20); (GC) judgment of 15 March 2022, Grzęda v. Poland (Appl. No. 43572/18); judgment of 6 July.2023, Tuleya v. Poland (Appl. Nos. 21181/19, 51751/20).

[148] Spieker (2023), p. 243 ff.

[149] ECtHR (GC), judgment of 9 April 2024, Verein KlimaSeniorinnen Schweiz and Others v. Switzerland (Appl. No. 53600/20), para. 412.

the other hand, if the judiciary gets involved in political disputes of this kind, it risks being politicised, its decisions being delegitimised and ultimately disregarded which suggests judicial restraint.[150]

The infringement procedure does have teeth: If the ECJ finds that the defendant Member State failed to fulfil an obligation under the Treaties, that State is required to take the necessary measures to comply with the Court's judgment (Art. 260 (1) TFEU). If it fails to do so, the Commission can refer the matter back to the ECJ for imposing a lump sum or a penalty payment on it (Art. 260 (2) TFEU). Any lump sum or penalty payment imposed on a Member State can be offset by the Commission against that State's claims for payments from the EU's budget.[151]

However, the infringement procedure does not involve any individual rights. According to the ECJ's settled case law, the Commission's decision whether or not to institute an infringement procedure against a Member State is discretionary and the exercise of that discretion is not reviewed by the Court.[152] The Commission exercises its discretion only in the public interest in the adequate enforcement of EU law obligations, not in anyone's individual interest. Therefore, any attempt by natural or legal persons to compel the Commission to institute such a procedure by an action for annulment pursuant to Art. 263 TFEU or an action for failure to act pursuant to Art. 265 TFEU is doomed to fail: such actions are inadmissible because Commission decisions made in the context of an infringement procedure are not of direct and individual concern to any natural or legal person in the sense of Art. 263 (4) TFEU and in the course of the infringement procedure, the Commission does not adopt any act of which they are the potential addressees in the sense of Art. 265 (3) TFEU.[153] For this reason, the action against the Commission in the aforementioned Georgescu case[154] was dismissed as manifestly inadmissible.[155]

Where instances of democratic backsliding involve interferences in democratic individual rights guaranteed by EU law, victims are entitled to remedies in national courts sufficient to ensure effective legal protection.[156] Pursuant to Art. 267 TFEU, all national courts may then request preliminary rulings from the ECJ regarding the interpretation of the democratic guarantees of EU law, and last-instance national courts are required to do so. Accordingly, the judiciaries of the Member States and the EU cooperate in order to protect the democratic rights enshrined in Union law.

---

[150] See Blauberger and Kelemen (2017).

[151] Pohjankoski (2021), p. 1341 ff.; id. (2023). GC, judgment of 29 May 2024 (Joined Cases T-200/22 and T-314/22), ECLI:EU:T:2024:329; judgment of 5 February 2025 (Joined Cases T-830/22 and T-156/23), ECLI:EUT:2025:131: Poland's actions were dismissed.

[152] ECJ, judgment of 6 December 1989 (C-329/88), ECR 1989, 4159, headnote 2; judgment of 1 June 1994 (C-317/92), ECR 1994, I-2039, para. 4; judgment of 10 May 1995 (C-422/92), ECR 1995, I-1097, para. 18.

[153] ECJ, judgment of 14 February 1989 (247/87), ECR 1989, 291, paras. 9 ff.; GC, order of 29 November 1994 (T-479/93 and T-559/93), ECR 1994, II-1115, para. 31; GC, order of 3 March 2025 (T-67/25), ECLI:EU:T:2025:200. See Pechstein, in: Pechstein et al. (2023c), vol. IV, Artikel 258 AEUV, para. 9.

[154] See above Sect. 4.2.1.2.1.4.2.

[155] GC, order of 3 March 2025 (T-67/25), ECLI:EU:T:2025:200.

[156] Art. 19 (1) subpara. 2 TEU.

On the other hand, as again the Georgescu case demonstrates, natural or legal persons cannot bring a direct action before the GC against national authorities to ward off possible encroachments on democratic rights guaranteed by EU law.[157] The GC dismissed Georgescu's action against Romania "on the ground of manifest lack of jurisdiction".[158] This left the plaintiff without any protection by the ECJ because the encroachment was made by the Romanian Constitutional Court, with no judicial remedies available under national law and no reference pursuant to Art. 267 TFEU.

5.4.2.3 Financial Sanctions

It is not yet clear, if and to what extent democratic backsliding, like rule of law backsliding, can trigger financial sanctions by the EU.[159] The Regulation 2020/2092 on a general regime of conditionality for the protection of the Union budget[160] focusses on the protection of that budget against breaches of the principles of the rule of law in the Member States.[161] The reason for the Regulation's narrow focus on the protection of the Union budget necessarily follows from the use of Art. 322 (1) lit. a TFEU as the basis for its enactment. But its narrow focus on breaches of the principles of the rule of law is not so clearly prescribed.

Accordingly, the definition of "the rule of law" in Art. 2 (a) of the Regulation includes "the principles of legality implying a transparent, accountable, democratic and pluralistic law-making process" as well as the separation of powers, adding that "[t]he rule of law shall be understood having regard to the other Union values and principles enshrined in Article 2 TEU". It may therefore be possible to sanction also breaches of the principle of democracy, but only if they "affect or seriously risk affecting the sound financial management of the Union budget or the protection of the financial interests of the Union in a sufficiently direct way."[162] But this will be difficult and has so far not been tried.

In any event, Art. 4 (1) of the Regulation states that "[a]ppropriate measures shall be taken where it is established ... that breaches of the principles of the rule of law in a Member State affect or seriously risk affecting the sound financial management of the Union budget or the protection of the financial interests of the Union in a sufficiently direct way." This indicates a legal obligation to act, but the indeterminate legal terms used include so much interpretative margin that it will be hard to find a case in which the political organs of the EU cannot avoid imposing sanctions.

There is another possibility to impose financial sanctions on Member States for failure to respect fundamental rights and comply with the CFR ("Charter

[157] Georgescu's general right to national democracy (see below Sect. 5.4.3) could have been violated.

[158] GC, order of 3 March 2025 (T-67/25), ECLI:EU:T:2025:200.

[159] For a general overview, see Fisicaro (2022), p. 697 ff.

[160] OJ L 433 I of 22 December 2020, p. 1. See Baquero Cruz and Keppenne (2022), p. 54 ff.

[161] See Article 1 of the Regulation.

[162] Article 6 (1) of the Regulation.

conditionality") which is provided by the new Common Provisions Regulation.[163] This could be used to counter democratic backsliding, provided that specific democratic fundamental rights are violated in connection with the implementation of one of the EU Funds, which is not inconceivable.

It is, however, quite clear that the imposition of financial sanctions on whatever basis is within the discretion of the EU organs. Since there are no respective individual rights, natural and legal persons cannot bring actions for annulment under Art. 263 (4) TFEU or actions for failure to act under Art. 265 TFEU.[164]

5.4.2.4 Exclusion of Undemocratic Member State from EU?

The most severe sanction against a Member State having turned undemocratic would of course be its exclusion from the EU. While the Treaties provide for the possibility of voluntary withdrawal in Art. 50 TEU, there is no basis for excluding an unwilling Member State. Two arguments speak against this option: Firstly, the ultimate sanction provided in the context of Art. 7 TEU is the temporary suspension of certain membership rights of a Member State that is seriously and persistently breaching the values referred to in Art. 2 TEU. Secondly, when the political sanctions procedure pursuant to Art. 7 TEU was introduced by the Treaty of Amsterdam (1997), the Statute of the CoE had long contained a provision permitting the exclusion of a Member State for seriously violating the fundamental values of the organisation in its Art. 8.[165] But that readily available model was not adopted by the EU. This suggests *a contrario* that the Treaties do not permit the suspension of the entire membership let alone the expulsion of a Member State having turned undemocratic.

Some authors have argued that in such a case the other Member States could fall back on devices provided by public international law for a material breach of a treaty or a fundamental change of circumstances, which permit the suspension or termination of the treaty relationship with the defaulting State.[166] But this is hard to square with the existence of special rules in the Treaties and the autonomy of Union law *vis-à-vis* international law which the ECJ has emphasised.[167]

---

[163] Articles 9 (1), 15 (1) and Annex III of the Regulation (EU) 2021/1060 of 24 June 2021 laying down common provisions on the European Regional Development Fund, the European Social Fund Plus, the Cohesion Fund, the Just Transition Fund and the European Maritime, Fisheries and Aquaculture Fund and financial rules for those and for the Asylum, Migration and Integration Fund, the Internal Security Fund and the Instrument for Financial Support for Border Management and Visa Policy (OJ L 231 of 30. June 2021 p. 159); consolidated version including later amendments at https://eur-lex.europa.eu/legal-content/EN/TXT/PDF/?uri=CELEX:02021R1060-20240301&qid=1717601024816 (22 January 2025).

[164] General Court, order of 4 June 2024 (Joined Cases T-530/22 to T-533/22), ECLI:EU:T:2024:363, appeal pending before the ECJ under C-555/24 P; order of 14 November 2024 (T-116/23), ECLI:EU:T:2024:832, appeal pending before the ECJ under C-50/25 P. See also GC, order of 3 February 2025 (T-1126/23), ECLI:EU:T:2025:138; Lobina and Maharaj (2025).

[165] See above Sect. 4.2.1.1.1.

[166] See Articles 60, 62 of the Vienna Convention on the Law of Treaties of 23 May 1969 (UNTS vol. 1155, p. 331) which are declaratory of customary international law.

[167] See Nowak, in: Pechstein et al. (2023a), vol. I, Artikel 7 EUV, para. 26 (with further references); Franzius (2025), p. 726 ff.

Ultimately, however, there is no doubt that, if a Member State, having degenerated into an autocracy, also persistently undermines the effective functioning of the EU by casting vetoes etc., the Treaties would permit its expulsion in order to save the European integration project from an existential threat. How to realise that possibility of self-defence in accordance with the rule of law principle is a question of legal technique.[168] The Treaties are not a "suicide pact".[169] I have suggested to use an unwritten general principle of EU law in the sense of the *clausula rebus sic stantibus*.[170] Undoubtedly, however, no individual rights would be involved in that legal technique at the level of high politics.

5.4.2.5 Conclusion: No Procedural Right to Enforcement of Democratic Standards

While there are relatively effective judicial and financial mechanisms to enforce EU law parameters for Member State democracy, none of these is connected with individual rights. Natural and legal persons therefore have no role in these mechanisms. In other words, there is no individual procedural right against EU organs to have democracy parameters enforced *vis-à-vis* Member States.

5.4.3 Substantive EU Law Right to National Democracy

5.4.3.1 Art. 10 (3) Sentence 1 TEU: Right to "Democratic Life" Also in the Member States

The Treaties do not contain any explicit substantive right to national democracy. But Art. 10 (3) sentence 1 TEU guarantees every citizen of the Union "the right to participate in the democratic life of the Union." This can be interpreted as implicitly including a right to the existence of such a "democratic life", beyond the explicitly enshrined participatory right, because democratic participation makes no sense without democracy. Since the right to participate in a democracy necessarily presupposes the existence of a democracy, it also implicates an entitlement to such an existence; otherwise it would be illusory.

This begs the question whether "democratic life of the Union", whose existence is thus guaranteed by Art. 10 (3) sentence 1 TEU, exclusively focusses on the EU level or also includes the national level, both levels being intertwined regarding democracy. A systematic perspective reveals the following: While Art. 10 (4) TEU expressly mentions only the European level of the Union, Art. 10 (2) TEU also regulates the

[168] For a political science perspective, see Theuns (2024), p. 191 ff.

[169] See Kennedy v. Mendoza-Martinez, 372 U.S. 144, 160 (1963): "the Constitution ... is not a suicide pact."

[170] Giegerich (2019), p. 85 ff.

national democratic accountability of the Heads of State or Government and the governments of the Member States, in addition to the parliamentary democracy at EU level. And in Art. 10 (1) TEU, which identifies representative democracy as the foundation of the Union's functioning, the term Union obviously addresses both the European and the Member State levels. The systematic interpretation thus leads to the conclusion that Art. 10 (3) sentence 1 TEU regulates both levels of the Union, the European and the Member State level. It entitles every citizen of the Union to the existence of a parliamentary-democratic system at the level of both the EU and the Member State of their own nationality,[171] where they enjoy comprehensive rights of political participation.[172] This entitlement is judicially enforceable in the national courts of the respective Member State,[173] under the conditions set out in the next section. It constitutes a general right to democracy that complements and invigorates specific democratic individual rights which are guaranteed separately.[174] Contrary to sentence 1, sentence 2 of Art. 10 (3) TEU does not extend to Member States, so that they are not required by Union law to decentralise or even federalise.[175]

In this context, it is worth mentioning the Commission Recommendation (EU) 2023/2836 of 12 December 2023 on promoting the engagement and effective participation of citizens and civil society organisations in public policy-making processes,[176] which is part of the "Defence of Democracy" package.[177] The recommendation expressly aims at ensuring such participation "at the local, regional, national, European and international level",[178] in order "to help building democratic resilience within the Union."[179]

5.4.3.2 Direct Effect of Art. 2 and Art. 10 (2) Subpara. 2 TEU

Another question is whether one can derive a substantive right of citizens of the Union to democracy in the Member States also from the objective values and standards of Art. 2, 10 (2) subpara. 2 TEU, if read in the light of Art. 10 (3) sentence 1

[171] See Art. 10 (2) subpara. 2, 12 TEU presupposing the existence of national parliaments that meet elementary democratic standards.

[172] See Article 10 (2) subpara. 2 *in fine* TEU. The partial participatory rights of EU foreign nationals in the Member State of their residence guaranteed in Article 22 (1) TFEU are an exception which cannot be the basis for recognising them as having a general right to democracy in that Member State.

[173] See in this sense also Schuler (2024b), Paving the way.

[174] On these specific rights, see below Sects. 5.4.3.3 (voting rights) and 5.4.3.4. (supplementary democratic rights).

[175] See further below Sects. 5.5.8.2.

[176] OJ L, 20.12.2023.

[177] See below Sect. 5.3.6.

[178] Recital 5 of the preamble (citing pertinent UN, CoE, OECD and OSCE guidelines and recommendations).

[179] Operative para. 1.

TEU. That would enable individual citizens to enforce the democracy parameters of EU law against their Member States in the national courts. According to the case law of the ECJ, dating back to the seminal *van Gend & Loos* judgment of 1963, rights of individuals "arise not only where they are expressly granted by the Treaty, but also by reason of obligations which the Treaty imposes in a clearly defined way upon individuals as well as upon the Member States and upon the institutions of the Community."[180] In a more recent formulation, the ECJ enquires whether a primary law provision "is sufficient in itself to confer on individuals a right which they may rely on as such in disputes between them in a field covered by EU law ... and does not need to be made more specific by provisions of EU or national law to confer on individuals a right which they may rely on as such".[181] The Court has lately extended the concept of directly effective provisions in primary and secondary law considerably, not least by reading together several provisions that are not directly effective, if taken separately, but that mutually amplify each other and together become judicially enforceable.[182] Based on the *van Gend & Loos* jurisprudence, "'the vigilance of the individuals concerned to protect their rights' has been a central instrument in assuring that the Member States observe EU law."[183] This instrument could also be used to enforce the requirements regarding national democracy.[184]

But do the democracy parameters of Art. 2, 10 (2) subpara. 2 TEU impose "clearly defined" obligations on Member States so that they can have direct effect or, in other words, confer rights on individual citizens that could be invoked in national courts?[185] In answering this question one cannot disregard that those parameters leave Member States a considerable margin in designing their democratic political structure. Democracy indeed works quite differently in the Member States—it may be federal or unitary, presidential or parliamentary and more or less direct. This margin is necessary in view of Art. 4 (2) TEU which requires the Union to respect Member States' "national identities, inherent in their fundamental structures, political and constitutional"; it ultimately preserves the right of self-determination of each of the Member States' peoples. On the other hand, Art. 4 (2) TEU does not give the Member States, including their judiciaries, *carte blanche* to disregard the primacy of EU law rules in favour of national constitutional principles. Rather, it is for the ECJ definitely to settle conflicts between EU law rules, including those setting democratic standards for the Member States, and core national

---

[180] Judgment of 5 February 1963 (Case 26/62), ECR 1963, p. 1, 12. See Court of Justice of the European Union (2013). Available via https://op.europa.eu/de/publication-detail/-/publication/de3db697-1f5c-4f83-8424-1663b43ac2d3 (22 January 2025). See below Sect. 5.5.6.1.

[181] Judgment of 17 April 2018 (Case C-414/16), ECLI:EU:C:2018:257, paras. 76, 78. For an overview of the case law, see Lenaerts et al. (2021), paras. 23.031 ff.

[182] Spieker (2021), p. 244 ff.; Kokott (2023), p. 496 ff.

[183] Spieker (2023), p. 201.

[184] Id., p. 197 ff.

[185] Bouzoraa (2023), p. 842 ff.

constitutional principles covered by Art. 4 (2) TEU.[186] As the ECJ has also made clear, it cannot be maintained that "the requirements arising, as conditions for both accession to and participation in the European Union, from respect for values and principles … enshrined in Article 2 …, are capable of affecting the national identity of a Member State, within the meaning of Article 4(2) TEU."[187] This is because Art. 2 TEU defines the constitutional identity of the EU that sets limits to the Member States' margin in designing their governmental systems. One has to remember in this context that "Article 4(2) TEU must be read in the light of provisions of the same rank, in particular Articles 2 and 10 TEU …".[188]

The ECJ has also been reluctant to grant Member States more than "a certain degree of discretion" in implementing the principles of Art. 2 TEU.[189] It emphasised in regard to the rule of law principle that the obligation as to the result to be achieved may not vary from one Member State to another. Rather, Art. 2 TEU expressly states that its values are common to the Member States and thus part of their own constitutional traditions and need to be respected at all times.[190] It is therefore necessary to identify the common democratic standards of Union law enshrined in Art. 2, 10 (2) subpara. 2 TEU which definitely limit Member States' discretion in designing their governmental structure, in full accordance with Art. 4 (2) TEU. Examples would be the prohibition of election fraud, manifestly unfair elections[191] and arbitrary interferences with the creation or functioning of political parties which "fulfil an essential function in the system of representative democracy, on which the functioning of the Union is founded, in accordance with Article 10 (1) TEU."[192] One can also add manifest violations of democratic principles regarding the composition, internal processes and constitutional position of national parliaments which, pursuant to Art. 12 TEU, play a subsidiary, but important role in the functioning of the EU's representative democracy, beyond their legitimising function under Art. 10

---

186 ECJ, judgment of 22 February 2022 (C-430/21), ECLI:EU:C:2022:99, paras. 68 ff.; judgment of 7 September 2022 (C-391/20), ECLI:EU:C:2022:638, paras. 83 ff. But see the German FCC's assertion of jurisdiction on whether EU acts are compatible with the core principles of the German Basic Law (so-called "identity review"—FCC, judgment of 30 June 2009 [2 BvE 2/08 et al.])—Treaty of Lisbon, paras. 234 ff. and headnote 5, English translation available via https://www.bundesverfassungsgericht.de/SharedDocs/Entscheidungen/EN/2009/06/es20090630_2bve000208en.html (22 January 2025); most recent affirmation by FCC, order of 6 February 2024 (2 BvE 6/23 et al.), paras. 90 ff. Available via https://www.bverfg.de/e/es20240206_2bve000623.html (22 January 2022) and the critique by Giegerich (2013), p. 49 ff.

187 ECJ, judgment of 5 June 2023 (C-204/21), ECLI:EU:C:2023:442, para. 72.

188 ECJ, judgment of 19 November 2024 (C-808/21), ECLI:EU:C:2024:962, para. 158; judgment of 19 November 2024 (C-814/21), ECLI:EU:C:2024:963, para. 155.

189 ECJ (Full Court), judgment of 16 February 2022 (C-156/21), ECLI:EU:C:2022:97, paras. 232 ff.; judgment of 16 February 2022 (C-157/1), ECLI:EU:C:2022:98, paras. 264 ff.

190 See Erlbacher and Herrmann (2022), p. 35.

191 Verellen (2022).

192 See Erlbacher and Herrmann (2022), p. 38. The quote is from ECJ, judgment of 19 November 2024 (C-808/21), ECLI:EU:C:2024:962, para. 121; judgment of 19 November 2024 (C-814/21), ECLI:EU:C:2024:963, para. 119.

(2) subpara. 2 TEU.[193] These elementary standards for Member States' democracies are directly effective and judicially enforceable. In this context, the non-retrogression rule can also be useful in the sense that individuals should be enabled to challenge any major reduction in Member State democratic standards in a court which should subject such reduction to strict scrutiny: While not completely excluded, retrogressions are suspect and therefore require particularly strong justification.[194]

Thus narrowing down of the right to national democracy in EU law also takes the sting out of the objection that making the rather indeterminate Art. 2, 10 (2) subpara. 2 TEU judicially enforceable would extend the influence of EU law (and the powers of ECJ) far beyond its ordinary scope into national sovereignty reserves protected by Art. 4 (2) TEU.[195] While the principle of democracy as such is opposed to giving supranational law and courts too much influence in the national political arena,[196] this does not exclude their use as ultimate guardrails and guardians against manifest democratic retrogressions in Member States that jeopardise the democratic character of the entire multilevel EU system. Art. 267 TFEU ensures that the ECJ will have the last word regarding the determination of the elementary Union law standards for national democracy which guarantees that they are equal throughout the EU, as required by Art. 4 (2) sentence 1 TEU. As the Court has confirmed, the EU can respect the equality of Member States before the Treaties "only if the Member States are unable, under the principle of the primacy of EU law, to rely on, as against the EU legal order, a unilateral measure, whatever its nature."[197] It will be for the ECJ to concretise the concept of "manifest democratic retrogressions" at Member State level, as it has concretised the rule of law requirements regarding the independence of national courts.[198]

This raises the question who can seek enforcement of those elementary parameters of EU law for Member State democracy in the national courts. In accordance with Art. 47 CFR, the immediate victims of Member State interferences in their democratic fundamental rights guaranteed by EU law, such as the right to vote or stand as a candidate or the right to establish and run a political party,[199] have a right to a judicial remedy as a matter of course, provided that the interfering Member

---

[193] See in particular Art. 12 lit. d TEU that requires the national parliaments' participation in the Treaty revision process under Art. 48 TEU. National parliaments that are not sufficiently democratic in their composition or operation would be unable to convey democratic legitimacy on Treaty revisions which are not subject to the consent of the European Parliament.

[194] See above Sect. 4.2.1.2.1.1. But see Erlbacher and Herrmann (2022), p. 35 f.; Assenbrunner (2023), p. 616.

[195] See Erlbacher and Herrmann (2022), p. 38.

[196] See Weiler (2013), p. 11 ff.; Möllers (2025), p. 842.

[197] ECJ, judgment of 21 December 2021 (Joined Cases C-357/19, C-379/19, C-547/19, C-811/19 and C-840/19), ECLI:EU:C:2021:1034, para. 249.

[198] See, *e.g.*, ECJ, judgment of 15 July 2021 (C-791/19), ECLI:EU:C:2021:596; judgment of 5 June 2023 (C-204/21), ECLI:EU:C:2023:442; judgment of 13 July 2023 (Joined Cases C-615/20 and C-671/20), ECLI:EU:C:2023:562.

[199] On these rights, see below Sects. 5.4.3.3 and 5.4.3.4.

States are implementing Union law (Art. 51 (1) CFR), *i.e.*, that the interferences come within the scope of EU law.[200] But can other citizens of the Union who are not such immediate victims also challenge democratic retrogressions in the national courts of their Member State, all the more since such retrogressions may not always produce immediate victims? This possibility certainly promotes the effectiveness of the democratic parameters. While at first glance it would look like an *actio popularis*, this does not hold true because Art. 10 (3) sentence 1 TEU entitles every citizen of the Union to a democratic system in the Member State of their own nationality.[201] Since the number of individual rights holders is large, so is the number of potential plaintiffs—which further enhances the effectiveness of the judicial remedies against democratic retrogression.

All in all, there is a general right to national democracy in current primary Union law in a limited sense only, namely a right of each Union citizen to challenge manifest retrogressions in national democratic standards in the courts of their respective Member States, even absent concrete interferences with their individual democratic rights. While covering only very elementary standards of national democracy, the right may be useful at a time of democratic backsliding, if taken together with the rule against retrogression.

5.4.3.3 Voting Rights at National Level Guaranteed by EU Law

5.4.3.3.1 EU Law Expressly Only Regulates Municipal Elections

Primary law guarantees certain individual voting rights at national level in Art. 20 (2) lit. b, 2nd variant, Art. 22 (1) TFEU and Art. 40 CFR, namely the right of EU foreign nationals (mobile Union citizens[202]) to vote and stand as a candidate in municipal elections in the Member State where they reside, subject to detailed arrangements for the exercise of those rights enacted by the Council.[203] As the ECJ recently made clear, the Council "cannot, even implicitly, limit the scope of the

[200] ECJ, judgment of 26 February 2013 (C-617/10), ECLI:EU:C:2013:105, paras. 17 ff. For an overview, see Lenaerts et al. (2021), para. 25.009. See also Bruti Liberati et al. (2022), p. 80. See below Sect. 5.4.3.4.

[201] See above Sect. 5.4.3.1.

[202] Term used by the Advocate General in his Opinions of 11 January 2024 in cases C-808/21, ECLI:EU:C:2024:12, and C-814/21, ECLI:EU:C:2024:15.

[203] See Council Directive 94/80/EC of 19 December 1994 laying down detailed arrangements for the exercise of the right to vote and to stand as a candidate in municipal elections by citizens of the Union residing in a Member State of which they are not nationals (as amended—available via https://eur-lex.europa.eu/legal-content/EN/TXT/?uri=CELEX%3A01994L0080-20130701&qid=1732006774487 [22 January 2025]). In November 2021, the Commission submitted a proposal to recast the Directive (see Report from the Commission under Article 25 TFEU—COM(2023) 931 final of 6.12.2023, p. 27 f. Available via https://eur-lex.europa.eu/resource.html?uri=cellar:b69763bf-94da-11ee-b164-01aa75ed71a1.0001.02/DOC_1&format=PDF (22 January 2025).

rights and obligations arising under Article 22 TFEU."[204] Rejecting a Member State claim to the contrary, the Court also underlined that "[t]he right to vote and to stand as a candidate ... is ... conferred by citizenship of the Union and ... it cannot, therefore, be construed as an exception to a purported rule that only nationals of a Member State may participate in the political life of that State, which would require Article 22 TFEU to be interpreted restrictively. Such an interpretation would be at odds with the fact that citizenship of the Union is intended to constitute the fundamental status of those nationals."[205] It remains to be seen how much regulatory margin the ECJ allows the Union legislator regarding the detailed arrangements for the exercise of the active and passive voting rights pursuant to Art. 22 (1) and (2) TFEU.[206]

But those voting rights at national level, which are automatically lost with the loss of Union citizenship,[207] are limited in two regards: Firstly, they seemingly merely prohibit discrimination on grounds of nationality as compared with citizens of the Member State of residence, but do not guarantee the right to vote and stand as a candidate as such.[208] Secondly, they only extend to municipal elections and not higher-level national elections, and within these limits are intended "to promote the gradual integration of the EU citizens concerned in the society of the host Member State".[209] Member States, some of which had to overcome constitutional problems before they could accept voting rights of EU foreign nationals even at municipal level,[210] are reluctant to extend these rights to third-country nationals. Only six of them have ratified the CoE Convention on the Participation of Foreigners in Public Life at Local Level[211] which guarantees active and passive voting rights at local level to all long-term foreign residents in Art. 6 and 7, and two of these Member States have permissbly excluded the application of exactly these articles.

---

[204] ECJ, judgment of 19 November 2024 (C-808/21), ECLI:EU:C:2024:962, para. 103; judgment of 19 November 2024 (C-814/21), ECLI:EU:C:2024:963, para. 102.

[205] ECJ, judgment of 19 November 2024 (C-808/21), ECLI:EU:C:2024:962, para. 111.

[206] For a critique of the reluctance of German courts to make references to the ECJ in cases regarding restrictions of the passive right to vote, see Giegerich (2020c), Unionsbürgerschaft, paras. 95 ff.

[207] ECJ, judgment of 9 June 2022 (C-673/20), ECLI:EU:C:2022:449: Loss of voting rights of mobile UK citizens due to UK withdrawal from the EU.

[208] See below Sect. 5.5.7.1.

[209] ECJ, judgment of 19 November 2024 (C-808/21), ECLI:EU:C:2024:962, para. 125; judgment of 19 November 2024 (C-814/21), ECLI:EU:C:2024:963, para. 123.

[210] For the situation in Germany, see Schönberger (2005), p. 446 ff., and Giegerich (2020c), Unionsbürgerschaft, paras. 87 f.

[211] Of 5 February 1992 (ETS No. 144).

5.4.3.3.2 Art. 22 TFEU Also Guarantees Substantive Right to Vote and Stand as Candidate

While the second limitation to municipal elections seems to be clear from the wording of Art. 22 (1) TFEU,[212] the first limitation is not. Art. 22 TFEU can very well be understood in the sense that it guarantees to EU foreign citizens in their Member State of residence both the substantive right to vote and stand as a candidate in municipal and European Parliament elections and the right not to be discriminated in these regards (right to national treatment). The ECJ has recently confirmed that this is the correct reading. When defining the objective of Art. 22 TFEU, the Court stated the following: "that article seeks, first, to confer on EU citizens residing in a Member State of which they are not nationals the right to participate in the democratic electoral process of that Member State. … that right extends to participation in that process through the right of vote and to stand for election at European and local level. Secondly, that article seeks to ensure equal treatment between EU citizens …"[213] In accordance with Art. 52 (2) CFR, this broad interpretation of Art. 22 TFEU extends to Art. 40 CFR.[214]

Art. 22 TFEU does not explicitly cover the relationship between citizens of the Union and the Member States of their nationality, neither with regard to municipal elections nor with regard to European Parliament elections. Accordingly, Art. 39, 40 CFR do not readily apply to that relationship either. But as we shall see, the active and passive right to vote in elections to the European Parliament of Union citizen who reside in the Member State of their nationality is also protected.[215]

According to the ECJ case law pertaining to European Parliament elections that are also valid in regard of municipal elections, the principle of non-discrimination as a general principle of Union law—now codified in Art. 20 CFR—prohibits Member States from excluding some of their own citizens from participating in these elections unless the exclusion can be objectively justified.[216] Regarding municipal and European Parliament elections, the disenfranchisement of Union citizens in their home State because they established residence in another Member State, having exercised their free movement rights under the TFEU, is justified because this group of persons acquires the right to vote at municipal and European level in their State of residence.[217]

---

[212] But see below Sect. 5.4.3.3.3.

[213] ECJ, judgment of 19 November 2024 (C-808/21); ECLI:EU:C:2024:962, paras. 123 f.; judgment of 19 November 2024 (C-814/21), ECLI:EU:C:2024:963, paras. 121 f.

[214] On Article 39 CFR, see below Sect. 5.5.7.1.

[215] See below Sect. 5.5.7.1.

[216] ECJ, judgment of 12 September 2006 (C-300/04), ECLI:EU:C:2006:545, paras. 56 ff.

[217] For the problematic disenfranchisement of expatriates at the national parliamentary level, see below under Sect. 5.4.3.3.5.2. But see Poptcheva (2015), p. 17 f., who argues that with regard to elections to the European Parliament, EU citizens should be left the choice between exercising their right to vote in their Member State of nationality or residence.

5.4.3.3.3 EU Law Implicitly Guarantees Active and Passive Right to Vote in National Parliamentary Elections

The Treaties and the CFR do not expressly protect Union citizens' right to vote in national parliamentary elections, neither in their Member State of nationality nor in their Member State of residence, and certainly not if they do not hold the latter's nationality.[218] All Member States reserve electoral rights in respect of their national parliaments (as well as regional parliaments, if applicable) for their own citizens and consider this as an element of their national identity in the sense of Art. 4 (2) TEU.[219] Accordingly, in a referendum held in Luxembourg in 2015, more than 70% of the voters were against putting foreigners on an equal footing with nationals in terms of voting rights.[220] While host State exclusion of resident EU foreign nationals from active and passive participation in national parliamentary elections certainly amounts to a discriminatory interference with their free movement rights, that limitation is generally considered as justified.[221] Even with regard to municipal elections, Art. 22 (1) sentence 2, 2nd half sentence TFEU permits the Council to "provide for derogations where warranted by problems specific to a Member State." On this basis, Art. 12 of Directive 94/80/EC contains special provisions for Luxembourg and Belgium, which have a particularly high proportion of EU-foreigner residents.[222]

Member States are apparently reluctant to accept rights under Union law even regarding participation of their own citizens in national parliamentary elections, because that would enable the European Commission and the ECJ to intervene in their constitutional systems. By implication of Art. 20 (2) lit. b, Art. 22 (1) TFEU and Art. 39, 40 CFR, national parliamentary elections seem to be completely outside the scope of application of the Treaties.[223] This gap left by EU law is filled by the regional and global international standards embodied in Art. 3 Prot. No. 1 and Art. 25 lit. b ICCPR, whose enforcement is left to the ECtHR and the Human Rights Committee.

But a good argument can be made that those international standards, which also correspond to the Member States' common constitutional traditions, are incorporated into primary Union law by virtue of Art. 6 (3) TEU.[224] The main argument for their supranationalisation is that in accordance with Art. 10 TEU, national

[218] See Schönberger (2005), p. 443 ff.

[219] This applies in particular to Germany: Federal Constitutional Court, BVerfGE 83, 37 (50 ff.); Constitutional Court of the City of Bremen (BremStGH), NVwZ-RR 2014, 497 ff. See also the opinion of the Advocate General of 11 January 2024 (C-808/21), para. 127; id. in C-814/21, para. 127.

[220] Available via https://www.luxtimes.lu/luxembourg/luxembourg-rejects-foreigner-voting-rights/1234796.html (22 January 2025).

[221] See Shuibhne (2023), p. 200 f.

[222] Lenaerts et al. (2021), para. 6.021.

[223] But see below Sect. 5.4.3.3.5.

[224] This has been suggested by Sonnevend (2023), p. 575 f.

parliamentary elections are simply too important for the democratic legitimacy of the EU as a whole to remain completely unregulated by EU law. Thus, while leaving a broad regulatory margin to the Member States, as required by Art. 4 (2) TEU, the general principles of Union law pertaining to national parliamentary elections draw certain red lines whose observance is subject to the supervision by the European Commission and the ECJ. It remains to be seen, however, if the Court accepts this construction based on the Art. 6 (3) TEU, the general gap-filler regarding fundamental rights in primary EU law.

5.4.3.3.4 Supplementary Right of EU Foreign Nationals to Become Members of Political Parties

Another important question was recently decided by the ECJ in two infringement proceedings against the Czech Republic and Poland: Does the right of mobile EU foreign nationals to stand as a candidate in municipal elections and elections to the European Parliament in their Member State of residence without discrimination pursuant to Art. 22 TFEU, read in conjunction with Art. 20, 21 TFEU, Art. 10 TEU and Art. 12 CFR, also include the right to become members of a political party or political movement? The Court held that the denial of that right to Union citizens who are not nationals of their State of residence, in contrast to nationals of that State, violates Art. 22 TFEU. Since such membership is a key component in promoting candidates at elections, the effectiveness of the rule of non-discrimination on grounds of nationality enshrined in that provision requires its extension to party membership.[225]

Countering the invocation by the Czech Republic and Poland of Art. 4 (2) TEU to justify the exclusion of EU foreign nationals from political party membership, the ECJ stated the following: "By guaranteeing EU citizens residing in a Member State of which they are not nationals the right to vote and to stand as a candidate in municipal and European Parliament elections in that Member State, under the same conditions as nationals thereof, Article 22 TFEU gives concrete expression to the principles of democracy [Art. 2, 10 TEU] and … of equal treatment of EU citizens, principles which are an integral part of the identity and common values of the European Union, to which the Member States adhere and whose observance they must ensure in their territories. Consequently, allowing such EU citizens to become members of a political party or political movement in their Member State of residence so as to implement in full the principles of democracy and equal treatment cannot be regarded as undermining the national identity of that Member State."[226] The Court added, however, that Member States remained free to adopt "specific rules on decision-making within a political party or political movement regarding the nomination of candidates in national elections, rules which would preclude

[225] ECJ, judgment of 19 November 2024 (C-808/21), ECLI:EU:C:2024:962; judgment of 19 November 2024 (C-814/21), ECLI:EU:C:2024:963. Peers (2024).

[226] C-808/21, paras. 162 f. (and para. 158). C-814/21, paras. 159 f. (and para. 155).

members of the party or movement who are not nationals of that State from taking part in such decision-making."[227] Such difference in treatment would be justified because EU law does not convey the right to vote and to stand as a candidate in national elections to EU foreign citizens nor require Member States to grant such a right.[228]

In the two cases which the ECJ decided against the Czech Republic and Poland, national laws prohibited membership of EU foreign nationals in political parties. The Court has not yet been called upon to decide whether Art. 22 TFEU and Art. 12 CFR also have horizontal effect, directly prohibiting political parties from excluding membership of EU foreign nationals in their statutes or whether Member States are obliged to protect the latter from such discrimination.[229]

5.4.3.3.5 Multiple National Voting and Disenfranchisement Problems: Attempt at Synthesis Solution

It would in any event be premature to assume that national parliamentary elections are of no concern to primary EU law. There are at least two issues related to national parliamentary elections which are relevant from the democratic perspective—the possibility under national law for one person to vote in more than one such elections (multiple voting) and the disenfranchisement by national law of citizens who reside in another Member State as EU foreign nationals, having exercised their free movement rights pursuant to EU law (disenfranchisement of mobile Union citizens).

5.4.3.3.5.1 Multiple Voting Possibility in Conflict with Democratic Equality of Citizens

One voting rights problem at the intersection of Member State and EU democracy remains unresolved by Union law, international human rights law and national law: The possibility of Union citizens who are nationals of more than one Member State to vote in more than one national election (multiple national voting problem). These Union citizens holding dual or multiple Member State nationalities[230] can thereby exercise dual or multiple influences on the composition of the European Council and the Council that constitute the national strand of democratic legitimation of the EU. This is hard to square with the fundamental principle "one person, one vote",

[227] C-808/21, paras. 155 ff.; C-814/21, para. 154.

[228] C-808/21, para. 155; C-814/21, para. 154.

[229] See Peers (2024). On the potential horizontal effect of EU fundamental rights, see Lenaerts et al. (2021), para. 25.010.

[230] There are no official statistics, but the number of those "multiple" Union citizens definitely is not small: In 2015, more than 700,000 German citizens also had the nationality of another EU Member State. See Gallagher-Teske and Giesing (2017), p. 46. Available via https://www.ifo.de/DocDL/dice-report-2017-3-gallagher-giesing-october.pdf%20%5b22 (22 January 2025).

an expression of the democratic equality of citizens that is enshrined in Art. 9 sentence 1 TEU.[231]

German citizenship law (like most European citizenship laws) accepts dual or even multiple nationalities and even permits the retention of foreign nationalities in the naturalisation process.[232] According to § 12 (2) of the Federal Election Law (Bundeswahlgesetz),[233] adult German citizens who reside outside the German territory may under (not particularly strict) conditions vote in the federal parliamentary elections.[234] They can thereby exercise indirect influence on the composition of the federal government[235] whose members represent Germany in the Council of the EU and whose chair—the Federal Chancellor—represents Germany in the European Council. If these German citizens are at the same time citizens and residents of EU Member State X, they can also vote in X which gives them another chance to influence the composition of the Council. Since only five EU Member States exclude or limit the possibility of their citizens to vote in national elections because of their residence abroad,[236] this problem of possible double or multiple voting within the national strand of democratic legitimation of the EU is potentially widespread.[237]

The EU legislature cannot address this democratic problem because the Treaties do not confer any competence on it to regulate voting at national parliamentary elections. This area would also seem to lie outside the framework of the policies defined in the Treaties, so that the flexibility clause (Art. 352 TFEU) cannot be used either

[231] See Kochenov and Lock, in: Kellerbauer et al. (2019), Article 9 TEU, para. 5.

[232] See § 10 of the Citizenship Law *(Staatsangehörigkeitsgesetz)* as amended by Article 1 of the Act on the Modernisation of Nationality Law of 22 March 2024 (BGBl. [Federal Law Gazette] I No. 104 of 26 March 2024), consolidated version available via https://www.gesetze-im-internet.de/stag/BJNR005830913.html (19 November 2024).

[233] Current version available via https://www.gesetze-im-internet.de/bwahlg/__12.html (22 January 2025).

[234] § 12 (2) of the Federal Election Law reads in part as follows: "… Germans within the meaning of Article 116 (1) of the Basic Law who live outside the Federal Republic of Germany on election day are also eligible to vote, provided that they 1. have resided or otherwise habitually stayed in the Federal Republic of Germany for an uninterrupted period of at least three months after reaching the age of fourteen and this stay does not date back more than 25 years, or 2. have, for other reasons, become personally and directly familiar with the political situation in the Federal Republic of Germany and are affected by it. …" (translation by the author). On the constitutional law background, see FCC, Order of 4 July 2012 (2 BvC 1/11 etc.). Available via https://www.bundesverfassungsgericht.de/SharedDocs/Entscheidungen/DE/2012/07/cs20120704_2bvc000111.html (in German) (22 January 2025).

[235] According to Article 63 BL, the Federal Chancellor who determines the composition of the federal government is elected by an absolute majority of the Federal Diet (Bundestag).

[236] See Poptcheva (2024), p. 4 ff. See, e.g., § 29 (1) of the Constitutional Act of Denmark of June 5, 1953 which limits the right to vote at Folketing (Parliament) elections to Danish subjects permanently domiciled in the realm. Available via https://www.thedanishparliament.dk/-/media/sites/ft/pdf/publikationer/engelske-publikationer-pdf/the_constitutional_act_of_denmark_2018_uk_web.pdf (22 January 2025).

[237] It is unclear how many dual or multiple citizens actually vote in more than one national parliamentary election. No official statistics exist in this regard.

for excluding multiple national voting by way of an act of secondary Union law. Rather, in accordance with Art. 4 (1), 5 (2) sentence 2 TEU, the pertinent competence has remained with the Member States. They could enact parallel legislation disenfranchising their citizens who reside in another EU Member State whose nationality they also have so that they could henceforth only vote in the national elections of their Member State of residence. Another option for the Member States would be to give Union citizens with more than one Member State nationality a choice where to vote in national parliamentary elections. But that option would be more difficult to implement due to the different legislative periods and election dates in the Member States.

The obvious tension with the democratic equality of Union citizens that some of them can and probably do cast more than one vote in the EU's national strand of legitimation begs the question: Can primary Union law be interpreted as obliging Member States to solve the multiple national voting problem in one way or another? There is much to suggest that the EU values of democracy and equality which are also common to the Member States (Art. 2 TEU), read together with the specific definition of the EU's dual-level/quasi-federal representative democracy in Art. 10 (2) TEU and the democratic equality of all Union citizens (Art. 9 sentence 1 TEU) imposes such a partial disenfranchisement obligation upon the Member States. While Art. 9 sentence 1 TEU is directly addressed to the EU only, and not the Member States, it also indirectly binds the Member States to the extent in which it is indispensable for guaranteeing the democratic legitimacy of the EU that Art. 2 TEU identifies as a foundational value of the EU and Member States. The interdependence between democracy at Union and Member State levels requires that also the Member States respect the fundamental principle of equality enshrined in Art. 9 sentence 1.[238] But this is not yet settled because no pertinent case law of the ECJ exists and the Commission does not seem to have become active on the basis of Art. 258 TFEU in this regard either.

On the other hand, dual or multiple nationals may have genuine connections with and vested interests in more than one Member State and thus a legitimate stake in the outcome of several national elections. Requiring them to choose in which one to cast their vote would be a hardship for them. Yet, democratic equality means strictly formal equality—one person, one vote, irrespective of their personal situation and interests. Looking at the German federal system for comparison, we find that the right to vote in the parliamentary elections of the constituent states (*Länder*) is bound to the main place of residence.[239] This means that one person can vote in only one of the sixteen constituent states. If they change their main place of residence sufficient time before the respective election date, they can vote in another constituent state, but always only in one at a time.

---

[238] See Heselhaus, in: Pechstein et al. (2023a), vol. I, Artikel 9 EUV, para. 23, who argues that Member States are indirectly bound by Article 9 sentence 1 TEU.

[239] See, e.g., § 8 (1) sentence 1 no. 2, sentence 2 Landtagswahlgesetz (Regional Parliamentary Election Law) of the Saarland.

All in all, the democratic guarantees of primary EU law are opposed to the exercise by Union citizens of the right to vote at national parliamentary elections in more than one Member State. Member States are therefore obliged to prevent their citizens from multiple voting. It is left to their discretion how to accomplish this.[240] The Commission, in its capacity as guardian of the Treaties,[241] is called upon to enforce the limits of that discretion pursuant to Art. 258 TFEU. But is there an individual entitlement under EU law of other Union citizens that Member States adequately fulfil this obligation deriving from primary Union law? Can they claim a judicially enforceable right to be protected from the excessive and undemocratic political influence of multiple nationals who vote in more than one national parliamentary election? Do they, in other words, have an enforceable right to democratic equality at Member State level? The answer is no, for several reasons: The obligation is too vague, in view of the Member States' discretion. Such a right would also constitute a very general right of the many millions of Union citizens who hold only one Member State nationality. There is no hint in the text of the Treaties and the CFR of such a right. The limited general right to national democracy in the sense of a right to challenge manifest retrogressions in national democratic standards[242] does in any event not include an enforceable right to democratic equality at Member State level.

5.4.3.3.5.2 Disenfranchisement of Mobile Union Citizens Discourages Free Movement

The Commission has taken up another related matter—the disenfranchisement by Member States of their own citizens who reside in another Member State as EU foreign nationals (*i.e.*, without the right to vote at national level), having exercised their free movement rights pursuant to EU law.[243] It is unclear how many EU citizens are thus disenfranchised and how many of these would actually wish to vote, but they presumably number in the tens of thousands.[244] Currently, the electoral laws of five Member States—Cyprus, Denmark, Germany, Ireland and Malta—can lead to a loss of voting rights, if citizens move abroad.[245] More than one million adult citizens of these five States are usually resident in another EU/EFTA Member State and thus potentially affected.[246]

In 2014, the Commission addressed a pertinent recommendation (based on Art. 292 TFEU) to the Member States to "enable their nationals who make use of their right to free movement and residence in the Union to demonstrate a continuing

[240] See below Sect. 5.4.3.3.5.3.

[241] Article 17 (1) sentences 2, 3 TEU.

[242] See above Sect. 5.4.3.2.

[243] Articles 21, 45, 49 or 56 TFEU.

[244] See the figures and estimates mentioned by Poptcheva (2015), p. 15 f.

[245] Kelly (2022).

[246] Id., p. 4.

interest in the political life in the Member State of which they are nationals, including through an application to remain registered on the electoral roll, and by doing so, to retain their right to vote."[247] The objective of the recommendation is stated as being "to enhance the right to participate in the democratic life of the Union and the Member States of EU citizens who make use of their right to free movement within the Union."[248] The Commission rightly explained that since no Member State grants EU foreign nationals the right to vote in national elections such disenfranchisement by their State of nationality results in their total disenfranchisement at the national level.[249]

This recommendation, which is not legally binding,[250] is cautiously formulated: It does not directly convey the impression of reflecting legal obligations of the Member States, but it comes close to it. Thus, it mentions the "founding premise of Union citizenship" to enhance the legal status of Member State nationals and give them additional rights such as free movement rights whose exercise should not result in the loss of a right of political participation.[251] It also deplores the gap in the political rights of mobile Union citizens[252] that removes their influence on the Council as the EU's co-legislator[253] so that they can no longer fully participate in the democratic life of the Union,[254] as envisaged in Art. 10 (3) TEU.[255] Moreover, it emphasises "the prime importance of the right to participate in the democratic life of the Union and the right to free movement."[256] Finally, invoking the case law of the ECtHR,[257] the right to vote is identified as "a basic civil right" whose deprivation "risks undermining the democratic validity of the legislature thus elected and the laws it promulgates". The presumption in a democratic State should therefore be against disenfranchisement.[258] In line with this, a clear trend could be observed "in favour of allowing voting by non-resident nationals, even though no common European approach exists yet."[259]

In other words, the recommendation stopped just short of finding that primary EU law—free movement rights read together with the principle of democracy enshrined in Art. 10 TEU—prohibits this kind of disenfranchisement. There is a lot

[247] Commission Recommendation of 29 January 2014 addressing the consequences of disenfranchisement of Union citizens exercising their rights to free movement (2014/53/EU) (OJ L 32 of 1 February 2014, p. 34), para. 1.

[248] 4th recital of the preamble.

[249] 6th recital of the preamble.

[250] Article 288 (5) TFEU.

[251] 7th recital of the preamble.

[252] 9th recital of the preamble.

[253] 8th recital of the preamble.

[254] 10th recital of the preamble.

[255] 1st recital of the preamble.

[256] 14th recital of the preamble.

[257] ECtHR, judgment of 7 May 2013, Shindler v. UK (Appl. No. 19840/09).

[258] 11th recital of the preamble.

[259] Id., citing the Shindler judgment of the ECtHR.

to be said in favour of this conclusion. It is true that in view of the still existing differences in national practice regarding voting rights for expatriates, the ECtHR continues to grant Convention States a broad margin of appreciation and therefore usually does not find any violation of Art. 3 Prot. No. 1 if they disenfranchise them.[260] But this does not preclude deriving stricter obligations of EU Member States from primary Union law. EU foreign nationals cannot vote at the national parliamentary elections in their Member State of residence. If they are also denied the right to vote in their home Member State, they have no possibility at all to participate in providing democratic legitimation to the EU in the national strand (Art. 10 (2) subpara. 2 TEU). This impairs the democratic legitimacy of the EU.[261] It also unacceptably discriminates against those Union citizens who have exercised their free movement rights which EU law prohibits[262]: They lose their right to vote for no other reason than having made use of their rights as Union citizens—this amounts to "punishing EU citizens for exercising their right to free movement in the EU".[263]

The Treaties and the CFR do not expressly guarantee the right to vote in national parliamentary elections as such. Rather, these elections are particularly sensitive in view of their close connection with Member State sovereignty and constitutional identity (Art. 4 (2) TEU).[264] But we have already seen that Art. 6 (3) TEU incorporates the international standards embodied in Art. 3 Prot. No. 1 and Art. 25 lit. b ICCPR into the general principles of Union law. Accordingly, certain elementary requirements regarding participation of citizens in national parliamentary elections are part of unwritten primary EU law while leaving Member States a broad regulatory margin, in accordance with Art. 4 (2) TEU. It is therefore reasonable to assume that Member States are not completely free to disenfranchise their citizens for having moved to another Member State. They cannot be permitted arbitrarily to impose a loss of political participation rights on mobile Union citizens and thereby diminish the democratic legitimacy of the EU. Since the free movement rights pursuant to Art. 21, 45, 49 and 56 TFEU undoubtedly have direct effect, they also implicitly guarantee a judicially enforceable right to vote in their home country national parliamentary elections to Member State nationals that reside in another Member State.

[260] ECtHR, judgment of 15 April 2014, Oran v. Turkey (Appl. Nos. 28881/07 and 37920/07), paras. 53, 60 ff. See the extensive studies by Lappin (2016), p. 859 ff., and de Guttry (2018), p. 933 ff.

[261] See Giegerich (2020b), Political Dimensions of Equality, p. 79 ff. See in that sense also the answer given by Mrs. Reding on behalf of the Commission to a written Parliamentary question in 2011. Available via https://www.europarl.europa.eu/doceo/document/E-7-2011-009269-ASW_EN.html?redirect (22 January 2025).

[262] ECJ, judgment of 11 July 2002 (C-224/98), ECR 2002, I-6191, paras. 30 ff.; judgment of 29 April 2004 (C-224/02), paras. 18 ff.; judgment of 17 January 2008 (C-152/05), ECR 2008, I-39, paras. 22 ff. See Kelly (2022), p. 20.

[263] Speech by European Commission Vice-President Viviane Reding "Disenfranchisement: defending voting rights for EU citizens abroad" on 29 January 2014. Available via ec.europa.eu/commission/presscorner/detail/de/SPEECH_14_73 (22 January 2025).

[264] See ECJ, judgment of 19 November 2024 (C-808/21), ECLI:EU:C:2024:962, para. 154; judgment of 19 November 2024 (C-814/21), ECLI:EU:C:2024:963, para. 153: "…the organisation of national political life … is part of national identity, within the meaning of Article 4(2) TEU."

For these expatriates, this constitutes a subsidiary right to the applicable free movement right without which the latter would be burdened with a liability making it less effective.

On the other hand, it does not seem unreasonable if a Member State disenfranchises those of its expatriates who have lost all connections with the political conditions in their State of nationality. Accordingly, the Commission's recommendation does not call for an unconditional retention of voting rights in favour of expatriates, but only of those who "demonstrate a continuing interest in the political life in the Member State of which they are nationals, including through an application to remain registered on the electoral roll".[265] The Commission is right in recommending that the proof of such a continuing interest should be made easy, such as by a simple application to remain registered on the electoral roll.

The Commission has only cautiously followed up on the disenfranchisement problem in recent years, probably because Member States continue to insist that electoral rights at national level are their sole competence.[266] Its most recent report under Art. 25 TFEU "On progress towards effective EU citizenship 2020-2023" again stopped short of denouncing an infringement of primary law: "EU citizenship rights do not grant mobile EU citizens the right to vote in national elections in their Member State of residence, even though they are active members of society and are affected by national policies. The 'EU Citizenship Report 2020' Communication noted that there was a certain public support to grant mobile EU citizens such a right. A European citizens' initiative on this subject was registered in 2020 but did not manage to gather the necessary support. Several EU Member States deprive their own nationals of the right to vote in national elections if they permanently reside in other countries. As reiterated in the 'EU Citizenship Report 2020' Communication, the Commission continues to call on the Member States concerned to abolish these rules."[267] The Commission also reported that it had registered a European Citizens' Initiative entitled "Voters without borders, full political rights for EU citizens" in March 2020 that wanted to extend EU citizens' rights to vote and stand in elections in their country of residence to regional and national elections as well as referenda. But the organisers had not managed to collect the necessary support by June 2022.[268]

While it is true that EU citizenship rights do not expressly grant mobile EU citizens the right to vote in national elections in their Member State of residence, this statement falls short because it does not consider those citizenship rights that are necessarily implied in the free movement rights. It has long been settled that mobile EU citizens are also protected from interferences by their State of nationality, such as measures that discourage them from exercising their free movement rights, unless

---

[265] See also the conditions formulated in § 12 (2) of the German Federal Election Law (note 231).

[266] See Poptcheva (2015) p. 18.

[267] COM(2023) 931 final of 6.12.2023, p. 29 – emphasis and footnote omitted. Available via https://eur-lex.europa.eu/legal-content/EN/TXT/?uri=celex%3A52023DC0931 (22 January 2025).

[268] Id,. p. 29 note 116. For a similar abortive citizen initiative in 2014, see Poptcheva (2015) p. 19. See also Kelly (2022), p. 5 f.

these are justified for overriding reasons.[269] This leads to the conclusion that the free movement rights include the entitlement of mobile EU citizens not to be deprived of their right to vote in the national elections of their State of nationality, if they express their wish to retain that right, unless the State can give good reasons.

5.4.3.3.5.3 Synthesis Solution: Coordination of National Legislation on Voting Rights

The conclusions to be drawn from the preceding sections are as follows: (1) Primary Union law does not expressly guarantee Union citizens' right to vote in national parliamentary elections, neither in their Member State of nationality nor in their Member State of residence, and certainly not, if they do not hold the latter's nationality. But it implicitly guarantees citizens' active and passive right to vote, in accordance with international requirements. (2) Primary Union law (democratic precepts) requires Member States to prevent their citizens with more than one nationality from multiple voting, *i.e.* voting at more than one national election in EU Member States. (3) Primary Union law (free movement rights) at the same time prohibits Member States from depriving their mobile citizens of their right to vote in national elections without good reason. The last two conclusions can be harmonised with each other, if one accepts that obligation (2) constitutes good reason for depriving dual or multiple nationals of some of their voting rights according to (3). Member States have a margin of discretion on how to accomplish goal (2) without going further than permitted by conclusion (3).

One way would be to give priority to voting in the Member State of residence, if the Union citizen also holds that State's nationality. Member States could also leave it to the dual/multiple EU nationals to decide in which national elections they want to vote. It must, however, be ensured that dual/multiple EU nationals can effectively participate in one national election without excessive burdens. There must in other words be some form of coordination between Member States. Since the EU has no competence regarding national elections, the open method of coordination could be applied, in which Member States cooperate in inter-governmental forms, encouraged and monitored by the Commission.[270] The outcome of the coordination can be a soft-law catalogue of regulatory examples or the identification of best practice.

---

[269] See Poptcheva (2015) p. 17, citing Kochenov (2009).

[270] Craig (2021a), Institutions, p. 63 f. See, e.g., Art. 156, 168 (2), 173 TFEU.

5.4.3.4 Supplementary Democratic Rights in the EU Charter of Fundamental Rights

The CFR, which invokes the principle of democracy in its preamble[271] and is closely interlinked with the ECHR,[272] enshrines the following supplementary democratic rights: the freedom of expression and information regardless of frontiers as well as the freedom and pluralism of the media (Art. 11); the freedom of peaceful assembly and association (Art. 12); the right to education (Art. 14, which indicates that privately founded educational establishments must pay due respect for democratic principles); equality and non-discrimination (Art. 20, 21 CFR); the right to an effective remedy against violations of the rights and freedoms guaranteed by EU law (Art. 47). Art. 54 CFR prohibits the abuse of CFR rights by anybody, such as their abuse for undemocratic purposes, in parallel with Art. 17 ECHR.

Invoking Art. 11 (1) ECHR, the case law of the ECtHR and Art. 52 (3) CFR, the ECJ has emphasised that the right to freedom of association enshrined in Art. 12 (1) CFR "is one of the essential foundations of a democratic and pluralist society, in that it allows citizens to act collectively in areas of common interest and, in doing so, contribute to the proper functioning of public life".[273] Regarding the freedom of expression, the Court has emphasised "the particular importance accorded to that freedom in any democratic society. That fundamental right, guaranteed in Article 11 of the Charter, constitutes one of the essential foundations of a pluralist, democratic society, and is one of the values on which, under Article 2 TEU, the Union is founded ...".[274]

It must be remembered, however, that the provisions of the CFR are addressed to Member States only when they are implementing Union law (Art. 51 (1) CFR). This means that the supplementary democratic rights are at best partly applicable to the Member States political processes. The general parameter of democracy for Member States in Art. 2, 10 (2) sentence 2, (3) sentence 1 TEU as such is definitely not specific enough to subject national democratic processes fully to the CFR, except in the few clear cases of manifest violations of elementary democratic standards.[275] It is necessary to identify other more specific EU law provisions in primary or secondary EU law[276] or international agreements of the EU in conjunction with Art. 216 (2) TFEU that govern the particular situation.[277]

---

[271] 2nd recital.

[272] See 5th recital of preamble and Article 52 (3) CFR.

[273] ECJ, judgment of 19 November 2024 (C-808/21), ECLI:EU:C:2024:962, para. 119; judgment of 19 November 2024 (C-814/21), ECLI:EU:C:2024:963, para. 117 (both judgments citing ECtHR, judgment of 17 February 2004, Gorzelik and Others v. Poland [Appl. No. 44158/98]). See in that sense already ECJ, judgment of 18 June 2020 (C-78/18), ECLI:EU:C:2020:476, para. 112.

[274] ECJ, judgment of 21 December 2016 (Joined Cases C-203/15 and C-698/15), ECLI:EU:C:2016:970, para. 93.

[275] See above Sects. 5.4.3.1 and 5.4.3.2.

[276] Such as Articles 21, 22 TFEU.

[277] See ECJ, judgment of 26 February 2013 (C-617/10), ECLI:EU:C:2013:105, para. 19.

Where the CFR's supplementary democratic rights bind the Member States pursuant to Art. 51 (1) CFR, they protect both nationals and foreigners. EU law does not include any provision similar to Art. 16 ECHR that would specifically authorise Member States to subject "the political activity of aliens" to additional restrictions.[278] Rather, nationals, EU foreign citizens as well as third-State nationals all enjoy equal protection by the CFR rights, except for those in Title V that are reserved for Union citizens. In the specific circumstances of each individual case, Art. 52 (1) CFR may, however, allow Member States to limit the exercise of those supplementary democratic rights by foreigners generally further than that by nationals. Yet, within the field of application of the Treaties, EU foreign citizens are specifically protected from discrimination on grounds of nationality either by the applicable freedom of the internal market or by Art. 18 in conjunction with Art. 21 TFEU. In a parallel development at the ECHR level, the ECtHR decided already in 1995 that EU Member States may not raise Art. 16 ECHR against nationals of other Member States, in particular if they are also members of the European Parliament.[279] This defines minimum standards which have an impact on the CFR level of protection, in accordance with Art. 52 (3) CFR.

5.4.3.5 Enforcement Procedures

Individual rights under EU law can be enforced in the national courts—they are directly applicable and enjoy primacy over national law. Art. 19 (1) subpara. 2 TEU obliges Member States to "provide remedies sufficient to ensure effective legal protection in the fields covered by Union law", such as with regard to the few directly applicable EU law parameters for democracy in Member States. If national law does not provide the necessary remedies to enforce the democratic rights guaranteed by EU law in a reasonable manner and cannot be interpreted in conformity with Art. 19 (1) subpara. 2 TEU, the national courts must derive a remedy directly from Union law, probably from the directly effective Art. 47 CFR, and disregard procedural hurdles in national law by virtue of the primacy of Union law.[280] Art. 267 TFEU permits all national courts and requires the last instance national courts to seek binding preliminary rulings from the ECJ on relevant questions of EU law, thereby ensuring the consistent and uniform interpretation and application of the EU law democratic precepts throughout the Union.[281]

---

[278] On the restrictive interpretation of Article 16 ECHR by the ECtHR, in particular within the EU context, see above Sect. 4.2.1.2.1.3.

[279] ECtHR, judgment of 27 April 1995, Piermont v. France (Appl. No. 15773/89 and 15774/89), para. 64.

[280] ECJ, judgment of 3 October 2013 (C-583/11 P), ECLI:EU:C:2013:625, paras. 103 f.; judgment of 14 April 2020 (Joined Cases C-924/19 PPU and C-925/19 PPU), ECLI:EU:C:2020:367, paras. 143 ff.

[281] ECJ, judgment of 2 September 2021 (C-741/19), ECLI:EU:C:2021:655, paras. 45 f.; judgment of 21 December 2021 (C-347/19), ECLI:EU:C:2021:1034, paras. 254 ff.

5.4.3.6 Conclusion: Only Aspects of a Right to National Democracy Are Protected by EU Law

All in all, it is still difficult to detect a written or unwritten general individual right to national democracy in EU law, but there is continuing further development in this regard which is promoted not least by instances of democratic backsliding. Only specific aspects of national democracy (such as non-discriminatory participation in municipal elections) are explicitly enshrined as enforceable individual rights. Some democratic minimum standards prescribed by EU law have also solidified into individual rights. The CFR contains the usual series of supplementary democratic individual rights, but they bind Member States only within the scope of application of other EU law provisions. While the ECJ is ready to expand these rights further by extensive interpretation or progressive development, while possible, it must avoid conflicts with Art. 4 (2) TEU that protects Member States' constitutional identities, in particular regarding the national parliamentary systems. Remaining individual rights gaps can partially be closed by recourse to pertinent ECHR and ICCPR rights which, however, leave States a broad regulatory margin.[282] While the use of ECHR rights as gap-fillers is expressly permitted by Art. 6 (3) TEU, the ECJ has also taken account of the ICCPR, which binds all Member States, in applying the general principles of the Union's law.[283]

5.5 EU Law Parameters for Democracy at Union Level and Pertinent Individual Rights

5.5.1 Art. 9, 10 TEU as Fundamental Provisions for EU Democracy

When formulating the Treaties and the CFR, Member States have taken great care to ensure that democracy at EU level, as a synthesis of the democratic essentials common to their own constitutional traditions,[284] is firmly entrenched in a way adapted to the Union's character as a supranational non-State polity. Some Member States have thereby fulfilled specific requirements formulated by their own constitutions. This is, *e.g.*, the case for Germany.[285] According to the Federal Constitutional

[282] See above Sects. 4.1.2.1, 4.2.1.2.1.1, 4.2.1.2.1.2, 4.2.1.2.1.3.

[283] ECJ, judgment of 27 June 2006 (C-540/03), ECR 2006, I-5769, para. 37.

[284] Heselhaus, in: Pechstein et al. (2023a), vol. I, Artikel 10 EUV, para. 15.

[285] See Article 23 (1) sentence 1 Basic Law (BL): "With a view to establishing a united Europe, the Federal Republic of Germany shall participate in the development of the European Union that is committed to democratic, social and federal principles, to the rule of law and to the principle of subsidiarity and that guarantees a level of protection of basic rights essentially comparable to that afforded by this Basic Law.". Available via https://www.gesetze-im-internet.de/englisch_gg/englisch_gg.html (22 January 2025) The FCC recently confirmed that Article 23 (1) BL requires that

Court, the Basic Law requires as a condition of Germany's EU membership that the democratic foundations of the Union are enhanced in step with the progress of integration.[286]

The provisions fundamental for EU democracy are Art. 9 and Art. 10 TEU. Art. 9 sentence 1 TEU obliges the Union to observe the principle of democratic equality of its citizens.[287] Art. 9 sentences 2 and 3 TEU define the citizenship of the Union as the personal substrate of EU democracy and its relation to Member State citizenship as the personal substrate of national democracy. Art. 10 (1) TEU, which "gives concrete form to the value of democracy referred to in Article 2 TEU",[288] bases the functioning of the EU on representative democracy. Art. 10 TEU "underscores, as regards elections to the European Parliament, the connection between the principle of representative democracy within the European Union and the right to vote and to stand as a candidate in European Parliament elections attached to citizenship of the Union, guaranteed by Article 22 (2) TEU."[289]

Pursuant to Art. 10 (2) TEU, the democratic legitimacy of the EU's quasi-federal decision-making process is based on the interaction of the directly elected European Parliament and the (European) Council consisting of Member State representatives who are democratically accountable in their respective Member State. Institutionally, two strands of democratic legitimation of Union action—a direct supranational and an indirect national one—are thereby established that interact and support each other.[290] This means that democracy at EU level depends on the effective implementation of democracy in each and every Member State. On the other hand, democracy in the Member States also depends on the effective implementation of democracy at EU level, in view of the direct applicability and primacy of Union law that therefore constitutes an important part of the legal order in force in each Member State.

---

the EU's democratic legitimacy must be sufficiently effective and imposes an "integration responsibility for the democratic principle in the EU" on the German State that includes a co-responsibility with the other Member States for securing the effective functioning of the European Parliament (order of 6 February 2024 [2 BvE 6/23 etc.], paras. 105, 126).

286 FCC, judgment of 12 October 1993 (2 BvR 2134, 2159/92), BVerfGE 89, 155, 186, para. 100.

287 See above Sect. 5.3.4.

288 ECJ, judgment of 19 December 2019 (C-502/19), ECLI:EU:C:2019:1115, para. 63. See also ECJ, judgment of 19 December 2019 (C-418/18 P), ECLI:EU:C:2019:1113, para. 64; judgment of 19 November 2024 (C-808/21), ECLI:EU:C:2024:962, para. 114; judgment of 19 November 2024 (C-814/21), ECLI:EU:C:2024:963, para. 112.

289 ECJ, judgment of 19 November 2024 (C-808/21), ECLI:EU:C:2024:962, para. 116; judgment of 19 November 2024 (C-814/21), ECLI:EU:C:2024:963, para. 114.

290 FCC, order of 6 February 2024 (2 BvE 6/23 etc.), para. 108.

5.5.2 *Different Concepts of Democracy at EU and Member State Level Generate Potential for Conflict*

It is generally agreed that differences between democracy at Union level and national levels are inevitable and in particular that the EU cannot simply adopt the peculiar democratic concepts of any one Member State without antagonising all the others.[291] Nevertheless, differences in the approach to democracy by the EU and the German Member State have sometimes caused irritations. One example concerns the establishment of independent agencies that are viewed critically in Germany because they remain largely outside the regular democratic legitimisation connection proceeding from the voters via parliament to the decision-making administrative body. In an infringement case under (now) Art. 258 TFEU concerning the obligation to establish an independent supervisory authority in every Member State for monitoring compliance with European data protection law, Germany had argued that the principle of democracy prevented a broad interpretation of the independence requirement. The ECJ responded that the principle of democracy in Community law did not preclude "conferring a status independent of the general administration" on data protection authorities, provided that the latter remained subject to the regulatory and appointment powers of parliament and could be obliged to submit regular reports to parliament and that they were "required to comply with the law subject to the review of the competent courts."[292]

In another infringement case against Germany concerning the establishment of national regulatory authorities in the internal markets in electricity and natural gas, the ECJ referred to its earlier judgment and stated "that the principle of democracy does not preclude the existence of public authorities outside the classic hierarchical administration and more or less independent of the government, which often exercise regulatory functions or carry out tasks which must be free from political influence, whilst still being required to comply with the law subject to the review of the competent courts. Conferring on NRAs a status independent of the general administration does not in itself deprive those authorities of their democratic legitimacy, in so far as they are not shielded from all parliamentary influence".[293]

German reluctance to accept this EU concept of democracy, which was endorsed by the ECJ, is based on the notion that the democratic principle of the sovereignty of the people requires "an unbroken chain of legitimisation from the people to the bodies and officials entrusted with state tasks."[294] This reluctance becomes clear from a judgment of the German FCC concerning the European Banking Union[295]

---

[291] On the different concepts of democracy in Europe, see Huber, in: Streinz (2018), Artikel 10 EUV, paras. 3 ff.

[292] ECJ, judgment of 9 March 2010 (C-518/07), ECLI:EU:C:2010:125, paras. 38 ff.

[293] ECJ, judgment of 2 September 2021 (C-718/18), ECLI:EU:C:2021:662, para. 126.

[294] FCC, judgment of 17 January 2017 (2 BvB 1/13), BVerfGE 144, 20, para. 545 (my translation).

[295] FCC, judgment of 30 July 2019 (2 BvR 1685/14 etc.), BVerfGE 151, 202, English translation available via https://www.bundesverfassungsgericht.de/SharedDocs/Entscheidungen/EN/2019/07/

that was handed down in between the two aforementioned ECJ decisions. While the FCC rejected the constitutional complaints against German participation in the EU legal acts underlying the European Banking Union,[296] it voiced criticism from a democratic perspective against independent authorities on EU level established by primary law (the European Central Bank),[297] the Europeanisation of national administrative structures and the establishment of independent bodies, offices and agencies of the EU by acts of secondary law.[298]

In the concrete case, secondary law required that the national supervisory authorities, such as the German Federal Financial Supervisory Authority, had to act independently when performing their tasks under the Single Supervisory Mechanism. The FCC referred to "drops in influence" of the German people that diminished the level of democratic legitimation of EU acts of public authority which was required by Art. 23 (1) sentence 3 in conjunction with Art. 79 (3) and Art. 20(1) and (2) of the Basic Law. These drops in influence had to be compensated by effective parliamentary oversight and judicial review. But the FCC underlined that "diminishing the level of democratic legitimation is not permissible without limits and requires

---

rs20190730_2bvr168514en.html (22 January 2025). See Heselhaus, in: Pechstein et al. (2023a), vol. I, Artikel 10 EUV, para. 19.

[296] Council Regulation (EU) No. 1024/2013 of 15 October 2013 conferring specific tasks on the European Central Bank concerning policies relating to the prudential supervision of credit institutions (OJ L 287 of 29 October 2013, p. 63); Regulation (EU) No. 1022/2013 of the European Parliament and the Council of 22 October 2013 amending Regulation (EU) No. 1093/2010 establishing a European Supervisory Authority (European Banking Authority) as regards the conferral of specific tasks on the European Central Bank pursuant to Council Regulation (EU) No. 1024/2013 (OJ L 287 of 29 October 2013, p. 5); Regulation (EU) No. 806/2014 of the European Parliament and the Council of 15 July 2014 establishing uniform rules and a uniform procedure for the resolution of credit institutions and certain investment firms in the framework of a Single Resolution Mechanism and a Single Resolution Fund and amending Regulation (EU) No. 1093/2010 (OJ L 331 of 30 July 2014, p. 12).

[297] In its judgment of 12 October 1993 on the constitutionality of the Treaty of Maastricht, the FCC already determined that the independence of the European Central Bank was a justifiable modification of the principle of democracy (BVerfGE 89, 155 [207 ff.]): "This modification of the principle of democracy in the service of ensuring confidence in a currency is acceptable, since it is a reflection of a special characteristic—that has been proven within the German legal order and is also supported by research—that an independent central bank can be a better guarantor of monetary stability, and thus of the general economic foundations of fiscal policy and private planning and arrangements in the exercise of economic freedoms, than state institutions that depend on the money supply and monetary value for their ability to act and are dependent on short-term approval by political forces. Therefore, entrusting the competence for monetary policy to an independent European Central Bank that is thereafter not subject to state authority—an authorisation that cannot be applied to any other policy area—satisfies the constitutional requirements subject to which the principle of democracy may be modified." (English translation of the judgment available via https://www.bundesverfassungsgericht.de/SharedDocs/Entscheidungen/EN/1993/10/rs19931012_2bvr213492en.html [22 January 2025]). As a matter of fact, the Treaty provision on the independence of the ECB (Article 130 TFEU) was inserted at the insistence of Germany, reflecting the independence of the German central bank guaranteed by Article 88 sentence 2 Basic Law.

[298] FCC (footnote 293), paras. 126 ff.

justification. While, based on this, there are no fundamental objections to the establishment of independent agencies of the European Union, such practice remains precarious in light of the principle of democracy."[299] It has been argued, however, that in this judgment the FCC moved closer to the ECJ's approach regarding democratic legitimacy.[300]

In this context, the FCC referred to the ECJ's *Meroni* doctrine that limited the delegation of executive powers to bodies outside the Commission hierarchy.[301] The Court also indicated that not only the principle of democracy in the German constitution, but also the EU's principle of democracy limited the disconnect of such bodies (including the ECB) from democratic oversight.[302] Ultimately, the FCC reluctantly determined that the Basic Law's requirements for democratic accountability of the supervisory bodies in the banking sector were still met[303] and that it was unnecessary to request a preliminary ruling from the ECJ according to Art. 267 (3) TFEU because of the *acte clair* exception.[304]

5.5.3 *Democratic Legitimacy as a General Principle of EU Law*

In the Interinstitutional Agreement between the European Parliament, the Council of the European Union and the European Commission on Better Law-Making,[305] that was expressly based on Art. 295 TFEU and is obviously intended to be legally binding,[306] "the three Institutions agree to observe general principles of Union law, such as democratic legitimacy, subsidiarity and proportionality, and legal certainty" in the exercise of their powers. They further agreed "to promote the utmost transparency in the legislative process."[307] It is notable that the most important political institutions of the EU on whom the latter's representative democracy rests,[308] jointly designate democratic legitimacy as an (unwritten) general principle of Union law, alongside the (written) principles of subsidiarity and proportionality,[309] and the fur-

---

299 Id., headnote 3.

300 Kahl (2022), p. 325 f.

301 FCC (footnote 293), para. 137, citing ECJ, judgment of 22 January 2014 (C-270/12), ECLI:EU:C:2014:18.

302 Id., para. 139. The FCC here only referred to German legal literature, but did not cite ECJ case law.

303 Id., paras. 285 ff.

304 Id., paras. 314 ff.

305 Of 13 April 2016 (OJ L 123 of 12 May 2016, p. 1).

306 This intention is confirmed by the publication of the Agreement in the L series of the Official Journal.

307 Para. I.2.

308 See Article 10 (1), (2) TEU.

309 Article 5 (1), (3) and (4) TEU.

ther unwritten principle of legal certainty. The ECJ uses the principles of democracy and of democratic legitimacy interchangeably, dispelling any doubts that it recognises both as principles of EU law.[310]

That general principle of democratic legitimacy, located at the primary law level, obviously complements Art. 9, 10 TEU. It is based on the corresponding principle of Community law that predates these provisions[311] and can serve as an interpretative background of primary and secondary Union law,[312] but cannot override concrete provisions of the TFEU.[313] It supports the interpretation and application of Union law provisions in a way that enhances the democratic legitimacy of the EU. It also favours the use of the ordinary legislative procedure, wherever possible, because that produces legislative acts with the best democratic credentials. But the Interinstitutional Agreement does not go that far. It is rather satisfied with the following: "If a modification of the legal basis entailing a change from the ordinary legislative procedure to a special legislative procedure or a non-legislative procedure is envisaged [during the legislative process], the three Institutions will exchange views thereon."[314] This cautionary approach is due to the pertinent case law of the ECJ which does not permit giving any precedence to the ordinary legislative procedure.[315] Unsurprisingly, the Interinstitutional Agreement does not contain any indication that the general principle of democratic legitimacy creates judicially enforceable individual rights.

5.5.4 *Entrenchment Problem at EU Level: Unanimity Requirements Are Inherently Undemocratic*

The question is whether the basic set-up of the EU's constitutional system corresponds to the aforementioned legal parameters of democracy/democratic legitimacy or whether it suffers from an undemocratic design flaw in the form of excessive unanimity requirements that overly limit political decision-making in EU matters.[316]

According to Abraham Lincoln's famous definition, a republic (which we would now call democracy) is characterised by "government of the people, by the people,

[310] ECJ, judgment of 2 September 2021 (C-718/18), ECLI:EU:C:2021:662, paras. 124 ff.

[311] ECJ, judgment of 29 October 1980 (138/79), ECLI:EU:C:1980:249, para. 33. Confirmed, *e.g.*, in the judgment of 10 June 1997 (C-392/95), para. 14.

[312] ECJ, judgment of 9 March 2010 (C-518/07), ECLI:EU:C:1997:289, para. 41.

[313] ECJ, judgment of 14 April 2015 (C-409/13), ECLI:EU:C:2015:217, paras. 37, 96. See also Ritleng (2016), p. 11 ff. and Möllers (2025), p. 833 ff.

[314] Para. IV.25. subpara. 3.

[315] See below Sect. 5.5.9.

[316] For the parallel question whether the excessive use of cardinal laws in Hungary which can only be changed by a two-thirds majority in parliament, contravenes the democracy parameters of Art. 2, 10 TEU for Member States, see Sonnevend (2023), p. 563 ff.

for the people",[317] demanding the social, input and output legitimacy of government. The definition presupposes that the people (or their representatives) can actually govern, *i.e.*, make political decisions according to what they consider best in the particular situation. Generally speaking, the larger the area in which such political decision-making can effectively take place, the more democratic the respective governmental system is. Conversely, this means that constraints on political decision-making translate into democratic deficits. Facilitating political decision-making therefore increases the level of democracy, while complicating it lowers that level and therefore requires justification from the perspective of the democracy parameter.

According to experience, the most effective and at the same time fairest political decision-making method is by majority, provided that today's outvoted minority has a realistic chance to become tomorrow's new majority, capable of reversing the decisions of the previous majority.[318] Effectively guaranteeing such changes in government is the hallmark of every true democracy. Systems of respresentative democracy—amongst which the EU counts itself pursuant to Art. 10 (1) TEU—are characterised by the time-limited transfer of governmental powers to the people's representatives that typically exercise them by majority decisions.[319] On this background, exceptions to the majority principle, such as the entrenchment of certain matters (e.g., minority rights) in a constitution (which is difficult to change),[320] removes these matters from the ordinary political decision-making process and thus from the reach of the democratic majority. The same applies if decision-making in certain areas requires unanimity: Granting veto powers to individual members of decision-making bodies, so that they can frustrate decision-making, gives excessive power to a small minority. It not only reduces the output, but also the input legitimacy of the decision-making process and is inherently undemocratic.[321]

At EU level, too many matters of ordinary law character (such as antitrust and State aids[322]) are "constitutionalised" by entrenchment in the Treaties which can only be revised with the consent of all the Member States (Art. 48 TEU).[323] Moreover, while decision-making by qualified majority in the Council has long

---

[317] Gettysburg Address, 19 November 1863 (Abraham Lincoln, Selected Speeches and Writings, First Vintage Books 1992, p. 405). See also Art. 2 of the French Constitution of 4 October 1958, according to which the principle of the French Republic is "gouvernement du peuple, par le peuple et pour le people".

[318] Möllers (2021), p. 342 f.

[319] See Frankenberg (2012), p. 258.

[320] Important parts of constitutions may even be unchangeable (see for Germany Art. 79 (3) BL). For a critique, see Thomas Jefferson, Letter to Major John Cartwright, 5 June 1824: "But can they [our state and federal constitutions] be made unchangeable? Can one generation bind another, and all others, in succession forever? I think not. The Creator has made the earth for the living, not the dead. … Nothing then is unchangeable but the inherent and unalienable rights of man." (reprinted in Merrill D. Peterson [ed.], The Portable Thomas Jefferson, Penguin Books 1977, p. 577, 580 f.)

[321] Giegerich (2015), p. 143 ff. See above Sect. 3.3 on the parallel problem at global level.

[322] Art. 101 ff. TFEU.

[323] This was pointed out by Grimm (2017), chapter 5 on the democratic costs of constitutionalisation); id. (2022), p. 248.

been the default option,[324] there are still too many areas in which it must act unanimously, first and foremost in the CFSP.[325] This situation does not make the EU undemocratic, not least because there have been constant endeavours to reduce unanimity requirements, beginning with the Single European Act. But it calls for their further reduction by using existing *passerelles* clauses[326] as far as possible and amendments to the Treaties where necessary. Maintaining unanimous decision-making demands compelling justification in order to be compatible with the principle of democracy.

All in all, it is a democratic postulate to phase out all unanimity requirements in EU law which cannot be justified by overriding concerns connected with either European or national identity. Political demands in this regard have often been made.[327] One may even construct an objective obligation to this effect arising from primary Union law. As we shall see, however, because of the broad margin of discretion left to the EU organs and the Member States, there is no corresponding individual right to improve EU democracy in general, and no right to remove unanimity requirements in particular.[328]

5.5.5 European Parliament: Primary Democratic EU Institution

"The EP is the first parliament 'beyond the state' – beyond state-constituted democracies: as the world's only supranational institution with genuine powers of action and representative functions that is directly elected by citizens, it represents a quantum leap in the – always open-ended and by no means necessarily successful – experiment of democracy."[329] The EP takes the development of international democracy that started with PACE to a qualitatively new supranational level.

While the European Parliament had traditionally been considered as the representation "of the peoples of the States brought together in the Community",[330] in other words the representation of the national electorates taken together in the sense of a demoicracy,[331] the Treaty of Lisbon now defines it as the representation of the

[324] Art. 16 (3) TEU.

[325] Art. 31 TEU.

[326] See, e.g., Art. 31 (3) TEU: Art. 81 (3) subpara. 2, Art. 192 (2) subpara. 2 TFEU.

[327] See, e.g., the 39th proposal of the Final Outcome of the Conference on the Future of Europe (below Sect. 5.7.1) and the EP's follow-up proposals (below Sect. 5.7.2).

[328] See below Sect. 5.5.6.2.

[329] Von Achenbach (2025), p. 863 (my translation).

[330] See Article 189 (1) EC-Treaty as amended by the Treaty of Nice of 2001 (OJ 2006 C 321 E, p. 130).

[331] See von Achenbach (2025), p. 867 (citing, e.g., Nicolaïdis [2013], p. 351 ff.).

Union's citizens as a whole,[332] in other words the representation of one multinational European electorate as an anticipation of a European *demos* which does not yet exist but may develop in the future.[333] This establishes a direct relationship of democratic legitimisation between the EU and the citizens of the Union, without the intermediate level of the peoples of the Member State.[334] Each Member of the European Parliament represents all citizens of the Union, irrespective of nationality and party affiliation, and not only their electorate (*i.e.*, the Union citizens of the one Member State in which they were elected).[335]

During the European integration process, the European Parliament has gained the most competences of all EU institutions.[336] In order to ensure adequate democratic legitimacy of EU legal acts, the EP's equal participation in EU decision-making is particularly essential in all cases in which the Council acts by a qualified majority, which has become the standard case.[337] This is because there, the national parliaments of the outvoted Member States cannot provide democratic legitimacy, a gap that needs to be filled by the European Parliament.[338] Therefore, the ECJ rightly emphasises the importance of "the genuine participation of the Parliament in the

[332] Article 14 (2) subpara. 1 sentence 1 TEU. This clear formulation supersedes the ECJ case law dating back to the time before the entry into force of the Treaty of Lisbon, according to which Member States were free to extend the right to vote and stand as a candidate in EP elections to persons who are not citizens of the Union (judgment of 12 September 2006 [C-145/04], ECR 2006, I-7961, paras. 65 ff.). This case is no longer good law. See in this sense also Huber (2022), § 24, para. 9 (with footnote 10).

[333] Giegerich (2020b), Political Dimensions of Equality, p. 81 f. See also Möllers (2025), p. 812 ff.; von Achenbach (2025), p. 872 ff.; Nettesheim (2024), in: Grabitz/Hilf/Nettesheim, Artikel 9 EUV paras. 9 ff. Huber, in: Streinz (2018), Artikel 10 EUV, paras. 28 f., criticises this "remarkable attempt to elevate the citizens of the Union to an independent source of legitimation alongside the Member States and to emancipate the EU to a certain extent from the 'masters of the treaties'." (my translation) For confirmation, Huber refers to the FCC's judgment of 30 June 2009 (2 BvE 2, 5/08 etc.), BVerfGE 123, 267 (372 f., paras. 280 ff.) where the FCC stated that "the European Parliament is not a representative body of a sovereign European people, despite the inference to this effect that appears in Art. 10(1) TEU – Lisbon. … the European Parliament remains a representative body of the peoples of the Member States [rather than of EU citizens] due to the use of national quotas." (English translation available via https://www.bundesverfassungsgericht.de/SharedDocs/Entscheidungen/EN/2009/06/es20090630_2bve000208en.html [22 January 2025]). While the Court's first statement is correct, the second is not, in view of Article 22 (2) TFEU.

[334] Heselhaus, in: Pechstein et al. (2023a), vol. I, Artikel 9 EUV, para. 26.

[335] See Sydow (2024), p. 320. But see Heselhaus, in: Pechstein et al. (2023a), vol. I, Artikel 10 EUV, para. 27, who limits the representation by each national contingent of MEPs to the electorate of their Member State.

[336] Von Achenbach (2025), p. 863 ff., who, however, also points out that the "new intergovernmentalism" regarding Euro crisis management bypassed the EP and that the latter's role in the EU's finances is limited (p. 910 ff.).

[337] Art. 16 (3) TEU.

[338] Giegerich (2020b), Political Dimensions of Equality, p. 74. Heselhaus, in: Pechstein et al. (2023a), vol. I, Artikel 10 EUV, paras. 24, 26. This is also recognised by Huber, in: Streinz (2018), Artikel 10 EUV, paras. 27 ff. (who deplores the continuous strengthening of the EP as "a unitary act at the expense of the Member States and their parliaments" [my translation]).

legislative process in compliance with the principles of representative democracy".[339] Furthermore, the Court has stressed that, "in accordance with the principle of representative democracy [in Art. 10 (1) TEU] and with Article 14 TEU, its composition must reflect faithfully and completely the free expression of choices made by the citizens of the European Union, by direct universal suffrage, as regards the persons by whom they wish to be represented during a given term, [and] that the European Parliament must be protected, in the exercise of its tasks, against hindrances or risks to its proper operation."[340]

In the ordinary legislative procedure, which is the most common case, the European Parliament and the Council interact on an equal footing,[341] while in special legislative procedures, the European Parliament only participates in the adoption of legislative acts by the Council which dominates these procedures and usually acts by unanimity.[342] But that participation also has democratic relevance. Thus, according to the settled case law of the ECJ, even the mere consultation of the EP "in the cases provided for by the Treaty constitutes an essential procedural requirement disregard of which renders the measure concerned void. Effective participation of the Parliament in the decision-making process, in accordance with the procedures laid down by the Treaty, represents an essential element of the institutional balance intended by the Treaty. This function reflects the fundamental democratic principle that the people should take part in the exercise of power through the intermediary of a representative assembly ...".[343] The European Parliament and the Council also jointly exercise budgetary functions.[344]

In the Common Foreign and Security Policy (CFSP) that includes the Common Security and Defence Policy,[345] decision-making is still completely dominated by the European Council and the Council, both acting unanimously (as a rule).[346] This is not unlike the situation in the Member States where external action is usually also dominated by the executive and the parliament plays a secondary role only.[347] The CFSP constitutes the last reserve of intergovernmentalism in the EU and is the most

[339] ECJ, judgment of 10 January 2006 (C-344/04), ECLI:EU:C:2006:10, para. 61.

[340] ECJ, judgment of 19 December 2019 (C-502/19), ECLI:EU:C:2019:1115, para. 83.

[341] Articles 289 (1), 294 TFEU. For a critique from a democratic perspective of the standard trilogue procedure in which the EP, the Council and the Commission hammer out compromises on legislative projects behind closed doors, see von Achenbach (2025), p. 901 f., 926 f. See also below Sect. 5.5.8.1.

[342] Article 289 (2) TFEU.

[343] ECJ, judgment of 6 September 2017 (Joined Cases C-643/15 and C-647/15), ECLI:EU:C:2017:631, para. 160 (with further references).

[344] Articles 312, 314, 319 TFEU.

[345] Article 42 (1) sentence 1 TEU.

[346] Article 24 (1) subpara. 2, sentence 2, Article 31 TEU.

[347] See Giegerich (2020a) Foreign Relations Law, paras. 17 ff. With regard to Germany, see FCC, judgment of 26 October 2022 (2 BvE 3/15 etc.), paras. 66 f., in contrast to the important role which the German parliament plays in the decision-making process concerning the EU – id., paras. 68 ff. (English translation available via https://www.bundesverfassungsgericht.de/SharedDocs/Entscheidungen/EN/2022/10/es20221026_2bve000315en.html [22 January 2025]).

democratically deficient of all Union policies.[348] There, the European Parliament is consulted by the High Representative of the Union for Foreign Affairs and Security Policy, but only on the main aspects and the basic choices (and not before concrete decisions are made), and it is later informed of how those policies evolve.[349] At least, the EP has a right of information pursuant to Art. 218 (10) TFEU at all stages of the procedure to negotiate and conclude even those international agreements which relate exclusively to the CFSP.[350] Yet, this minimisation of the EP's role is the exception that proves the rule which applies throughout all the other EU policy areas.

The situation is mitigated by the norm, set forth twice in identical wording, that in the CFSP "[t]he adoption of legislative acts shall be excluded".[351] This means that CFSP acts must not directly interfere with fundamental rights or other individual rights.[352] It must also be remembered that much of the EU's external action takes place on the basis of Art. 205 ff. TFEU in supranational forms that fully include the European Parliament, such as the Common Commercial Policy, development cooperation and humanitarian aid. Restrictive measures under Art. 215 TFEU straddle the TEU and the TFEU and there, the role of the European Parliament is also marginalised to being informed *ex post* of decisions made by the Council. This is all the more troubling because of the serious consequences of those sanctions. Another aspect that connects the EU's democratically deficient CFSP and the democratically better organised supranational external action are the goals set by Art. 21 (1) TEU and Art. 205 TFEU, one of them being the "export "of democracy.

One can paraphrase the dual democratic legitimation of the EU as deriving from the sovereignty of the Union citizens in their entirety, made up of the aggregated sovereign peoples of the sovereign Member States.[353] It is reflected in the EU's quasi-bicameral decision-making process bringing together the Council and the still not completely equal European Parliament.[354]

Art. 10 (2) TEU identifies the European Parliament and the (European) Council as the two institutions on which the EU's representative democracy is based. The directly elected European Parliament is mentioned first, the (European) Council, whose members are mostly indirectly legitimised via the national parliaments,[355] is mentioned only second. This indicates that the Treaties consider the European Parliament as the primary source of the EU's democratic legitimacy and the (European) Council only as the secondary source. As a matter of fact, the European Court of Human Rights already in 1999 characterised the European Parliament as

[348] Giegerich (2015), p. 135, 139 ff.

[349] Article 36 TEU.

[350] ECJ, judgment of 24 June 2014 (C-658/11), ECLI:EU:C:2014:2025, paras. 64 ff. See below Sect. 5.5.9.

[351] Article 24 (1) subpara. 2 sentence 3 and Article 31 (1) subpara. 1 sentence 2 TEU.

[352] Giegerich (2024), p. 623 ff.

[353] Giegerich (2020b), Political Dimensions of Equality, p. 66, 72.

[354] Id., p. 73 f.

[355] Article 10 (2) subpara. 2 TEU at the end indicates that members of the European Council, such as the French President, can also be directly elected.

follows: "[T]he European Parliament represents the principal form of democratic, political accountability in the Community system. The Court considers that whatever its limitations, the European Parliament, which derives democratic legitimation from the direct elections by universal suffrage, must be seen as that part of the European Community structure which best reflects concerns as to 'effective political democracy".[356]

By contrast, the German Federal Constitutional Court has continued to insist that the democratic legitimacy of the EU is primarily guaranteed by the democratically constituted Member States via the Council and that this legitimisation provided by national parliaments and governments is only complemented and supported by the directly elected European Parliament.[357] The German Court has, however, not explained how this would work for Member States that are outvoted in the Council—for them, the primary source of democratic legitimacy simply fails and everything depends on the European Parliament as the secondary source that allegedly only complements and supports something which does not exist in cases of outvoting.[358]

5.5.6 Citizenship of the Union and Associated General Democratic Rights

5.5.6.1 Citizenship of the Union as Fundamental Status of Member State Nationals

In the seminal *van Gend & Loos* judgment, the Court of Justice stated that "the Community constitutes a new legal order of international law for the benefit of which the states have limited their sovereign rights, albeit within limited fields, and the subjects of which comprise not only Member States but also their nationals."[359] That formula—which was also based on the argument "that the nationals of the states brought together in the Community are called upon to cooperate in the functioning of this Community through the intermediary of the European Parliament and the Economic and Social Committee"[360] gave birth to the concept of "market citizens" *(bourgeois)* of the Community[361] which was later extended by also including a political component, upgrading market citizens from freely moving economic

356 Judgment of 18 February 1999, Matthews v. UK (Appl. No. 24833/94), para. 52.

357 BVerfGE 89, 155, 184 (1993); 123, 267, 364 para. 262 (2009) – for an English translation, see: https://www.bundesverfassungsgericht.de/SharedDocs/Entscheidungen/EN/2009/06/es20090630_2bve000208en.html (22 January 2025). See in this sense also Huber, in: Streinz (2018), Artikel 10 EUV, paras. 40 f. The FCC's most recent pertinent order of 6 February 2024 (2 BvE 6/23 etc.) neither repeats nor abandons this approach expressly.

358 See Giegerich (2009a), The Last Word, p. 34.

359 ECJ, judgment of 5 February 1963 (Case 26/62), ECR 1963, p. 1, 12.

360 Id., p. 12. See von Achenbach (2025), p. 864.

361 The concept goes back to Hans Peter Ipsen (see von Bogdandy [2012], p. 324).

actors to citizens of the Union *(citoyen)* and political actors.[362] On this background, the *status activus processualis* of individuals according to the *van Gend & Loos* judgment is not only an important aspect of the rule of law in the EU, because it promotes the effective enforcement of Union law, but also of democratic participation, at least as far as Union citizens are concerned, *i.e.* a partial aspect of the right to democracy in the EU[363]: It symbolises the ownership by Union citizens of the entire integration process, both directly (as citizens of the Union) and indirectly (as citizens of their respective Member State).[364]

One year after *van Gend & Loos*, the ECJ handed down its judgment in the Costa v. ENEL case in which it held that Community law had primacy over national law, superseding without nullifying incompatible national provisions.[365] Read together, the two judgments, that were further developed by later case law,[366] federalised and constitutionalised the European Economic Community to a considerable extent.[367] In substance, the primacy of EU law means primacy of democratic law-making at Union level (*i.e.*, Union citizenship) over democratic law- making at Member State level. Consequently, the individuals' position as co-sovereigns in the EU's democratic system has priority over their position as co-sovereigns in their Member States' democratic systems (*i.e.*, national citizenship)—their common European will precedes the particular national wills.[368]

The citizenship of the Union was formally introduced by the Treaty of Maastricht,[369] together with the establishment of the political European Union, which complemented the economic European (Economic) Community. The Treaty of Lisbon merged the EU and the EC to form the new EU.[370] Union citizenship summarises the subjective legal status—both economic and political—under primary EU law of all persons holding the nationality of a Member State.[371] According to the settled case-law of the ECJ "Union citizenship is destined to be the fundamental

[362] See Kadelbach (2010), p. 445 ff.; Shuibhne (2023), p. 28 ff.

[363] See also Alemanno (2024a), Beyond EU Law Heroes, p. 822 ff.

[364] But see Grimm (2022), p. 242, pointing out that the constitutionalisation of the Treaties by virtue of the ECJ's van Gend & Loos and Costa v. ENEL judgments produced "a power shift from the democratically legitimated and accountable institutions to the judiciary." In reality, the power shift occurred from the national political institutions trying to renege on their Treaty commitments to the citizens preventing that with the help of the national and EU courts.

[365] ECJ, judgment of 15 July 1964 (C-6/64), ECR 1964, 1141.

[366] See, e.g., ECJ, judgment of 9 March 1978 (106/77), ECR 1978, 629.

[367] Schorkopf (2023) speaks of a normative re-foundation (*normative Umgründung*) by the ECJ, while acknowledging that, contrary to the prevailing view, the Court did not invent this normative supranationality; rather, it was inherent in the treaties, p. 106.

[368] See Schorkopf (2023), p. 117.

[369] Of 7 February 1992 (OJ C 191).

[370] Article 1 (3) TEU, as amended by the Treaty of Lisbon of 13 December 2007 (OJ C 306).

[371] Article 9 TEU; Article 20 (1), (2) TFEU.

status of nationals of the Member States".[372] It complements without replacing national citizenship to which it remains accessory.[373] Since the Treaty of Maastricht, the citizens of every Member State have a dual political identity as citizens of their respective Member State and citizens of the Union. That parallels the situation in federal States in which the citizens of all the constituent States are at the same time also citizens of the federation.[374]

The accessory character of Union citizenship makes Member States the gatekeepers of individuals' fundamental status and attached political rights in the EU, because they determine access to and retention of Union citizenship through the enactment and execution of their various citizenship laws. The Member States undoubtedly retain the exclusive competence to regulate their citizenship, including conditions for acquisition and loss, a competence whose exercise is closely connected with their sovereign statehood and national identity.[375] Accordingly, the Intergovernmental Conference of Maastricht of 1992 adopted a Declaration (no. 2) on nationality of a Member State, together with the Treaty of Maastricht and attached to the Final Act, that stated the following: "…the question whether an individual possesses the nationality of a Member State shall be settled solely by reference to the national law of the Member State concerned. Member States may declare, for information, who are to be considered their nationals for Community purposes by way of a declaration lodged with the Presidency and may amend any such declaration when necessary."[376]

On the other hand, it has long been recognised that public international law imposes certain limits on the discretion of States to grant and withdraw citizenship, limits that prevent arbitrariness. Other States are bound to accept the award of citizenship to an individual by a State only if there is a genuine connection between that State and the individual.[377] And States may not deprive anyone arbitrarily of their nationality.[378] To this limited extent, international law protects an individual right to nationality and the associated rights to democratic participation. Relying on the Member States with regard to the acquisition and loss of Union citizenship, the EU

---

[372] ECJ, judgment of 20 September 2001 (C-184/99), ECLI:EU:C:2001:458, para. 31. This settled case-law was reconfirmed recently, e.g., by ECJ, judgment of 25 April 2024 (Joined Cases C-684/22, C-685/22 and C-686/22), ECLI:EU:C:2024:345, para. 35; judgment of 19 November 2024 (C-808/21), ECLI:EU:C:2024:962, paras. 109, 111; judgment of 29 April 2025, ECLI:EU:C:2025:283, paras. 92, 100.

[373] Article 9 TEU, Article 20 (1) TFEU.

[374] See, e.g., Amendment XIV section 1 sentence 1 to the U.S. Constitution.

[375] Article 4 (2) TEU.

[376] OJ C 191, p. 98.

[377] ICJ, judgment of 6 April 1955, Nottebohm Case (Liechtenstein v. Guatemala), Second Phase, I.C.J. Reports 1955, p. 4, 23. The scope of this judgment is controversial – see Dörr (2019), paras. 18, 54.

[378] Article 15 (2) UDHR. Article 7 of the European Convention on Nationality of 6 November 1997 (ETS No. 166). There is a corresponding rule of customary international law (Dörr [2019], para. 32).

assumes as a matter of course that they will comply with the aforementioned international law limits in designing and applying their citizenship laws.

But according to the case law of the ECJ, Union law imposes stricter limits than international law on Member State discretion regarding the withdrawal of citizenship where this results in the loss of Union citizenship. The Court has determined that the loss of Union citizenship and its consequences must be consistent with the EU law principle of proportionality and that the proportionality of these consequences must in each case be individually assessed regarding the person concerned and his or her family.[379] To this extent, there is an individual right to retain Union citizenship and the associated democratic rights which enable participation in EU democracy, but that right is limited, protecting only from disproportionate consequences caused by the loss of Union citizenship.

The question whether EU law also imposes limits on the granting of Member State nationality (with the automatic consequence of acquisition of Union citizenship) was recently answered by the ECJ in the context of an infringment procedure by the Commission concerning the Maltese citizenship by investment ("golden passports").[380] The main thrust of the European Commission's infringement action had been the claim that Malta has failed to fulfil its obligations under Article 20 TFEU and Article 4(3) TEU by selling its citizenship in an "unlawful citizenship investor scheme" to persons without any genuine link with the country. The Court held that "by establishing and operating an institutionalised citizenship investment scheme … which establishes a transactional naturalisation procedure in exchange for predetermined payments or investments and thus amounts to the commercialisation of the grant of nationality of a Member State and, by extension, that of Union citizenship", Malta had violated Art. 20 TFEU and Art. 4 (3) TEU. The ECJ was not called upon to decide whether there may be an individual right of access to Union citizenship and ensuing democratic participation via Member State nationality, but on the contrary, to determine Member States' obligations under EU law to limit such access. In this context, the Court emphasised that "the provisions relating to citizenship of the Union are among the fundamental provisions of the Treaties which are part of the framework of a system that is specific to the European Union and which are structured in such a way as to contribute to the implementation of the process of integration that is the *raison d'être* of the European Union itself and thus form an integral part of its constitutional framework".[381]

[379] ECJ, judgment of 2 March 2010 (C-135/08), ECLI:EU:C:2010:104; judgment of 12 March 2019 (C-221/17), ECLI:EU:C:2019:189; judgment of 18 January 2022 (C-118/20), ECLI:EU:C:2022:34; judgment of 5 September 2023 (C-689/21), ECLI:EU:C:2023:626; judgment of 25 April 2024 (Joined Cases C-684/22 to 686/22), ECLI:EU:C:2024:345. Shuibhne (2023), p. 110 ff. For a critique of the ECJ case law, see Nettesheim (2024), in: Grabitz/Hilf/Nettesheim, Artikel 9 EUV paras. 17, 23.

[380] ECJ, judgment of 29 April 2025, C-181/23, ECLI:EU:C:2054:283 in an infringement procedure concerning the Maltese citizenship by investment ("golden passports"). See Weiler (2024); Chamon (2024).

[381] Id., para. 91.

5.5.6.2 Central Democratic Human Right of Union Citizens: Art. 10 (3) Sentence 1 TEU

The central democratic human right is set forth in Art. 10 (3) sentence 1 TEU, giving every citizen "the right to participate in the democratic life of the Union", in particular at EU level, but also at Member State level.[382] While formulated as an individual right, the provision is rather vague[383] and the ECJ has not yet ruled on its direct effect, which is controversial in the legal literature.[384] It is argued that using Art. 10 (3) sentence 1 TEU as a reservoir of unwritten individual democratic rights would be difficult to reconcile with Art. 25 (2) TFEU which has introduced a cumbersome (and so far unused) procedure for complementing the list of Union citizens' rights in the Treaties.[385]

In parallel to what has been explained above regarding that provision's function at the Member State level,[386] Art. 10 (3) sentence 1 TEU, read together with Art. 2 and Art. 10 (1) TEU, can be interpreted as containing a judicially enforceable individual entitlement to the maintenance of elementary standards of democracy at EU level. But this will only protect from severe forms of democratic backsliding which have so far never occurred at EU level (in contrast to the Member State level). One can imagine that Art. 10 (3) sentence 1 TEU at least contains a non-retrogression rule in the sense that it prohibits the dismantling of democratic standards which have already been established at EU level. In cases concerning rule of law backsliding by Member States, the ECJ found the non-retrogression rule to be part of the guarantee of values in Art. 2 TEU and the Treaty provisions which give concrete expression to those values.[387] There is no reason why the rule should not equally apply to instances of democratic backsliding and also extend to the EU that is bound by Art. 2 TEU, too. If a case of prohibited democratic backsliding by the EU can be identified, Art. 10 (3) sentence 1 TEU could produce a subjective entitlement enabling individuals to challenge that retrogression in the courts. While direct actions for annulment against retrogressive EU acts by natural or legal persons would usually not meet the strict standing requirement of individual concern pursuant to Art. 263 (4) TFEU in the sense of the *Plaumann* formula,[388] indirect actions before Member State courts, which have to be made available in accordance with Art. 19 (1) subpara. 2 TEU and Art. 47 CFR, would enable the ECJ to give preliminary rulings (Art. 267 TFEU).

---

[382] See above Sect. 5.4.3.1.

[383] Huber, in: Streinz (2018), Artikel 10 EUV, para. 20.

[384] See Heselhaus, in: Pechstein et al. (2023a), vol. I, Artikel 10 EUV, paras. 32 ff.; Ruffert, in: Calliess and Ruffert (2022), Artikel 10 EUV, paras. 11 f.

[385] Heselhaus, in: Pechstein et al. (2023a), vol. I, Artikel 10 EUV, para. 32.

[386] See above Sects. 5.4.3.1 and 5.4.3.2.

[387] ECJ, judgment of 20 April 2021 (C-896/19) ECLI:EU:C:2021:311, paras. 63–64; judgment of 15 July 2021 (C-791/19), ECLI:EU:C:2021:596, para. 51.

[388] ECJ, judgment of 15 July 1963 (25/62), ECR 1963, p. 95, 107.

Another question is whether Art. 10 (3) sentence 1 TEU includes a right of EU citizens to steady improvements of the democratic life of the Union in the sense of a right to a constantly enhanced state of democracy and better individual democratic participation at EU level. This would be in accordance with the Union's aim to promote its values, including democracy.[389] There is a corresponding obligation of the Member States pursuant to Art. 4 (3) TEU to support the EU's endeavours to realise its aims which continues their accession-related commitment under Art. 49 TEU to promote the values referred to in Art. 2 TEU. However, in this respect Art. 10 (3) sentence 1 TEU is certainly too vague to provide a basis for any judicially enforceable individual claim. But there may be a parallel individual right under national constitutional law to the effect that the democratic foundations of the Union are enhanced in step with the progress of integration.[390]

The main function of Art. 10 (3) sentence 1 TEU, however, is to serve as a paraphrase of the subjective legal status of citizens of the Union as political actors (*status activus*), following the classical formula of the Court of Justice in *van Gend & Loos*.[391] For the most part, it therefore requires specification by concrete democratic rights enshrined elsewhere in the Treaties and the CFR. Although mostly devoid of direct effect, Art. 10 (3) sentence 1 TEU sets forth a legally binding principle guiding the pro-democratic and pro-participatory interpretation of other primary and secondary law provisions.[392] It constitutes the bridge between the concrete democratic rights that are enshrined elsewhere in the Treaties and the CFR[393] and the democratic system of the EU which Art. 10 TEU defines in general terms. It also serves as interpretative background of these specific rights which are obviously relevant to that system as a whole and should therefore be accorded as much practical effect and protection as possible *vis-à-vis* both the EU and the Member States.[394]

Art. 10 (3) sentence 1 TEU also constitutes a constant reminder that the Union's system of representative democracy is no longer founded on the separate peoples of the Member States,[395] but on the community of Union citizens who exercise their individual political rights at EU level, irrespective of their specific national citizenship. Accordingly, the European Parliament is no longer defined as composed of "representatives of the peoples of the States brought together in the Community"[396]

---

[389] Article 3 (1), Article 2 TEU. See also the 7th recital of the preamble of the TEU.

[390] See FCC, judgment of 12 October 1993 (2 BvR 2134, 2159/92), BVerfGE 89, 155, 186, para. 100.

[391] ECJ, judgment of 5 February 1963, Case 26/62, ECR 1963, p. 1, 12.

[392] Heselhaus, in: Pechstein et al. (2023a), vol. I, Artikel 10 EUV, para. 33.

[393] See below Sects. 5.5.7 and 5.5.8.

[394] See below Sect. 5.5.9 on the existence of a general right to democracy at EU level.

[395] To which the judgment in the *van Gend & Loos* case referred, citing the preamble of the EEC Treaty. See also Article 1 (2) TEU and the first recital of the preamble of the TFEU that speak of "an ever closer union among the peoples of Europe".

[396] Article 189 (1) EC Treaty as amended by the Treaty of Nice of 26 February 2001 (consolidated version in OJ 2002 C 325).

but of "representatives of the Union's citizens",[397] giving up the national compartmentalisation of the European electorate. This is a necessary consequence of the fact that since the entry into force of the Treaty of Maastricht on 1 November 1993, EU citizens residing in a Member State of which they are not nationals have the right to vote and to stand as a candidate in elections to the European Parliament in that Member State.[398] The source of the Union's democratic legitimacy now is the aggregation of Union citizens (*i.e.*, the European electorate as a European people in *statu nascendi*), and no longer the community of the peoples of the Member States (*i.e.*, the collectivity of national electorates).[399]

5.5.6.3 Democratic Equality Pursuant to Art. 9 Sentence 1 TEU as an Individual Right

As already explained, Art. 9 sentence 1 TEU obliges the EU to observe the principle of democratic equality of its citizens.[400] This begs the question whether the provision gives Union citizens a justiciable general individual right to democratic equality at EU level. Such an assumption is countered by the vagueness of that article that seems to be far from imposing obligations on the EU institutions "in a clearly defined way", in the sense of the *van Gend & Loos* judgment. On the other hand, the application of any equality standard always includes a margin of uncertainty because, according to the case law of both the ECtHR and the ECJ, unequal treatment can be justified if it pursues a legitimate aim and is a proportionate means towards that end.[401] This has not prevented the ECJ from directly applying numerous prohibitions of discrimination in primary and secondary EU law.

Accordingly, it is possible to derive a human right to democratic equality from Art. 9 sentence 1 TEU which is directed against the EU and includes a justiciable claim against instances of unreasonable or disproportionate discrimination regarding citizens' participation in the Union's political processes.[402] This right covers the elections to the European Parliament and the citizens' initiative pursuant to Art. 11 (4) TEU, while the right to petition the European Parliament, the right to apply to the European Ombudsman and the right to communicate with the institutions and bodies of the EU, to which Union citizens are also entitled, are regulated separately, including protection against discrimination.[403]

---

[397] Article 14 (2) sentence 1 TEU.

[398] Article 22 (2) TFEU.

[399] See Heselhaus, in: Pechstein et al. (2023a), vol. I, Artikel 9 EUV, para. 5.

[400] See above Sect. 5.3.4.

[401] ECtHR, judgment of 30 September 2003, Koua Poirrez v. France (Appl. No. 40892/98), para. 46; ECJ, judgment of 15 March 2005 (C-209/03), ECLI:EU:C:2005:169, para. 54.

[402] See Heselhaus, in: Pechstein et al. (2023), vol. I, Artikel 9 EUV, paras. 9, 24; Haag, in: von der Groeben et al. (2015), vol. 1, Artikel 9 EUV, para. 6; Magiera, in: Streinz (2018), Artikel 9 EUV, para. 11; Nettesheim (2024), in: Grabitz/Hilf/Nettesheim, Artikel 9 EUV paras. 26 ff.

[403] Articles 24 (4), 227, 228 TFEU; Article 41 (4), 43, 44 CFR.

The right to democratic equality regarding EP elections arising from Art. 9 sentence 1 TEU must of course be interpreted in the context of the special provisions on EP elections in Art. 14 (2), (3), Art. 22 (2) TFEU and Art. 39 CFR. It complements them without displacing them.[404]

5.5.7 *Voting Rights at EP Elections as Particular Rights Associated with Union Citizenship*

5.5.7.1 Active and Passive Voting Rights—Prohibition of Discrimination and Substantive Rights

Art. 10 (3) sentence 1 TEU is concretised by Art. 20 (2) (b), 22 (2) TFEU and Art. 39 CFR that protect the Union citizens' right to vote and to stand as a candidate at elections to the European Parliament in the Member State of residence, if they have the nationality of another Member State,[405] under the same conditions as nationals of their State of residence, subject to detailed arrangements for the exercise of those rights enacted by the Council.[406] As the ECJ recently made clear, the Council "cannot, even implicitly, limit the scope of the rights and obligations arising under Article 22 TFEU", but only regulate their exercise.[407]

Those primary law provisions definitely have direct effect. The rights guaranteed in Art. 22 (2) TFEU are a corollary of the right to move and reside freely throughout the Union enshrined in Art. 21 TFEU.[408] The passive voting right in Art. 22 (2) TFEU also protects EU foreign nationals from discrimination regarding membership in political parties.[409] Moreover, the ECJ applied the principle of non-discrimination as a general principle of Community law—now codified in Art. 20 CFR as a general principle of Union law—to require that a national rule excluding

[404] On the right to equality of suffrage, see below Sect. 5.5.7.2.

[405] According to Article 52 (2) CFR, the personal and substantive scope of Articles 39, 40 CFR corresponds to Article 22 TFEU.

[406] See Council Directive 93/109/EC of 6 December 1993 laying down detailed arrangements for the exercise of the right to vote and to stand as a candidate in elections to the European Parliament for citizens of the Union residing in a Member State of which they are not nationals (as amended – available via https://eur-lex.europa.eu/legal-content/EN/TXT/?uri=CELEX%3A01993L0109-20130127&qid=1732176714474 [22 January 2025]). In November 2021, the Commission submitted a proposal to recast the Directive (see Report from the Commission under Article 25 TFEU – COM(2023) 931 final of 6.12.2023, p. 27 f. Available via https://eur-lex.europa.eu/resource.html?uri=cellar:b69763bf-94da-11ee-b164-01aa75ed71a1.0001.02/DOC_1&format=PDF [22 January 2025).

[407] ECJ, judgment of 19 November 2024 (C-808/21), ECLI:EU:C:2024:962, para. 103; judgment of 19 November 2024 (C-814/21), ECLI:EU:C:2024:963, para. 102.

[408] See in this sense ECJ, judgment of 19 November 2024 (C-808/14); ECLI:EU:C:2024:962, paras. 16, 113.

[409] See above Sect. 5.4.3.3.4.

citizens of that same State residing in overseas territories from participating in elections to the European Parliament had to be objectively justified.[410]

The ECJ has held that Art. 39 (1) CFR "is confined to applying the principle of non-discrimination on grounds of nationality to the exercise of the right to vote in elections to the European Parliament".[411] By contrast, the electoral principles enshrined in Art. 39 (2) CFR also protect Union citizens that have the nationality of the Member State of their residence from the deprivation of the right to vote, in parallel with Art. 14 (3) TEU.[412] Art. 39 (2) CFR thus transforms Art. 14 (3) TEU into a fundamental right that is addressed to both the Member State of residence and the Member State of nationality. In order to confirm this interpretation, the ECJ refers to the explanation relating to Art. 39 CFR, according to which Art. 39 (2) CFR "takes over the basic principles of the electoral system in a democratic State."[413] The same interpretation must apply to the right to stand as a candidate. In other words, the two paragraphs of Art. 39 CFR enshrine both the right of EU foreign nationals not to be discriminated against on grounds of nationality by their Member State of residence with regard to active and passive voting rights at elections to the European Parliament (para. 1) and the substantive right to vote and to stand as a candidate in EP elections held in compliance with the basic electoral principles *vis-à-vis* their Member State of residence as well as their Member State of nationality (para. 2). The ECJ's interpretation of Art. 39 CFR as including both a prohibition of discrimination and substantive rights corresponds to its more recent interpretation of both paragraphs of Art. 22 TFEU,[414] as it should, pursuant to Art. 52 (2) CFR.

This interpretation is also in line with the case-law of the ECtHR, according to which Art. 3 of Prot. No. 1 protects the right to vote in elections to the European Parliament in the State of the voter's nationality.[415] Pursuant to Art. 52 (3) CFR, Art. 39 CFR must be interpreted conformously. Since the Member States are responsible for organising the EP elections, the dependence of EU democracy on national democracies becomes particularly clear.[416] This makes the implementation of Union law democratic standards *vis-à-vis* the Member States indispensable, especially those that define themselves as "illiberal democracies".[417]

The ECJ has also indicated that the passive voting right guaranteed in Art. 39 CFR also protects the exercise of their mandate by elected Members of the European Parliament.[418]

---

[410] ECJ, judgment of 12 September 2006 (C-300/04), ECLI:EU:C:2006:545, paras. 56 ff.

[411] ECJ, judgment of 6 October 2015 (C-650/13), ECLI:EU:C:2015:648, paras. 42 f.

[412] Id., paras. 44 ff.

[413] Id., paras. 41, 44.

[414] See above Sect. 5.4.3.3.2.

[415] GC, judgment of 18 February 1999, Matthews v. UK (Appl. No. 24833/94).

[416] See ECJ, judgment of 19 December 2019 (C-502/19), ECLI:EU:C:2019:1115.

[417] See Szabó (2023).

[418] ECJ, judgment of 19 December 2019 (C-502/19), ECLI:EU:C:2019:1115, para. 86. That judgment is, however, mainly based on Article 9 of Protocol (No. 7) on the privileges and immunities of the EU.

5.5.7.2 Right to Equality of Suffrage in European Parliament Elections

Art. 14 (3) TEU and Art. 39 (2) CFR stipulate that members of the European Parliament shall be elected "by direct universal suffrage in a free and secret ballot." Equal suffrage is conspicuously missing and that gap cannot simply be closed by the general democratic equality standard enshrined in Art. 9 sentence 1 TEU, because Art. 14 TEU and Art. 39 (2) CFR are more special and *prima facie* exhaustive.[419] Art. 21 UDHR, Art. 25 lit. b ICCPR and Art. 23 (1) lit. c ACHR expressly guarantee equal suffrage, but it is not mentioned in Art. 3 Prot. No. 1 to the ECHR. The ECtHR has indeed determined that "the phrase 'conditions which will ensure the free expression of the opinion of the people in the choice of the legislature' implies essentially … the principle of equality of treatment of all citizens in the exercise of their right to vote and their right to stand for election."[420] Yet, this does not mean "that all votes must necessarily have equal weight as regards the outcome of the election or that all candidates must have equal chances of victory." Rather, Art. 3 Prot. No. 1 permits the choice of an electoral system adapted to the peculiarities of the specific country (or polity), "at least so long as the chosen system provides for conditions which will ensure the 'free expression of the opinion of the people in the choice of the legislature'."[421]

Accordingly, neither the ECHR system nor EU law include a comprehensive right to equality of suffrage, in contrast to the global level. But, as we shall see, there is a partial right to equality of suffrage in European Parliament elections, both pursuant to EU law and Art. 3 Prot. No. 1 to the ECHR, which corresponds to the special characteristics of the representation of Union citizens in the EP and also complies with Art. 21 UDHR and Art. 25 lit. b ICCPR.[422]

5.5.7.2.1 Degressive Proportional Representation of Union Citizens in the EP

The elections to the European Parliament do indeed not meet the equality standard. One reason is that these elections are conducted by the Member States according to standards that are only partly harmonised by the Act concerning the Elections of the Members of the European Parliament by Direct Universal Suffrage (Electoral Act),[423] for instance by requiring all Member States to conduct the election accord-

---

[419] See Heselhaus, in: Pechstein et al. (2023a), vol. I, Artikel 9 EUV, paras. 4, 17 f. But see also below Sect. 5.5.7.2.2.2.

[420] ECtHR (Plenary), judgment of 2 March 1987, Mathieu-Mohin and Clerfayt v. Belgium (Appl. No. 9267/81), para. 54; decision of 29 November 2007, Partija 'Jaunie Demokrāti' v. Latvia (Appl. No. 10547/07) and Partija 'Mūsu Zeme' v. Latvia (Appl. No. 34049/07).

[421] ECtHR (Plenary), judgment of 2 March 1987, Mathieu-Mohin and Clerfayt v. Belgium (Appl. No. 9267/81), para. 54.

[422] See below Sect. 5.5.7.2.4.

[423] Of 20 September 1976, as amended. Available via https://eur-lex.europa.eu/legal-content/EN/TXT/PDF/?uri=CELEX:01976X1008(01)-20020923&qid=1715938728555) (22 January 2025).

ing to the proportional representation system.[424] The Electoral Act is based on Art. 223 (1) TFEU which expressly leaves the EU legislature a choice between "a uniform procedure in all Member States or … accordance with principles common to all Member States" for regulating EP elections.[425] Since the EU legislature opted for the second alternative of only partial harmonisation, important differences have remained in the national rules that affect the composition of the EP, such as with regard to the minimum thresholds for the allocation of seats which only some Member States use, and at various levels.[426] These remaining differences also impair electoral equality. The call for further harmonisation of EU electoral laws should be heeded in order to improve the Union's democratic legitimacy, not least by turning the EP elections into a truly European democratic event focussing on European political issues.[427]

But the main reason preventing genuine electoral equality is the degressively proportional representation of Union citizens in the European Parliament laid down in Art. 14 (2) subpara. 1 TEU, with an allocation of seats to the Member States in a range from 6 to 96.[428] Degressive proportionality means "that each Member of the European Parliament from a more populous Member State represents more citizens than each Member of the European Parliament from a less populous Member State and, conversely, that the larger the population of a Member State, the greater its entitlement to a large number of seats in the European Parliament".[429] In other words, citizens in less populous Member States are overrepresented compared with citizens in more populous Member States.[430]

According to Art. 14 (2) subpara. 2 TEU, the European Council makes the actual allocation by unanimity, on the initiative of the European Parliament and with its consent. In the current European Parliament, Germany (the most populous Member State with more than 83 million inhabitants) has 96 representatives, while Malta (the least populous Member State with a little over 500,000 inhabitants) has six.[431] This means that an MEP from Germany represents ca. 865,000 voters, whereas an

See Article 8 of the Act.

[424] Article 1 (1) Electoral Act.

[425] See below Sect. 5.5.7.3 on an EP proposal to make EP elections more equal by increasing harmonisation through EU law.

[426] See below Sect. 5.5.7.2.2.

[427] See, e.g., Report of Franco-German Working Group on EU Institutional Reform (2023), p. 23.

[428] See the criticism voiced in this regard by the German FCC, judgment of 30 June 2009 (2 BvE 2/08 etc.), paras. 279 ff. Available via https://www.bundesverfassungsgericht.de/SharedDocs/Entscheidungen/EN/2009/06/es20090630_2bve000208en.html (22 January 2025). FCC, order of 6 February 2024 (2 BvE 6/23 etc.), para. 110, is now less critical.

[429] Article 1 of European Council Decision (EU) 2023/2061 of 22 September 2023 establishing the composition of the European Parliament (OJ L 238 of 27 September 2023, p. 114).

[430] Technically, the allocation of seats in the EP is based on population (*i.e.*, inhabitants) of Member States, not citizens with voting rights, but the latter constitute the large majority of the former. See Giegerich (2020b), Political Dimensions of Equality, p. 78 f.

[431] Article 3 of European Council Decision (EU) 2023/2061 (note 427) for the 2024–2029 parliamentary term.

MEP from Malta represents only ca. 87,000. In other words, the weight of a vote cast in Malta equals almost ten times the weight of a vote cast in Germany, giving every voter in Malta ten times as much influence on the composition of the European Parliament as every voter in Germany.[432] This means that there is no equal suffrage from a transnational perspective, comparing the weight of votes cast in different Member States.

Degressive proportionality is a compromise mechanism that ensures both size limitation of the European Parliament in order to guarantee functionality[433] and adequate representation of the less populous Member States that prevents their domination in the parliamentary process by the large Member States, which is a democratic imperative and *conditio sine qua non* of non-hegemonic supranational integration.[434] The small Member States' national delegations, comprising at least six MEPs, can reasonably well represent the main political currents in these States, and not only the governing majority that is already represented in the Council.[435] The overrepresentation of the less populous Member States in the European Parliament is "a step towards maintaining political equality among the European electorates (*i.e.* resident Union citizens) in the various Member States, irrespective of their numbers" and, correspondingly, of the national electorates from whom the democratic legitimacy of the national governments is derived.[436] This means that there is a democratic reason for the deviation from the principle of equal suffrage which is connected with the special character of the EU's supranational polity: the primacy of national citizenship (*i.e.*, the belonging to a national electorate) *vis-à-vis* the Union citizenship (*i.e.*, the belonging to a European electorate).[437] The resulting loss regarding individual electoral equality of Union citizens at EU level is partly compensated by the second element of the required double majority in the Council's standard procedure of qualified majority voting (*i.e.* population size) which gives the more populous Member States greater voting power and their citizens accordingly greater political influence in the EU's decision-making process.[438] All in all, the compromise struck by Union law between Member State equality and citizen equality is an adequate adaptation of democratic requirements to the specific circumstances of the dual-level/quasi-federal democracy of the EU.[439]

While compromises of that kind are common in federal systems,[440] the deviation from electoral equality in the EU is particularly pronounced, because of the com-

---

[432] See Giegerich (2020b), Political Dimensions of Equality, p. 86 f.

[433] Article 14 (2) subpara. 1 sentence 2 TEU limits the number of MEP to 751. According to Article 3 of European Council Decision (EU) 2023/2061 (note 427), the current EP has only 720 members.

[434] Von Achenbach (2025), p. 891 f. (citing Nicolaïdis [2013], p. 358).

[435] Article 16 (2) TEU. See Giegerich (2020b), Political Dimensions of Equality, p. 85.

[436] Giegerich (2020b), Political Dimensions of Equality, p. 87.

[437] See also von Bogdandy (2023), p. 28 ff.

[438] Article 16 (3), (4) TEU. See Giegerich (2020b), Political Dimensions of Equality, p. 78 ff., 87 f.

[439] Heselhaus, in: Pechstein et al. (2023a), vol. I, Artikel 9 EUV, para. 17.

[440] See *id.*

paratively low level of integration between the peoples of the Member States.[441] It therefore continues to present a legitimacy dilemma[442] which could only be solved after the utopian merger of the peoples of the Member States into one true European people that would enable proportional representation of Union citizens in the European Parliament. According to general opinion such a European people does not exist today and will not come into being in the foreseeable future.[443] In view of that continuing legitimacy dilemma, the power of the EP to legitimise decisions which the Council takes by a qualified majority is not unlimited.[444] But it is difficult exactly to define that limit and determine the areas where unanimity in the Council cannot yet be abolished.

5.5.7.2.2 Minimum Threshold for Allocation of Seats in the European Parliament

Within each Member State, the votes cast for candidates competing for the number of seats allocated to that Member State carry equal weight.[445] And yet, even in this regard, there is an exception to the equality of suffrage in the form of minimum thresholds. According to the current Art. 3 of the Electoral Act, Member States may set a minimum threshold for the allocation of seats in the EP, but at national level, this threshold may not exceed 5 per cent of votes cast. If such a threshold is introduced, the votes cast for a list that does not surpass it will have no effect on the composition of the EP, in contrast to all the other votes cast. These votes are practically "lost" in the sense that they carry no weight at all, whereas all the other votes carry equal weight in the sense that they are equally reflected in the composition of the EP.

5.5.7.2.2.1 German Federal Constitutional Court's Opposition to Minimum Threshold

Germany introduced a 5 per cent threshold by law in time for the first direct EP elections in 1979.[446] The constitutionality of this rule was immediately, but unsuccessfully challenged before the Federal Constitutional Court. The Court ruled in 1979 that the threshold did not violate the fundamental right to equality (including electoral equality regarding EP elections) in Art. 3 (1) of the Basic Law because it was

---

[441] Heselhaus, in: Pechstein et al. (2023a), vol. I, Artikel 10, para. 1.

[442] Müller (2024), p. 7.

[443] See Article 1 (2) TEU: "process of creating an ever closer union among the peoples of Europe". Heselhaus, in: Pechstein et al. (2023a), vol. I, Artikel 10 EUV, para. 27, who cites BVerfGE 89, 155 (184 f.).

[444] Ruffert, in: Calliess and Ruffert (2022), Artikel 9 EUV, para. 7; Heselhaus, in: Pechstein et al. (2023), vol. I, Artikel 10 EUV, para. 15.

[445] See FCC, order of 6 February 2024 (2 BvE 6/23), para. 110.

[446] § 2 (6) [later (7)] of the Europawahlgesetz of 16 June 1978 (BGBl. I p. 709).

justified by the goal to avoid excessive fragmentation and in this way safeguard the functioning of the EP.[447] In 2011, however, the FCC struck down that same 5 per cent threshold, finding that it was incompatible with Art. 3 (1) read together with Art. 21 (1) of the Basic Law, the latter provision guaranteeing political parties' equal chances in elections, regardless of the number of votes received.[448] The Court now argued that the serious interference with the principles of electoral equality and equal chances for political parties caused by that threshold could not be justified under the given legal and factual circumstances. The impediment to the formation of majorities caused by fragmentation did not impair the functioning of the EP, in contrast to the German Parliament where preventing fragmentation was still considered as necessary for ensuring government stability.[449] The German legislature reacted by introducing a new 3 per cent threshold for EP elections. But the FCC annulled that threshold, too, for the same reason.[450] In the judgments of 2011 and 2014, the FCC emphasised that EU law permitted, but did not require the introduction of thresholds for the allocation of seats in the EP. Both judgments were supported by a 5:3 majority of judges and supplemented by dissenting opinions.

In those two cases, the FCC used the basic right to electoral equality guaranteed by German constitutional law to prevent the German legislature from taking measures aimed at preventing fragmentation and thus ensuring the functionality of the EP, a task which Union law had long left to the discretion of the Member States. But this is about to change: Council Decision (EU, Euratom) 2018/994 of 13 July 2018[451] amends the Electoral Act by replacing the current Art. 3 (which only permits but does not oblige Member States to set a minimum threshold not exceeding 5 per cent of votes cast) by the following new Art. 3:

1. Member States may set a minimum threshold for the allocation of seats. At national level, this threshold may not exceed 5 per cent of valid votes cast.
2. Member States in which the list system is used shall set a minimum threshold for the allocation of seats for constituencies which comprise more than 35 seats. This threshold shall not be lower than 2 per cent, and shall not exceed 5 per cent, of the valid votes cast in the constituency concerned, including a single-constituency Member State.
3. Member States shall take the measures necessary to comply with the obligation set out in paragraph 2 no later than in time for the elections to the European Parliament which follow the first ones taking place after the entry into force of Council Decision (EU, Euratom) 2018/994 …

---

[447] FCC, order of 22 May 1979 (2 BvR 193, 197/79), BVerfGE 51, 222.

[448] FCC, judgment of 9 November 2011 (2 BvC 4/10 etc.), BVerfGE 129, 300.

[449] On the continuous constitutionality of the 5 per cent threshold regarding federal elections in Germany, see FCC, order of 19 September 2017 (2 BvC 46/14), BVerfGE 146, 327, 354 ff, paras. 68 ff.; judgment of 30 July 2024 (2 BvF 1/23 etc.), paras. 219 ff.

[450] FCC, judgment of 26 February 2014 (2 BvE 2/13 etc.), BVerfGE 135, 259. For a critique, see Giegerich (2016), p. 37 ff.

[451] OJ 2018 L 178, p. 1 (not yet in force).

Para. 2 of this new provision now requires the five most populous Member States—France, Germany, Italy, Poland and Spain—to set a minimum threshold of at least 2 per cent of the valid votes cast.[452] According to Art. 223 (1) subpara. 2 sentence 2 TFEU, the entry into force of that Council Decision depends on approval by all the Member States in accordance with their respective constitutional requirements. In Germany, the approval must be given in the form of a federal law, based on Art. 23 (1) BL.[453] The corresponding German law[454] was adopted by the supermajorities in both chambers of the federal legislature required for constitutional amendments because it had to overcome the constitutional obstacles identified by the FCC judgments of 2011 and 2014. Opponents of the threshold tried to prevent the law's entry into force with the help of the FCC, but to no avail—the Court rejected their applications as inadmissible because the applicants had not sufficiently substantiated their claim that the law violated their constitutional rights.[455]

In this most recent decision, the FCC applied the reduced standard of review provided by Art. 23 (1) sentence 3, Art. 79 (3) BL, the same that it uses *vis-à-vis* constitutional amendments, because the proceedings now concerned an EU law obligation to introduce the threshold, in difference to the previous cases. In this context, it reaffirmed that, according to Art. 23 (1) BL, the Federal Republic of Germany participated in the development of the European Union that was particularly committed to democratic principles. This prohibited the relinquishment of core elements of democratic legitimacy at EU level. Rather, a sufficiently effective level of democratic legitimacy had to be achieved in the EU. The Court went on to identify the safeguards to ensure democratic rule in primary Union law that constituted the framework into which the threshold provision as an element of the secondary-law Electoral Act must fit. The FCC acknowledged the legitimate interest of the Union legislature to introduce the threshold as a safeguard to protect the functionality of the EP and indicated that it was ready to grant the EU legislature a certain margin of appreciation as to what was necessary in this regard.

With reference to the dissenting opinions annexed to its judgments of 2011 and 2014, the FCC stated that according to Art. 223 (1) subpara. 2 sentence 2 TFEU, electoral regulations only came into force after all Member States had given their consent. Primary EU law thus entrusted the Member States with joint responsibility for maintaining the EP's ability to function. For the Federal Republic of Germany, such responsibility also followed from the responsibility for integration enshrined in Art. 23 (1) of the Basic Law. Each Member State was therefore obliged to formulate its requirements for the structures of electoral law in such a way that they could also be a maxim for the election of the entire European Parliament. This precluded

---

[452] For an assessment, see Giegerich (2018b), Die Verflechtungsfalle des Europawahlrechts, p. 145 ff.

[453] See § 3 (1), (2) of the Integration Responsibility Law (Integrationsverantwortungsgesetz) of 22 September 2009 (BGBl. 2009 I, p. 3022).

[454] Gesetz zu dem Beschluss (EU, Euratom) 2018/994 des Rates der Europäischen Union vom 13. Juli 2018 of 6 March 2024 (BGBl. 2024 II No. 87).

[455] FCC, order of 6 February 2024 (2 BvE 6/23 etc.).

Germany from claiming a "special path" ("Sonderweg") with regard to the minimum threshold (as it had practically done by virtue of the two earlier FCC judgments). This FCC decision is more positive towards European integration in general and the EP in particular than the previous case-law.[456]

5.5.7.2.2.2 Compatibility of Minimum Threshold with Primary EU Law

Although the procedure for enacting and amending the Electoral Act is reminiscent of the Treaty revision procedure (Art. 48 TEU), because both require the approval by all the Member States, the Treaty of Lisbon amended the text of Art. 223 (1) subpara. 2 TFEU in the sense that a special legislative procedure shall be used for enacting electoral provisions. This makes clear that the Electoral Act and its amendments constitute legislative acts of the Union ranking as secondary law.[457] Accordingly, the introduction of the obligatory minimum threshold by the Council Decision of 2018 that amends the Electoral Act must comply with primary Union law precepts. The German Federal Constitutional Court used the principles of electoral equality and equal chances for political parties, having the status of basic rights in German constitutional law, as standards of review. This raises the question whether parallel guarantees can be identified in primary EU law and whether the Electoral Act amendment of 2018 is compatible with them.

As has already been explained, Art. 39 (2) CFR does not expressly guarantee electoral equality. On the contrary, the degressive proportional representation of EU citizens in the European Parliament makes electoral inequality an inherent structural part of EU electoral law. Yet, this does not give the Union legislature *carte blanche* to enact further non-inherent restrictions on electoral equality, because such restrictions partially devalue the individual right to vote which Art. 22 (2) TFEU and Art. 39 CFR obviously intend to protect as comprehensively as possible within the basic structure of EU electoral law. For the equal right to vote is an essential element in the EU's system of representative democracy (Art. 10 TEU), which is characterised by the equal right of all citizens to participate in political life (Art. 10 (3) in conjunction with Art. 9 sentence 1 TEU).[458] Therefore, the introduction of an obligatory minimum threshold by an amendment to the Electoral Act is subject to judicial review by the equal right to vote enshrined in Art. 22 (2) TFEU and to the same extent in Art. 39 CFR,[459] always read together with Art. 10 (3) and Art. 9 sentence 1 TEU.

This interpretation of Art. 39 CFR also corresponds to the jurisprudence of the ECtHR regarding Art. 3 Prot. No. 1 which does not expressly guarantee electoral equality either. The Court has nevertheless categorised minimum thresholds as

[456] See Classen (2024), p. 322 ff.

[457] See Article 289 (2) and (3) TFEU in the Treaty section on the legal acts of the Union.

[458] On Article 9 sentence 1 TEU as a general pro-equality interpretative background of other rules of EU law, see Huber, in: Streinz (2018), Artikel 10 EUV, para. 16.

[459] See Article 52 (2) CFR.

interferences with the right to free elections that require adequate justification. According to Art. 52 (3) CFR, Art. 39 CFR must not lag behind that provision in its protective effect. However, the ECtHR considers minimum thresholds of 5% or less (*i.e.*, on the scale provided by EU electoral law) to be unobjectionable.[460] There is much to suggest that Art. 39 CFR does not impose stricter requirements, although Art. 52 (3) CFR would permit this, because the EU legislature must retain a margin of appreciation.[461]

The counterpart in primary EU law of the second standard of review used by the German Federal Constitutional Court—equal chances for political parties –could be Art. 12 (1) CFR which guarantees the right to freedom of association also in political matters. Since Art. 12 (2) CFR mentions only political parties at Union level, it cannot be used as a standard of review for EU measures affecting national political parties which participate in EP elections. But it supports the inclusion of national political parties in the ambit of Art. 12 (1) CFR ("right … to freedom of association … in political … matters").[462] The activities of those political parties, including their participation in EP elections on an equal footing with competing parties, is probably protected by Art. 12 (1) CFR.[463] According to the case law of the ECtHR pertaining to the parallel provision in Art. 11 ECHR, which sets the minimum standard of protection valid also for Art. 12 (1) CFR,[464] the activities of political parties are also protected by that Convention right.[465] Although there is no ECtHR case concerning equal chances for political parties in parallel to the FCC cases, it is unlikely that the Strasbourg Court would consider a minimum threshold provision which is compatible with Art. 3 Prot. No. 1 as violating Art. 11 ECHR.

5.5.7.2.2.3 European Parliament's 2022 Proposal to Increase Minimum Threshold

Although the 2018 reform of the Electoral Act has still not entered into force, because the Spanish approval is the last one missing, the European Parliament in 2022 already launched a further and much more ambitious electoral reform project which not even the Council has approved yet: the proposal for a new Council Regulation on the election of members of the European Parliament by direct universal suffrage.[466] Art. 13 of that Regulation entitled "Electoral threshold" in para. 2

---

[460] ECtHR (GC), judgment of 8 July 2008, Yumak and Sadak v. Turkey (Appl. No. 10226/03); decision of 29 November 2007, Partija "JAUNIE DEMOKRĀTI" v. la Lettonie (Appl. No. 10547/07) and Partija "MŪSU ZEME" v. la Lettonie (Appl. No. 34049/07).

[461] See Giegerich (2018a), 5%-Klausel.

[462] See Richter (2022), §17 para. 53.

[463] But see Sauer (2023), p. 794.

[464] See Article 52 (3) CFR.

[465] See, e.g., ECtHR, judgment of 10 May 2022, Yeşiller ve Sol Gelecek Partisi v. Turquie (Appl. No. 41955/14); judgment of 14 February 2006, Christian Democratic People's Party v. Moldova (Appl. No. 28793/02).

[466] See below Sect. 5.5.7.3.

reads as follows: "For national constituencies, which comprise more than 60 seats a threshold shall be set and shall not be lower than of 3,5 % of the valid votes cast in the constituency concerned." This would increase the obligatory threshold considerably, but affect only four Member States, namely France, Germany, Italy and Spain. Art. 13 (3) would permit Member States to grant exemptions to "political parties or associations of voters that represent recognised national or linguistic minorities." Art. 13 (4) exempts European electoral entities from the threshold, creating an incentive for smaller parties to establish transnational associations and run under their logo. Pursuant to Art. 13 (5), "there shall be no minimum threshold for the allocation of seats in the Union-wide constituency referred to in Article 15."[467]

That higher threshold proposed by the EP would also be compatible with both Art. 3 Prot. No. 1 and Art. 39 CFR.

5.5.7.2.3 Exclusion of Active and Passive Double Voting

There is one transnational aspect of equal suffrage that is guaranteed in the elections to the European Parliament: every Union citizen, including those who reside in a Member State of which they are not nationals, can cast only one vote and stand as a candidate in only one Member State. If their Member State of nationality gives expatriates the active and passive right to vote in the European elections, they must choose whether they vote or stand as a candidate in that Member State or in the Member State in which they reside. They are not permitted to vote more than once or stand as a candidate in more than one Member State at the same election.[468] This is the obvious consequence of the "one person, one vote" rule at EU level, an expression of the democratic equality of citizens enshrined in Art. 9 sentence 1 TEU.[469]

The Council Decision of 13 July 2018 amending the Electoral Act (that is not yet in force) adds a second paragraph to Art. 9 of the Electoral Act according to which "Member States shall take measures necessary to ensure that double voting in elections to the European Parliament is subject to effective, proportionate and dissuasive penalties."[470] This amendment indicates that the prohibition of double voting has so far not been effectively enforced by the Member States.[471] In view of the importance of the "one person, one vote" rule, one can assume that all Union citizens are generally entitled to effective protection by the EU and Member States against electoral fraud in the form of double voting by some Union citizens. But individual Union citizens have no right to any specific measures in this regard.

[467] On that Union-wide constituency, see below Sect. 5.5.7.3.

[468] Article 9 of the Electoral Act; Article 4 of the Council Directive 93/109/EC (note 404).

[469] On the parallel problem of double voting in national parliamentary elections, see above Sect. 5.4.3.3.5.1.

[470] OJ 2018 L 178 of 16 July 2018, p. 1.

[471] For a prominent case in Germany, see Joos and Droste (2024), p. 293 f.

5.5.7.2.4 Conclusion: Partial Right to Equality of Suffrage in European Parliament Elections

All in all, primary EU law does not guarantee a comprehensive right to equality of suffrage in European Parliament elections, primarily because the degressive proportional representation of Union citizens makes electoral inequality an inherent structural part of EU electoral law. But there is a partial right to equality of suffrage, to the extent in which it fits into these structural parameters. It derives from Art. 22 (2) TFEU and Art. 39 CFR, read together with Art. 10 (3) and Art. 9 sentence 1 TEU, and protects Union citizens from restrictions of electoral equality that are not inherent in the electoral system.[472] It also includes a general entitlement to protection against double voting.

5.5.7.3 Future Electoral Reform: Enhancing Democracy at EU Level

In 2022, the EP took the initiative for a far-reaching reform of the EP elections, based on Art. 223 (1) TFEU.[473] Since electoral reform in the EU can only enter into force after having been unanimously adopted by the Council and then approved by all the Member States in accordance with their respective constitutional requirements, it is impossible to predict, if, when and to what extent the EP's proposal will be realised.[474] In the Council, several Member States have rated many aspects of that proposal as unacceptable.[475]

The EP considers that the adoption of its proposal would henceforth make the elections to the EP "equal".[476] It would certainly improve equality by harmonising many more elements of the EP elections that have so far been regulated differently by the Member States, such as the minimum age for voting and eligibility, the possibility of postal voting and voting by persons with disabilities as well as expatriates and the introduction of one common election day (9th May). The EP also proposes the establishment of a European electoral roll for the purpose of detecting and avoiding double voting and of a European Electoral Authority for ensuring the correct implementation of the EU electoral law.[477] But the EP's reform proposal cannot

---

[472] For a similar view, see Schroeder (2023), p. 528 ff.

[473] European Parliament legislative resolution of 3 May 2022 on the proposal for a Council Regulation on the election of the members of the European Parliament by direct universal suffrage, P9_TA(2022)0129. Available via https://www.europarl.europa.eu/doceo/document/TA-9-2022-0129_EN.pdf (22 January 2025). On the proposed increase in the minimum threshold for the allocation of seats, see above Sect. 5.5.7.2.2.3.

[474] For an overview, see Giegerich (2022a), Die Verflechtungsfalle des Europawahlrechts; id. (2022a), Europawahlreform als unendliche Geschichte; Gitzen (2024); Joos and Droste (2024), p. 293 ff.

[475] Council Working Document WK 7750/2023 INIT of 16 June 2023. Available via https://www.politico.eu/wp-content/uploads/2024/06/03/Council-questionnaire_cleanned.pdf (22 January 2025).

[476] See Article 12 (1) of the proposed Regulation.

[477] Articles 9, 28 of the proposed Regulation.

do away with the principle of degressive proportional representation which constitutes the main challenge to electoral equality and is entrenched in Art. 14 (2) sub-para. 1 TEU.

Regarding the selection of candidates, Art. 10 (1) sentence 1 of the EP's proposed Regulation provides as follows: "All political parties, associations of voters, electoral alliances and European electoral entities participating in elections to the European Parliament shall observe democratic procedures, transparency and gender equality, through measures that aim to ensure that all eligible persons have an equal opportunity to be elected, and a composition of the European Parliament that reflects the diversity of the European Union, when selecting their candidates for election to the European Parliament."

Democratic equality specifically between women and men at EU level is required by Art. 9 sentence 1 TEU read together with Art. 8, 10 TFEU and Art. 21, 23 CFR. It also constitutes an essential democratic right of both women and men that can be derived from Art. 39 in conjunction with Art. 21 (1), 23 CFR. In its electoral reform proposal, the EP "[c]onsiders gender equality to be a key element for improving representation in elections" and "stresses that there are significant differences between Member States, with some not having elected to Parliament a single woman", obviously calling for harmonisation.[478] The representativeness of the EP also in gender terms obviously is an essential factor in its capacity to bestow democratic legitimacy on the EU's decision-making process.[479] Enhancing female representation in the EP therefore goes along with reinforcing democracy at EU level. In this regard, the EP, invoking Art. 8 TFEU,[480] proposes to promote gender equality in the selection of candidates by all political parties and other entities participating in EP elections in Art. 10 (1) sentence 2 of the proposed Regulation: "Gender equality shall be reached depending on the Member States electoral systems and in any event in the Union-wide constituency by the use of zipped lists or quotas, without infringing the rights of non-binary people."[481]

Interestingly, Art. 10 (2) of the EP's draft Regulation provides that "[a] member of a political party, an association of voters or a European electoral entity may file a reasoned complaint of non-compliance with the democratic procedures, transparency and gender equality criteria laid down in this Article with the responsible national authority or the European Electoral Authority." This translates the

[478] Legislative resolution, para. 9. On women's equal participation in political decision-making as a democratic requirement, see Beijing Declaration and Platform for Action of the Fourth World Conference on Women, 15 September 1995: Platform for Action, para. 181. Available via https://www.un.org/womenwatch/daw/beijing/pdf/BDPfA%20E.pdf (22 January 2025).

[479] According to the ECtHR, a law requiring political parties to include a minimum of 35% of female and male candidates in their electoral lists for national parliamentary elections pursued "the legitimate aim of strengthening the legitimacy of democracy by ensuring a more balanced participation of women and men in political decision-making." (Decision of 12 November 2019, Zevnik and Others v. Slovenia [Appl. No. 54893/18], para. 34).

[480] Proposed Regulation, recital (3) of the preamble.

[481] See Giegerich (2023), p. 155.

requirements for candidate selection that political parties etc. have to observe according to Art. 10 (1) of that Regulation into enforceable rights.

One important goal of the EP is to "to improve the transparency and democratic accountability of the Parliament, by strengthening the European dimension of the elections, notably by transforming the European elections into a single European election, especially through the establishment of a Union-wide constituency, as opposed to the collection of 27 separate national elections, which is the way that European elections are organised today".[482] In this constituency, 28 EP-Members would be elected from geographically balanced Union-wide (transnational) lists submitted by European electoral entities using their logo and in accordance with a uniform electoral procedure, in addition to the EP-Members elected in each Member State.[483] This is intended "to enhance the democratic and pan-European dimension of the European elections".[484] It would give every voter two votes, one for a national list and one for the Union-wide list (with no minimum threshold for the allocation of seats).[485] But because of the small number of additional MEPs, it would only marginally mitigate the negative effect on electoral equality caused by the degressively proportional representation of Union citizens in the European Parliament.

The proposal also wants to codify the lead candidate practice[486] in soft form, in order to enable Union citizens to vote for their preferred candidates for the President of the Commission who would head each European political family's list for the Union-wide constituency.[487] This would strengthen the democratic legitimacy of the Commission.[488]

5.5.8 *Supplementary Democratic Rights*

5.5.8.1 Right of Access to Documents

There are further provisions relevant to democracy at EU level: Pursuant to Art. 10 (3) sentence 2 TEU, decision-making processes have to be as open/transparent and take place as close to the citizen as possible.[489] As a consequence, Art. 16 (8) TEU stipulates that "[the Council shall meet in public when it deliberates and votes on a

[482] Para. 2 of the EP's legislative resolution (note 471).

[483] Article 15 of the proposed Regulation.

[484] Recital (9) of the preamble of the proposed Regulation.

[485] Article 13 (5) of the proposed Regulation.

[486] See Lenaerts et al. (2021), para. 12.014; Citino (2024). See also Nemitz and Ehm (2019), p. 354 ff.

[487] Paras. 12, 16 and 18 of the EP's legislative resolution (note 471); Article 18 of the proposed Regulation.

[488] See in this sense also the Report of Franco-German Working Group on EU Institutional Reform (2023), p. 24 f.

[489] See also Article 1 (2) TEU.

draft legislative act." Regarding the openness/transparency requirement, Art. 10 (3) sentence 2 TEU does not enshrine any individual right,[490] but Art. 15 TFEU takes up that requirement again, establishing a connection with good governance and participatory democracy in para. 1 and in para. 3 introducing an individual right of access to documents of the EU's institutions etc.,[491] subject to conditions to be included in a regulation.[492] Art. 42 CFR identifies access to documents as a fundamental right.[493]

The democratic roots of that right have been recognised by the ECJ.[494] The Court recalled that the principle of transparency was inextricably linked to the principle of openness enshrined in Art. 10 (3) TEU, Art. 15 (1) and Art. 298 (1) TFEU as well as Art. 42 CFR.[495] This principle "makes it possible ... to ensure that the administration enjoys greater legitimacy and is more effective and more accountable to the citizen in a democratic system".[496] The right's particular relevance regarding access to legislative documents has been emphasised by the General Court: "Openness in that respect contributes to strengthening democracy by allowing citizens to scrutinize all the information which has formed the basis of a legislative act. The possibility for citizens to find out the considerations underpinning legislative action is a precondition for the effective exercise of their democratic rights ... If citizens are to be able to exercise their democratic rights they must be in a position to follow in detail the decision-making process within the institutions taking part in the legislative procedures and to have access to all relevant information ... Furthermore, Article 10(3) TEU states that every citizen is to have the right to participate in the democratic life of the Union and that decisions are to be taken as openly and as closely as possible to the citizen. Thus, the expression of public opinion in relation to a particular provisional legislative proposal or agreement agreed in the course of a trilogue and reflected in the fourth column of a trilogue table forms an integral part of the exercise of EU citizens' democratic rights, particularly since ... such agreements are generally subsequently adopted without substantial amendment by the co-legislators."[497]

---

[490] Heselhaus, in: Pechstein et al. (2023a), vol. I, Artikel 10 EUV, para. 35.

[491] Heselhaus, in: Pechstein et al. (2023b), vol. II, Artikel 15 AEUV, para. 37 (explaining that the direct effect of Article 15 (3) TFEU is controversial but that the counterarguments are unconvincing).

[492] Regulation (EC) No. 1049/2001 of 30 May 2001 regarding public access to European Parliament, Council and Commission documents (OJ L 145 of 31 May 2001, p. 43).

[493] For a critical account of the current Commission's practice regarding access to documents, see Leino-Sandberg (2025).

[494] See, e.g., ECJ, judgment of 21 September 2010 (Joined Cases C-514/07 P, C-528/07 P and C-532/07 P), ECLI:EU:C:2010:541, para. 68. See also recital 2 of the preamble of Regulation (EC) No. 1049/2001 (note 490).

[495] Article 296 (2) TFEU which provides that all legal acts, including legislative acts, shall state the reasons on which they are based, could additionally have been mentioned (see von Bogdandy [2012], p. 330).

[496] ECJ, judgment of 5 March 2024 (C-588/21 P), ECLI:EU:C:2024:201, para. 83.

[497] General Court, judgment of 22 March 2018 (T-540/15), ECLI:EU:R:2018:167, paras. 80, 98.

Relying on the principle of openness laid down in Art. 1 (2), 10 (3) TEU and Art. 15 (1), 298 (1) TFEU, the ECJ has extended that right of access even to legal opinions of the Council's legal service relating to a legislative procedure, unless there are particularly strong reasons for refusing to disclose a specific legal opinion. The Court held that "[i]t is precisely openness in that regard which, by allowing divergences between various points of view to be openly debated, contributes to reducing doubts in the minds of citizens, not only as regards the lawfulness of an isolated legislative measure but also as regards the legitimacy of the legislative process as a whole … and contributes to strengthening the principles of democracy and respect for fundamental rights as laid down in Article 6 TEU and in the Charter".[498]

As a matter of fact, both Art. 15 (3) TFEU and Art. 42 CFR extend the right of access to documents beyond Union citizens to natural and legal persons residing or having their registered office in a Member State. This can be explained either by a modern concept of democracy that accords participatory rights to all those subject to the respective authority[499] or by the rule of law aspect of transparency that also promotes effective control of authorities regarding the legality of their conduct.[500]

5.5.8.2 Right to Subsidiarity?

The requirement of decision-making as close as possible to the citizen in Art. 10 (3) sentence 2 TEU reflects the principle of subsidiarity (Art. 5 (3) TEU). Contrary to Art. 10 (3) sentence 1 TEU, sentence 2 only applies in the relationship between the EU and the Member States, and not within each Member State.[501] This corresponds to the EU's obligation to respect the constitutional structures of its Member States, pursuant to Art. 4 (2) TEU, which can be more or less centralised, in accordance with the right of self-determination of each Member State's people. EU law does not require Member States to decentralise or federalise their systems. Pursuant to Art. 5 (3) TEU, subsidiarity means that problems should preferably be solved at Member State and not EU level, which reaffirms the importance of national democratic processes. This concern is reinforced by Art. 12 TEU providing that national parliaments "contribute actively to the good functioning of the Union".[502] Their most important task is to "seeing to it that the principle of subsidiarity is respected".[503]

The EU law principle of subsidiarity, together with the primary principle of conferral set forth in Art. 5 (2) TEU[504] and the principle of proportionality (Art. 5 (4)

[498] ECJ, judgment of 16 February 2022 (C-157/21), ECLI:EU:C:2022:98, paras. 43 ff., 57.

[499] See Heselhaus, in: Pechstein et al. (2023b), vol. II, Artikel 15 AEUV, para. 41.

[500] See Heselhaus, in: Pechstein et al. (2023a), vol. I, Artikel 10 EUV, para. 35.

[501] On the applicability of Article 10 (3) sentence 1 TEU within Member States, see above Sect. 5.4.3.1.

[502] See also Protocol (No. 1) on the Role of National Parliaments in the EU.

[503] Article 12 (b) and Protocol (No. 2) on the Application of the Principles of Subsidiarity and Proportionality. See Lenaerts et al. (2021) para. 15.010.

[504] The relationship between the two principles is clarified in Article 5 (1) TEU.

TEU), takes up a concern of the right of self-determination of peoples, namely that as much as possible should be left to the autonomous decision-making of individual peoples within their national democratic systems.[505] In the EU system, a distribution and use of competences that counteracts excessive centralisation is essential for maintaining a proper federal power balance. This is also important for ensuring adequate democratic legitimacy which is enhanced, if decisions are made as close as possible to the citizen, as required by Art. 10 (3) sentence 2 TEU. This gives the principles of conferral and subsidiarity a decidedly democratic effect in the sense of maintaining as much as possible of democratic autonomy at Member State level, but does not make them directly applicable: There is no individual right to compliance with the two principles as such.[506]

On the other hand, whenever any act of an EU institution etc. interferes with individual rights otherwise guaranteed by Union law, the holders of that right can challenge the validity of that act by arguing that it is incompatible with the principles of conferral or subsidiarity. If the strict conditions of Art. 263 (4) TFEU are met, the right holders can bring an action directly before the CJEU (General Court); otherwise, the Member States are obliged by Art. 19 (1) subpara. 2 TEU to give them access to their national court systems.[507] In accordance with Art. 267 TFEU, national courts cooperate with the ECJ that monopolises the power to strike down EU acts in order to guarantee legal unity throughout the EU.[508] If the ECJ then finds that the challenged EU act violates the principles of conferral or subsidiarity, the Court will declare it to be void and thereby also remove any interference with individual rights. However, the Court rarely annuls an EU legal act for a complete lack of EU competence,[509] and its review of compliance with the principle of subsidiarity is deferential.[510]

5.5.8.3 Right to Citizens' Participation?

Art. 10 TEU is complemented by Art. 11 TEU on civil society participation in all areas of Union action, including the citizens' initiative as an element of direct democracy in Art. 11 (4) TEU, "the objective of which is to encourage the participation of citizens in the democratic process and to promote dialogue between citizens and the EU institutions."[511] Civil society participation in the sense of Art. 11 TEU is

[505] See above Sect. 3.3.

[506] Nettesheim (2024), in: Grabitz/Hilf/Nettesheim, Artikel 10 EUV para. 87. But see Huber, in: Streinz (2018), Artikel 10 EUV, para. 52, who assumes that Article 10 (2) sentence 2 TEU provides a "subjective dimension" to those two principles.

[507] ECJ, judgment of 3 October 2013 (C-583/11 P), ECLI:EU:C:2013:625, paras. 89 ff.

[508] ECJ, judgment of 22 October 1987 (C-314/85), ECR 1987, 4199.

[509] Lenaerts et al. (2021), para. 5.013.

[510] Id., para. 5.033.

[511] See ECJ, judgment of 19 December 2019 (C-418/18 P), ECLI:EU:C:2019:1113, para. 65. Christopoulou (2024).

based on both individual citizens and representative associations. While it constitutes an important element of democracy at EU level, Art. 11 TEU as such is not directly applicable. But it is concretised by Art. 41–44 CFR (right to good administration, right of access to documents, right to refer cases of maladministration to the European Ombudsman,[512] right to petition the European Parliament[513]) that do provide enforceable individual rights. However, there is no individual right under primary EU law to carry out a citizens' initiative pursuant to Art. 11 (4) TFEU, but individual rights may derive from the Regulation (EU) 2019/788 on the European citizens' initiative that was enacted on the basis of Art. 24 (1) TFEU.[514]

There have been calls to strengthen participatory democracy at EU level further, such as by institutionalising citizens' panels.[515] The Commission wants to make European Citizens' Panels "a regular feature of our democratic life".[516] But there seem to be no plans to create any new individual entitlements in this regard.

5.5.8.4 Other Democratic Rights

The other supplementary democratic rights enshrined in the CFR that were already mentioned above in the context of the top-down perspective on Member States (where they are only applicable to the extent that these are implementing Union law), guaranteeing the freedom of expression and information, the freedom and pluralism of the media as well as the freedom of peaceful assembly and association,[517] are fully applicable to the EU in the bottom-up perspective.[518] This holds in particular true for the right to establish political parties at Union level that is expressly guaranteed.[519] Their "fundamental role … in expressing the will of EU citizens" and their "essential function in the system of representative democracy" has been recognised by the ECJ.[520] Based on Art. 224 TFEU, the Regulation (EU, EURATOM) No. 1141/2014 on the statute and funding of European political parties and European

---

[512] See also Article 228 TFEU.

[513] See also Article 227 TFEU.

[514] Of 17 April 2019 (OJ L 130 of 17 May 2019, p. 55). See Huber (2022), paras. 80 f.

[515] Report of Franco-German Working Group on EU Institutional Reform (2023), p. 25 f.

[516] Report from the Commission to the European Parliament, the Council, the European Economic and Social Committee and the Committee of the Regions under Article 25 TFEU: On progress towards effective EU citizenship, COM(2023) 931 final of 6 December 2023, p. 34. Available via https://eur-lex.europa.eu/resource.html?uri=cellar:b69763bf-94da-11ee-b164-01aa75ed71a1.0001.02/DOC_1&format=PDF (22 January 2025).

[517] See above Sect. 5.4.3.4.

[518] Article 51 (1) sentence 1 CFR.

[519] Article 12 (2) CFR; Article 10 (4) TEU. See Huber, in: Streinz (2018), Artikel 10 EUV, paras. 56 f.; id. (2022), para. 33.

[520] ECJ, judgment of 19 November 2024 (C-808/21), ECLI:EU:C:2024:962, paras. 120 f.; judgment of 19 November 2024 (C-814/21), ECLI:EU:C:2024:963, paras. 118 f.

political foundations was enacted.[521] According to recital 4 of the preamble, "[t]ruly transnational European political parties and their affiliated European political foundations have a key role to play in articulating the voices of citizens at European level by bridging the gap between politics at national level and at Union level."

Among the conditions for registration of a European political party in Art. 3 (1) Regulation No. 1141/2014, lit. c includes the following: "it must observe, in particular in its programme and in its activities, the values on which the Union is founded, as expressed in Article 2 TEU, namely respect for human dignity, freedom, democracy, equality, the rule of law and respect for human rights, including the rights of persons belonging to minorities".[522] Art. 10 Regulation No.1141/2014 establishes a procedure in which the independent Authority for European political parties and European political foundations "shall regularly verify that the conditions for registration laid down in Article 3 … continue to be complied with by registered European political parties and European political foundations." If it finds "a manifest and serious breach as regards compliance with" Art. 3 (1) lit. c or Art. 3 (2) lit. c Regulation No. 1141/2014, it can (and is probably obliged to) de-register that party or foundation, which is the functional equivalent at EU level of a prohibition of such a European political party or foundation.[523]

Pursuant to Art. 3 (3) Regulation No. 1141/2024, the "European Parliament, acting on its own initiative or following a reasoned request from a group of citizens … may lodge with the Authority a request for verification of compliance by a specific European political party or European political foundation with the conditions laid down in point (c) of Article 3(1) and point (c) of Article 3(2)." The Authority must ask a committee of independent eminent persons for an opinion before making its decision. Needless to say that there is no individual entitlement to the initiation of such a verification procedure or the de-registration of a European political party or foundation.

If the EU fulfils its obligation under Art. 6 (2) TEU to accede to the ECHR,[524] it will become directly subject to the supervision of the ECtHR, thereby enhancing its human rights credibility also with regard to democratic rights.[525] Even before that accession, however, the democratic guarantees of the ECHR and the Prot. No. 1 (that bind all EU Member States) play an important role because CFR rights that

---

[521] Of 22 October 2014 (OJ L 317 of 4 November 2014, p. 1), amended version via https://eur-lex.europa.eu/legal-content/EN/TXT/?uri=CELEX%3A02014R1141-20190327&qid=1709649301916 (22 January 2025).

[522] Article 3 (2) lit. c Regulation 1141/2014 imposes the same condition for registration of a European political foundation.

[523] Gutmann and Kohlmeier (2024).

[524] See the revised draft accession instruments of 2023 (that provide for the EU's accession to the ECHR as well as Prot. No. 1 and No. 6) in the appendix to CoE—Steering Committee for Human Rights, Interim to the Committee of Ministers, CDDH(2023)R_EXTRA ADDENDUM, 4 April 2023. Available via https://rm.coe.int/steering-committee-for-human-rights-cddh-interim-report-to-the-committ/1680aace4e (22 January 2025).

[525] On the current state of play in this respect, see Øby Johansen et al. (2024), p. 641 ff.

correspond to Convention rights shall have the same meaning and scope as the latter, except that they may provide more extensive protection.[526] Moreover, according to Art. 6 (3) TEU, the ECHR and Protocols binding all Member States can always serve as a point of reference for fundamental rights in the form of unwritten general principles of EU primary law.[527] The Convention guarantees therefore constitute the minimum standards of European fundamental rights protection also within Union law, including with regard to democratic standards.[528]

5.5.9 General Right to Democracy at EU Level?

From a synthesis of the aforementioned specific rights to democratic participation one can arguably derive an unwritten general individual right to democracy at EU level that is available to citizens of the Union. It is the subjective derivative of the aforementioned general principle of democratic legitimacy.[529] This general right promotes the pro-democratic interpretation of the specific democratic rights and other EU law provisions, increases the demands on justification of limitations and can perhaps even generate further supplementary unwritten democratic rights. One could link it to Art. 10 (3) sentence 1 TEU.

The ECJ has accordingly interpreted the “provisions on democratic principles” in Title II of the TEU (such as Art. 11 (4) TEU) and pertinent secondary law provisions in a pro-democratic way, in order to encourage participation by citizens in the democratic life of the EU and make the EU more accessible.[530] It has also relied on the value of democracy referred to in Art. 2 TEU and the preamble of the CFR for giving Art. 50 TEU a pro-democratic interpretation in the sense that a Member State having notified its intention to withdraw from the EU pursuant to Art. 50 (2) TEU remains free to revoke that notification unilaterally before the entry into force of the withdrawal agreement or the expiration of the two-year period laid down in Art. 50 (3) TEU. For it would be inconsistent with the value of democracy, if a “Member State could be forced to leave the European Union despite its wish — as expressed through its democratic process in accordance with its constitutional requirements — to reverse its decision to withdraw and, accordingly, to remain a Member of the European Union.”[531]

But the Court has so far refused to adopt a general and coherent pro-democracy interpretative approach to primary law provisions that would correspond to such a general right to democracy. It is true that the Court prohibits basing an EU measure

526 Article 52 (3) CFR.

527 Bruti Liberati et al. (2022), p. 76.

528 See FCC, order of 6 February 2024 (2 BvE 6/23 etc.), para. 116.

529 See above Sect. 5.5.3.

530 ECJ, judgment of 22 February 2024 (C-54/22 P), ECLI:EU:C:2024:164.

531 ECJ, judgment of 10 December 2018 (C-621/18); ECLI:EU:C:2018:999, para. 66.

simultaneously on two otherwise appropriate legal bases in the Treaties where that "is liable to undermine the rights of the Parliament."[532] This approach was based on the intention to protect the participation rights of the EP that had long been weak and needed a boost because "that participation reflects a fundamental democratic principle that the peoples should take part in the exercise of power through the intermediary of a representative assembly".[533] But after the position of the EP was strengthened by various Treaty reforms, the Court has refused to go further down his path, even though the EP has not yet caught up with the Council in terms of powers, which denotes a continuing democratic deficit.

Thus, the ECJ ruled that in choosing the correct legal basis for a measure, the fact that one of two bases in question gives the European Parliament a greater role in the adoption of the measure, which enhances its democratic legitimacy, was irrelevant.[534] In a more recent case, the ECJ struck down Regulation (EU) 2019/1157[535] for having been adopted on an incorrect legal basis.[536] The Regulation had been adopted jointly by the European Parliament and the Council in accordance with the most democratic ordinary legislative procedure on the basis of Art. 21 (2) TFEU. The Court, however, in contrast to the Opinion of the Advocate General,[537] found that Art. 77 (3) TFEU should have been used as the more specific legal basis, requiring a special legislative procedure in which the Council has to act unanimously after consulting the European Parliament. The democratic differential between the two legal bases was not discussed by either the Advocate General or the ECJ, even though the question which of the two Treaty provisions is more specific is obviously difficult to answer, because they both make a reservation in favour of other Treaty provisions conferring the necessary powers and the political organs of the EU had agreed on using the provision with the more democratic procedure. This was a lost opportunity for the ECJ.

Along a similar line, the General Court refused to recognise an individual right of a Member of the European Parliament to bring an action for annulment pursuant to Art. 263 (4) TFEU against a delegated regulation adopted by the Commission.[538]

---

532 ECJ, judgment of 10 January 2006 (C-94/03), ECLI:EU:C:2006:2, para. 52 (with further references). This approach goes back to the famous titanium dioxide case (judgment of 11 June 1991 [C-300/899], ECLI:EU:C:1991:244, paras. 17 ff.).

533 ECJ, judgment of 11 June 1991 (C-300/899), ECLI:EU:C:1991:244, para. 20.

534 ECJ, judgment of 19 July 2012 (C-130/10), ECLI:EU:C:2012:472, paras. 79 ff.

535 Regulation (EU) 2019/1157 of 20 June 2019 on strengthening the security of identity cards of Union citizens and of residence documents issued to Union citizens and their family members exercising their right of free movement (OJ L 188 of 12 July 2019, p. 67). On grounds of legal certainty, the ECJ ordered that the effects of the Regulation were "to be maintained until the entry into force, within a reasonable period … of a new regulation" based on the correct TFEU provision. This amounts to an analogous application of Article 264 (2) TFEU in the preliminary reference procedure (Article 267 TFEU).

536 ECJ, judgment of 21 March 2024 (C-61/22), ECLI:EU:C:2024:251, paras. 45 ff.

537 Of 29 June 2023, ECLI:EU:C:2023:520.

538 General Court, order of 21 June 2023 (T-628/22), ECLI:EU:T:2023:353. See Chamon et al. (2022); Krenn (2022).

The MEP claimed that the Commission should instead have initiated an ordinary legislative procedure pursuant to Art. 114, 294 TFEU that would have enabled the European Parliament to co-decide on the measure. He further claimed "that the legal status of Member of the Parliament confers on him, under EU law and the principle of representative democracy, voting and initiative rights, a right to participate in a lawful legislative procedure, procedural rights to respect for the provisions on competence and procedure, and a right to defend the democratic powers of the Parliament". But the General Court denied his standing because it found that the contested delegated regulation was not of direct concern to him so that his action was inadmissible. The MEP's appeal to the ECJ was recently retracted,[539] which may amount to another lost opportunity.

Unsurprisingly, the ECJ has not recognised any functional equivalent in primary EU law of the German constitutional principle that interferences in fundamental rights must always be based on an Act of Parliament.[540] While pursuant to Art. 52 (1) CFR "[a]ny limitation on the exercise of the rights and freedoms recognised by" the CFR "must be provided for by law", the term "law" covers any act of secondary EU law, even if, in accordance with the correct legal basis in the Treaties, that secondary was adopted by the Council without the consent of the EP. Thus, Art. 215 (2) TFEU on individualised restrictive measures, read together with Art. 29 TEU, authorises the Council to interfere in fundamental rights on its own and inform the EP only later. In cases where the pertinent Charter right corresponds to a right guaranteed by the ECHR, this is also in accordance with the requirement that restrictions on the exercise of Convention rights be "prescribed by law", a requirement which the ECtHR has interpreted as also covering rules of unwritten law, if they are sufficiently precise and foreseeable in their application.[541] This guarantees the conformity prescribed by Art. 52 (3) CFR.

It has been suggested that in such a case, the principle of democracy would operate at national level in the sense that the Council members must obtain authorisation by their national parliaments before approving the CFSP decision and the subsequent regulation, at least if the national constitution requires parliamentary consent for interferences in fundamental rights.[542] This would be a good example for the complementarity between EU democracy and national democracies, reciprocally closing gaps and each reinforcing the other so that an adequate overall level of democracy is guaranteed. That suggestion of democratic gap-filling on Member State level was not presented as an obligation enshrined in primary EU law, which

[539] See ECJ, order of 30 October 2024 (C-552/23 P).

[540] See von Achenbach (2025), p. 932. See, e.g., ECJ, judgment of 19 July 2012 (C-130/10), ECLI:EU:C:2012:472, para. 83, where the Court emphasised that "the duty to respect fundamental rights is imposed, in accordance with Article 51(1) of the Charter of Fundamental Rights of the European Union, on all the institutions and bodies of the Union". This includes the Council so that EP participation in the decision-making process is not indispensable for ensuring respect for fundamental rights.

[541] Grabenwarter (2014), Article 10 ECHR, paras. 23 f.

[542] Lenaerts (2013), p. 285 f.

would indeed be difficult to justify. One could refer to the general provisions on democracy in Art. 2 and Art. 10 (1) TEU or a general right to democracy, each read together with Art. 4 (3) TEU. But Art. 12 TEU strictly limits the role of national parliaments in the functioning of the EU. The only pertinent variant would be Art. 12 lit. a TEU in conjunction with the Protocol (No. 1) on the Role of National Parliaments in the European Union,[543] but that limits the information given to national parliaments to draft legislative acts and therefore does not cover Art. 29 TEU and Art. 215 (2) TFEU.[544] Indeed, in Germany, where constitutional law does require that interferences in fundamental rights be based on an Act of Parliament, constitutional and statutory law only stipulate that the Federal Government shall provide Parliament (the Bundestag) with an opportunity to state its position and take that position into account during the negotiations in the Council.[545] The Federal Government is not bound by that position which is not adopted in the form of a legislative act either.

On the positive side, the ECJ has strengthened the minor role of the European Parliament within the CFSP to a certain extent, for the sake of democracy.[546] Before the Council concludes an international agreement for the EU, Art. 218 (6) TFEU requires it either to ask the EP for its consent or at least consult it, depending on the subject-matter of that agreement. But the provision exempts agreements that relate exclusively to the CFSP, which are thus neither subject to the consent nor the consultation of the EP. However, in the Court's view, the EP's right under Art. 218 (10) TFEU to be "immediately and fully informed at all stages of the procedure" also applies to such CFSP-only agreements.[547] When the EP brought an action for annulment against the Council, because it had not complied with Art. 218 (10) TFEU, the Court initially confirmed its jurisdiction, despite Art. 24 (1) subpara. 2 TEU and Art. 275 (1) TFEU. It then determined that the Council had infringed Art. 218 (10) TFEU, which constituted an essential procedural requirement within the meaning of Art. 263 (2) TFEU so that the Council decision had to be annulled. In its reasoning, the ECJ referred as far back as its 1980 *Roquette Frères* judgment[548] to substantiate that the procedural rule of Art. 218 (10) TFEU was "an expression of the democratic principles on which the European Union is founded. In particular, the Court has already stated that the Parliament's involvement in the decision-making process is the reflection, at EU level, of the fundamental democratic principle that the people should participate in the exercise of power through the intermediary of a representative assembly". Although the EP was excluded from the procedure for negotiating

[543] OJ 2016 C 202, p. 203.

[544] See Article 289 (3) TFEU.

[545] Article 23 (3) BL; Sec. 8 of the Law on Co-operation between the Federal Government and the German Federal Parliament in EU Matters of 4 July 2013 (BGBl. I p. 2170). None of the provisions of the Integration Responsibility Act of 22 September 2009, as amended (BGBl. I p. 3022 and p. 3822) that require statutory authorisation before the German member may consent to certain decisions by the Council covers Art. 29 TEU, Art. 215 (2) TFEU.

[546] ECJ, judgment of 24 June 2014 (C-658/11), ECLI:EU:C:2014:2025.

[547] Id., para. 85.

[548] ECJ, judgment of 29 October 1980 (138/79), ECR 1980, 3333, para. 33.

and concluding a CFSP-only agreement, it had a right of scrutiny in respect of the CFSP.[549]

It remains to be seen if the regular annual dialogue recently established between the European Parliament and the ECJ and the GC will induce the EU judiciary to bolster the important democratic role of the European Parliament further wherever possible. The Press Release by the ECJ's Press and Information Unit on the first annual dialogue states this: "Thanks to the establishment of this annual forum for exchange and discussion, the European Parliament and the CJEU now have a platform that promotes continuous dialogue between two institutions whose complementary missions, lying at the heart of European democracy, contribute every day to bringing justice closer to European citizens."[550]

All in all, the ECJ has not yet recognised any general right to democracy at EU level for EU citizens. It should do so and adopt a more pronounced general pro-democracy stance in interpreting and applying EU law provisions, wherever possible. At a time of democratic backsliding, the EU institutions should do all they can to bolster EU democracy.

5.5.10 Enforcement Procedures

Individuals can challenge EU acts that violate directly effective democratic standards by initiating actions for annulment in the General Court,[551] provided that they fulfil the strict standing requirements in Art. 263 (4) TFEU. Otherwise, they need to use the judicial remedies which the Member States are required to provide under Art. 19 (1) subpara. 2 TEU, giving them only indirect access to the ECJ via Art. 267 TFEU. Any Member State, the Commission, the Council and the European Parliament always have standing to lodge actions for annulment against undemocratic EU acts in the ECJ.[552] Exceptionally, however, the ECJ does "not have jurisdiction with respect to the provisions relating to the common foreign and security policy nor with respect to acts adopted on the basis of those provisions."[553] As a matter of fact, CFSP decision-making is executive-heavy and not very democratic because the European Parliament plays only a minor role,[554] which is only partly compensated by enhanced roles of national parliaments *vis-à-vis* Member State

[549] ECJ, judgment of 24 June 2014 (C-658/11), ECLI:EU:C:2014:2025, paras. 81, 84.

[550] Press Release No. 58/24 of 21 March 2024. Available via https://curia.europa.eu/jcms/upload/docs/application/pdf/2024-03/cp240058en.pdf (22 January 2025).

[551] Article 256 (1) TFEU.

[552] Article 256 (1) TFEU in conjunction with Article 51 of the Protocol (No. 3) on the Statute of the Court of Justice of the European Union.

[553] Article 275 TFEU.

[554] Articles 31 36 TEU. See above Sects. 5.5.5 and 5.5.9.

governments in CFSP matters.[555] The CFSP, as it is structured today, falls afoul of the EU's own values of democracy and the rule of law (Art. 2 TEU).[556]

5.6 Right to Adequate Overall Standard of Democracy in the Multilevel EU System?

5.6.1 Mitigating Negative Effects of European Integration on Member States' Democracies

The strict standards for democracy at EU level pursue the secondary goal of mitigating negative repercussions of supranational integration on Member State democracies. The EU has tried to compensate the reduction of national parliaments' influence on matters within EU competences by strengthening the influence of the directly elected European Parliament in all cases in which the Council decides by qualified majority. It has also given national parliaments a certain role at Union level[557] and introduced direct citizen participation in the EU.[558] Finally, it has tried to maintain a balanced distribution of competences that preserves a broad enough range of democratic autonomy for Member States by the principles of conferral, subsidiarity and proportionality.[559]

Member States have added their own adaptation mechanisms to preserve national democracy, such as by strengthening the influence of parliaments on the formulation of national EU policy and the voting behaviour of ministerial representatives in

[555] See, e.g., with regard to Germany FCC, judgment of 26 October 2022 (2 BvE 3/15, 2 BvE 7/15) – EUNAVFOR MED, paras. 68 ff. Available via https://www.bundesverfassungsgericht.de/SharedDocs/Entscheidungen/EN/2022/10/es20221026_2bve000315en.html (English translation) (22 January 2025).

[556] See Giegerich (2024), p. 590 ff.

[557] Article 12 TEU; Protocol (No. 1) on the Role of National Parliaments in the European Union; Protocol (No. 2) on the Application of the Principles of Subsidiarity and Proportionality. See Grimm (2017), chapter 9. The proposal to establish a new institution, alongside the Council and the European Parliament, in which the national parliaments would participate in the EU's decision-making process in order to improve the democratic input (see the European Council's Laeken Declaration on the future of the European Union of 15 December 2001. Available via https://www.cvce.eu/content/publication/2002/9/26/a76801d5-4bf0-4483-9000-e6df94b07a55/publishable_en.pdf (22 January 2025)), was ultimately abandoned, probably because it would have rendered that process too complicated.

[558] Article 11 (4) TEU, Article 24 TFEU and Regulation (EU) 2019/788 of 17 April 2019 on the European citizens' initiative, OJ L 130 of 17 May 2019, p. 55.

[559] See above Sect. 5.5.8.2.

the Council based thereon.[560] This has rightly been called compensatory constitutionalism,[561] and in our context, it amounts to compensatory democracy. One can argue that Member States are under an EU law obligation to pursue compensatory democracy (Art. 2, 10 (2) subpara. 2, 10 (3) sentence 1 TEU).

5.6.2 The "Right to Democracy" of the German Federal Constitutional Court and Its Drawbacks

But the interdependence problem has not been completely resolved in the relation between the EU and Member States. It also underlies the conflict between the ECJ and national courts, such as the German Federal Constitutional Court.[562] The latter clearly characterised that problem already in its judgment on the constitutionality of the Treaty of Maastricht where it derived an obligation from the Basic Law to the effect that both the democratic foundations of the Union be enhanced and a vibrant democracy maintained in the Member States as integration progressed.[563] On this background, national courts and the ECJ compete for the right of final decision with regard to the delimitation of competences between the EU and Member States and thus between EU democracy and national democracies.[564] These national courts claim that their taking action against *ultra vires* acts of the EU was indispensable for maintaining democracy, both in their Member State and the EU as a whole.[565] In

[560] See, e.g., Article 23 (3) of the German BL and the implementing laws (Gesetz über die Zusammenarbeit von Bundesregierung und Deutschem Bundestag in Angelegenheiten der Europäischen Union [Act on Cooperation between the Federal Government and the German Bundestag in European Union Affairs] of 4 July 2013; Gesetz über die Wahrnehmung der Integrationsverantwortung des Bundestages und Bundesrates in Angelegenheiten der Europäischen Union [Act on the Exercise of the Integration Responsibility of the Bundestag and Bundesrat in European Union Affairs] of 22 September 2009; Gesetz über die Zusammenarbeit von Bund und Ländern in Angelegenheiten der Europäischen Union [Act on Cooperation between the Federation and the *Länder* in European Union Affairs] of 12 March 1993 with later amendments). For an overview of the situation in other Member States, see Lenaerts et al. (2021), para. 15.008.

[561] See Peters (2006), p. 579 ff. On the necessity of compensatory constitutionalism at UN level, see Giegerich (2009b), The *Is* and the *Ought* of International Constitutionalism, p. 59 ff.

[562] Calliess (2020), p. 153 ff. Other contributions in this volume address the situation in further Member States.

[563] See FCC, judgment of 12 October 1993 (2 BvR 2134, 2159/92), BVerfGE 89, 155, 186, para. 100.

[564] FCC, order of 6 July 2010 (2 BvR 2661/06), BVerfGE 126, 286. Available via https://www.bundesverfassungsgericht.de/SharedDocs/Entscheidungen/EN/2010/07/rs20100706_2bvr266106en.html (English translation) (22 January 2025); judgment of 5 May 2020 (2 BvR 859/15 etc.), BVerfGE 154, 17. Available via https://www.bundesverfassungsgericht.de/SharedDocs/Entscheidungen/EN/2020/05/rs20200505_2bvr085915en.html (English translation) (22 January 2025). See Grimm (2017), chapter 10. For a critique, see Giegerich (2010), p. 867 ff.

[565] See in this sense, *e.g.*, FCC, judgment of 21 June 2016 (2 BvR 2728/13 etc.), English translation available via https://www.bundesverfassungsgericht.de/SharedDocs/Entscheidungen/EN/2016/06/

essence, they have tried to gain a veto position on the applicability of EU law within their respective jurisdictions which the ECJ and the European Commission have never accepted, because it is incompatible with their concept of the autonomy, primacy and uniformity of Union law.[566]

There is no enforceable individual right under EU law to an adequate overall standard of democracy in the EU system, comprising the Union and Member State levels. But there may well be corresponding individual rights under Member State law. This is the case in Germany where the Federal Constitutional Court has interpreted the basic right to vote in federal parliamentary elections[567] as including the right to be protected against excessive power transfers from the German parliament to the EU (which would make the German elections practically meaningless), from *ultra vires* acts of EU institutions as well as infringements of the German constitutional identity caused by the European integration.[568] In truth, however, that "right to democracy", as it is sometimes called,[569] amounts to a basic right to national democracy in the sense of preserving national sovereignty,[570] embodied in the German national parliament, at the expense of both European integration and EU democracy.[571] By way of example, it prevents the transition to Treaty revisions by a majority of Member States, because that would bring the Union to close to a federal state which the Basic Law allegedly prohibits.[572] Since the FCC has attached that

rs20160621_2bvr272813en.html (22 January 2025).

[566] ECJ, judgment of 26 September 2024 (C-792/22), ECLI:EU:C:2024:788; opinion of the Advocate General of 11 March 2025 (C-448/23), ECLI:EU:C:2025:165. See also the infringement procedure which the Commission initiated against Germany because of an FCC judgment disregarding a preliminary ruling by the ECJ and later terminated (Giegerich [2021a], All's well that ends well?; id. [2022b], Das PSPP-Urteil des BVerfG, p. 49 ff.).

[567] Article 38 of the German Basic Law.

[568] Settled case law since the 1993 FCC judgment on the Treaty of Maastricht (BVerfGE 89, 155). See the FCC judgment of 5 May 2020 (2 BvR 859/15 etc.), BVerfGE 154, 17. Available via https://www.bundesverfassungsgericht.de/SharedDocs/Entscheidungen/EN/2020/05/rs20200505_2bvr085915en.html (English translation) (22 January 2025). For a critique of the latter judgment see Müller-Graff (2022), p. 405 ff. with further references. See the overview by Giegerich (2016), p. 23 ff. For a critique of the German jurisprudence and parallels in some other Member States, together with an attempt to transform them into a more constructive approach fostering constitutional homogeneity in the EU, see Spieker (2023), p. 223 ff. See also the more restrained *ultra vires* review in FCC, judgment of 6 December 2022 (2 BvR 547/21 etc.), BVerfGE 164, 193. Available via https://www.bundesverfassungsgericht.de/SharedDocs/Entscheidungen/EN/2022/12/rs20221206_2bvr054721en.html (English translation) (4 March 2025). Anagnostaras (2024), p. 578 ff.

[569] See, e.g., FCC, judgment of 21 June 2016 (2 BvR 2728/13 etc.), para. 133 (English translation available via https://www.bundesverfassungsgericht.de/SharedDocs/Entscheidungen/EN/2016/06/rs20160621_2bvr272813en.html [22 January 2025]). Huber (2024), p. 428 f. For a critique, see Möllers (2021), p. 331 f.

[570] See Nettesheim (2009), p. 2867 ff.

[571] For a critique, see, e.g., Schönberger (2009), p. 539 ff. ("unlimited expansion of the scope of application of Art. 38 (1) sentence 1 BL" [my translation]).

[572] BVerfGE 123, 267 (355 f., para. 243; 384 ff., paras. 306 ff.).

right to the principle of democracy in Art. 20 (2) BL, the obstacle it poses to the further deepening of European integration and EU democracy cannot even be overcome by a constitutional amendment, as a consequence of Art. 79 (3) BL. The only way forward would be for the FCC to relax its opposition to further decisive steps towards "creating an ever closer union among the peoples of Europe" (Art. 1 (2) TEU).

According to the FCC, every person entitled to vote in the German federal elections can individually enforce that "right to (national) democracy" by an *actio popularis*-like constitutional complaint procedure in the FCC, which thereby reserves for itself a guardianship position over the development of the European integration process.[573] But such a mechanism seems misplaced in a constitution which, like the German Basic Law, favours European integration and expressly obliges Germany to participate in the development of the European Union.[574] It also gives German voters privileged influence on the European integration process that voters in other Member States do not have and that therefore is incompatible with democratic equality.[575] The FCC has at least mitigated the effects of its "right to democracy" case-law by placing high demands on the presentation of arguments by *actio popularis*-complainants as to why that right was violated in their particular case. If these demands are not met, the constitutional complaint will be inadmissible.[576]

Moreover, the FCC has recognised an enforceable right to EU democracy in the sense of an individual entitlement to challenge democratic deficits at EU level that it has also derived from Art. 38 BL.[577] This builds on earlier case law according to which Art. 23 (1) BL makes it a condition of Germany's EU membership that the democratic foundations of the Union are enhanced in step with the progress of integration.[578] So far, the FCC has used this right as another obstacle to the deepening of European integration and not as a right to enhance EU democracy which would be tantamount to such deepening.

More recently, however, the FCC interpreted Art. 23 (1) BL as requiring that the EU's democratic legitimacy must be sufficiently effective and imposing an "integration responsibility for the democratic principle in the EU" on the German State that included a co-responsibility with the other Member States for securing the effective functioning of the European Parliament.[579] This may be considered as a cautious first step towards formulating a general constitutional obligation of the German State organs to improve EU democracy, such as by switching from unanimous decision-making in the Council to qualified majority voting, or by abandoning the requirement that Treaty revisions need to be ratified by every single Member State.

---

573 Richter, in: Dörr et al. (2022), Kapitel 25 para. 63.

574 Article 23 (1) BL.

575 Kadelbach (2025), p. 781 f.

576 See, e.g., FCC (Chamber), order of 23 July 2024 (2 BvR 557/19), paras. 60 ff.

577 BVerfGE 123, 267 (331, paras. 176 f.).

578 FCC, judgment of 12 October 1993 (2 BvR 2134, 2159/92), BVerfGE 89, 155, 186, para. 100.

579 FCC, order of 6 February 2024 (2 BvE 6/23 etc.), paras. 105, 126.

If such an obligation were recognised, a further step would be required to develop a corresponding individual entitlement in the form of a basic right enforceable through a constitutional complaint.[580] Such a right to EU democracy would constitute a counterbalance to the right to national democracy, in recognition of the interdependence of the democratic structures at Member State and Union level. There is an outright tension between a right to national democracy requiring the maintenance of national veto positions and a right to EU democracy requiring their abolition. The FCC has not yet come to recognising this tension, not to mention to striking a proper balance between the two conflicting democratic entitlements.

Currently, we are therefore stuck with the FCC's EU-sceptical "right to democracy" based on a narrow nationalistic concept of democracy which qualifies European integration as a threat to the national self-determination of the German people. Yet, this is a misconception, because under present-day global conditions dominated by existing and emerging superpowers, the national self-determination of European peoples is no longer conceivable in the form of completely autonomous decision-making, but only in the form of joint self-determination regarding common questions of destiny. This must also have consequences for the concept of democracy in the integration-friendly Basic Law. European integration has from its beginnings been an attempt at self-assertion by the small and medium-sized European States.[581] For them, joining forces and pooling their resources is the only way effectively to preserve and strengthen peace and liberty, reinforce European identity and independence as well as protect and promote their values and interests as well as those of their citizens.[582] This was most clearly stated by the French President in his 2017 speech at Sorbonne University on a sovereign, united and democratic Europe: "La seule voie qui assure notre avenir … c'est … la refondation d'une Europe souveraine, unie et démocratique. … l'Europe seule peut nous donner une capacité d'action dans le monde, face aux grands défis contemporains. L'Europe seule peut … assurer une souveraineté réelle, c'est-à-dire notre capacité à exister dans le monde actuel pour y défendre nos valeurs et nos intérêts. Il y a une souveraineté européenne à construire, et il y a la nécessité de la construire … dans cette mondialisation."[583]

In other words, the transfer of powers to the EU permits Member States and their peoples to co-determine the conditions of economic well-being and social progress

[580] One could fall back on Article 2 (1) BL (the general right to liberty), read together with Article 23 (1) BL, which would include a basic right to the fulfilment of the constitutional obligations set forth in Article 23 (1) BL (just as Article 2 (1) in conjunction with Article 25 BL is used to enforce the obligations deriving from the general rules of international law [see FCC (Chamber), order of 15 March 2028 (2 BvR 1371/13), para. 33 with further references]).

[581] See Schuman (2010), p. 28: "Il est de l'intérêt de l'Europe d'être maîtresse de sa destinée. Le morcellement de l'Europe est devenue un absurde anachronisme." The text was written in 1963.

[582] See the preambles of the TEU and TFEU.

[583] Speech of 26 September 2017 (https://www.elysee.fr/emmanuel-macron/2017/09/26/initiative-pour-l-europe-discours-d-emmanuel-macron-pour-une-europe-souveraine-unie-democratique [30 January 2025]).

in Europe, to protect and promote human rights and democracy, to exert greater influence on the global level and to realise their right of self-determination better. From this perspective, jointly exercising their sovereignty translates into more rather than less autonomy for the European States.[584] It is certainly more democratic to participate in joint decision-making within the EU than "autonomously" (*i.e.*, for better or worse, out of weakness) to follow decisions taken by others outside the EU.[585] Undermining European integration by reasserting autonomous national decision-making therefore amounts to a Pyrrhic victory for democracy and democratic rights in Europe as well as the self-determination of the individual European peoples that risk becoming subject to external hegemony, if they opt for splendid isolation.[586]

5.7 "Export" of Democracy to Third States and the International Community

5.7.1 External Value Promotion by EU

The EU adds a special, partly horizontal and partly vertical, perspective to democracy because it is actively trying to "export" democratic standards to other parts of the world,[587] having actually done so for decades.[588] Pursuant to Art. 3 (5) TEU, the Union shall "promote its values" in its relations with the wider world, but also contribute to the "strict observance and the development of international law, including respect for the principles of the United Nations Charter". The EU's value "export" must therefore always respect the limits of international law and the UN Charter, including the peoples' right of self-determination. It must in other words remain peaceful and free from coercion, respecting the prohibition of the threat or use of force (Art. 2 No. 4 UNCh) and the principle of non-intervention in customary international law. Moreover, it is important to remember the statement in the TEU preamble that "from the cultural, religious and humanist inheritance of Europe … have developed the universal values of the inviolable and inalienable rights of the human person, freedom, democracy, equality and the rule of law."[589] This means that the EU is not actually promoting its intrinsic values and trying to impose them on others

---

[584] See Kotzur (2024), p. 434 ff.

[585] See Schuman (2010), p. 21: "La loi démocratique de la majorité, librement acceptée dans des conditions et des modalités préalablement fixées, limitée aux problèmes essentiels de l'interêt commun, sera en définitive moins humiliante à subir que les décisions imposées par le plus fort." The text was written in 1963.

[586] See von Bogdandy (2012), p. 323.

[587] See Bouzoraa (2023), p. 829 ff.

[588] See Freigang (2015), p. 283 ff.

[589] 2nd recital.

as foreign values. Rather, the object of the EU's promotion efforts are shared values whose maintenance and implementation constantly require joint efforts.

More specifically, Art. 21 (1) TEU sets forth that "the Union's action on the international scene shall be guided by the principles which have inspired its own creation, development and enlargement, and which it seeks to advance in the wider world: democracy, the rule of law, … human rights …" Art. 21 (2) (b) TEU obliges the Union to pursue the goal of the consolidation and support of "democracy, the rule of law, human rights and the principles of international law".[590] On this basis, the Council has by now adopted three consecutive action plans on human rights and democracy in relation to third States, the most recent one in 2020.[591] More specifically, the European Neighbourhood Policy has since 2004 tried to strengthen the EU's relations with sixteen Eastern and Southern neighbouring States. Among the joint priorities for cooperation are "good governance, democracy, rule of law and human rights."[592] It comes as no surprise that the EU's efforts regarding worldwide promotion of democracy mostly take the forms of leadership by example, cooperation and dialogue.

But the EU is also using unilateral measures (*i.e.*, sanctions) in reaction to undemocratic behaviour, such as electoral fraud, in third States (*e.g.*, Belarus, Nicaragua, Venezuela) whose compatibility with international law, in particular the prohibition of intervention as well as human rights in the target States, is contested.[593] This draws attention to the recent EU global human rights sanctions regime (European Magnitsky Act), which consists of a Council Decision based on Art. 29 TEU and a Council Regulation based on Art. 215 TFEU.[594] This regime establishes a framework for targeted restrictive measures (travel restrictions and asset freezes) against both State actors and non-State actors in reaction to serious human rights violations and abuses worldwide.[595] The European Magnitsky Act's first priority is certainly not the protection of democracy, but the suppression of genocide, crimes against humanity and other human rights violations of similar magnitude.[596] But the first and fifth recitals of the preamble of the Council Decision also mention the value

[590] Articles 205, 208, 214 TFEU concerning EU external action in supranational forms refer to Article 21 TEU.

[591] European Union (2020).

[592] Available via https://neighbourhood-enlargement.ec.europa.eu/european-neighbourhood-policy_en (22 January 2025). See Gawrich et al. (2024), p. 120 ff.

[593] See Prezas (2023), p. 235, 241 f., 257 ff.

[594] Council Decision (CFSP) 2020/1999 of 7 December 2020 concerning restrictive measures against serious human rights violations and abuses (OJ L 410 I of 7 December 2020, p. 13) and Council Regulation (EU) 2020/1998 of 7 December 2020 concerning restrictive measures against serious human rights violations and abuses (OJ L 410 I of 7 December 2020, p. 1). See the overview by Strothteicher (2022). Available via https://opendata.uni-halle.de/bitstream/1981185920/80386/1/BeitraegeEVR_24.pdf (22 January 2025).

[595] Article 1 (3), Article 2, Article 3 f. Council Decision; Article 2 (3), Articles 3 ff. Regulation.

[596] See Article 1 (1) Council Decision and Article 2 (1) Regulation.

of (national) democracy that the targeted restrictive measures will contribute to consolidating and supporting, in pursuit of CFSP objectives as set out in Art. 21 TEU and particularly "in accordance with point (b) of Article 21(2) TEU." The serious human rights violations addressed by the European Magnitsky Act include some that typically go along with an overthrow of or a grave interference with democratic systems of government: enforced disappearances of persons; arbitrary arrests and detentions; violations or abuses of freedom of peaceful assembly and of association as well as freedom of opinion and expression.[597] Needless to say, the use of sanctions pursuant to the European Magnitsky Act is entirely left to the discretion of the Council, acting by unanimity upon a proposal from a Member State or from the High Representative[598]; there is no corresponding individual entitlement.

5.7.2 *Horizontal "Export" of Democracy*

Efforts to advance democracy in the EU's external relations have a long history.[599]

5.7.2.1 Association Relationships and Strategic Partnerships

The direction of the EU's democracy "export" is primarily towards third States (horizontal perspective), such as neighbouring countries[600] and States parties of association or partnership agreements,[601] but also States parties of trade agreements in general.[602] Such agreements routinely include provisions making respect for democratic principles an essential element of the association or partnership or market access conditionality and permitting swift suspension of the agreements in cases of violation, which constitutes a material breach of treaty,[603] such provisions usually invoking the UDHR and relevant international human rights instruments in force

[597] Article 1 (1) lit. c (iv), (v), lit. d (iii), (iv) Council Decision; Article 2 (1) lit. c (iv), (v), lit. d (iii), (iv) Regulation.

[598] Article 5 (1) Council Decision. The unanimity requirement is incompatible with Article 31 (2) third indent TEU (see Giegerich [2020d], 75 Jahre Internationale Menschenrechtsrevolution, p. 13 ff.

[599] See Council conclusions on Democracy Support in the EU's External Relations of 17 November 2009. Available via https://www.consilium.europa.eu/uedocs/cms_data/docs/pressdata/en/gena/111250.pdf (24 February 2025). Council Conclusions on Democracy of 14 October 2019. Available via https://data.consilium.europa.eu/doc/document/ST-12836-2019-INIT/en/pdf (24 February 2025).

[600] Article 8 TEU.

[601] Article 217 TFEU.

[602] Article 207 (3) TFEU. See Bruti Liberati et al. (2022), p. 85 ff.

[603] Art. 60 (3) lit. b of both the Vienna Convention on the Law of Treaties of 23 May 1969 (UNTS, vol. 1155, p. 331) and the Vienna Convention on the Law of Treaties between States and International Organizations or between International Organizations of 21 March 1986 (UN Doc.

between the parties, and working on a reciprocal basis.[604] This horizontal "export" of democracy is particularly important in association relationships with the candidate countries in the Western Balkans which are striving to fulfil the political criteria laid down in Art. 49, 2 TEU and have all acceded to the ECHR and Prot. No. 1.[605]

The recent EU-Western Balkans Summit produced the Brussels Declaration of 18 December 2024 which reconfirmed the strategic partnership between the EU and the Western Balkans, based on shared principles and values.[606] In para. 5, "[t]he EU welcomes the resolve of the Western Balkans partners to respect and commit to core European values and principles, in line with international law and the restated commitment to the primacy of democracy, fundamental rights and values and the rule of law. The rule of law, freedom of expression, independent and pluralistic media, gender equality, and a strong role for civil society are crucial to ensure a functioning democracy. In this respect, actions will speak louder than words as partners take ownership and implement the necessary reforms, notably in the area of fundamentals. …".

Democracy plays but a different role in the treaty-based strategic partnerships which the EU and its Member States have entered into on an equal footing with other advanced democracies—Canada and Japan.[607] These relationships are characterised by the mutual respect for each other's democratic achievements and the joint endeavour to advance democracy elsewhere, and not democracy "export" in their mutual relationship.[608] In another, political agreement-based, quasi-strategic part-

---

A/CONF.129/15—not yet in force) which codify a rule of customary international law. See Freigang (2015), p. 285.

[604] See, e.g., Article 1 of the Cooperation Agreement between the European Community and the Republic of India on partnership and development of 20 December 1993 (OJ 1994 L 223, p. 24); Articles 1, 8 (3) of the Trade Agreement between the European Union and its Member States, of the one part, and Colombia and Peru, of the other part, of 26 June 2012 (OJ L 354, p. 3); Articles 1 (1), 57 of the Framework Agreement on Comprehensive Partnership and Cooperation between the European Union and its Member States, of the one part, and the Socialist Republic of Viet Nam, of the other part, of 27 June 2012 (OJ 2016 L 329, p. 8); Articles 2, 478 of the Association Agreement between the EU and European Atomic Energy Community and their Member States, of the one part, and Ukraine, of the other part of 27 June 2014 (OJ L 161, p. 3); Art. 1, 44 of the Partnership and Cooperation Agreement between the EU and its Member States, of the one part, and the Republic of Singapore, of the other part, of 19 October 2018 (https://www.bundeskanzleramt.gv.at/dam/jcr:59b15b71-6bfd-4d79-a7e9-40d158655d56/29_7_abk_en.pdf [29 August 2025])—not yet in force (see OJ 2018 L 189, p. 2).

[605] See, e.g., Articles 1 (2), 2 of the Stabilisation and Association Agreement between the European Communities and their Member States, of the one part, and the Republic of Albania, of the other part of 12 June 2006 (OJ 2009 L 107, p. 166).

[606] Available via https://www.consilium.europa.eu/media/wvld5ka1/brussels-declaration-2024-en.pdf (22 January 2025).

[607] Strategic Partnership Agreement between the EU and its Member States, of the one part, and Canada, of the other part, of 30 October 2016 (OJ 2016 L 329, p. 45); Strategic Partnership Agreement between the EU and its Member States, of the one part, and Japan, of the other part, of 17 July 2018 (OJ 2018 L 216, p. 4).

[608] See the respective Art. 2 of each of the two agreements cited in the preceding footnote. See also Art. 2 of the Framework Agreement between the European Union and its Member States, of the

nership which the EU has entered into with the African Union on peace, security and governance, democratic principles are also invoked as guidance.[609] The participants state their commitment to "to promote inclusive, participatory, accountable and transparent institutions at all levels as a foundation for good governance, respect for human rights, and the rule of law, in accordance with their respective instruments".[610] Among the areas of cooperation, the Memorandum of Understanding lists "[s]trengthening democratic institutions and promotion of good governance" and "[s]trengthening cooperation and dialogue with regard to good governance, the promotion and protection of human rights, the rule of law and democracy, including support in electoral matters for inclusive, transparent and fair elections, in line with Participants' respective instruments and decision making organs, and the provision of technical assistance in election observation and monitoring processes".[611]

5.7.2.2 Samoa Agreement with ACP States as Example

But the horizontal "export" of democracy extends far beyond actual and potential accession candidacies to the non-European area, as part of the EU's development cooperation.[612] In the special relationship between the EU and its Member States and the former colonies of some of the latter in Africa, the Caribbean and the Pacific, the "export" of democratic standards has always played an important role, together with the promotion of sustainable development, which are closely connected. This relationship had long been based on the Partnership Agreement between the members of the African, Caribbean and Pacific Group of States of the one part, and the European Community and its Member States, of the other part, signed in Cotonou on 23 June 2000.[613] The Cotonou Agreement is currently being replaced by the new Partnership Agreement between the European Union and its Member States, of the one part, and the Members of the Organisation of African, Caribbean and Pacific States, of the other part (Samoa Agreement) which the EU and its Member States signed on 15 November 2023.[614] While the Samoa Agreement has not yet entered into force, it is for the most part being applied on a provisional basis from 1 January 2024 between the EU and the OACPS Members, "to the extent that its provisions cover matters falling within the Union's competence, including matters falling

one part, and Australia, of the other part, of 7 August 2017 (OJ 2017 L 237, p. 7) which establishes a "strengthened partnership" between the Parties that is also called "strategic relationship" (see Art. 1 (1) lit. a, Art. 2 (1)).

[609] Memorandum of Understanding Between The African Union And The European Union On Peace, Security and Governance of 23 May 2018, para. 1 (3) (https://www.eeas.europa.eu/sites/default/files/medghme_2018.05.23_16.31.36_5c4n7108_1_0.pdf [3 February 2025]).

[610] Id., para. 1 (4).

[611] Id., para. 3 lit. n, o.

[612] See the overview by Castellarin (2023), p. 191 ff.

[613] OJ 2000 L 317, p. 3.

[614] OJ Series L, No. 2023/2862 of 28 December 2023 (not yet in force).

within the Union's competence to define and implement a common foreign and security policy, and are applicable to the Union".[615] The Samoa Agreement contains no provision excluding the direct applicability of any of its provisions. But it remains to be seen whether the future Council Decision pursuant to Art. 218 (6) TFEU will include such a rule which would make it impossible to derive individual rights from the Agreement.

The Samoa Agreement, which confirms the parties' "commitment to democratic principles and human rights as laid down in the Universal Declaration of Human Rights and other relevant international human rights instruments, as well as to the principles of the rule of law and good governance" in its preamble,[616] raises the advancement of democracy in the relationship between the EU and its Member States and the ACP States to a new level. Among the Agreement's objectives, Art. 1 (3) lit. a first mentions the promotion, protection and fulfilment of "human rights, democratic principles, the rule of law and good governance, paying particular attention to gender equality". Accordingly, Art. 7 (1) Samoa Agreement mentions democracy among the cross-cutting themes of the parties' cooperation, and Part II, Title I identifies "Human Rights, Democracy and Governance in People-Centred and Rights-Based Societies" as the Parties' number one strategic priority. In Art. 8, the first provision of this Title, the "Parties reaffirm their determination to promote, protect and fulfil human rights, fundamental freedoms and democratic principles, and to strengthen the rule of law and good governance, in compliance with the UN Charter, the Universal Declaration of Human Rights and international law, in particular international human rights law and, where relevant, international humanitarian law" (para. 1). In Art. 8 (2) Samoa Agreement, they also "recognise that respect for democracy, human rights, fundamental freedoms, the rule of law and good governance is an integral part of sustainable development."

The Parties' commitment to national democracy is reconfirmed many times in the text of the Samoa Agreement as well as the three attached African, Caribbean and Pacific Regional Protocols.[617] Among these provisions, Art. 9 of the Agreement is particularly important.[618] In Art. 9 (4), the Parties "reaffirm that the universally recognised democratic principles underpinning the organisation of the State ensure the legitimacy of its authority, the legality of its actions reflected in its constitutional, legislative and regulatory system, and the existence of participatory mechanisms. They shall preserve and strengthen the application of those principles by ensuring inclusive, transparent and credible elections with due respect for sover-

[615] Article 4 of Council Decision (EU) 2023/2861 on the signing, on behalf of the European Union, and provisional application of the Partnership Agreement between the European Union and its Member States, of the one part, and the Members of the Organisation of African, Caribbean and Pacific States, of the other part, of 20 July 2023 (OJ Series L, No. 2023/2861 of 28 December 2023).

[616] 7th recital.

[617] See Articles 65 ff. (in particular Article 67) African Regional Protocol and (less pronounced) Articles 32 ff. Caribbean Regional Protocol as well as Articles 38 ff. Pacific Regional Protocol.

[618] See also Article 101 (7) Samoa Agreement on the consequences of a particularly serious and flagrant violation of Article 9.

eignty, as well as by allowing and supporting participatory decision-making processes. The Parties shall promote the upholding of electoral best practices and cooperation between them, including on electoral observation within the EU Party and OACPS Members, as appropriate." The Parties also promise actively to "support the consolidation of the rule of law at national, regional and international levels, acknowledging its crucial importance for the protection of human rights and for the effective functioning of democratic institutions."[619] They furthermore "agree that respect for human rights, democratic principles and the rule of law shall underpin their domestic and international policies and constitute an essential element of this Agreement."[620]

While Art. 9 Samoa Agreement regulates the Parties' objective commitments to national democracy and an adequate electoral system as its cornerstone,[621] and not corresponding individual rights, the Parties in Art. 11 Samoa Agreement on "[i]nclusive and pluralistic societies" turn their attention to the human rights basis of a functioning democracy.[622] In Art. 11 (2) Samoa Agreement, the Parties promise to "protect freedom of expression, freedom of opinion, freedom of assembly, and media independence and pluralism as pillars of democracy, noting that these are not only human rights but also prerequisites for democracy, development and dialogue." This is a reference to specific democratic human rights (the freedom of association being conspicuously absent), and not to a general right to democracy. Moreover, the provision is apparently not intended to re-guarantee those democratic rights regulated elsewhere in the sense of providing additional judicially enforceable individual entitlements.

Interestingly, the Parties also undertake to cooperate for enhancing democracy in other parts of the world. Pursuant to Art. 80 (3) Samoa Agreement, "[t]he Parties shall engage in international forums to uphold international norms and agreements to promote and protect human rights for all, to achieve gender equality, and to enhance democracy and the rule of law. They shall cooperate with the UN's human rights bodies and mechanisms and fully support the work of the UN Human Rights Council. They shall establish cross-regional alliances to serve common values and interests, as appropriate."

In the institutional framework established by the Samoa Agreement, the three Regional Parliamentary Assemblies for Africa, the Caribbean and the Pacific in Art. 94, and the OACPS-EU Joint Parliamentary Assembly in Art. 90 stand out. Each of the Regional Parliamentary Assemblies consists of an equal number of parliamentarians from Africa, the Caribbean or the Pacific respectively, and Members of the European Parliament. The OACPS-EU Joint Parliamentary Assembly[623] comprises

---

[619] Article 9 (5) Samoa Agreement.

[620] Article 9 (7) Samoa Agreement.

[621] See also Article 12 Samoa Agreement on good governance that is deemed to be "critical to the respect of all human rights, democratic principles and the rule of law."

[622] See also Article 28 (2) Samoa Agreement on the democratic goal of education.

[623] For its predecessor, the Joint Parliamentary Assembly, see Article 17 of the Cotonou Agreement (note 611).

all the members of the three Regional Parliamentary Assemblies. All four assemblies are consultative bodies whose main task is to promote democratic processes, foster cooperation between parliaments and facilitate greater understanding between the peoples of the Parties.

Already in 1975, the ACP States established their own transcontinental international organisation with currently 79 Member States—the Organisation of African, Caribbean and Pacific States (OACPS).[624] While the OACPS as such is not a party to the Samoa Agreement, it is taken note of in this Agreement. The revised Georgetown Agreement establishing the OACPS's statute pays only limited attention to national democracy. In the preamble, the States parties reaffirm "their commitment to adherence to the fundamental human rights defined in the Universal Declaration of Human Rights, particularly with regard to compliance with democratic principles, the rule of law, the right to development, as well as the right to self-determination".[625] According to Art. 5 lit. c, one of the OACPS's objectives is to "consolidate, strengthen, and maintain peace and stability as a precondition for improving the well-being of the peoples of the OACPS, in a democratic and free environment". Art. 25 permits the creation of subsidiary and consultative organs which shall, among others, "promote democratic processes through dialogue and consultation".[626] Art. 6 on membership in the OACPS does not formulate any requirements regarding national democracy. On the other hand, Art. 21 counts a Parliamentary Assembly among the organs of the OACPS which consists of one member of each Parliamentary House of each Member State, but its functions are unclear. These findings indicate that the EU is the driving force behind the inclusion of standards of national democracy in the Cotonou and Samoa Agreements.

5.7.3 Vertical "Export"

A secondary direction of the EU's "export" of democracy is the international community as a whole (vertical bottom-up perspective): The EU is obliged to join forces with like-minded States in order to promote the precepts of a democratic international order and in particular the democratic legitimacy and accountability of international organisations. This becomes clear from various formulations in Art. 21 TEU: that the EU "shall seek to develop relations and build partnerships with third countries, and international, regional or global organisations which share the principles referred to in the first subparagraph"[627]—such as democracy as well as the

[624] Available via https://www.oacps.org (22 January 2025). The OACPS is based on the revised Georgetown Agreement of 2019. Available via https://www.oacps.org/wp-content/uploads/2022/05/ACP-Brochure-Revised-Georgetown-Agreement-UK-def.pdf (22 January 2025) which entered into force on 5 April 2020.

[625] 4th recital.

[626] Lit. d.

[627] Article 21 (1) sentence 2 TEU.

principles of equality and solidarity. The EU shall also "promote multilateral solutions to common problems, in particular in the framework of the United Nations."[628] One of the goals of EU action on the international scene is to "promote an international system based on stronger multilateral cooperation and good global governance".[629] In practice, this vertical "export" is less developed than the horizontal one, but one can detect at least some EU activities.

5.7.3.1 Samoa Agreement with ACP States as Sponsor of International Democracy

The aforementioned Samoa Agreement[630] also regulates cooperation between the EU and its Member States and the OACPS Member States in promoting international democracy. This is made clear in Part III on global alliances and international cooperation.[631] There, the Parties "reaffirm the importance of cooperating at the international level with a view to … preserving and strengthening multilateralism. They commit to joining forces for a more peaceful, cooperative and just world which rests solidly on the common values of peace, democracy, human rights, the rule of law, gender equality, sustainable development, preservation of the environment and the fight against climate change ..."[632] A world that rests solidly on the common value of democracy is an international democracy. A "rules-based global order, with multilateralism as its key principle and the United Nations as its core", which the Parties define as their common goal and agree to promote,[633] characterises a world much closer to an international democracy than a lawless world of unilateral power politics.[634]

Art. 78 Samoa Agreement tunes in: According to para. 1, "[t]he Parties are committed to the rules-based international order with multilateralism as its key principle and the UN at its core. They shall promote international dialogue and seek multilateral solutions to drive global action forward." Art. 78 (3) Samoa Agreement is even more to the point: "The Parties shall endeavour to strengthen global governance and to support necessary reforms and the modernisation of multilateral institutions to make them more representative, responsive, effective, efficient, inclusive, transparent, democratic and accountable." This is a direct call for the democratisation of the UN and other international organisations, from the International Monetary Fund to the World Trade Organisation. Finally, according to Art. 78 (4) Samoa Agreement, "[t]he Parties shall deepen their multi-stakeholder approach to multilateralism by

[628] Article 21 (1) sentence 3 TEU.

[629] Article 21 (2) (h) TEU.

[630] See above Sect. 5.7.2.2.

[631] Articles 77 ff. See also the 3rd recital of the preamble and Article 1 (5).

[632] Article 77.

[633] 3rd recital of the preamble and Article 1 (5).

[634] See Sands (2005).

more effectively engaging civil society, the private sector and social partners in developing responses to global challenges." This is a call for citizens' participation in global governance.

5.7.3.2 Western Sahara Cases of the ECJ

Recalling that international democracy is based on the free and equal exercise by peoples of their right to external self-determination,[635] EU measures to ensure this therefore constitute examples of democracy "export" in the vertical direction. This draws attention to the ECJ judgments in the Western Sahara cases.[636] In its 2016 judgment, the Court had already invoked the ICJ's judgment in the East Timor Case to justify its finding that self-determination was "a legally enforceable right *erga omnes* and one of the essential principles of international law."[637] In the most recent case, the Court, relying on the ICJ's pertinent Advisory Opinion of 1975[638] and resolutions of the UN Security Council,[639] determined that the Sahraoui people of Western Sahara, a non-self-governing territory in the sense of Art. 73 UN Charter administered by Morocco, had the right of self-determination. Therefore, their at least implicit consent was required with regard to international agreements which Morocco concluded with the EU to the extent in which they applied to the territory of Western Sahara. Since such consent was missing in the case at hand, the ECJ confirmed the GC judgment that had annulled the Council Decision pursuant to Art. 218 (6) TFEU on the conclusion of the agreement at issue amending the Association Agreement with Morocco.[640] However, based on Art. 264 (2) TFEU, the ECJ ordered that the effects of that Council Decision were to be maintained for twelve months, in order to avoid serious negative consequences for the external action of the EU and the legal certainty of its international commitments.

This judgment is both introverted—because it annulled a Council Decision—and extroverted—because it enforced the Sahraoui people's right to external self-determination (and international democracy) also against Morocco (which has long been the main obstacle to successful decolonisation of Western Sahara). In this case, the ECJ could, but did not, also have referred to Art. 2 of the Euro-Mediterranean Agreement establishing an association between the European Communities and their Member States, of the one part, and the Kingdom of Morocco, of the other

---

[635] See above 3.

[636] See in particular ECJ, judgment of 21 December 2016 (C-104/16 P), ECLI:EU:C:2016:973; judgment of 4 October 2024 (Joined Cases C-779/21 P and 799/21 P), ECLI:EU:C:2024:835. Odermatt (2024).

[637] ECJ, judgment of 21 December 2016 (C-104/16 P), ECLI:EU:C:2016:973, para. 88, citing ICJ, judgment of 30 June 1995, East Timor (Portugal v. Australia), ICJ Reports 1995, p. 90, para. 29.

[638] ICJ, Advisory Opinion on Western Sahara of 16 October 1975, ICJ Reports 1975, p. 12.

[639] The most recent one cited is UN Security Council Resolution 2703 of 30 October 2023 (S/RES/2703 [2023]).

[640] Council Decision (EU) 2019/217 of 28 January 2019 (OJ L 34 of 6 February 2019, p. 1).

part.[641] Art. 2 stipulates that "[r]espect for the democratic principles and fundamental human rights established by the Universal Declaration of Human Rights shall inspire the domestic and external policies of the Community and of Morocco and shall constitute an essential element of this Agreement." This provision quite generally commits the EU and Morocco to democratic principles, which can be interpreted as covering both national and international democracy. Even though it lacks direct effect, it could have been used to confirm the findings which the ECJ made on the basis of customary international law.[642]

5.7.3.3 European Council and UN Pact for the Future

A recent example regarding the promotion of international democracy by the EU are the European Council Conclusions of 17 October 2024. In part III., the European Council reaffirmed "its unwavering commitment to effective multilateralism and to the rules-based international order with the United Nations at its core, steadfastly upholding the UN Charter and the rules and principles enshrined in the UN Charter, including those of sovereignty and territorial integrity, political independence and self-determination."[643] In this context, the European Council also welcomed the adoption of the Pact for the Future by the UN General Assembly which contains extensive promises to enhance international democracy.[644]

5.7.4 Individual Rights Regarding Democracy "Export"

Regarding democracy "export" by the EU to third States and the international community, there is no enforceable individual right to democracy pursuant to primary Union law. Because the "export" of democracy can only succeed to the extent in which other States agree, the EU enjoys such a broad margin of discretion that it will be difficult to demonstrate that it has not adequately fulfilled its obligations under Art. 3 (5), 21 TEU in this respect. Moreover, these "export" obligations are incumbent on the EU in the general interest and not in the interest of individuals. Accordingly, individuals usually have no standing to challenge Council decisions pursuant to Art. 218 (6) TFEU on the conclusion of association or partnership agreements or statutes of international organisations which they consider as inadequately

---

[641] Of 26 February 1996 (OJ 2000 L 70 of 18 March 2000, p. 2).

[642] ECJ, judgment of 4 October 2024 (Joined Cases C-779/21 P and 799/21 P), ECLI:EU:C:2024:835, para. 139.

[643] EUCO 25/24, paras. 27 ff. Available https://www.consilium.europa.eu/media/2pebccz2/20241017-euco-conclusions-en.pdf (22 January 2025).

[644] See above Sect. 2.2.

"exporting" democracy, because such decisions are not of direct and individual concern to them.[645]

But the ECJ made an exception in respect of the Front Polisario, as the representative of the people of Western Sahara which seeks to establish a sovereign State. As the Court explained, Front Polisario is a "privileged interlocutor in the process conducted under the auspices of the United Nations with a view to determining the future status of Western Sahara". The Court therefore permitted Front Polisario to protect the people of Western Sahara's right to self-determination by bringing an action for annulment pursuant to Art. 263 (4) TFEU against the Council Decision under Art. 218 (6) TFEU on the conclusion of an agreement with Morocco also affecting Western Sahara.[646]

Another question is whether international agreements concluded by the EU with third States and international organisations, which become part of EU law pursuant to Art. 216 (2) TFEU, ranking between secondary and primary law,[647] enshrine judicially enforceable individual rights regarding the protection or promotion of democracy in the treaty parties of the EU, or in the EU. This question can only be answered in respect of each particular agreement. It is hard to imagine that such rights could be successfully invoked in actions for annulment against EU acts (Art. 263 TFEU) or actions for failure to act (Art. 265 TFEU) before the GC. Perhaps the national courts of the respective treaty partner would show greater readiness to enforce those rights *vis-à-vis* their own State.

5.8 Conference on the Future of Europe—More Democracy in the EU?

The Conference on the Future of Europe took place in 2021–2022 as a citizen-focussed and bottom-up exercise that was intended to give all Europeans a say on how to improve the EU. It was an "opportunity to underpin the democratic legitimacy and functioning of the European project as well as to uphold the EU citizens support for our common goals and values, by giving them further opportunities to express themselves."[648] The main challenge was "the organisation, for the first time, of a transnational, multilingual and interinstitutional exercise of deliberative

[645] Article 263 (4) TFEU.

[646] ECJ, judgment of 4 October 2024 (Joined Cases C-779/21 P and 799/21 P), ECLI:EU:C:2024:835, paras. 58 ff.

[647] Article 218 (11) TFEU makes clear that the EU's international agreements rank below primary Union law.

[648] Joint Declaration of the Presidents of the European Parliament, the Council and the European Commission "Engaging with Citizens for Democracy – Building a more resilient Europe" of 10; March 2021 (OJ C 91 I of 18 March 2021, p. 1).

democracy, involving thousands of European citizens as well as political actors, social partners, civil society representatives and key stakeholders".[649]

5.8.1 Democratic Ingredients of the Final Outcome

On this background, it is unsurprising that the Report on the Final Outcome of 9 May 2022 also considers ways to improve the EU's democratic system. "European Democracy" is the specific focus of proposals 36–40. The 36th proposal suggests "[i]mproving the effectiveness of existing and developing new citizens' participation mechanism", thus enhancing the elements of direct democracy in the Union's representative system and ensuring that Europeans can effectively participate in EU policy-making.[650] The 37th proposal is concerned with making "the European Union more understandable and accessible and strengthen a common European identity", such as by bringing Europe closer to citizens.[651]

The 38th proposal "Democracy and elections" is of course most central, its objective being to "[s]trengthen European democracy by bolstering its foundations, boosting participation in European Parliament elections, fostering transnational debate on European issues and ensuring a strong link between citizens and their elected representatives".[652] It is concretely proposed to strengthen common democratic values within the EU in order to be more credible in advertising the EU's democratic model to third States. It is further proposed to enable the European Parliament to trigger an EU wide referendum "in exceptional cases on matters particularly important to all European citizens". Moreover, EU electoral law should be amended to harmonise electoral conditions for the European Parliament election, which would also constitute a step towards more electoral equality. Another suggestion is to introduce Union-wide or transnational lists with candidates from several Member States which would be voted on in all Member States.[653] This is based on the intention to transform the EP elections—that are currently conducted as 27 parallel national ballots[654]—into a European event and trigger a true European democratic debate.[655] In order to strengthen the link between citizens and their elected representatives, it is proposed that "European citizens should have a greater say on

[649] Conference on the Future of Europe: Report on the Final Outcome (May 2022), p. 5. Available via https://www.europarl.europa.eu/resources/library/media/20220509RES29121/20220509RES29121.pdf (22 January 2025).

[650] Id., p. 79.

[651] Id., p. 89 (footnote omitted).

[652] Id., p. 81.

[653] See above Sect. 5.5.7.3 for a pertinent proposal by the EP in 2022.

[654] Alemanno (2024b), Pause Button.

[655] See in this sense, e.g., Discours du Président de la Republique sur l'Europe à la Sorbonne, 25 avril 2024. Available via https://www.elysee.fr/front/pdf/elysee-module-22625-fr.pdf (22 January 2025).

who is elected as President of the Commission. This could be achieved either by the direct election of the Commission President or a lead candidate system".[656] The European Parliament should also be given the right of legislative initiative and the right to decide on the EU budget, like its national counterparts.[657]

The 39th proposal on the EU decision making process also relates to democratic progress. Its objective is to "[i]mprove the EU's decision-making process in order to ensure the EU's capability to act, while taking into account the interests of all Member States and guaranteeing a transparent and understandable process for the citizens".[658] It is proposed to replace unanimous decision-making by qualified-majority voting (with few exceptions) which would enhance democracy.[659] It is further proposed to increase the transparency of the decision-making process and institutions as well as the involvement of "national, regional, local representatives, social partners and organised civil society … and [n]ational parliaments."[660] Finally, the 40th proposal concerns effectuating the subsidiarity principle that is identified as a key feature for the EU's democratic accountability.[661]

Other democracy-related suggestions can be found outside the chapter on "European Democracy", in particular promoting media independence and pluralism as well as media and digital literacy and combating fake news and disinformation online as well as offline.[662] In this regard, the European Media Freedom Act (EMFA) has meanwhile been enacted in the form of a Regulation based on Art. 114 TFEU.[663] While the Act's main thrust therefore is to lay down "common rules for the proper functioning of the internal market for media services", it also strives to "safeguarding the independence and pluralism of media services."[664] It does so in acknowledging that, "[g]iven the unique role of media services, the protection of media freedom and media pluralism as two of the main pillars of democracy and of the rule of law constitutes an essential feature of a well-functioning internal market for media services." Art. 3 EMFA accordingly guarantees the "right of recipients of media services to have access to a plurality of editorially independent media content and ensure that framework conditions are in place in line with this Regulation to safeguard that right, to the benefit of free and democratic discourse." It has been argued that Art. 3 EMFA, read together with Art. 11 CFR and Art. 56 TFEU, may guarantee a justiciable individual right to have access to pluralistic media.[665] The EMFA is an

[656] See note 647, p. 81 (footnotes omitted).

[657] Id., p. 81.

[658] Id., p. 83.

[659] See above Sect. 5.5.4 See above Sect. 3.3 on the parallel problem at global level.

[660] See note 647, p. 83.

[661] Id., p. 84.

[662] 27th and 33rd proposal (id., p. 70, 75).

[663] Regulation (EU) 2024/1083 of 11 April 2024 establishing a common framework for media services in the internal market … (OJ L 2024/1083 of 17 April 2024).

[664] Article 1 (1) EMFA.

[665] Malferrari and Gerhold (2024), p. 893 ff. See also Mastroianni (2022), p. 393 ff.

important element in the European Commission's new defence of democracy package.[666] But it is controversial whether Art. 114 TFEU constitutes a sufficient legal basis for EU media regulation.[667]

5.8.2 *European Parliament Follow-up Proposals to Enhance EU's Democratic Legitimacy and Accountability*

In reaction to the Conference Outcome, the European Parliament adopted a resolution including proposals for the amendment of the Treaties that it submitted to the Council, pursuant to Art. 48 (2) TEU.[668] The resolution was only narrowly adopted by a vote of 291:274, with 44 abstentions.[669] The EP stated that the proposed amendments were necessary for reshaping "the Union in a way that will enhance its capacity to act, as well as its democratic legitimacy and accountability".[670] In particular, it tried to realise the inherent connection between enhanced effectiveness and more democratic legitimacy by drastically reducing the instances in which the Council can act only unanimously, while simultaneously further empowering the EP.[671] It also called for "the strengthening of instruments for citizens' participation in the EU decision-making process within the framework of representative democracy".[672]

Among many others, the EP made the following concrete suggestions that are particularly relevant to supranational democracy: to oblige the Union to ensure that there are instruments that enable citizens to exercise their right to participate in the democratic life of the Union[673]; to empower the EP and the Council, acting in accordance with ordinary legislative procedure, "to adopt provisions to guarantee … the adherence to the principles set out in Articles 10 and 11 [TEU]"[674]; to enhance the role of the EP and reduce the role of the European Council in the election of the President of the European Commission[675]; to give the EP the power of voting on a

666 Communication from the Commission to the European Parliament, the Council, the European Economic and Social Committee and the European Committee of the Regions on Defence of Democracy, COM(2023) 630 final of 12 December 2023. Available via https://eur-lex.europa.eu/resource.html?uri=cellar:d0c78e96-99c5-11ee-b164-01aa75ed71a1.0001.02/DOC_1&format=PDF (13 February 2025).

667 Roß (2023), p. 458 f. This question is currently pending before the ECJ under the file number C-486/24 (annulment action brought by Hungary).

668 Resolution of 22 November 2023, P9_TA(2023)0427. Available via https://www.europarl.europa.eu/doceo/document/TA-9-2023-0427_EN.html (13 February 2025).

669 Müller (2023).

670 See note 666, preamble, B.

671 Id., para. 3 and 4.

672 Id., para. 12.

673 Id., proposed amendment 13 regarding Article 10 (3) TEU.

674 Id., proposed amendment 19 adding a new para. 4a to Article 11 TEU.

675 Id., proposed amendment 41 regarding Article 17 (7) TEU.

motion of individual censure of a member of the Commission[676]; to use qualified majority voting in the European Council and the Council throughout the Common Foreign and Security Policy, including in the Common Security and Defence Policy, while making those decisions subject to EP consent, in order to maintain adequate democratic legitimacy[677]; to require EP consent for ordinary treaty revisions[678]; to have the European Council adopt decisions by a qualified majority in the simplified treaty revision procedure of Art. 48 (7) TEU[679]; to introduce the ordinary legislative procedure in Art. 22 (1) and (2) TFEU concerning detailed arrangements for EU foreign nationals' right to vote in municipal and European Parliament elections in their Member State of residence[680]; to include a further aim in the EU education policy, namely "developing common objectives and standards of an education that promotes democratic values and the rule of law ..."[681]; to include "the promotion of democratic values, good governance, human rights and sustainability … in the scope of the common commercial policy"[682]; to have the EP and the Council, acting by a reinforced qualified majority,[683] adopt a regulation harmonising the rules for EP elections[684]; to give the EP the right of initiative for legislation[685]; to enable the Council to make use of the flexibility clause (Art. 352 (1) TFEU) by a qualified majority, with the consent of the EP, and extend that clause to the Common Foreign and Security Policy.[686]

The Commission, the Council and the European Council have so far been hesitant to pursue the ordinary revision procedure according to Art. 48 (2)–(5) TEU on the basis of the EP proposals. Rather, there seem to be considerations to use the accession clause in Art. 49 TEU to put at least some amendments into effect together with the next EU enlargement.[687] In any event, the fate of the EP proposals for enhancing the EU's democratic legitimacy is currently unclear.

---

[676] Id., proposed amendment 42 regarding Article 17 (8) TEU.

[677] Id., proposed amendments 45 and 47 regarding Article 24 (1) subpara. 2, Article 31 (1) TEU and proposed amendment 53 regarding Article 42 (4) TEU.

[678] Id., proposed amendment 62 adding a new subpara. 1a to Article 48 (4) TEU.

[679] Id., proposed amendment 64.

[680] Id., proposed amendments 88 and 89.

[681] Id., proposed amendment 143 regarding Article 165 (2) TFEU.

[682] Id., para. 29 and proposed amendment 169 regarding Article 206 TFEU.

[683] The definition of "reinforced qualified majority" is missing because the pertinent proposal by the Committee on Constitutional Affairs was deleted by the Plenary (see Müller [2023]).

[684] Id., proposed amendment 187 regarding Article 223 (1) TFEU.

[685] Id., proposed amendment 189 regarding Article 225 TFEU.

[686] Id., proposed amendment 238.

[687] See the criticism by Duff (2024). See also the call for a Convention to "ensure a deep and democratic reform" of the Treaties in a 2024 Memorandum by the Union of European Federalists: Why we need a Convention to change the Treaties. Available via https://federalists.eu/wp-content/uploads/2024/02/Memorandum-ENG-2024-UEF-Campaign.pdf (29 August 2025).

5.8.3 Limits to Democratic Backsliding at EU Level?

Having presented various proposals to enhance EU democracy, it is appropriate to also discuss what limits EU law sets to democratic backsliding at EU level. Since democratic standards are firmly entrenched in primary Union law, including in the form of actionable individual rights,[688] the only serious question is whether Treaty amendments pursuant to Art. 48 TEU which reduce democratic standards would be prohibited. Such an undemocratic amendment could certainly not be introduced through the narrowly tailored simplified revision procedure of Art. 48 (7) TEU. Through the second simplified revision procedure pursuant to Art. 48 (6) TEU, democratic standards in Art. 26 – 197 TFEU, such as the participation of the European Parliament, could be reduced. Severe forms of democratic backsliding, such as the abolition of the European Parliament, could, however, only be accomplished through the ordinary revision procedure in Art. 48 (2)–(5) TEU.

This begs the question whether EU law contains implicit substantive limitations to Treaty amendments in favour of maintaining the values enshrined in Art. 2 TEU, which define the Union's constitutional identity, and in particular democracy, in parallel to the constraints on constitutional amendments well known in several national constitutions.[689] The ECJ has indicated but never clearly determined the existence of such implicit substantive limits on the Treaty amending power.[690] Is there perhaps a non-retrogression rule preventing at least a massive reduction of the EU's democratic *acquis,* is that rule justiciable and can it be enforced by individuals, invoking their right to democracy under Union law? One can make an argument for answering all three questions in the affirmative.[691]

Concentrating on the third question, the general right to democracy in the EU, derived from Art. 10 (3) TEU, read together with Art. 10 (1) and (2) as well as Art. 2 TEU, can be used as a basis for Union citizens' actions against Treaty amendments undermining the EU's democratic system. If such actions against democratic backsliding by Treaty revision do not meet the strict standards of Art. 263 (4) TFEU for a direct action for annulment against an EU component of the Treaty revision process, they can instead be lodged in the Member State courts, pursuant to Art. 19 (1) subpara. 2 TEU. For that purpose, plaintiffs should choose a Member State, like Germany, whose constitution formulates a specific requirement regarding realisation of the democratic principle in the EU.[692] Such a Member State would be constitutionally prohibited from ratifying any Treaty amendment scaling back the

---

[688] See above Sect. 5.5.

[689] Spieker (2023), p. 145 ff. For national constitutional parallels, see, *e.g.*, Article 79 (3) of the German Basic Law.

[690] ECJ, Opinion 1/91 of 14 December 1991, ECR 1991, I-6079, paras. 70 f.; judgment of (Joined Cases C-401/05 P and C-415/05 P), ECLI:EU:C:2008:461, paras. 303 f. The interpretation of these decisions is controversial (see Spieker [2023], p. 148 ff.)

[691] See Spieker (2023), p. 150 ff. (concerning the first two questions).

[692] On the German situation, see above Sect. 5.3.3.

democratic *acquis* at EU level and its national judiciary could be used to enforce that constitutional prohibition and thereby frustrate the entire Treaty revision process, thereby preserving the current level of EU democracy.[693]

5.9 Conclusion: EU Democracy and Individual Democratic Rights in an Era of Democratic Backsliding

In the EU's quasi-federal (supranational) constitution, democracy at EU and Member State levels are interdependent and therefore closely intertwined. This is why EU law formulates democratic requirements for both the EU and the Member States, something typical for (quasi-) federal constitutional systems. From a bottom-up perspective, Member States (such as Germany) also provide in their constitutions that a sufficiently effective level of democratic legitimacy must exist at EU level and that their national democracy must remain effective in the process of supranational integration.

EU law's supranationality is characterised by the direct effect also of those of its provisions which are not formulated as individual rights, but impose clearly defined objective obligations on EU institutions or Member States.[694] Consequently, the democratic standards of EU law for both the Union and Member States are more likely to constitute judicially enforceable individual rights than those in regional or global international law. As a further difference, the EU standards also command primacy over conflicting national—including constitutional—standards. On the other hand, Art. 4 (2) TEU obliges the EU to respect the constitutional identity of Member States, which therefore retain a broad margin of discretion in designing their concrete democratic structures.

EU law parameters for national democracy have partly consolidated into individual rights: Art. 10 (3) sentence 1 TEU enshrines a judicially enforceable general right of all citizen of the Union to the existence of a democratic system also in the Member State of their own nationality, where they enjoy comprehensive rights of political participation. Art. 2 and Art. 10 (2) sentence 2 TEU, that also have direct effect, provide a second leg for this general right to national democracy. But the right is limited to elementary democratic standards which definitely limit Member States' discretion under Art. 4 (2) TEU in designing their governmental structure. At a time of democratic backsliding, such a very general, but directly effective and judicially enforceable, right (which the ECJ has not yet recognised) can be useful, if taken together with the non-retrogression rule. More specific democratic individual rights are guaranteed separately, such as the active and passive right to vote in municipal elections of EU foreign nationals in their Member State of residence and, by virtue of Art. 6 (3) TEU, implicitly and only to a certain extent also the

[693] See Spieker (2023), p. 151.

[694] See above Sect. 5.4.3.2.

active and passive right to vote in national parliamentary elections.[695] The CFR contains the usual series of supplementary democratic individual rights (*e.g.*, to communicative freedoms), but they bind Member States only within the scope of application of other EU law provisions.

Regarding democracy at EU level, Art. 10 (3) sentence 1 TEU enshrines the central democratic right of Union citizens to EU democracy. Read together with Art. 2 and Art. 10 (1) TEU, the provision can be interpreted as containing a judicially enforceable individual entitlement to the maintenance of elementary standards of democracy at EU level. In conjunction with the non-retrogression rule, this will, however, only protect from severe forms of democratic backsliding. In this sense, Art. 10 (3) sentence 1 TEU for the most part sets forth a legally binding principle guiding the pro-democratic and pro-participatory interpretation of other primary and secondary law provisions. Art. 9 sentence 1 TEU adds a general individual right of Union citizens to democratic equality *vis-à-vis* the EU and includes a justiciable claim against instances of unreasonable or disproportionate discrimination regarding their participation in the Union's political processes.

Art. 22 (2) TFEU and Art. 39 CFR enshrine individual rights of Union citizens to vote and stand as a candidate at EP elections, both as substantive rights addressed to their Member State of nationality as well as their Member State of residence (if different) and as rights of EU foreign nationals against discrimination based on nationality by their Member State of residence. There is a partial right to equality of suffrage, protecting Union citizens from restrictions of electoral equality which are not inherent in the degressively proportional composition of the EP. It also includes a general entitlement to protection against double voting by other Union citizens.

Primary EU law codifies a host of supplementary democratic rights of Union citizens as well as third-State nationals residing in the EU, such as the right of access to documents (Art. 15 (3) TFEU, Art. 42 CFR), the right to petition the European Parliament (Art. 227 TFEU, Art. 44 CFR) and the usual series of rights to communicative freedoms in the CFR. These individual rights deriving from primary EU law are complemented by further individual rights granted by secondary acts, such as the EMFA.

From a synthesis of all these democratic rights, one can arguably derive an unwritten general individual right of Union citizens to democracy at EU level. This general right, which can be linked to Art. 10 (3) sentence 1 TEU, promotes the pro-democratic interpretation of the specific democratic rights and other EU law provisions, increases the demands on justification of limitations and can perhaps even generate further supplementary unwritten democratic rights. The ECJ has, however, so far not recognised any such right.

EU law does not include any judicially enforceable individual right regarding the adequacy of the federal and democratic balance between the EU and Member States (subsidiarity) or to constant enhancements of the state of democracy and better individual democratic participation at EU level. Nor is there any individual right

[695] See above Sect. 5.4.3.3.3.

accompanying the primary law obligation of the EU to "export" democracy horizontally to third States and vertically to the international community as a whole. But there is an individual right against massive democratic backsliding by way of Treaty revisions pursuant to Art. 48 TEU.

All in all, the human right to democracy in general and in its specific aspects is more firmly entrenched and more easily and effectively enforceable within the multilevel EU system than outside. Remaining gaps can be closed by recourse to regional European and global human rights instruments which can be used to identify unwritten general principles of EU law, based on Art. 6 (3) TEU. Union law thus harbours a great potential to counteract democratic backsliding both in individual Member States and at EU level, but also in candidate countries and treaty partners; that potential must be used actively and wisely to preserve democratic achievements within the Union and beyond.

References

Alemanno A (2024a) Beyond EU law heroes: unleashing strategic litigation as a form of participation in the Union's democratic life. German Law J 25:822–839

Alemanno A (2024b) Hitting the pause button on the EU project?. Available via Verfassungsblog. https://verfassungsblog.de/hitting-the-pause-button-on-the-eu-project/. Accessed 22 Jan 2025

Anagnostaras G (2024) Acquitted on the benefit of doubt … but not proven innocent! The judgment of the German Federal Constitutional Court on the next generation EU program. German Law J 25:578–596. https://www.cambridge.org/core/journals/german-law-journal/article/acquitted-on-the-benefit-of-doubt-but-not-proven-innocent-the-judgment-of-the-german-federal-constitutional-court-on-the-next-generation-eu-program/08FB1667795FCE512E6C9845555846DC. Accessed 4 March 2025

Assenbrunner B (2023) Struktursicherung im europäischen Verfassungsverbund durch Art. 2 EUV. Die Öffentliche Verwaltung 76:609–618

Baquero Cruz J, Keppenne J-P (2022) Fundamental values, constitutional identity and the protection of the European Union budget against breaches of the rule of law. In: European Commission (ed) 70 years of EU law, 1st edn. Publications Office of the European Union, Luxemburg, pp 54–71

Bárd P (2023) Can the Hungarian council presidency be postponed – legally?. Available via Verfassungsblog. https://verfassungsblog.de/can-the-hungarian-council-presidency-be-postponed-legally/. Accessed 22 Jan 2025

Blanke H-J, Sander A (2023) Enforcing the rule of law in the EU: the case of Poland and Hungary. Zeitschrift für Europarechtliche Studien 26:239–276

Blauberger M, Kelemen RD (2017) Can courts rescue national democracy? Judicial safeguards against democratic backsliding in the EU. J Eur Publ Policy 24:321–336

Bonelli M, Claes M (2023) Crossing the Rubicon? The commission's use of article 2 TEU in the infringement action on LGBTQ+ rights in Hungary. Maastricht J Eur Comp Law 30:3–14

Bouzoraa Y (2023) The value of democracy in EU law and its enforcement: a legal analysis. Eur Pap 8:809–851

Bradley K (2020) Showdown at the last chance saloon. Available via Verfassungsblog. https://verfassungsblog.de/showdown-at-the-last-chance-saloon/. Accessed 22 Jan 2025

Bruti Liberati M, Ramopoulos T, Bianchi D (2022) The European Union as a worldwide promoter of the universality and indivisibility of human rights. In: European Commission (ed) 70 years of EU law, 1st edn. Publications Office of the European Union, Luxemburg, pp 72–90

Calliess C (2020) Constitutional identity in Germany. In: Calliess C, Van der Schyff G (eds) Constitutional identity in a Europe of multilevel constitutionalism, 1st edn. Oxford University Press, Oxford, pp 153–181
Calliess C, Ruffert M (eds) (2022) EUV/AEUV, 6th edn. C.H. Beck, Munich. (quoted by: Author)
Castellarin E (2023) Democracy promotion and development cooperation. In: Khan D-E, Lagrange E, Oeter S et al (eds) Democracy and sovereignty. Rethinking the legitimacy of public international law, 1st edn. Brill Nijhoff, Brill/Leiden, pp 183–211
Chamon M (2024) A rejoinder to citizenship for Sale (commission v Malta). Available via Verfassungsblog. https://verfassungsblog.de/a-rejoinder-to-citizenship-for-sale/. Accessed 22 Jan 2025
Chamon M, Eliantonio M, Volpato A (2022) Repasi vs Plaumann: an individual MEP's standing before the EU courts. Available via Verfassungsblog. https://verfassungsblog.de/repasi-vs-plaumann/. Accessed 22 Jan 2025
Chelini-Pont B (2025) The European Union and national sovereignty: a new democratic challenge? Available via Schuman Paper No. 790, 6th May 2025. https://server.www.robert-schuman.eu/storage/en/doc/questions-d-europe/qe-790-en.pdf. Accessed 29 Aug 2025
Christopoulou A-E (2024) Towards a Golden age of the European citizens' initiative?. Available via European Law Blog. https://www.europeanlawblog.eu/pub/oqrjrv7h/release/1. Accessed 22 Jan 2025
Churchill W (1946) Speech at the University of Zurich. https://rm.coe.int/16806981f3. Accessed 4 Dec 2024
Citino YM (2024) The Spitzenkandidaten practice in the spotlight. Available via Verfassungsblog. https://verfassungsblog.de/the-spitzenkandidaten-practice/. Accessed 22 Jan 2025
Classen CD (2024) Frieden mit Europa? – Anmerkung zum Beschluss des BVerfG v. 6.2.2024. Europarecht 59:322–330
Cotter J (2020) The last chance saloon: Hungarian representatives may be excluded from the European council and the council. Available via Verfassungsblog. https://verfassungsblog.de/the-last-chance-saloon/. Accessed 22 Jan 2025
Cotter J (2022) To everything there is a season: Instrumentalising article 10 TEU to exclude undemocratic member state representatives from the European council and the council. Eur Law Rev 47:69–84
Court of Justice of the European Union (ed) (2013) 50th anniversary of the judgment in Van Gend en Loos 1963–2013. https://op.europa.eu/de/publication-detail/-/publication/de3db697-1f5c-4f83-8424-1663b43ac2d3. Accessed 22 Jan 2025
Craig P (2021a) Institutions, power, and institutional balance. In: Craig P, De Búrca G (eds) The evolution of EU law, 3rd edn. Oxford University Press, Oxford, pp 46–89
Craig P (2021b) Integration, democracy, and legitimacy. In: Craig P, De Búrca G (eds) The evolution of EU law, 3rd edn. Oxford University Press, Oxford, pp 12–45
Cramér P, Wrange P (2001) The Haider Affair, Law and European Integration. Faculty of Law, Stockholm University Research Paper No. 19. Available via https://papers.ssrn.com/sol3/papers.cfm?abstract_id=3048316. Accessed 27 February 2025
de Cecco F (2024) Added value(s)?. Available via Verfassungsblog. https://verfassungsblog.de/commission-v-hungary/. Accessed 22 Jan 2025
de Guttry A (2018) The right of aliens to vote and carry out political activities: a critical analysis of the relevant international obligations incumbent on the state of origin and on the host state. Zeitschrift für ausländisches öffentliches Recht und Völkerrecht 78:933–1001
Díez Sarasola M (2024) EU'S involvement in the renewal of the Spanish Council of the Judiciary: the European Commission's new role in the internal constitutional Affairs of the Member States. Available via Verfassungsblog. https://verfassungsblog.de/renewal-of-the-judiciary/. Accessed 22 Jan 2025
Dörr O (2019) Nationality. Max Planck encyclopedia of public international law (OUP online edition)

Dörr O, Grote R, Marauhn T (eds) (2022) EMRK/GG. Konkordanzkommentar zum europäischen und deutschen Grundrechtsschutz, vol.II 3rd edn. 2022 Mohr Siebeck, Tübingen (quoted by: Author)

Duff A (2024) How to avoid another botched EU enlargement by sticking to the rules. Available via Verfassungsblog. https://verfassungsblog.de/sticking-to-the-rules/. Accessed 22 Jan 2025

Erlbacher F, Herrmann K (2022) Fundamental values of the European Union: from principles to legal obligations. In: European Commission (ed) 70 years of EU law, 1st edn. Publications Office of the European Union, Luxemburg, pp 30–53

European Parliament (2022) Conference on the Future of Europe: Report on the Final Outcome (May 2022). https://www.europarl.europa.eu/resources/library/media/20220509RES29121/20220509RES29121.pdf. Accessed 22 Jan 2025

European Union (2020) EU Action Plan on Human Rights and Democracy 2020–2024. https://www.eeas.europa.eu/sites/default/files/eu_action_plan_on_human_rights_and_democracy_2020-2024.pdf. Accessed 22 Jan 2025

European Union Agency for Fundamental Rights (2024) Fundamental Rights Report 2024. https://fra.europa.eu/sites/default/files/fra_uploads/fra-2024-fundamental-rights-report-2024_en.pdf. Accessed 22 Jan 2025

Fassbender B (2023) Are the EU member states still sovereign states? The perspective of international law. Eur Pap 8:1629–1643. https://www.europeanpapers.eu/fr/system/files/pdf_version/EP_eJ_2023_3_SS2_1_Bardo_Fassbender_00733.pdf. Accessed 21 Feb 2025

Feisel FM (2023) Walking a democratic tightrope: EU militant democracy and the infringement action against Lex tusk. Available via Verfassungsblog. https://verfassungsblog.de/walking-a-democratic-tightrope/. Accessed 22 Jan 2025

Fisicaro M (2022) Beyond the rule of law conditionality: exploiting the EU spending power to Foster the Union's values. Eur Pap 7:697–719

Franco-German Working Group on EU Institutional Reform (2023) Sailing on High Seas: Reforming and Enlarging the EU for the 21st Century. https://www.auswaertiges-amt.de/resource/blob/2617206/4d0e0010ffcd8c0079e21329bbbb3332/230919-rfaa-deu-fra-bericht-data.pdf. Accessed 22 Jan 2025

Franzius C (2025) Europäische Verfassungsaufsicht. In: Bast J, von Bogdandy A (eds) Unionsverfassungsrecht, 1st edn. Nomos, Baden-Baden, pp 671–734

Freigang L (2015) EU-Demokratie- und Menschenrechtsförderung im auswärtigen Handeln nach dem Vertrag von Lissabon, 1st edn. Nomos, Baden-Baden

Gallagher-Teske K, Giesing Y (2017) Dual Citizenship in the EU ifo DICE Report 15

Gawrich A, Schöppner F, Achrainer C et al (2024) Ein neuer Ansatz der EU-Demokratieförderung für die EU-Nachbarschaftspolitik: Ambitionen, Konzepte. Lernkurven integration 47:120–136

Giegerich T (2009a) The Federal Constitutional Court's judgment on the treaty of Lisbon—the last word (German) wisdom ever has to say on a united Europe? German Yearb Int Law 10:9–44

Giegerich T (2009b) The *is* and the *ought* of international constitutionalism: how far have we come on Habermas's road to a "Well-Considered Constitutionalization of International Law"? German Law J 10:31–62

Giegerich T (2010) The Federal Constitutional Court's non-sustainable role as Europe's ultimate arbiter. German Yearb Int Law 11:867–884

Giegerich T (2013) The German Federal Constitutional Court's misguided attempts to guard the European guardians in Luxemburg and Strasbourg. In: Breuer M, Epiney A, Haratsch A et al (eds) Der Staat im Recht. Festschrift für Eckart Klein zum 70. Geburtstag, 1st edn. Duncker & Humblot, Berlin, pp 49–64

Giegerich T (2015) Wege zu einer vertieften Gemeinsamen Außen- und Sicherheitspolitik: Reparatur von Defiziten als "kleine Lösung". In: Kadelbach S (ed) Die Europäische Union am Scheideweg: mehr oder weniger Europa? 1st edn. Nomos, Baden-Baden, pp 132–185

Giegerich T (2016) Zwischen Europafreundlichkeit und Europaskepsis—Kritischer Überblick über die bundesverfassungsgerichtliche Rechtsprechung zur europäischen Integration. Zeitschrift für Europarechtliche Studien 19:3–47

Giegerich T (2018a) Bringt das EU-Recht den Europawahlen in Deutschland die 5%-Klausel zurück?. Available via Verfassungsblog. https://verfassungsblog.de/bringt-das-eu-recht-den-europawahlen-in-deutschland-die-5-klausel-zurueck/. Accessed 22 Jan 2025

Giegerich T (2018b) Die Verflechtungsfalle des Europawahlrechts: Nationale Ratifikationen des geänderten EU-Direktwahlakts mit obligatorischer Sperrklausel und ihre rechtlichen Hürden. Zeitschrift für Europarechtliche Studien 21:145–164

Giegerich T (2019) Die Unabhängigkeit der Gerichte als Strukturvorgabe der Unionsverfassung und ihr effektiver Schutz vor autoritären Versuchungen in den Mitgliedstaaten. Zeitschrift für Europarechtliche Studien 22:61–111

Giegerich T (2020a) Foreign relations law. Max Planck Encyclopedia of Public International Law (OUP online edition)

Giegerich T (2020b) The political dimension of equality in the European Union: equality of citizens and equality of member states in a supranational representative democracy. In: Giegerich T (ed) The European Union as protector and promoter of equality, 1st edn. Springer, Cham, pp 45–95

Giegerich T (2020c) Unionsbürgerschaft, politische Rechte (§ 9). In: Schulze R, Janssen A, Kadelbach S (eds) Europarecht, 4th edn. Nomos, Baden-Baden, pp 395–451

Giegerich T (2020d) 75 Jahre Internationale Menschenrechtsrevolution: Von der UN-Charta zur EU-Sanktionsregelung im Bereich Menschenrechte. Available via Jean Monnet Saar. https://jean-monnet-saar.eu/wp-content/uploads/2020/12/Giegerich_75-Jahre-Internationale-Menschnerechtsrevolution.pdf. Accessed 22 Jan 2025

Giegerich T (2021a) All's well that ends well?. Available via Jean Monnet Saar. https://jean--monnet-saar.eu/?page_id=125638. Accessed 22 Jan 2025

Giegerich T (2021b) The Rule of Law in the European Union – Countering Recent Challenges to Self-Evident Truths Politically, Judicially, and Financially. In: SEE | EU Cluster of Excellence in European and International Law (ed) South Eastern Europe and the European Union – Legal Developments, 1st edn. Saarbrücken, pp 9–23

Giegerich T (2022a) Europawahlreform als unendliche Geschichte: Wir müssen auch dort die Vetomacht einzelner Mitgliedstaaten eliminieren. Available via Jean Monnet Saar. https://jean--monnet-saar.eu/?page_id=212894. Accessed 22 Jan 2025

Giegerich T (2022b) Das PSPP-Urteil des BVerfG und seine diversen Nachspiele. In: Hilpold P, Steinmair W, Raffeiner A (eds) Österreich und die EU im Umbruch—eine Nachlese zur Festschrift für Heinrich Neisser, 1st edn. Facultas, Vienna, pp 49–60

Giegerich T (2023) Gendering political participation in Germany and beyond: should quotas ensure gender parity in parliaments? In: Gstrein OJ, Fröhlich M, Van den Berg C et al (eds) Modernising European legal education, 1st edn. Springer, Cham, pp 141–166

Giegerich T (2024) The rule of law, fundamental rights, the EU'S common foreign and security policy and the ECHR: Quartet of Constant Dissonance? Zeitschrift für Europarechtliche Studien 27:590–633

Gitzen RM (2024) Quo vadis europäischen Wahlrecht?. Available via Jean Monnet Saar. https://jean-monnet-saar.eu/wp-content/uploads/2024/02/Expert-Paper-Quo-vadis-europaeisches-Wahlrecht-Von-Spitzenkandidaten-Sperrklauseln-und-Quoten-im-Mehrebenensystem.pdf. Accessed 22 Jan 2025

Grabenwarter C (2014) European convention on human rights—commentary. C.H. Beck, Munich

Grabitz E, Hilf M, Nettesheim M (eds) (2024) Das Recht der Europäischen Union. C.H.Beck, München (quoted by: Author)

Griffiths RT (1994) Europe's First Constitution: The European Political Community, 1952–1954. In: Martin S (ed) The construction of Europe. Essays in honour of Emile Noël, 1st edn. Kluwer Academic Publishers, Dordrecht/Boston/London, pp 19–41

Griffiths RT (2000) Europe's First Constitution: The European Political Community, 1952–1954. Federal Trust, London

Grimm D (1995) Does Europe need a constitution? Eur Law J 1:282–302

Grimm D (2017) The constitution of European democracy. Oxford University Press, Oxford

Grimm D (2022) Enhancing the European Union's legitimacy. In: Deliyanni-Dimitrakou C, Gaudin H, Prévédourou E et al (eds) Mélanges Vassilios Skouris, 1st edn. Mare & Martin, Paris, pp 241–250

Gutmann A, Kohlmeier N (2024) Transnational wehrhafte Demokratie: Zu den Voraussetzungen eines Parteiverbotsverfahrens im Mehrebenensystem. Available via Verfassungsblog. https://verfassungsblog.de/transnational-wehrhafte-demokratie/. Accessed 22 Jan 2025

Hailbronner M (2018) Beyond legitimacy: Europe's crisis of constitutional democracy. In: Graber MA, Levinson S, Tushnet M (eds) Constitutional democracy in crisis? 1st edn. Oxford University Press, New York, pp 277–293

Halmai G (2025) Can the Rule of Law Be Restored by Violating Its Principles? Available via Verfassungsblog. https://verfassungsblog.de/can-the-rule-of-law-be-restored-by-violating-its-principles/. Accessed 22 Jan 2025

Haltern U (2017) Europarecht, Band I, 3rd edn. Mohr Siebeck, Tübingen

Hatje A (2019) The value of constitutionalism in the European Union. In: Garben S, Govaere I, Nemitz P (eds) Critical reflections on constitutional democracy in the European Union, 1st edn. Hart Publishing, Oxford, pp 115–126

Huber PM (2022) Politische Grundrechte der Unionsbürger. In: Grabenwarter C (ed) Europäischer Grundrechteschutz, 2nd edn. Nomos, Baden-Baden, pp 1081–1118

Huber PM (2024) Die Verfassungsprinzipien nach 75 Jahren Grundgesetz. Die Öffentliche Verwaltung 77:426–432

Joos K, Droste H (2024) Aktuelle Reform des EU-Wahlrechts. Europäische Zeitschrift für Wirtschaftsrecht 35:293–295

Kadelbach S (2010) Union citizenship. In: Von Bogdandy A, Bast J (eds) Principles of European constitutional law, 2nd edn. Hart Publishing, Oxford, pp 443–478

Kadelbach S (2025) Unionsbürgerschaft. In: Bast J, von Bogdandy A (eds) Unionsverfassungsrecht, 1st edn. Nomos, Baden-Baden, pp 735–794

Kahl W (2022) Democratic legitimacy of the EU Administration. In: Deliyanni-Dimitrakou C, Gaudin H, Prévédourou E et al (eds) Mélanges Vassilios Skouris, 1st edn. Mare & Martin, Paris, pp 311–326

Kaiser L, Knecht A, Spieker LD (2024) European society strikes Back. Available via Verfassungsblog. https://verfassungsblog.de/european-society-strikes-back/. Accessed 22 Jan 2025

Kaźmierska K (2024) In favour of the Hungarian council presidency. Available via Verfassungsblog. https://verfassungsblog.de/the-hungarian-council-presidency/. Accessed 22 Jan 2025

Kelemen RD (2019) The 'democratic deficits' of the US and the EU compared. In: Garben S, Govaere I, Nemitz P (eds) Critical reflections on constitutional democracy in the European Union, 1st edn. Hart Publishing, Oxford, pp 47–62

Kellerbauer M, Klamert M, Tomkin J (eds) (2019) The EU treaties and the charter of fundamental rights, 2nd edn. Oxford University Press, Oxford

Kelly A (2022) Disenfranchisement in EU Member States: An Analysis of the loss of voting rights on the basis of non-residence, Research Paper for ECIT Foundation (European Citizens' rights, Involvement and Trust). https://ecit-foundation.eu/wp-content/uploads/2022/09/Report-on-Disenfranchisement-in-EU-Member-States.pdf. Accessed 22 Jan 2025

Kochenov D (2009) Free movement and participation in the parliamentary elections in the member state of nationality: an ignored link? Maastricht J Eur Comp Law 16:197–223

Kokott J (2023) Zur unmittelbaren Wirkung des Unionsrechts. Archiv des öffentlichen Rechts 148:496–520

Kotzur M (2024) Das Grundgesetz in seinen internationalen Wirkungszusammenhängen – Resilienz durch Offenheit. Die Öffentliche Verwaltung 77:432–440

Krenn C (2022) A Chernobyl Case for our Times: Repasi v. Commission and the legal protection of minority rights in the European Parliament. Available via Verfassungsblog. https://verfassungsblog.de/a-chernobyl-case-for-our-times/. Accessed 22 Jan 2025

Kristan V (2025) Beyond Formal Legality – The Restorative Effect of an Episodic Infringement. Available via Verfassungsblog. https://verfassungsblog.de/beyond-formal-legality/. Accessed 15 Feb 2025

Lappin R (2016) The right to vote for non-resident citizens in Europe. Int Comp Law Q 65:859–894

Leino-Sandberg P (2025) Who can guard the guardian? Available via European Law Blog. https://www.europeanlawblog.eu/pub/aehrtxyf/release/2. Accessed 21 Feb 2025

Lenaerts K (2013) The principle of democracy in the case law of the European court of justice. Int Comp Law Q 62:271–315

Lenaerts K (2024) Verfassungsrechtliche Eckpunkte für die weitere Entwicklung der Europäischen Union. Europarecht 59:380–388

Lenaerts K, van Nuffel P, Corthaut T (2021) EU constitutional law. Oxford University Press, Oxford

Lincoln A (1992) Selected speeches and writings. Vintage Books, New York

Lobina B, Maharaj CM (2025) The dismissal of the Romanian prosecutors annulment action. A critical take. Available via Verfassungsblog. https://verfassungsblog.de/romanian-association-of-prosecutors/. Accessed 2 Mar 2025

Malferrari L, Gerhold M (2024) Ein Unionsrecht auf Empfang pluraler Medien? Europäische Zeitschrift für Wirtschaftsrecht 35:893–900

Mangas A (2024) The European Union's response to the Catalan secessionist process. Hague J Rule Law 16:63–88

Mastroianni R (2022) Freedom and pluralism of the media: an European *value* waiting to be discovered? In: Deliyanni-Dimitrakou C, Gaudin H, Prévédourou E et al (eds) Mélanges Vassilios Skouris, 1st edn. Mare & Martin, Paris, pp 393–404

Möllers C (2021) Demokratie. In: Herdegen M, Masing J, Poscher R et al (eds) Handbuch des Verfassungsrechts, 1st edn. C.H. Beck, Munich, pp 317–382

Möllers C (2025) Demokratie und Gewaltenteilung. In: Bast J, von Bogdandy A (eds) Unionsverfassungsrecht, 1st edn. Nomos, Baden-Baden, pp 795–859

Morijn J (2024) Polish Re-Democratisation as "Building Back Better". Available via Verfassungsblog. https://verfassungsblog.de/polish-re-democratisation-as-building-back-better/. Accessed 22 Jan 2025

Müller M (2023) Update: How the European Parliaments wants to reform the EU Treaties. Available via Der (europäische) Föderalist https://www.foederalist.eu/2023/12/parliament-eu-treaty-reform.html. Accessed 22 Jan 2025

Müller M (2024) A permanent system for seat allocation in the EP – Reconciling degressive proportionality and electoral equality through proportional completion. https://www.europarl.europa.eu/cmsdata/280848/PolDepC%20_A%20Permanent%20System%20for%20Seat%20Allocation%20in%20the%20EP_Muller.pdf. Accessed 22 Jan 2025

Müller-Graff P-C (2022) Consequences of Karlsruhe's PSPP-judgment for the EU's community of law? In: Deliyanni-Dimitrakou C, Gaudin H, Prévédourou E et al (eds) Mélanges Vassilios Skouris, 1st edn. Mare & Martin, Paris, pp 405–420

Nemitz P, Ehm F (2019) Strengthening democracy in Europe and its resilience against autocracy: daring more democracy and a European democracy charter. In: Garben S, Govaere I, Nemitz P (eds) Critical reflections on constitutional democracy in the European Union, 1st edn. Hart Publishing, Oxford, pp 345–385

Nettesheim M (2009) Ein Individualrecht auf Staatlichkeit? Die Lissabon-Entscheidung des BVerfG. Neue Juristische Wochenschrift 62:2867–2869

Nettesheim M (2024) Die föderale Homogenitätsklausel des Art. 2 EUV. Europarecht 59:269–299

Nicolaïdis K (2013) European Demoicracy and its crisis. J Common Mark Stud 51:351–369

Øby Johansen S, Ulfstein G, Follesdal A et al (2024) The revised draft agreement on the accession of the EU to the ECHR. Eur Pap 9:641–646

Odermatt J (2024) Whose consent?. Available via Verfassungsblog. https://verfassungsblog.de/commission-v-front-polisario/. Accessed 22 Jan 2025

Oeter S (2009) Federalism and democracy. In: Von Bogdandy A, Bast J (eds) Principles of European constitutional law, 2nd edn. Hart Publishing, Oxford, pp 55–83

Okunrobo S (2023) Case C-769/22: a further step in the protection of the fundamental rights within the European Union?. Available via European Law Blog. https://www.europeanlawblog.eu/pub/case-c-769-22-a-further-step-in-the-protection-of-the-fundamental-rights-within-the-european-union/release/1. Accessed 22 Jan 2025
Pechstein M, Nowak C, Häde U (eds) (2023a) Frankfurter Kommentar zu EUV, GRC und AEUV, vol I, 2nd edn. Mohr Siebeck, Tübingen. (quoted by: Author)
Pechstein M, Nowak C, Häde U (eds) (2023b) Frankfurter Kommentar zu EUV, GRC und AEUV, vol II, 2nd edn. Mohr Siebeck, Tübingen. (quoted by: Author)
Pechstein M, Nowak C, Häde U (eds) (2023c) Frankfurter Kommentar zu EUV, GRC und AEUV, vol IV, 2nd edn. Mohr Siebeck, Tübingen. (quoted by: Author)
Peers S (2024) EU Citizens' Right to Join Political Parties. Available via Verfassungsblog. https://verfassungsblog.de/eu-citizens-right-to-join-political-parties/. Accessed 22 Jan 2025
Peters A (2006) Compensatory constitutionalism. Leiden J Int Law 19:579–610
Peukert A (2024) Risky recommendations. Available via Verfassungsblog. https://verfassungsblog.de/risky-recommendations/. Accessed 22 Jan 2025
Pohjankoski P (2021) Rule of law with leverage: policing structural obligations in EU law with the infringement procedure, fines, and set-off. Common Mark Law Rev 58:1341–1364
Pohjankoski P (2023) Contesting the ultimate leverage to enforce EU law. Available via Verfassungsblog. https://verfassungsblog.de/contesting-the-ultimate-leverage-to-enforce-eu-law/. Accessed 22 Jan 2025
Poptcheva E-M (2015) Disenfranchisement of EU citizens resident abroad, European Parliamentary Research Service. https://www.europarl.europa.eu/RegData/etudes/IDAN/2015/564379/EPRS_IDA(2015)564379_EN.pdf. Accessed 22 Jan 2025
Potacs M (2016) Wertkonforme Auslegung des Unionsrechts? Europarecht 51:164–176
Prezas I (2023) Democratic sanctions and international law. In: Khan D-E, Lagrange E, Oeter S et al (eds) Democracy and sovereignty. Rethinking the legitimacy of public international law, 1st edn. Brill Nijhoff, Brill/Leiden, pp 235–268
Reding V (2014) Speech by European Commission Vice-President Viviane Reding "Disenfranchisement: defending voting rights for EU citizens abroad" on 29 January 2014. https://ec.europa.eu/commission/presscorner/detail/de/SPEECH_14_73. Accessed 22 Jan 2025
Richter D (2022) Versammlungs- und Vereinigungsfreiheit. In: Grabenwarter C (ed) Europäischer Grundrechteschutz, 2nd edn. Nomos, Baden-Baden, §17
Riedl B (2024) Keine allgemeine Verfassungsaufsicht über die Unionswerte im Vertragsverletzungsverfahren. Available via Verfassungsblog. https://verfassungsblog.de/eugh-lgbtqi-ungarn-werte/. Accessed 22 Jan 2025
Ritleng D (2016) Does the European court of justice take democracy seriously? Common Mark Law Rev 59:11–33
Roß L (2023) European media freedom act und Kernfragen der europäischen integration. Europarecht 58:450–475
Sadurski W (2023) The law to take out tusk. Available via Verfassungsblog. https://verfassungsblog.de/the-law-to-take-out-tusk/. Accessed 22 Jan 2025
Safradin B, Groenendijk K, Morijn J (2023) An Honest Broker?. Available via Verfassungsblog. https://verfassungsblog.de/an-honest-broker/. Accessed 22 Jan 2025
Sands P (2005) Lawless world: America and the making and breaking of global rules. Viking Press, New York
Sauer H (2023) Unions- und verfassungsrechtliche Fragen einer Sperrklausel bei der Wahl zum Europäischen Parlament. Europäische Zeitschrift für Wirtschaftsrecht 34:792–796
Scheppele KL (2024) Blinded by Legality: The Venice Commission's Change of Heart on Restoring the Rule of Law in Poland. Available via Verfassungsblog. https://verfassungsblog.de/blinded-by-legality/. Accessed 22 Jan 2025
Schmidt R (2024) Die Rückkehr Polens in die Rechtsstaatlichkeit. Die Öffentliche Verwaltung 77:969–975
Schmitt C (2020) Die Tyrannei der Werte, 4th edn. Duncker & Humblot, Berlin

Schönberger C (2005) Unionsbürger: Europas föderales Bürgerrecht in vergleichender Sicht, 1st edn. Mohr Siebeck, Tübingen
Schönberger C (2009) Die Europäische Union zwischen "Demokratiedefizit" und Bundesstaatsverbot. Der Staat 48:535–558
Schorkopf F (2001) Die Maßnahmen der XIV EU-Mitgliedstaaten gegen Österreich. Springer, Berlin
Schorkopf F (2020) Der Wertekonstitutionalismus der Europäischen Union. Juristen Zeitung 75:477–485
Schorkopf F (2023) Die unentschiedene Macht: Verfassungsgeschichte der Europäischen Union, 1948–2007. Vandenhoeck & Ruprecht, Göttingen
Schroeder W (2023) Wahlrechtsgrundsätze für Wahlen zum Europäischen Parlament. Europarecht 58:517–535
Schuler M (2023a) Taking democracy seriously: The Commission's Infringement Action against Poland. Available via European Law Blog. https://www.europeanlawblog.eu/pub/taking-democracy-seriously-the-commissions-infringement-action-against-poland-for-violating-eu-law-with-the-new-law-in-poland-on-the-state-committee-for-the-examination-of-russian-influence/release/1. Accessed 22 Jan 2025
Schuler M (2023b) Why the EU should care about national elections. Available via European Law Blog. https://www.europeanlawblog.eu/pub/why-the-eu-should-care-about-national-elections/release/1. Accessed 22 Jan 2025
Schuler M (2024a) Regime Defence Disguised as a Defence of Sovereignty: The Hungarian Defence of National Sovereignty Bill as a violation of European values. Available via European Law Blog. https://www.europeanlawblog.eu/pub/zur3yq9e/release/1. Accessed 22 Jan 2025
Schuler M (2024b) Paving the way for an enforcement of democracy under Article 10 TEU?. Available via European Law Blog. https://www.europeanlawblog.eu/pub/fsca541k/release/2. Accessed 22 Jan 2025
Schuman R (2010) Pour l'Europe. Fondation Robert Schuman, Paris
Shuibhne NN (2023) EU citizenship law. Oxford University Press, Oxford
Sonnevend P (2023) How to make Article 10 TEU operational? The right to influence the exercise of state power and cardinal law in Hungary. In: Bobek M, Bodnar A, Von Bogdandy A et al (eds) Transition 2.0: re-establishing constitutional democracy in EU member states, 1st edn, Nomos, Baden-Baden, pp 563–584
Spieker LD (2021) Defending Union values in judicial proceedings. On how to turn article 2 TEU into a judicially applicable provision. In: Von Bogdandy A, Bogdanowicz P, Canor I et al (eds) Defending checks and balances in EU member states, 1st edn. Springer, Berlin, pp 237–269
Spieker LD (2023) EU values before the court of justice: foundations, potential, risks. Oxford University Press, Oxford
Streinz R (ed) (2018) EUV/AEUV, 3rd edn. C.H.Beck, Munich. (quoted by: Author)
Strothteicher L (2022) Das neue EU-Sanktionsregime zur Ahndung schwerer Menschenrechtsverletzungen unter Beachtung der Werte und Ziele der EU: Analyse und Vergleich zum US-"Magnitksy-Act". Beiträge zum Europa-und Völkerrecht 24
Sydow G (2024) "In Deutschland gewählte" statt "deutsche" Abgeordnete. Juristen Zeitung 79:313–321
Szabó DG (2023) Protecting the Fairness of European Parliament Elections via Preliminary Ruling. Available via Verfassungsblog. https://verfassungsblog.de/protecting-the-fairness-of-european-parliament-elections-via-preliminary-ruling/. Accessed 22 Jan 2025
Theuns T (2024) Protecting democracy in Europe. Oxford University Press, Oxford
Verellen T (2022) Hungary's lesson for Europe: democracy is part of Europe's constitutional identity. It Should be Justiciable. Available via Verfassungsblog. https://verfassungsblog.de/hungarys-lesson-for-europe/. Accessed 22 Jan 2025
Vissers N (2023) Enforcing democracy. Available via Verfassungsblog. https://verfassungsblog.de/enforcing-democracy/. Accessed 22 Jan 2025
von Achenbach J (2025) Das Europäische Parlament – ein transnationales Repräsentationsorgan. In: Bast J, von Bogdandy A (eds) Unionsverfassungsrecht, 1st edn. Nomos, Baden-Baden, pp 863–933

von Bogdandy A (2012) The European lesson for international democracy: the significance of Articles 9-12 EU treaty for international organizations. Eur J Int Law 23:315–334

von Bogdandy A (2019) Tyrannei der Werte? Herausforderungen und Grundlagen einer europäischen Dogmatik systemischer Defizite. Zeitschrift für ausländisches öffentliches Recht und Völkerrecht 79:503–551

von Bogdandy A (2023) Ein Demokratiebegriff für die Europäische Gesellschaft. In: Heger A, Malkmus M, Gourdet S (eds) Zur Zukunft der Demokratie in der Europäischen Union, 1st edn. Nomos, Baden-Baden, pp 23–47

von Bogdandy A Spieker LD (2022) Transformative constitutionalism in Luxembourg: how the court can support democratic transitions. Max Planck Institute for Comparative Public Law & International Law, Research Paper Series No. 2022-14

von Bogdandy A, Spieker LD (2023) EU values as constraints and facilitators in democratic transitions. In: Bobek M, Bodnar A, Von Bogdandy A et al (eds) Transition 2.0: re-establishing constitutional democracy in EU member states, 1st edn. Nomos, Baden-Baden, pp 113–142

von der Groeben H (2015) In: Schwarze J, Hatje A (eds) Europäisches Unionsrecht, vol 1, 7th edn. Nomos, Baden-Baden. (quoted by: Author)

Walker N (2012) The European Union's unresolved constitution. In: Rosenfeld M, Sajó A (eds) The Oxford handbook of comparative constitutional law, 1st edn. Oxford University Press, Oxford, pp 1185–1208

Weiler JHH (1995) The State "über alles". Demos, Telos and the German Maastricht decision. In: Due O, Lutter M, Schwarze J (eds) Festschrift für Ulrich Everling, vol II, 1st edn. Nomos, Baden-Baden, pp 1651–1689

Weiler JHH (2011) Editorial: 60 years since the first European Community – reflections on political Messianism. Eur J Int Law 22:303–311

Weiler JHH (2013) Revisiting *Van Gend en loos*: Subjectifying and objectifying the individual. In: ECJ, 50th anniversary of the judgment in Van Gend en loos 1963–2013. Publications Office, Luxemburg

Weiler JHH (2018) The crumbling of European democracy. In: Graber MA, Levinson S, Tushnet M (eds) Constitutional democracy in crisis? 1st edn. Oxford University Press, New York, pp 629–638

Weiler JHH (2024) Citizenship for Sale (Commission v Malta). Available via Verfassungsblog. https://verfassungsblog.de/citizenship-for-sale/. Accessed 22 Jan 2025

Chapter 6
General Conclusions: Human Right to Democracy Ensures Comprehensive Legal Toolbox against Democratic Backsliding

Moving from the specific scenario of the EU's multilevel system to the general situation, one can state that neither the global nor the various regional levels of government expressly guarantee any "human right to democracy" as such. While both national democracy and international democracy are part and parcel of the right of self-determination of peoples, these components need further concretisation in order to be transformed into directly applicable rights. This is where civil and political human rights guarantees on the global and regional level come in. Together, they require States to guarantee the most important elements of democratic government, such as free and fair elections, free and pluralistic media and an informed and active civil society, whose members freely express themselves, assemble and associate, all of which have to be protected by independent and impartial courts under the rule of law. This all constitutes the human rights foundation of democracy that is firmly entrenched at the global level as well as at the world's various regional levels of government. Democratic human rights turn their holders—natural and (where applicable) legal persons—into actors as well as guardians of democratic systems. Their active participation brings these systems to life and their judicial action helps in effectively preventing their degeneration into authoritarianism.

There thus is a whole bouquet of legally binding democratic human rights on whose effective implementation the democratic system of government within States (national democracy) depends. These internationally or supranationally guaranteed rights can be enforced *vis-à-vis* States in proceedings before national courts as well as international courts or quasi-judicial bodies which global and regional human rights treaties establish. Protecting these democratic rights in each and every individual case helps protecting democracy as a whole against dying by the slice instead of a sudden coup. But the democratic rights can also be used to mitigate the undemocratic effects of such a coup and support the return to democracy.

The synthesis of these specific democratic rights produces an unwritten general human right to national democracy which promotes the pro-democratic

T. Giegerich, *The Human Right to Democracy in Multilevel Systems at a Time of Democratic Backsliding: Global, Regional and European Union Perspectives*, European Union and its Neighbours in a Globalized World 24,
https://doi.org/10.1007/978-3-032-01689-8_6

interpretation of the specific rights and may even generate further unwritten democratic rights. This unwritten general right to national democracy is in the background of the "democratic society" counterbalance mentioned in the limitation clauses of the UDHR, ICCPR and ECHR. While it has not yet been recognised as such by international courts or quasi-judicial treaty bodies, its discovery as another bastion against democratic backsliding will hopefully come and its added value make itself felt in particular in cases of systemic threats, *i.e.* threats against the democratic system as a whole that transcend isolated instances of violations of democratic rights.

There is an obvious interdependence and complementarity of—a symbiotic relationship between—democracy, human rights and the rule of law. Human rights enforced by independent and impartial courts or quasi-judicial bodies help protect and implement as well as restore democracy, while democratic systems are generally conducive to the effective implementation of human rights under the rule of law. However, in democratic systems political majorities also need to be limited by human rights and the rule of law, in order to protect the democratic *acquis* from backsliding. These limits on majority rule are inherent in the principle of democracy and reinforced by the rule of law principle. For democracy does not exhaust itself in the effective implementation of majority decisions at whatever cost. The democratic majority is not empowered to abolish democracy or any of its necessary ingredients, *i.e.*, the democratic rights that enable changes of majority at the ballot box and the subsequent reorientation of democratic politics. This principle of restraining political majorities is clearly enshrined in the human rights treaty provisions prohibiting destructive abuse of both human rights and governmental powers. The necessary human rights mechanisms to prevent and reverse democratic backsliding are thus available, but must be used more effectively, in particular by the ECtHR that still tends to grant States an overbroad margin of appreciation regarding their constitutional construction.

In multilevel systems, democracy must also be realised at governmental levels above the States, in particular in international and supranational organisations, but also more generally in the basic structure of the international legal and political order as a whole, both at the regional and the global level. International democracy—democracy between States—requires that the international order be an expression of the self-determination of the equal peoples of the world, *i.e.* the "nations large and small" to whom the preamble of the UN Charter attributes equal rights. Accordingly, the equally sovereign States established by those peoples must collectively and consensually remain the masters of the international legal order, so that none of them becomes subject to alien domination or subjugation in the disguise of international legal developments. On the other hand, democracy is not opposed to the increasing institutionalisation of the international community at regional and global levels. Rather, States are generally free to transfer decision-making powers to international and supranational organisations with regard to regional or global problems that they individually cannot solve effectively. Nor does democracy prohibit majority decisions in these organisations. But it requires that they have transparent, democratic, just and accountable decision-making processes that enable the full, equal and effective participation of the peoples of all Member

States through their democratically accountable representatives as well as adequate (preferably judicial) mechanisms to protect the outvoted minority.

The bouquet of democratic human rights, whose important role in the context of national democracy was already mentioned, also supports international democracy. As in the national context, so in the international context, too, the synthesis of these specific rights produces an unwritten general human right to international democracy, although admittedly, there is little case law yet recognising its existence. That right requires States to guarantee the democratic legitimacy of international and supranational organisations of which they are members and fend off threats to national democracies and the respective democratic rights of their citizens emanating from the transfer of powers to those organisations. Increasing the organisations' own democratic legitimacy will normally mitigate such threats. So will a reasonable distribution of competences between the organisations and their Member States and an adequate level of participation of Member State representatives in the decision-making processes of the organisations.

National democracy and international democracy are interdependent and should be mutually reinforcing, but there is potential for conflict in both directions: International or supranational decision-making may weaken democratic decisions-making at Member State level by disrupting the national balance of powers. Thus, power transfers to international or supranational organisations where the Member States are usually represented by their executives may disadvantage national parliaments. On the other hand, democratic decisions made in Member States may impair international or supranational democracy, if they entail the exercise of a national veto that blocks decision-making at the organisational level or, even worse, deny the bindingness of international or supranational decisions. The general human right to national democracy read together with the general human right to international democracy and the States' obligation to protect their citizens' democratic rights generates a further general human right to an adequate overall standard of democracy in systems of multiple interdependent democratic levels. The latter requires the best possible balance between national and international democracy. This permits and even requires a limited set-off between the levels of democratic legitimacy in the national and the international or supranational system in the sense that a deficit here can to a certain extent be compensated by a surplus there (and vice versa). It also requires compensatory adaptation mechanisms within each system in order to mitigate negative impacts of the international and supranational institutionalisation on national democracies.

The EU constitutes the most advanced supranational multilevel democratic system of government with strict top-down requirements for national democracy and bottom-up requirements for supranational democracy enshrined in primary Union law, both in the form of far-reaching objective standards and less far-reaching judicially enforceable individual rights. Despite its imperfections, the EU can serve as a model of democratic institutionalisation for other world regions and the UN level, although the direct transfer of EU solutions is impossible because of the very specific conditions in Europe. Primary Union law obliges the EU to "export" democratic standards horizontally to third States as well as vertically (bottom up) to the international community as a whole. But this is an objective obligation not accompanied by judicially enforceable individual rights.

The right to national democracy and supplementary democratic rights are much better entrenched in global and regional international law as well as in EU law than the right to international democracy and supplementary democratic rights. The reason is that national democracy has traditionally been much more in the focus of public attention than international democracy. In EU law again, the right to supranational democracy and supplementary democratic rights is much better entrenched than the right to international democracy and supplementary democratic rights, for a similar reason.

Returning to the indexes cited at the beginning which at best painted a mixed picture of the current state of democracy around the globe,[1] there is an obvious and growing gap between, on the one hand, the firm entrenchment and further expansion in international law of the explicitly guaranteed specific democratic rights and the implicit right to national democracy based on them and, on the other hand, the increasingly autocratic reality. But this gap between noble standards and ugly facts also exists with regard to other human rights, including most fundamental ones, such as the protection from torture and inhuman treatment. It provides no reason to doubt the existence of the norms, which no State calls in question, but rather an incentive to improve their implementation. States should actively be held on to their democratic commitments deriving from the human rights treaties they ratified as well as the UDHR. As with human rights in general, the realisation of democratic rights experiences ups and downs. After the up we experienced post-1989/90, we are currently witnessing a downward movement. This means that we now have to prove ourselves.

For the purpose of reversing that downward movement, democrats of all countries should unite in order to help enforce democratic parameters everywhere and at all levels. They can build on good legal and political foundations: All members of the human family enjoy a series of specific democratic human rights that are explicitly entrenched in the various global and regional human rights treaties as well as the truly universal and often confirmed UDHR; they are also part of supranational EU law. These guarantees, which are more or less effectively enforceable in national, international and supranational courts and treaty bodies, support an implicit general individual right to both national and international democracy at all levels that overlaps with the collective peoples' right of self-determination. While this general right will rarely be enforceable as such, it informs the pro-democratic interpretation of those specific rights and may generate further specific pro-democratic rights functioning as gap-fillers. Autocratic government and even more, retrogression from established democratic standards into autocracy, is presumptively incompatible with international and supranational law. Each and every holder of democratic rights can contribute to uphold national and democracy by resolutely exercising their rights.

[1] See above Sect. 1.4.2.

In conclusion, we have all the necessary legal and political instruments at our disposal at all governmental levels to counteract and reverse democratic backsliding. We need to use them with determination.

MIX
Papier aus verantwortungsvollen Quellen
Paper from responsible sources
FSC® C105338

If you have any concerns about our products,
you can contact us on
ProductSafety@springernature.com

In case Publisher is established outside the EU,
the EU authorized representative is:
Springer Nature Customer Service Center GmbH
Europaplatz 3, 69115 Heidelberg, Germany

Printed by Libri Plureos GmbH
in Hamburg, Germany